BJ Miller

Sams **Teach Yourself**

Swift

in **24**
Hours

SAMS 800 East 96th Street, Indianapolis, Indiana, 46240 USA

ISBN-13: 978-0-672-33724-6

ISBN-10: 0-672-33724-X

Library of Congress Control Number: 2014948978

Printed in the United States of America

First Printing December 2014

Trademarks

All terms mentioned in this book that are known to be trademarks or service marks have been appropriately capitalized. Sams Publishing cannot attest to the accuracy of this information. Use of a term in this book should not be regarded as affecting the validity of any trademark or service mark.

Warning and Disclaimer

Every effort has been made to make this book as complete and as accurate as possible, but no warranty or fitness is implied. The information provided is on an "as is" basis. The author and the publisher shall have neither liability nor responsibility to any person or entity with respect to any loss or damages arising from the information contained in this book or from the use of the programs accompanying it.

Special Sales

For information about buying this title in bulk quantities, or for special sales opportunities (which may include electronic versions; custom cover designs; and content particular to your business, training goals, marketing focus, or branding interests), please contact our corporate sales department at corpsales@pearsoned.com or (800) 382-3419.

For government sales inquiries, please contact governmentsales@pearsoned.com.

For questions about sales outside the U.S., please contact international@pearsoned.com.

Editor-in-Chief
Mark Taub

Senior Acquisitions Editor
Trina MacDonald

Senior Development Editor
Chris Zahn

Managing Editor
Kristy Hart

Senior Project Editor
Betsy Gratner

Copy Editor
Geneil Breeze

Indexer
Lisa Stumpf

Proofreader
Leslie Joseph

Technical Editors
Valerie Shipbaugh
Hank Turowski

Editorial Assistant
Olivia Basegio

Cover Designer
Mark Shirar

Compositor
Nonie Ratcliff

Contents at a Glance

Table of Contents

About the Author

BJ Miller is an iOS developer for a consultancy in the Cleveland, Ohio, area. BJ earned his B.S. in Computer Science from Baldwin-Wallace College (now called Baldwin-Wallace University) in Berea, Ohio, the town where he grew up. His latest career path encompasses large-scale enterprise network administration, SQL database administration, and Microsoft SharePoint Server and Microsoft Project Server administration and integration as a contractor for the United States Department of Defense, with all the Microsoft certifications that come along with that. Before that, he spent several years in LAN engineering, designing and implementing network infrastructure, as a Cisco Certified Network Associate.

BJ began iOS development in 2009 after not having programmed for a few years, and he developed a passion for the platform and the Objective-C language. Now, his love has expanded to include Swift, and there is still yet room in his heart for more. In 2013 he released his first app into the iOS App Store, called MyPrayerMap, as a simple tool for managing prayer requests.

When he is not writing in Objective-C or Swift for either work or this book, he enjoys spending time with his wife and two boys, reading, listening to music or podcasts, and playing The Legend of Zelda (any game on any system will do). He also co-organizes the Cleveland CocoaHeads Meetup with Daniel Steinberg, http://www.meetup.com/Cleveland-CocoaHeads/, and organizes a submeetup of that group called Paired Programming Fun, which is a casual meetup where the focus is on Test-Driven Development (TDD) in Swift and Objective-C in paired-programming style. BJ often presents iOS-related topics at CocoaHeads and also speaks at other conferences such as CocoaConf (Columbus, Ohio) and CodeMash v2.0.1.5. He also blogs from time to time at http://bjmiller.me and is on Twitter as @bjmillerltd.

Dedication

This book is dedicated to my wonderful family and friends who have been incredibly supportive throughout this entire process. Thank you all for your love and encouragement.

Acknowledgments

I would like to thank my wife and two boys for putting up with me while I wrote this book. I am excited to spend more time with you. I would also like to thank whoever invented coffee; may the Lord bless your soul and keep you. Speaking of the Lord, it is pretty close to not humanly possible that this book would have been completed in time, with all the other obstacles going on in my life, without his loving arms around me and my family; thank you, Jesus.

I would also like to thank my friends, coworkers, and the rest of the Mac/iOS community for all their love and encouragement. If I had not been introduced to someone, who introduced me to someone, who introduced me to Daniel Steinberg, I might not have pursued iOS development further and I might not have written this book. If you ever get the chance to meet that man, your life will be enriched.

Also, I cannot go without thanking the fine people who helped this book come to be: Trina MacDonald (Acquisitions Editor), Chris Zahn (Senior Development Editor), Olivia Basegio (Editorial Assistant), Hank Turowski (Technical Editor), Geneil Breeze (Copy Editor), and Betsy Gratner (Project Editor).

We Want to Hear from You!

As the reader of this book, you are our most important critic and commentator. We value your opinion and want to know what we're doing right, what we could do better, what areas you'd like to see us publish in, and any other words of wisdom you're willing to pass our way.

We welcome your comments. You can email or write to let us know what you did or didn't like about this book—as well as what we can do to make our books better.

Please note that we cannot help you with technical problems related to the topic of this book.

When you write, please be sure to include this book's title and author as well as your name and email address. We will carefully review your comments and share them with the author and editors who worked on the book.

Email: errata@informit.com

Mail: Sams Publishing
           ATTN: Reader Feedback
           330 Hudson Street
           7th Floor
           New York, New York 10013

Reader Services

Visit our website and register this book at informit.com/register for convenient access to any updates, downloads, or errata that might be available for this book.

Introduction

At Apple's yearly World Wide Developer Conference (WWDC) in June 2014, Apple announced a new programming language called Swift that the company had been developing since 2010. This was a huge announcement; Objective-C had been the primary language of choice for developing most Mac and iOS apps for many years. The excitement surrounding this language was palpable. Twitter lit up with tweets about Swift, domain names with Swift in the title were being bought up left and right, and within 24 hours of the announcement more than 300,000 copies of Apple's Swift iBook had been downloaded. People were ready for change.

But a new language brings not only syntactic differences but also idiomatic differences and new conventions. Swift is not just an object-oriented language, but it introduces features gleaned from other languages, such as C#, Haskell, Ruby, and more. Touted to be "Objective-C without the C," Swift builds upon familiar concepts from Objective-C but includes a more modern, safer syntax and multiple paradigms such as object-oriented, functional, imperative, and block structured.

Swift is officially at version 1.0 but is still evolving, and even as this book is being written more changes are entering beta. With that said, this book is current as of Swift 1.0 and Xcode 6.0.1. If there are changes that you find in these examples that do not work as described or with screenshots, please check Apple's release documentation and electronic versions of this book as they can get updated a lot faster than the printed book you may have in your hands. Also, all the code examples from this book are available and will be kept up-to-date in the GitHub repository, https://github.com/STYSwiftIn24H/Examples.

Swift is already proving to be a great language and as of its release is compatible with iOS 7 and up. Swift can be written for apps running on OS X Yosemite, but as of Xcode 6.0.1, the option for adding Swift files to an Objective-C project, or even creating a Mac app using Swift are not available. More Mac support is coming in future releases. Updates are coming from Apple rather quickly, so if something is not available that you need or if something is not working as expected, consider filing a bug or feature request at http://bugreport.apple.com.

Who Should Read This Book?

This book is designed for a beginner-intermediate level programmer. Even advanced programmers who are not yet familiar with Swift can benefit from this book. You do not have to have a background in software development to make your way through this book, although it may help. If you are not familiar with software development whatsoever, you may benefit from more fundamental books first, although with the examples inside this book you may be able to follow along just fine.

In this book, I assume you have a passion to learn about Swift and to develop apps for the Mac and/or iOS platforms. I also assume that you are willing to carve out time in your schedule to take this book seriously and learn the concepts herein.

What Should You Expect from This Book?

This book is a guided tour of the Swift programming language, discussing some of the ins-and-outs of Swift, best practices, do's-and-don'ts, and more. It is not just a language reference. By the time you complete this book you should have a firm grasp on many of the concepts in Swift including the syntax to make them come to fruition.

You should not expect to be able to write award-winning iOS or Mac apps right out of the gate by just reading this book alone, as this book is not meant to be a one-stop-shop for learning everything about app creation. Such a book would be thousands of pages long. Rather, there are more components to writing apps, particularly the Cocoa and Cocoa Touch frameworks, which deserve books in their own right (and many exist). Apps should be written with careful planning and development, and depending on how many different technologies your app includes, you may need more resources.

You also do not need to read this book from cover to cover before attempting to write apps of your own using Swift. Feel free to experiment along the way with your own apps, or use this book for reference if you are stuck in an app of your own and need some guidance.

Also remember that this book is current as of Swift 1.0 and Xcode 6.0.1, so please understand that changes may be made after this book has gone through final edits and been printed. Code examples will be updated as progressions in the Swift language and Xcode environment change. They are available on GitHub at https://github.com/STYSwiftIn24H/Examples.

NOTE

Code-Continuation Arrows and Listing Line Numbers

You'll see code-continuation arrows ➥ occasionally in this book to indicate when a line of code is too long to fit on the printed page.

Also, many listings have line numbers and some do not. The listings that have line numbers have them so that I can reference code by line; the listings that do not have line numbers are not called out by line.

HOUR 1

Introducing the Swift Development Environment

What You'll Learn in This Hour:

▶ What Swift is and where it came from

▶ How to install Xcode 6 from the Mac App Store

▶ How to navigate the Xcode Integrated Development Environment (IDE)

▶ How to use playgrounds

▶ How to use Swift's Read-Eval-Print-Loop (REPL)

▶ How to write your first Swift app

Since the introduction of the iPhone in 2007, Apple seems to have lit a fire in the industry for not only consumer-based electronics but also the opportunity for most anyone to be able to write apps for their platform, be it Mac or iOS. This has had a dramatic effect on culture, as you cannot go to a coffee shop or to any business now and not see a slew of MacBook Airs, MacBook Pros, iPhones, and iPads. Chances are, if you're reading this book, you are wondering how you can write an app that could appear on the screens of the very people you see at those coffee shops and businesses.

This book is about the Swift programming language, the new programming language announced by Apple at the 2014 World Wide Developer Conference (WWDC). Prior to Swift's introduction, Mac and iOS apps were mainly written in a language called Objective-C, which is a strict superset of the C programming language, meaning that you could write apps in both languages, and sometimes had to. In this book we explore the Swift programming language and learn its fundamentals, structure, and syntax, which gives you a foundation to write great Mac and iOS apps.

What Is Swift?

Swift is a programming language customized by Apple and introduced as Objective-C without the C. Indeed, this is true, but Swift has also taken cues from other languages such as Haskell, Ruby, Python, C#, and several others. Swift is tuned to work with the existing Cocoa and Cocoa Touch frameworks, which contain all the familiar classes used in modern Mac and iOS apps, to support their interoperability.

Swift is built on three pillars: being safe, powerful, and modern. Swift provides a lot of safety in terms of type checking, constants for immutability, requiring values to be initialized before use, built-in overflow handling, and automatic memory management. With respect to power, Swift was built using the highly optimized LLVM compiler, includes many low-level C-like functions such as primitive types and flow control, and of course was built with Apple's hardware in mind for optimal performance. Swift is also modern in that it adopted many features from other languages to make the language more concise yet expressive, such as closures, generics, tuples, functional programming patterns, and more that we cover in later hours.

Getting Started

The biggest assumption at this point is that you have a Mac computer already, as without that, you cannot install Xcode, Apple's Mac and iOS Integrated Development Environment (IDE).

NOTE

Download Xcode

Xcode 6 is a free download from the Mac App Store. You must have Mac OS X 10.9.3 or later.

Launch the App Store app on your Mac, search for Xcode, and click to install the software. Once the installation is complete, Xcode is listed in your /Applications directory.

Take a Look Around

When you open Xcode, you may be greeted with prompts asking whether you want to install extra tools; go ahead and install them. This should only happen the first time you launch Xcode. Once Xcode is open, you see a standard menu window with options to create a playground, create a new project, or open an existing project, and on the right side is a list of recent projects and playgrounds you've opened (if you've opened any). The window should look like Figure 1.1.

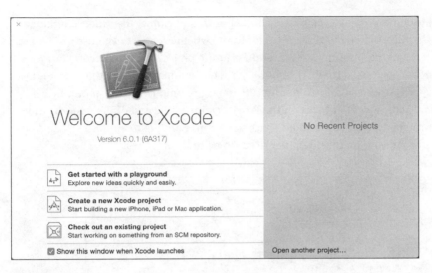

FIGURE 1.1
The Welcome to Xcode screen, where you can choose to create or edit projects and playgrounds.

Although in this book we predominantly work in playgrounds, it is good to become familiar with the IDE, so let's do that quickly. Click Create a New Xcode Project to create a new Xcode project. The next screen asks you what type of project you want to create, and for this experiment, just use Single View Application, as seen in Figure 1.2, and click Next.

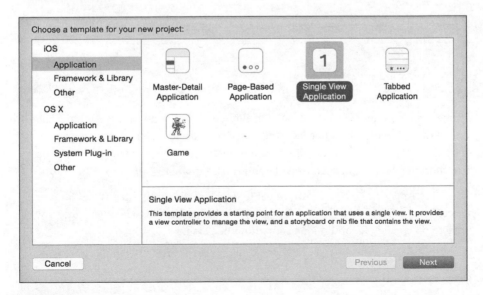

FIGURE 1.2
The project template chooser screen.

Next you are asked to name your project. Choose an Organization Name, Identifier, Language (Swift or Objective-C), and Device(s) to run on, and indicate whether you want to use Core Data, as shown in Figure 1.3. All this information is useful for future projects you will create, but for our testing purposes, we don't need to worry about it yet. The Organization Identifier is usually a reverse-DNS name of your personal or company URL to ensure uniqueness at an organizational level, and the Bundle Identifier tacks on the Project Name to the end of the Organization Identifier to ensure uniqueness per app bundle. Once you submit an app to either the Mac App Store or the iOS App Store, your bundle identifier needs to be unique.

Choose options for your new project:

Product Name:	TestApp
Organization Name:	BJ Miller
Organization Identifier:	com.sixfivesoftware
Bundle Identifier:	com.sixfivesoftware.TestApp
Language:	Swift
Devices:	iPhone
	☐ Use Core Data

Cancel   Previous   Next

FIGURE 1.3
Enter your project-related information.

Here you also have the choice for device type, such as iPhone or iPad, and that is so that Xcode can properly create the Storyboard files needed for the device or devices you plan to write your app to be used on. This way you can target different interfaces on different devices, but still use the same code to manage them both, such as with Universal apps.

Name your project TestApp, since we just want to get to Xcode to get acclimated (you can remove this project later), choose Swift for the language, and click Next. Xcode opens, and you see the new project you created. It should look something like Figure 1.4.

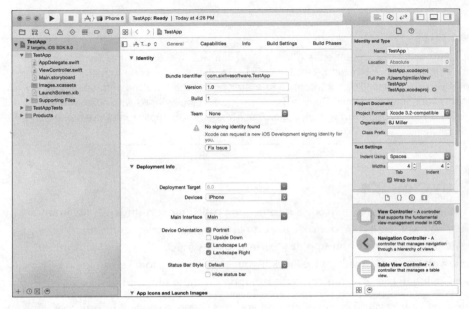

FIGURE 1.4
The initial Xcode IDE layout. The Navigation Pane is on the left, Inspector Pane is on the right, and main content area is in the center. In the top toolbar are buttons to run or stop a build, see error and warning info, and show or hide views.

Xcode is nicely partitioned off into logical sections, as you may be accustomed to from other IDEs; however, it also has some nice features to note. The pane on the left-hand side is called the Navigator Pane. Here, you can choose between different Navigators to view files in your project, warnings and errors, breakpoints, Unit Tests, and more. The pane on the right-hand side is called the Inspector Pane. This dynamic pane changes depending on what element is clicked, such as editing a selected button's text property, or adjusting a control's position in a window.

The main content area in the center is where you'll spend most of your time when working on an actual Mac/iOS project. The content area is where you can change project settings, and most importantly create your app by either writing code or designing the interface in a Storyboard.

The bar along the top left has several useful functions available. Toward the left, you have your standard Mac Red/Yellow/Green buttons for window management. Next, the play and stop buttons are actually *Build and Run* and *Stop* when referring to compiling, building, and running your apps on the Simulator or devices. To the right of that is where Xcode notifies you of current information, such as how many warnings or errors are in your project, and build status.

Finally, the upper right-hand set of buttons can adjust the views you see to show or hide the Navigator Pane, Inspector Pane, Debug Pane, or Assistant Editor, as well as view code comparisons, source code "blame" views, and logs.

NOTE

Viewing Two Files

The Assistant Editor splits the content area in half so you can view two files at the same time. This is helpful, for instance, when you might be writing Unit Tests and also the code to make the Unit Tests pass, or if you are creating a user interface in a Storyboard and have the corresponding View Controller open to connect Actions and Outlets. For more on developing apps with custom interfaces, I recommend reading John Ray's book *Sams Teach Yourself iOS Application Development in 24 Hours*, Sams Publishing.

Xcode Playgrounds

One of the excellent new features of Xcode 6 is something called **playgrounds**. A playground is a scratch pad, if you will, for testing out code to ensure you receive proper results from code segments, before adding the code to your app. It is because of this functionality that playgrounds are so powerful; you can get immediate feedback if your code is going to give you the results you expect without having to compile your code and run it on the Simulator or a device.

You can create a new playground at any time, and you can choose to have it be a part of your project or just as an independent playground file. Since we're already in an open project, click File > New > File, and then in the Source set of files (for either iOS or Mac), choose playground, then click Next. In the Save As dialog, name your playground file (the name MyPlayground is fine for our purposes), and then click Create. Don't worry about the Group or the Targets for now, we aren't building an app yet so we don't care about that.

NOTE

Mac or iOS Playgrounds

There is a difference in file structure when creating a playground from the Mac section or iOS section. Creating a Mac playground adds the `import Cocoa` statement at the top of the file, and makes Mac frameworks and modules available to you. Creating an iOS playground adds the `import UIKit` statement at the top of the file, and makes iOS framekworks and modules available to you. There is nothing visually different about either playground at first. If you create an iOS playground, but instead want to test Mac app code, or vice-versa, simply create a new playground of the desired type.

Notice that your new playground comes equipped with a few lines of Swift code for your learning convenience. Let's touch on a few of these basics first before moving on. Your playground should look something like this:

```
// Playground - noun: a place where people can play
import UIKit
var str = "Hello, playground"
```

The first line in the preceding code is a comment and is ignored by the compiler. You can use comments to annotate certain parts of code to be human readable, perhaps explaining for other coworkers (or even yourself) what this particular section of code is for. The // (double forward slash) signifies that the remainder of the line is to be treated as a comment. You can also comment entire sections of code or paragraphs of text, either on the same line or on multiple consecutive lines by enclosing them in /* and */. Swift even allows you to nest comment blocks inside comment blocks, such as /* ... /* ... */ ... */.

The remainder of the preceding code performs a simple task in that it assigns the string "Hello, playground" to a variable str. Even though the code doesn't directly print any output, the playground by default displays "Hello, playground" in the playground's results pane to show the contents of the variable and any subsequent variables or constants you create. This comes in handy when you want to test logic, math, and other operations.

TRY IT YOURSELF ▼

Create Your First Lines of Swift in the Playground

At this point, it makes sense to try out your first lines of code while you're in the playground, so let's do it together here.

1. Type the following onto a new line in the playground:

```
let myNewValue = 40 + 2
```

2. Notice the right-hand side of the playground displays "42". Type the following line of code as-is, to insert the value inside a sentence.

```
println("My new value is \(myNewValue).")
```

Congratulations! You have written your very first lines of Swift.

In the preceding Try It Yourself example, you assigned a value of 42 to myNewValue in Step 1. Then, in Step 2 you inserted the value inside a sentence, using something called **string interpolation**, which is a convenient way to interpolate variables or constants inside output. The next hour discusses string interpolation in more detail. The println() statement prints output to the console, which is handy for quick debugging or viewing contents of data.

The Swift Read-Eval-Print-Loop (REPL)

Swift also comes packaged with a nice feature called a **Read-Eval-Print-Loop**, or a **REPL** for short. The REPL is an interactive command-line based version of what we just experienced with playgrounds. Using the REPL is nice for quick tests to make sure code works the way you expect, similar to what you get with a playground, but rather than creating a new file in your project, you can just use this ephemeral REPL to get in, test your code, and get out. Whether to use a playground or the REPL is largely a matter of preference of what you feel comfortable with. If you are already using Terminal.app, or some other command-line utility, it may be easier for you to just open the REPL. On the other hand, if you're already in Xcode, it may be quicker for you to just create a playground and go from there.

To access the REPL, you simply type the following:

```
$> xcrun swift
```

xcrun is a command-line tool provided by Xcode for running or locating development tools or properties. So in the preceding line, we're telling xcrun to run the Swift REPL. When you press the Return key, you see the following:

```
Welcome to Swift!  Type :help for assistance.
  1>
```

The 1> is the Swift REPL prompt where you can start typing Swift code, one instruction per line, and it interprets your code for you, much like the playground did. Let's try another example of writing code, this time in the Swift REPL.

▼ TRY IT YOURSELF

Combine Two Strings Together

Let's do another example of some Swift code here; hopefully this one isn't too difficult yet. If you don't fully understand it, don't worry; we cover this in great detail in the next hour.

1. Open Terminal.app on your Mac.

2. Type xcrun swift in the Terminal; then press Return.

3. At the 1> prompt, enter the following:

   ```
   let firstHalf = "I'm writing Swift code,"
   let secondHalf = " and I'm so excited!"
   let combined = firstHalf + secondHalf
   ```

4. Notice how each time you press Return, Swift's REPL displays the name of the constant or variable we used, its data type of String (we cover data types in Hour 2, "Learning Swift's Fundamental Data Types"), and its value.

5. Take a look at how using the + operator concatenates the two strings together. Swift is smart enough to know that even though we're dealing with letter characters (as opposed to adding numbers), the + operator adds String instances together. More on operators in Hour 3, "Using Operators in Swift."

You're doing great! The Swift REPL keeps constants and variables (as well as Classes, Structs, Enums, and others) in memory for the duration of your REPL session. This means that you can reference variables, constants, classes, and so on, several lines later, which helps you work on tackling problems quickly and easily before you write the code in your actual app. The completed Try It Yourself example should look like Figure 1.5.

```
●  ●  ●                    1. xcrun swift (lldb)
➜  ~  xcrun swift
Welcome to Swift!  Type :help for assistance.
  1> let firstHalf = "I'm writing Swift code,"
firstHalf: String = "I'm writing Swift code,"
  2> let secondHalf = " and I'm so excited!"
secondHalf: String = " and I'm so excited!"
  3> let combined = firstHalf + secondHalf
combined: String = "I'm writing Swift code, and I'm so excited!"
  4> █
```

FIGURE 1.5
The completed Try It Yourself example using the Swift REPL.

To quit the Swift REPL, type a colon (:) to invoke command mode; then type q for quit and press Return. You are returned to your regular Unix shell prompt.

Summary

In this first hour, you learned a brief background on the Swift programming language and what it is built upon. We walked through opening the Xcode environment for the first time and explored some of Xcode's layout, as well as the Swift REPL. You also created your first lines of Swift code and saw how Xcode and the REPL give you instant feedback on what your code is doing.

In the next hour, we cover the difference between variables and constants, and explore some of Swift's native data types, such as `String`, `Int`, `Bool`, `Character`, `Double`, and `Float`.

Q&A

Q. **Can I have a playground without having to create a full Xcode project?**

A. Absolutely. Xcode treats playgrounds as interpretable files, independent of any project.

Q. **I am still running OS X Mountain Lion, can I still use Xcode?**

A. OS X Mountain Lion (v. 10.8) can run Xcode, but the latest version of Xcode that can run on Mountain Lion is Xcode 5.x.

Q. **I just started learning iOS development in Objective-C, but now Apple announced the Swift programming language. Should I still learn Objective-C?**

A. Objective-C is still heavily used in many Mac and iOS apps and will still be used for some time to come. This book predominantly teaches the Swift programming language, but if you want to be a developer full-time or in some sort of capacity, you may encounter Objective-C code from an existing code base, so you may benefit from learning some Objective-C. A great introduction to iOS programming in Objective-C is John Ray's book *Sams Teach Yourself iOS Application Development in 24 Hours* from Sams Publishing.

Workshop

The workshop contains quiz questions and exercises to help you solidify your understanding of the material covered. Try to answer all questions before looking at the answers that follow.

Quiz

1. What command opens the Swift REPL?

2. Use a playground to write Swift code that multiplies the numbers 3 and 19 and stores the value in a variable named `result`. What does the code look like?

3. How do you quit the Swift REPL?

4. What is the minimum Mac OS X version that runs Xcode 6?

5. What would be the output of the following Swift code?

```
let age = 33
let outputString = "Someone you know is \(age) years old"
```

Answers

1. `xcrun swift.`

2. `var result = 3 * 19` (The playground result pane displays 57.)

3. Type a colon (:) then q, and then press Return.

4. Mac OS X 10.9.3 is the minimum version to run Xcode 6.

5. The output would be: "Someone you know is 33 years old".

Exercise

Try creating a playground or use the Swift REPL to combine two strings together, and then use the `lowercaseString` method on your combined string to convert the string to all lowercase letters. (HINT: Import Cocoa first. In a playgroud, press the period key (.) immediately after typing the combined variable name to get a list of actions you can take on that string.)

HOUR 2

Learning Swift's Fundamental Data Types

What You'll Learn in This Hour:

- ▸ Understand the differences between constants and variables
- ▸ How to declare and use constants and variables
- ▸ How Swift uses type inference for automatic type setting
- ▸ Swift's common data types
- ▸ How to specifically declare data types with type annotation

In the first hour, we walked through setting up the Xcode and Swift Read-Eval-Print-Loop (REPL) environment and exposed the Xcode layout to you. We also examined some brief examples of Swift code to show how these environments can be used to help you code and even test your code. We briefly used the Swift keyword `let`, when declaring constants in code and assigned different types of data to them (such as the number `42` or the string `"Hello, playground"`). During this hour, we take a closer look at how Swift uses the `var` and `let` keywords (called **introducers**) and also how Swift knows how to handle different types of data.

There are two fundamental ways in Swift that we declare data types, and they are **constants** and **variables**. Let's take a look at that now.

Constants in Swift

Constants are a way of telling Swift that a particular value should not and will not change, hence the term constant. This is also called **immutable**, since something that is constant cannot mutate. Swift's compiler optimizes memory used for constants to make code perform better because if Swift knows that the size and/or contents of that memory will not change, it can eliminate a lot of potential mutability aspects it may normally have to check for when working with these values. Constants also provide you, the programmer, with a safety net by providing protection from accidentally overwriting the contents of a constant value.

Think of some times when constants may be necessary. For example, say you're writing an app that calculates distances, and you know that there are 5,280 feet in a mile. You could set a constant called `feetPerMile` and set its value to 5280. That way, whenever you need to reference that value in your code, you can use `feetPerMile` in your calculations.

Because of the immutability of constants, if you try to change the value of a constant, Xcode provides a compiler error, stating that you cannot assign to a `let` value. Now, let's take a look at variables.

NOTE

When To Use Constants

Because Swift is a safe language, it is a suggested best practice to use constants with the `let` introducer as often as necessary. This greatly improves safety by preventing accidental data manipulation and even helps Swift's compiler improve performance. Only use constants, however, when you know the value of your constant will never change.

Variables in Swift

As you can see, with as dynamic as apps are and have to be, we wouldn't get far by working with only constants. Swift provides an equally simple way to declare variables as it does constants, and that is with the `var` introducer. Variables, as the name implies, can be variable and are **mutable** by nature. This means that the value of the variable can change whenever you use the = operator, called the **assignment operator** (we discuss operators in Hour 3, "Using Operators in Swift").

Variables are particularly useful for when you know that data could or will change. For instance, if you are building a pedometer app, you know that with every step you or the user of your app takes (assuming the user has a device with the M7 motion coprocessor or newer), the number of steps will increase. That variable will continue to be updated with the number of steps taken up to that very moment.

▼ TRY IT YOURSELF

Assigning Constants and Variables

Using a playground or the Swift REPL (whichever you are more comfortable with), try these steps to visualize your knowledge of constants and variables.

1. Assign a constant named `feetPerMile` to a value of `5280`.

```
let feetPerMile = 5280
```

2. Assign a variable named `totalFeet` to a value of `0`, just to initialize it.

```
var totalFeet = 0
```

3. Imagine you walk 3 miles, and you want to know how many feet you traveled. Now, make `totalFeet` equal to 3 times what is stored in `feetPerMile`.

```
totalFeet = 3 * feetPerMile
```

4. Suppose the global standard for number of feet per mile changes from 5280 to 6000, due to a standards disagreement. Try to change `feetPerMile` to `6000`.

```
feetPerMile = 6000
```

You get an error trying to change `feetPerMile`, don't you?

In the last experiment, you noticed that you can declare a constant, `feetPerMile`, and give it an initial value (of 5280) with no problem. You also declared a variable, `totalFeet`, with an initial value (of zero), equally as easily. Then, you changed the value of the variable, and Swift was okay with that. Now, when you tried to change the value of `feetPerMile`, you received an error that you were trying to change a constant `let` value. This is an example of how Swift's compiler helps keep your code safe from mutation issues.

Keep a few things in mind when naming your constants and variables. You can use any Unicode character in the name of your constants and variables, except that they cannot begin with a number and must begin with a letter. This is an excellent feature if you need to express something in a different language that would not so easily be done with an English keyboard. Names also cannot have punctuation or special characters, as those are often reserved for keywords or operators. You can also now use Emoji for names of constants or variables, such as setting the chicken face character to the string "chicken," and Swift infers the chicken face Unicode character to be of type `String`. As cute as that may seem, a lot of programmers tend to shy away from using Emoji or other special characters for names as it makes referencing those variables and constants difficult while typing, and you have to pause your train of thought to hunt down a particular Unicode character or key combination.

Now that we've discussed constants and variables, let's learn about Swift's data types.

Introducing Data Types

One of Swift's primary safety features is related to handling data types. In this section, we cover four basic data types, their composition, and how Swift infers data types when they aren't explicitly stated.

Type Inference

So far we have not explicitly stated the types of data we want Swift to use for our constants and variables, and we haven't needed to. Swift uses something called **type inference** when a data type is not explicitly declared. Swift does this by analyzing the value that is set to the constant or variable we are declaring and setting the type accordingly. Let's take a quick look at our example from the last hour, where we added 40 and 2:

```
let myNewValue = 40 + 2
```

42 is obviously an integer, so Swift inferred it to be of type Int. The way we explicitly declare the type of a constant or variable in Swift is by appending a colon (:) and then the type (such as Int) to the constant or variable name. This is called **type annotation**. Here is what the code now looks like with type annotation:

```
let myNewValue: Int = 40 + 2
```

Because of type inference, we haven't needed to explicitly state a type, but our examples have been small. In real apps, you may have situations where you need to declare the type for many reasons: so that the compiler can help you for safety reasons, as self-documentation to clearly see what value a constant or variable should hold, or even in stating the return types of values in functions (we explore functions in Hour 8, "Using Functions to Perform Actions").

Data Types

Quite a few data types in Swift can be useful in your apps. The most common ones we talk about here are

- ▶ Int for integers, which are whole numbers without a fractional component

- ▶ Double and Float for floating-point numbers

- ▶ String for working with a collection of characters, words, and so on

- ▶ Bool for working with true and false values

NOTE

Other Data Types

Many other data types in Swift are available for use to further refine the scope of the data you need to manage. When possible we outline the data types to know about with relation to the current data type.

CAUTION
_____

Data Types Cannot Be Changed Once Assigned

Once you declare a variable or constant to be of a particular data type, it cannot be changed. Also, you cannot declare a new variable or constant with the same name as an existing variable or constant.
_____

The `Int` Data Type

Integers are a common data type to use in Swift. Integers are used for things like counting or enumerating through an ordered list or array, counting iterations over a section of code a particular amount of times, and many other practical uses. As you've seen already, the keyword for defining an integer is simply `Int`. On a 32-bit platform, `Int` is a 32-bit integer (or `Int32`), and on 64-bit platforms, `Int` is a 64-bit integer (or `Int64`). This is yet another example of how safe Swift is with its data types.

Another way of using integers is to use an **unsigned integer**, or `UInt`. Unsigned integers are just integers with no negative numerical range, meaning they go from 0 to whatever the upper bound is of the integer you choose. The max upper bound of an `Int` is nine quintillion and change, and its minimum bound is negative nine quintillion and change, so chances are you may never need a number bigger than that. A better illustration is `UInt8`, which is an 8-bit integer. Swift provides 8-, 16-, 32-, and 64-bit versions of `UInt`. Go ahead and see for yourself in this Try It Yourself section.

TRY IT YOURSELF ▼

Find the Minimum and Maximum Ranges of Integers

Open up a playground in Xcode, and try the following examples.

1. Assign a new constant of type `Int` to `Int.max`. What value do you see?

```
let intMax: Int = Int.max
```

2. Assign new constants from `UInt8.max` and `UInt8.min`. Try two more constants, `Int8.max` and `Int8.min`. What values do you see?

```
let uint8Max = UInt8.max
let uint8Min = UInt8.min
let int8Max = Int8.max
let int8Min = Int8.min
```

3. Repeat Step 2 for `UInt16` and `UInt32`. What values do you see?

```
let uint16Max = UInt16.max
let uint32Max = UInt32.max
```

4. Now try with `UInt64`. What do you see?

```
let uint64Max: UInt64 = UInt64.max
```

Now you can see the value is 18,446,744,073,709,551,615. That's 18 quintillion.

The completed Try It Yourself section should look like that in Figure 2.1.

```
●  ●  ●                      Ch02 Int TIY.playground
⊞   <   >    Ch02 Int TIY.playground ⟩ No Selection
1  let intMax: Int = Int.max         9,223,372,036,854,775,807
2  let uint8Max = UInt8.max          255
3  let uint8Min = UInt8.min          0
4  let int8Max = Int8.max            127
5  let int8Min = Int8.min            -128
6  let uint16Max = UInt16.max        65,535
7  let uint32Max = UInt32.max        4,294,967,295
8  let uint64Max = UInt64.max        18446744073709551615
9
```

FIGURE 2.1
The completed Try It Yourself example finding upper and lower bounds.

TIP

Use `Int` When Possible

Although all these types are available for you to use, Apple strongly suggests using `Int` whenever possible, even if you may only need an 8-bit integer, only positive integers (unsigned), and so on. This keeps code consistent, and ensures better interoperability with functions and methods with `Int` return types, preventing you from needing to cast return types to their proper annotation.

The `Double` Data Type

`Double`s are also a common data type to use in Swift. Akin to `Double`s are `Float`s, which are similar but with a few differences to note:

▶ `Double` represents a 64-bit floating-point value, and `Float` represents a 32-bit floating-point value.

▶ `Double` has at least 15 decimal digit precision, and `Float` has at least 6 decimal digit precision.

NOTE

When Swift Infers `Double`

Swift always infers `Double` over `Float` when using type inference with floating-point numbers. Because of this, it is suggested to always use `Double` when you need a floating-point number, unless you are working with something designated as a `Float` in another framework. It is also worth noting that if you have a statement in code that involves using an arithmetic operator on integer and floating-point literals, a `Double` return type is inferred. A **literal** is a value that is literally typed into your code as a fixed value, such as 42, -3.14, or "foo".

NOTE

Converting Between Integers and Floating-Point Numbers

There will be times when you need to convert a typed value from one type to another. This is sometimes referred to as **casting**, in that you are casting a variable to behave like another compatible type. For instance, say you have an `Int` with a value of 5, and you need to work with that value as if it were a `Double`. Since a variable cannot change its type once it has been assigned, you must declare a new variable or constant to equal the casted value of the source variable or constant. Consider the following example:

```
let myInt = 5  // this is inferred to be of type Int
let myDouble = Double(myInt)  // myDouble is a Double with the value of 5
```

You can cast a variable or constant by typing the type name and surrounding the variable or constant in parentheses. You can also use casting of variables or constants while adding that value to a value of a different type, so that Swift creates a new variable or constant with the agreed type from the return value, such as the following example:

```
let myNewDouble = Double(myInt) + 1.5
```

Since both `Double(myInt)` and `1.5` are of type `Double`, `myNewDouble` is inferred to be of type `Double`. You can do the same with numeric literals, but since literals don't have a type until they are assigned, you do not need to cast them. Take this example, with an integer and a floating-point number:

```
let gravity = 9 + 0.8
```

In this case, `gravity` is inferred to be of type `Double`, since Swift operates on the values first (to get 9.8) and then assigns it to `gravity`.

The `Bool` Data Type

Boolean data types are simple because they can only hold the logical values true or false. Boolean types are annotated by the `Bool` keyword. Boolean types are ideal for controlling the flow of app execution, covered in Hour 6, "Controlling Program Flow with Conditionals," and to verify whether a certain condition is `true` or `false`, which then executes a particular block of code. The following is a clear example of how `Bool` values are assigned:

```
let swiftIsCool = true
let objectiveCIsDead = false
```

The preceding example assigns `true` to `swiftIsCool`, and assigns `false` to `objectiveCIs-Dead`. As there are only `true` or `false` values in Boolean logic, these are the only values that can be assigned.

The `String` Data Type

The next data type to cover is the widely used **`String`** data type. A `String` is a logical grouping of characters, and those are, you guessed it, **`Character`** data types. Strings are most often what we output to consoles, use as input to text fields, or use as output to screens in labels, text fields, or extended text views.

A `String`, like every type we've talked about thus far, is actually something called a **struct**. A struct is a value type and is a structure that adds functionality to an entity by adding properties and methods. You briefly saw this by getting the maximum value of the `Int` type by calling `Int.max`. An `Int` data type doesn't just hold a number, it also has properties such as `min` and `max`, and methods such as `convertFromIntegerLiteral(value: Int)`.

▼ TRY IT YOURSELF

Find the Properties and Methods on Data Types

Since we know that `Strings`, `Bools`, `Ints`, and `Doubles` (and all variants discussed so far) are structures, you can easily find out what properties and methods are available to use for each data type.

1. Open Xcode 6 and open a playground.

2. Type the following code:

```
let myInt: Int = 5
let myBool: Bool = true
let myString: String = "Hi"
let myDouble: Double = 1.5
```

3. Hold down the Command key on your keyboard and click the `Int` keyword. Xcode takes you to the definition of `Int`, where you can see, in Swift language, how `Int` was created and what properties and methods are available on the `Int` struct and instances of `Ints`.

4. Click the Back button (a left-pointing arrow) in the bar immediately above the playground's text area, and that takes you back to your code. Hold down the Command key on your keyboard, and this time click the `Bool` keyword. Xcode takes you to the definition of `Bool`, where you can see properties and methods for the `Bool` type.

5. Click the Back button in the bar immediately above the playground's text area, and repeat the previous steps for the `String` and `Double` types. Do you see the differences in how these data types are structured and what is available to you?

`Strings` are a mechanism for storing a sequence of values of the `Character` data type. `Characters` are just that, one single character stored in its memory space. This allows us to do many things easily in Swift with regard to strings; we can easily count the number of characters in a `String` instance by using Swift's global function `countElements(someStringValue)`, and it returns however many Unicode characters represent that `String` called `someStringValue`. We can also quickly iterate over strings to get each character value at a time with fast enumeration in a for-in loop (we cover loops in Hour 7, "Iterating Code with Loops"). The following example shows a string and how its data is stored:

```
let myStr = "Hi!"

// myStr contains the following: "H", "i", "!"
```

Strings also can easily be concatenated, or joined together, much like adding numbers with the + operator. You already saw an example of this in Hour 1, "Introducing the Swift Development Environment," but it deserves mention here with the `String` discussion. This is a powerful feature and allows for concise but readable code. To concatenate two strings, simply add them when you are assigning them to a new value or using them together for output to the user:

```
let firstString = "Four score"
let secondString = " and seven years ago"
let newString = firstString + secondString
```

The `newString` constant now contains "Four score and seven years ago".

Because strings are so fundamental to Swift, it is now incredibly easy to insert string values, as well as other non-string values, into strings when creating some text to display to the user or to the output console, with something called **string interpolation**. String interpolation allows you to insert the values directly inline in a string literal, by typing the \ (backslash) key, and then surrounding the value with parentheses. Here is an example:

```
let year = 2014
let currentYearText = "The current year is \(year)"
```

The output of the preceding code is a string that contains "The current year is 2014", and sets it to the constant `currentYearText`. Compared to Objective-C, Apple's language of choice for Mac and iOS apps that has been around for almost 30 years, Swift's `String` implementation is a dream. Take a quick look at how the year example looked in Objective-C:

```
NSInteger year = 2014;
NSString *currentYearText = [NSString stringWithFormat:@"The current year is %d",
➥year];
```

NOTE

Differences Between Swift and Objective-C

Notice that each statement in Objective-C ends with a semicolon (;). This was to indicate to the compiler that it had reached the end of the statement. Swift infers the end of each statement when you press Return, so you do not need to explicitly type a semicolon, although you can.

Also, Objective-C relied on you, the programmer, to utilize the asterisk (*) character when using **pointers**. All Objective-C objects were pointers to memory in the heap. Swift does not require you to use the pointer indicator, and in fact, you don't use it. We discuss instances in Swift further in Hour 10, "Learning About Structs and Classes."

Before you go off on your own to explore more of these types and how you can work with them, there are a few other smaller things to mention. Swift allows string mutability, simply by declaring a String with the var introducer instead of the let introducer. That way, you can change the contents of a String variable simply by setting it to another String literal, concatenating one or more strings to it, or setting it to another string variable's value.

Swift's String struct also provides a property that returns a Bool value called isEmpty. This is convenient if you need to check whether a String instance has any characters in it, such as in an if-else block.

Initializing Values

Swift requires that constants and variables be declared before they are used. That means that you use the let or var introducer to declare a constant or variable with a name and a type (optionally, unless it can't be inferred or you specifically use type annotation). You also can immediately initialize your constants and variables, which is common. You can do this in two ways. First, you can directly assign a literal value to the new constant or variable. Second, you can use that structure's or class's **initializer**. We cover initializers in more depth in Hour 13, "Customizing Initializers of Classes, Structs, and Enums." Here's a brief example of some sample initializers:

```
let wheelsOnABicycle = 2 // assigns the numeric literal 2
let wheelsOnATricycle = Int(3)  // uses Int's initializer, with the parameter of 3
let emptyString = String() // the open and close parentheses indicate an empty
➥String
let piVal = Double(3.14)  // uses Double's initializer, with the parameter of 3.14
```

These seem a little redundant, since you could just as easily type let piVal = 3.14 instead of using Double's initializer, but you need to get used to this syntax for future lessons, so it was worth explaining now.

One last item to mention for the `String` data type is that since we discovered how to use string interpolation to use non-string values inside strings, you can convert strings with only integers in them to actual `Int` types by using the `toInt()` method on an instance of a `String`. For example:

```
let degreesOutsideString = "80"
  // inferred to be a String because of the double-quotes
let degreesOutsideInt = degreesOutsideString.toInt()!
  // returns 80 to degreesOutsideInt as an Int
```

NOTE

Unwrapping Optional Values

Swift has a concept called **optionals**, where a variable may have a value, or it may not. In that case, to remain safe from runtime errors, Swift introduced optionals as a way to wrap values, or lack of values, in a wrapper to be safely passed around and used. The exclamation point (!) in the preceding example tells Swift to explicitly unwrap what is returned from `toInt()` because theoretically `degreesOutsideString` could have a value with any character, such as the degree symbol, which is not convertible to an integer. We discuss optionals more in Hour 5, "Understanding Optional Values."

Summary

In this hour we covered a lot of material regarding the basic data types in Swift, including `Int`, `Double`, `Bool`, and `String`. We learned what types of data each one stores, how to initialize them with proper data, and even how to investigate the full list of data type properties and methods by command-clicking the data type's keyword in Xcode. We even covered some more in-depth topics such as type conversion and string interpolation.

We also really learned how Swift can derive types by using type inference based on the value or values given to a constant or variable, and what it means to have a constant or variable in your code.

In the next hour, we discuss operators, such as +, -, =, ==, and more, and how to work with operators with the data types discussed in this hour. It will be beneficial to jump to operators first before diving into more advanced data types like arrays and dictionaries. Arrays and dictionaries are discussed in Hour 4, "Working with Collection Types."

Q&A

Q. Will I harm anything by trying out data types with different values?

A. Absolutely not. Playgrounds offer a great way to test your code while providing immediate feedback. Have fun!

Q. Should I always explicitly declare a data type?

A. Not necessarily. There may be situations where it is best to declare a data type, but in simple applications it is not always necessary to do so. Generally you decide this on a case-by-case basis.

Q. Do all variables have to contain values?

A. No. Swift allows us to use optionals, where a variable can either have a value or not. Optional variables are declared with a question mark: `var myOptInt : Int?`. We learn more about optionals in Hour 5.

Workshop

The workshop contains quiz questions and exercises to help you solidify your understanding of the material covered. Try to answer all questions before looking at the answers that follow.

Quiz

1. What is the difference between `let` and `var`?
2. In the following code, what will Swift infer the data type as?

   ```
   var hasComment = false
   ```

3. What is an unsigned integer?
4. In the following code, what will Swift infer the data type as?

   ```
   var customerAge = "25"
   ```

5. What character is used to concatenate strings in Swift?

Answers

1. The introducer `let` indicates a constant. The introducer `var` indicates a variable.
2. Swift will infer the data type as `Bool`.
3. Unsigned integers can hold a large positive number but cannot contain negative values.

4. Swift will infer the data type as `String`. The actual value is an `Int`, but since the value is wrapped in quotes Swift will assign the `String` data type.

5. The plus sign (+) is used to join (or concatenate) strings in Swift.

Exercise

Create a new playground. Create two constants to hold your first and last name. Create another constant to hold your favorite quote. Join and display the variables by using concatenation and string interpolation.

Using Operators in Swift

What You'll Learn in This Hour:

- ► How to identify unary, binary, and ternary operators
- ► How to use arithmetic operators
- ► How to use logical operators
- ► How to use assignment and equality operators
- ► How to use operators with strings
- ► How to use range operators

Operators are a key ingredient to every app. In fact, it's difficult to write an app—other than the standard "Hello, world!" example—that doesn't contain at least one operator. Operators are symbols or a set of symbols that change or assign values, combine values, or check or verify values in your code. In this hour, we learn about most of the basic operators in Swift and understand why and how to use them.

All operators in Swift can be categorized as **unary**, **binary**, or **ternary**. Unary operators perform an action upon a single variable or constant, binary operators perform an action upon two variables and/or constants, and ternary operators perform an action involving three variables and/or constants.

Unary Operators

A unary operator operates on a single value. A unary operator can be **prefix** or **postfix**, meaning that it can come before a variable or constant (prefix, such as ++count), or immediately follow a variable or constant (postfix, such as count++). Some unary operators can be either (prefix or postfix), while some can be only one or the other. A unary operator cannot have any whitespace between itself and the variable or constant. Unary operators act upon numeric and Boolean types in Swift. Let's take a look at Swift's unary operators.

Increment and Decrement Operators

Two similar operators are the **increment operator** and the **decrement operator**. The increment operator, denoted by ++, increases a numeric value by 1, and the decrement operator, denoted by --, decreases a numeric value by 1. The increment operator is short-hand for a longer expression; a++ is the same as a = a + 1, and a-- is the same as a = a - 1. Both the increment and decrement operators can be prefix or postfix.

There is a key difference in behavior, however, between the increment and decrement operators concerning prefix and postfix. That is the order in which the value is incremented or decremented and when assignment occurs. A prefixed decrement operator decrements the numeric value by 1 and returns the newly assigned value. Likewise, a prefixed increment operator increments the numeric value by 1 and returns the newly assigned value. The postfixed decrement operator first returns the numeric value before decrementing; likewise, the postfixed increment operator returns the numeric value before incrementing. Take a look at the following code example to see this behavior in action.

```
var x = 1
println(++x)
// ++x - x increments first, new value is displayed
x = 1
// just resetting value for demonstration
println(x++)
// now x is incremented, but after the print function has already occurred
println(x)
//notice the different value now when this line is printed?
```

Logical NOT Operator

The logical **NOT** operator inverts the value of a Boolean variable. In other words, if a variable's value is true, the variable will not be false, and vice versa. The logical NOT operator is always a prefix operator. We discuss the logical NOT operator and other logical operators a little more in depth later in this hour. Here is what the logical NOT operator looks like in code.

```
let a = true  // a is a Bool equaling true
let b = !a  // b is a Bool equaling false
```

CAUTION

The Logical NOT Operator Must Be a Prefix Operator

Using (!) after a variable has another meaning, which is covered in Hour 5, "Understanding Optional Values."

Unary Minus Operator

The unary **minus** operator is short-hand for multiplying a variable's value by -1, and returning the result. The unary minus operator is always a prefix operator and can prefix variables, constants, or numeric literals. Here is what the unary minus operator looks like in code.

```
let c = 5
let d = -c  // d is equal to -5
let e = -42  // e is equal to -42
```

Swift also has a unary **plus** operator, by prefixing a + before any variable or constant, but it doesn't actually change the value of a numeric variable, because any negative multiplied by a positive is still a negative. The unary plus operator is more for distinction in your code to show that a certain value should be positive.

Binary Operators

Binary operators are operators that affect **operands**, which are the values on either side of the operator. For example, take a + b. In this expression, a and b are operands, and + is the operator. All Binary operators are **infix**, meaning they are in between two operands.

Standard Arithmetic Operators

Swift provides the four standard arithmetic operators that are binary operators for all numeric types, which are addition (+), subtraction (-), division (/), and multiplication (*). To use these operators in code, you use them exactly the way you would write them in a math equation.

```
let a = 5 + 5  // a equals 10
let b = 3 - 2  // b equals 1
let c = 8.0 / 5.0  // c equals 1.6
let d = 4 * 4  // d equals 16
```

Remainder Operator

Swift includes a **remainder operator**, annotated by the % sign. In other languages, this operator is called the **modulo operator**, which has slightly different behavior. Swift calculates the remainder operator by figuring out how many times b evenly divides a, and returns the remainder. In other words, a = (b * multiplier) + remainder, with multiplier being the largest number b could multiply against to not produce a value higher than a.

In languages like C and Objective-C, the modulo operator behaved similarly, but unlike Swift, it could not perform against floating-point numbers; you would get a compiler error as the modulo operator cannot take floating-point numbers as its operands. This is another reason that Swift's remainder operator is truly a remainder operator, because Swift gives the remainder of what is left over from a - (b * multiplier). Listing 3.1 displays the modulo operator in C.

LISTING 3.1   Modulo Operator in C and Objective-C

```
int a = 8;
int b = 6;
int c = a % b;  // returns 2, as expected
int d = -8;
int e = d % b;  // returns -2, as expected
```

In C and Objective-C, the modulo operator is pretty straightforward, as long as you're providing integers. Listing 3.2 displays the remainder operator in Swift, which not only works with integers like C, but can also operate on Double types.

LISTING 3.2   Remainder Operator in Swift

```
let a = 8
let b = 6
let c = a % b  // returns 2, just as in C
let d = 8.0
let e = 2.5
let f = d % e  // returns 0.5, Swift allows remainders for Double types
```

The Assignment Operator

There is just one **assignment operator** in Swift, as in other languages, and that is the equal sign (=). The assignment operator takes the calculated or literal value on the right side of the equal sign and assigns it to the variable or constant on the left side of the equal sign. We have seen the assignment operator many times throughout this book already, and every single line in Listing 3.1 and Listing 3.2 utilizes the assignment operator.

Compound Assignment Operators

Compound assignment operators in Swift utilize the previously mentioned assignment operator (=), coupled with another operator, to perform a combined effect. Table 3.1 details each operator, what code it is short for, and a description.

TABLE 3.1   Compound Assignment Operators

Operator	Example	Longer Expression	Description
+=	a += b	a = a + b	Add, then assign
-=	a -= b	a = a - b	Subtract, then assign

Operator	Example	Longer Expression	Description
*=	a *= b	a = a * b	Multiply, then assign
/=	a /= b	a = a / b	Divide, then assign
%=	a %= b	a = a % b	Compute remainder, then assign

Table 3.1 shows some of the basic compound operators. However, there are many more compound operators, all of which are more advanced than the scope of this book, such as bitwise and logical compound operations. For more information on these operators, see the chapter on expressions in *The Swift Programming Language*, Apple, 2014.

Comparison Operators

Comparison operators in Swift are similar to those of other programming languages. Table 3.2 lists the basic comparison operators.

TABLE 3.2 Comparison Operators

Operator	Example	Description
>	a > b	Returns true if a is greater than b, else false
<	a < b	Returns true if a is less than b, else false
>=	a >= b	Returns true if a is greater than or equal to b, else false
<=	a <= b	Returns true if a is less than or equal to b, else false
==	a == b	Returns true if a is equal to b, else false
!=	a != b	Returns true if a is not equal to b, else false

As with comparison operators, there are other advanced operators. We cannot discuss them all in this book, but we cover two more of them in Hour 10, "Learning About Structs and Classes."

NOTE

Using Comparison Operators

Most often, comparison operators are used in conditional statements, such as an if block, or in loop statements, such as a while block. Examples would be if a > b { println("a is greater than b" }, or while a < 100 { ++a }. We cover conditionals and control flow in Hour 6, "Controlling Program Flow with Conditionals," and loops in Hour 7, "Iterating Code with Loops."

Range Operators

Range operators in Swift are denoted by two dots and a left angle bracket (. .<) or three dots (. . .) depending on what type of range you need. There are two types of range operators: **half-closed range operators** and **closed range operators**.

A half-closed range operator uses two dots and a left angle bracket to indicate a range of integers from its left-hand operand up to but not including the right-hand operand. The expression 1..<5 defines a range of four integers, 1 through 4, but not including 5. You can also use variables or constants with range operators, such as 1..<a. The half-closed operator is called such because its range contains its initial value but not the final value.

A closed range operator uses three dots to indicate a range of integers from its left-hand operand up to and including the right-hand operand. The expression -2...2 defines a range of five integers, from -2 to +2. The closed range operator can also use variables or constants as operands, such as a...b. The closed range operator is called closed range because the range is closed on each end by including both operands.

Both half-closed range operators and closed range operators are useful in iterative expressions. Closed range operators are good for ranges where you want both the first and last values of the range to be included. Half-closed range operators are especially good for zero-based lists such as arrays, where the index of the first element is 0, followed by 1, then 2, and so on. Arrays are discussed in more detail in Hour 4, "Working with Collection Types." Consider the code in Listing 3.3—it illustrates the differences in the two range operators.

LISTING 3.3 Different Range Operators

```
for a in 1...5 {
    println(a)
}
// This closed range prints the following:
// 1
// 2
// 3
// 4
// 5
let arrayLength = 3
for b in 0..<arrayLength {
    println(b)
}
// This half-closed range prints the following:
// 0
// 1
// 2
```

CAUTION
___

Ranges Must Progress in a Positive Direction

Ranges in Swift must progress in a positive direction. The starting index (left-hand operand) must be less than or equal to the ending index (right-hand operand). Attempting to progress in a negative direction will result in a compiler error if detected when coding or a run-time error and crash if detected while the app is running. You might want to validate that the left-hand operand is less than the right-hand operand if your operands are not known at compile time.
___

Logical Operators

Swift provides three **logical operators**, AND (&&), OR(||), and NOT (!). These operators are called logical operators because they evaluate upon and return Boolean value types based on logic. The three logical operators compare the bits inside their given operands, perform the operation against them, and then return the result. These three operators are similar to those you would find in other languages, but we discuss them here if you're not familiar.

Logical AND Operator

The **logical AND operator**, sometimes referred to as just AND, performs a logical AND operation against both operands and returns the result. Let's illustrate how AND operates and comes up with a return value. Look at the truth table in Table 3.3.

TABLE 3.3   Logical AND Operator Truth Table

Operand 1	Operand 2	AND Result
True	True	True
True	False	False
False	True	False
False	False	False

Let's say you're comparing two Boolean values, a and b, in the following code sample.

```
let a = true
let b = false
let c = a && b
```

What value does c have? You're right, c is `false`. The AND operator is useful when every value in a certain set of conditions needs to be met first before executing an expression or set of expressions. For example, the following code snippet illustrates what use of the AND operator looks like if you were to try to get access to a device's motion data.

```
if CMPedometer.isStepCountingAvailable() && userAcceptedUseOfM7Processor {
    /* it's now ok to get step data */
} else {
    println("cannot get step data")
}
```

If step counting is not available (known by the Boolean return value of `CMPedometer.isStep-CountingAvailable()`) or if the user has explicitly stated it's not okay for us to have access to the device's motion coprocessor, then we cannot count the user's steps.

Logical OR Operator

The logical OR operator is similar in syntax to the AND operator but behaves slightly differently. The OR operator evaluates two operands and decides whether either one is true or not, no matter which one, and then returns its result. The truth table in Table 3.4 details the OR operator's behavior.

TABLE 3.4 Logical OR Operator Truth Table

Operand 1	Operand 2	OR Result
True	True	True
True	False	True
False	True	True
False	False	False

The OR operator returns true if either operand in the expression is true. Let's take another look at a simple code snippet to illustrate OR.

```
let a = true
let b = false
let c = a || b
```

What is the value of `c`? Again, you're right; the value is `true`. A more realistic example might look something like this:

```
if userHasCellularConnectivity || userHasWifiConnectivity {
    // assume user has an internet connection, start talking to web service
} else {
    // warn user to enable connectivity hardware
}
```

In the previous example, if either of the two operands (`userHasCellularConnectivity` or `userHasWifiConnectivity`) is true, then the first block of code executes. If neither operand is true, the second block of code executes. We cover conditionals with `if` statements in Hour 6.

Logical NOT Operator

The last logical operator, NOT, as mentioned earlier, simply inverts the value of a Boolean variable or constant. Although not a binary operator, NOT is listed here in the logical operators section for completeness. For example, see Table 3.5 for the truth table illustrating the values resulting from the NOT operator.

TABLE 3.5 Logical NOT Operator Truth Table

Operand	NOT Result
True	False
False	True

Combining Logical Operators

Logical operators can be combined into larger expressions where multiple lines of logic may be required. The expression `a && b || !c` combines all three logical operators and can be read as "a and b must be true, or not c". While not required, you can insert parentheses to explicitly state the order of operations you want in your code, such as `(a && b) || (!(c && d))`.

Ternary Conditional Operators

Swift has only one ternary conditional operator, and it is written as short-hand for a longer expression that checks a particular case or condition and provides a value for the true branch and another value for the false branch. We cover the ternary conditional operator in greater detail in Hour 6, since it is a more succinct substitution for a longer conditional expression.

Summary

In this hour, we covered a lot of material regarding operators. Most operators are straightforward, but if you don't understand any, don't worry; operators are used frequently throughout the book, and you will pick it up by repetition. Logical operators manipulate and/or combine Boolean values `true` and `false`. Unary operators act upon a single target, binary operators act upon two targets, and ternary operators compare a Boolean value to execute one of two expressions. Operators can be prefix, postfix, or infix, meaning they can be written immediately in front of an operand, immediately after an operand, or in between two operands, respectively. Most of these types of operators are familiar from other languages.

New to Swift (as compared to C or Objective-C) are range operators. These prove to be powerful for iterating over ranges of values, items in a list, and others. Range operators come in two types:

half-closed range operators, which include the first but not the last values given, and closed range operators, which include the first and the last values given. We use these operators multiple times throughout this book.

In the next hour, we discuss collection types including `Arrays` and `Dictionaries`. `Arrays` and `Dictionaries` are crucial to many apps, in that they keep lists of multiple objects in memory to be used for things such as data sources, data retrieved from networks, or even to store preferences between app launches.

Q&A

Q. Is it faster to use postfix or prefix?

A. This is a matter of opinion, but the truth is that in most cases the difference between the two is negligible in terms of processing speed in compiled languages.

Q. Why are there two range operators? Wouldn't it be simpler to just use one?

A. Having two range operators allows you to express intent a lot more clearly in code. In the case of a zero-based list, you may have 10 items but the last item's index is 9, so a half-closed range operator (`0..<count`, for instance) would be a better fit. If you know you have a finite number of times something should loop, a closed-range operator (`1...10`, for instance) clearly indicates a range of 1 to 10.

Q. What is a practical example of using remainder?

A. Imagine an app that shows a progress bar when loading. In this case, the progress is only checked occasionally (every nth time) throughout the loading loop, or when the count of the loop % n is equal to 0. This becomes clearer in later hours when we cover conditionals and control flow in Hour 6 and loops in Hour 7.

Workshop

The workshop contains quiz questions and exercises to help you solidify your understanding of the material covered. Try to answer all questions before looking at the answers that follow.

Quiz

1. What is the difference between postfix and prefix unary operators?

2. In the following code, what is the value of the variable named `c`?

```
let a = 11
let b = 5
let c = a % b
```

3. In the following code, what is the value of the variable named a?

```
var a = 5
let b = 6
a *= b
```

4. In the following code, what is the value of the variable named b?

```
let a = 5
let b = -a
```

5. What is the difference between two dots with a left angle bracket (..<) and three dots (...) in a range operation?

Answers

1. The postfix increment does not increase the value of its operand until after it has been evaluated. The prefix decrement increases the value of its operand before it has been evaluated.

2. The value of c after the modulo operator is 1.

3. The value of a after the compound assignment is 30.

4. The value of b after the unary minus operation is -5.

5. The two dot with left angle bracket range (..<) is a half-closed range because the upper limit is noninclusive. The three dot range (...) is a closed range because the upper limit is inclusive.

Exercise

Create a new playground. Create two variables to hold two separate numbers, 1 and 10. Use different comparison operators to compare the two values. Next, display the numbers using both the half-closed and closed ranges.

Working with Collection Types

What You'll Learn in This Hour:

▶ The structure of arrays

▶ The structure of dictionaries

▶ How to create arrays and dictionaries

▶ How to use subscripts and keys to access data

▶ How to use tuples to access key-value pairs

In this hour, we explore the two types of collections in Swift, **arrays** and **dictionaries**. We also cover a data structure called a **tuple**, which isn't a declarable data type like an array or dictionary but can be used to get data of varying types from dictionaries and other structures. Arrays and dictionaries are common structures used in everyday apps because they are great for things like storing data source information, storing retrieved data from a network resource, storing ordered or even unordered lists of information, and more. We can do a lot of things with arrays and dictionaries, so let's get started.

Arrays

Let's start by learning about arrays. Arrays are ordered sets of data, and every member inside an array must be of the same type. This means that if you have an array of integers, all the members must be of the integer type, and you cannot insert a double, character, string, or any other data type into the array. Swift's array structures behave this way to help with type safety to prevent the incorrect data type from entering an array and having potentially harmful side effects.

Declaring an array in Swift is simple. As you have done already with types such as `Int`, `Double`, `String`, and so on, you do something similar with the array type, with one small twist. You have to specify the type of data that will be stored in the array, and that type is placed inside open- and closed-chevrons. Here is what an array declaration looks like in Swift.

```
let myArray: Array<Int> = [1, 2, 3]
```

As you are familiar with by now, the `let` introducer signifies that the array is a constant. `myArray` is the name of the constant, and `Array<Int>` tells Swift that `myArray` is an array of `Int`s. Placing comma-separated values inside square brackets, as you see with `[1, 2, 3]`, is an array literal and is a way to provide elements to an array quickly.

CAUTION

Array Member Types Cannot Change

Keep in mind that once you declare an array, even with the `var` introducer to make it a mutable array, its member's types cannot change. This helps keep type safety consistent, and Swift warns you even before compiling if it notices you are trying to insert a value of a different type. If you need an array to store different types than an array you currently have, declare a new array with that desired member type.

As with many things in Swift, there is another way (and yes, an even shorter way) to declare an array of a particular type. From the previous example, let's declare `myArray` as an array of `Int`s again but now using Swift's short-hand syntax for declaring an array.

```
let myArray: [Int] = [1, 2, 3]
```

`[Int]` is Swift short-hand for declaring `myArray` of type `Array<Int>`. The same could be done for `[Double]`, `[String]`, `[Bool]`, or even if you had a custom class, struct, or other type, you could create an array of that type too, such as `[MyCustomClass]`. However, because of Swift's tremendous power to infer types, we can shorten this declaration even further.

```
let myArray = [1, 2, 3]
```

Excellent! Because of the square brackets, Swift infers `myArray` to be an array. Then, Swift analyzes the data inside the square brackets and senses that they are all integers, so it declares `myArray` to be `[Int]` for us.

NOTE

Best Practice for Declaring Instances of `Array`

Unless necessary, it is suggested for consistency and readability to use `Array` short-hand syntax with the enclosing square braces, such as `[Int]` rather than `Array<Int>`. This is because it visually models more closely the structure of an `Array`.

In the event you just want to declare an empty array, you can use the open- and close-parentheses after the open- and close-brackets when declaring an array.

```
var todoItems = [String]()
```

[String] indicates to Swift that you want a variable array to hold instances of type String, and the () short-hand syntax indicates to Swift to initialize the array with no items, as an empty array.

NOTE

All Values Must Be Initialized to Be Used

Remember that all instances in Swift must be initialized before they are used, thus the short-hand initializer syntax is common. You may find yourself using it frequently when you don't know the values needing to be stored in an array yet.

Indexes and Subscripts for Accessing Values

Each member in a Swift array has an associated **index**. This behavior is the same as C and Objective-C, as well as many other languages, in case you have experience there. You can use this index to reference a member inside the array. All arrays in Swift are **zero-based**, which means that the first index in an array is always zero (0), the second index is 1, the third is 2, and so on. Why is that important to mention? If you have an array that has five elements, let's say "A", "B", "C", "D", and "E", to get the value "E" you ask the array for the value at index 4, because index 4 is actually the fifth element's index in the array. To access the data in an array, you use a **subscript**. Subscripts are indexes enclosed inside square brackets immediately following the name of the array in code. Let's take a minute to try this out.

TRY IT YOURSELF ▼

Create and Access Data in an Array

We just learned a lot about creating arrays, how arrays handle member types, and setting initial data. Walk through these exercises to get comfortable with arrays and their syntax.

1. Open Xcode 6 and create a new playground.

2. In the playground, declare a variable array named myArray to hold String values and initialize the array to have the values "Foo", "Bar", and "Baz".

   ```
   var myArray = ["Foo", "Bar", "Baz"]
   ```

3. On the next line, type just the name of your array and watch the results pane to see how Xcode displays the contents of arrays.

   ```
   myArray
   ```

4. Use subscript syntax to access the second element in the array. Did Xcode return "Bar"?

   ```
   myArray[1]
   ```

5. This time use subscript syntax to change the value for the first element to "Dog", by using the assignment operator we learned about in Hour 3, "Using Operators in Swift." Then type the name of the array again to see the resulting array.

```
myArray[0] = "Dog"
myArray
```

Manipulating Arrays

In the preceding Try It Yourself section, step 5 walks you through changing the value of one of an array's members. You can use subscripts to change a value inside an array. Just be sure that you are inserting data of the proper type.

Adding Elements to Arrays

Another action you may want to take on arrays is appending elements to an array. For instance, say you're building a To Do manager, where the user inserts tasks to remind himself to do things. It wouldn't be an effective app if the user wasn't allowed to add tasks. Thankfully, Swift gives us an easy method to use on an array instance to append a value, and it is called **append**. Take a look at Listing 4.1 to see how appending to an array works.

LISTING 4.1   Appending an Element to an Array

```
var tasks = [String]()  // initializes empty array to tasks
tasks = ["Clean house", "Walk dog"]  // tasks now has 2 elements
tasks.append("Wash the car")  // tasks now has 3 elements
println(tasks)  // displays: [Clean house, Walk dog, Wash the car]
```

You can append items to arrays by not only using the append(someValue) method on your array instance, but you can also use the addition-assignment compound operator, discussed in Hour 3. To add items this way, you must enclose them inside square brackets as an array literal, even if you are appending one item. Using the code in Listing 4.1, see Listing 4.2 for a continuation.

LISTING 4.2   Appending an Array with the Addition-Assignment Operator

```
tasks += ["Milk the cow"]  // tasks now has 4 elements
tasks += ["Rake leaves", "Mow lawn"] // tasks now has 6 elements
tasks.count  // displays 6
```

In the previous example, we used the addition-assignment operator to add array literals to our existing array. This illustrates some of Swift's power, with concise syntax.

CAUTION

Be Careful with Subscript Syntax

You cannot append items to an array by using subscript syntax. Doing so, such as assigning "Fill gas tank" to index subscript 10, would result in an **out of bounds** error because the compiler checks first to see whether an element at that index exists, which it doesn't. You can always determine how many elements are in an array by using the `count` property on an array. It returns the number of elements in that array. Just remember, if there are five elements in an array, the last index is 4, because arrays are zero-based.

Inserting Elements into Arrays

Remember that arrays are ordered lists, and when you append an item to an array, it tacks the new item on to the end of the array. Table 4.1 illustrates an abstract representation of how an array can be visualized.

TABLE 4.1 Array Visualization

Index	Value
0	`"Clean house"`
1	`"Walk dog"`
2	`"Wash the car"`
3	`"Milk the cow"`
4	`"Rake leaves"`
5	`"Mow lawn"`

Suppose in our To Do app, our user wants to take a shower after milking the cow. We could change the value at index 4, but then he or she wouldn't be reminded to rake the leaves. Swift provides a way to insert elements into an array at a particular index, with the `insert(someValue)` method. Building upon Listing 4.1 and Listing 4.2, Listing 4.3 illustrates how to insert an item into our existing list of tasks.

LISTING 4.3 Inserting an Element into an Array

```
tasks.insert("Take a shower", atIndex: 4)  // tasks now has 7 elements
```

Now our array of tasks should look like Table 4.2.

TABLE 4.2　Array Visualization after Insertion

Index	Value
0	"Clean house"
1	"Walk dog"
2	"Wash the car"
3	"Milk the cow"
4	"Take a shower"
5	"Rake leaves"
6	"Mow lawn"

Replacing and Updating Items in an Array

Replacing values at a particular index is as easy as using subscript syntax denoting the index you want to update, and using the assignment operator (=) to set the new value. For example, to update "Walk dog" to "Walk Boudreau", simply type the following code.

```
tasks[1] = "Walk Boudreau"
```

Swift even has syntax for replacing ranges of values inside arrays. The range lengths don't have to be the same either, as Swift resizes the array to fit the new length. Perhaps you know that "Wash the car", "Milk the cow", and "Take a shower" are all part of your daily routine, and you don't need them spelled out for you. You could replace them with a new array literal or values from another array. The inserted value must be an array of the same type as the receiving array, even if you're only inserting one value. The following example illustrates the concept of replacing ranges.

```
tasks[2...4] = ["Daily routine"]
```

Removing Items in an Array

Swift's array structure provides many ways to remove elements from an array instance. Removing an item in an array deletes the item itself, and if necessary, shifts all the affected indexes so that they are once again sequential from 0 to count-1. Before we move on to dictionaries, let's try removing some items from our tasks list.

Remove Items from the Tasks List

Use several different methods to remove items from the tasks list.

1. Open Xcode 6 and create a new playground.

2. Create and populate the array `tasks` by writing all the code from Listings 4.1, 4.2, and 4.3.

3. Our user cleaned the house, so remove the first item in the `tasks` list:

```
tasks.removeAtIndex(0)
```

4. Our user decided not to mow the lawn, and since it's the last item in our array, we can simply remove the last item:

```
tasks.removeLast()
```

5. Our user just got lazy, and decided not to do anything. Clear the tasks array all at once:

```
tasks.removeAll(keepCapacity: false)  // or...
tasks = []  // either line would remove all items and set size to 0
```

Common Array Methods and Properties

Swift's array structure provides many methods for getting information from an array instance. Probably the most common is `count`. `count` is an instance property of type `Int` that tells you how many items are in the array. You can simply use `myArray.count` to return to you the number of items.

Another helpful instance property of arrays is the property `isEmpty`. `isEmpty` returns a `Bool` (true or false) as to whether the array is empty or not. This is commonly used in conditional statements (more on conditional statements in Hour 6, "Controlling Program Flow with Conditionals"), such as an `if` statement, because `if` statements evaluate Boolean expressions. Consider the following code example to illustrate the `isEmpty` and `count` properties.

```
if myArray.isEmpty {
    println("There are no items in myArray!")
} else {
    println("There are \(myArray.count) items in myArray.")
}
```

Arrays have many methods as well, where you can tell the array instance to perform a particular task. One such method is the `reverse()` method. `reverse()` is pretty self-explanatory; it returns a copy of the array instance in reverse order. `reverse()` does not actually alter the contents of the instance.

```
let reverseArray = myArray.reverse()
```

To get a look at what all you can do with arrays, as well as with any types, hold down the Command key and click the type (in this case, type `Array<Int>` and Command-click the word "Array" in Xcode), and Xcode takes you directly to the type's definition. Anything you see with a `var` introducer is a property, and anything that starts with `func` is a function or method. Most often, too, Apple provides documentation in its code in the form of comments above methods or properties that need explanation. This is a great way to learn what's available if you are the type of person who likes digging through code!

Dictionaries

Dictionaries in Swift are similar to arrays in that they hold lists of data, except dictionaries are unordered lists, and instead of accessing them via indexes, dictionary values are accessed via **keys**. A key is a unique identifier for every value in a dictionary. Keys can be `Ints`, `Doubles`, `Strings`, `Bools`, and even enum members, because a key must be **hashable**. Hashable means that the value can be made uniquely identifiable via a hash algorithm. Swift uses hashes for keys behind the scenes because this makes finding values for keys perform better. Don't worry about hashes, though; you won't have to interact with them directly.

NOTE

Enum Members As Dictionary Keys

A value type we've not yet discussed are enumerations, sometimes referred to as simply enums. Enums hold a unique group of related values. We discuss enums in Hour 12, "Harnessing the Power of Enums."

Key-Value Pairs

Data is stored in dictionaries in **key-value pairs**. A key-value pair is similar in concept to arrays where a value has an associated index, although dictionaries are unordered, and data members are referenced by their keys. Each key and value in a dictionary must have a data type, and it must remain consistent throughout the life of the dictionary. For instance, to declare a dictionary with keys of type `String` and values of type `Double`, it would look like the following code example.

```
var myDictionary: Dictionary<String, Double> = [ "pi" : 3.14 ]
```

The preceding dictionary declaration is similar to arrays in that you specify the types to be used inside the dictionary in between the open- and closed-chevrons. The differences here are that there are two types inside the chevrons rather than just one, represented as <key-type, value-type>, and the dictionary literal we assigned as our initial value uses "pi" as the key string, and the literal 3.14 as the value. This satisfies Swift's type safety requirements.

Dictionaries in Swift are slightly different than Objective-C's NSDictionary and NSMutableDictionary classes, which can store any type of object as their keys and values, and no information was provided about the type of data stored in these dictionaries. Often you, the developer, had to perform introspection on a retrieved object, meaning you asked it what type of class it was first before you could do anything with the returned value. Swift allows you to do something similar by telling a dictionary to use the Any type for the value type, but it is not the default behavior, and you should make sure you explicitly state the data type if it is known.

NOTE

Using Swift's Any and AnyObject Types

Swift provides two generic data types, Any and AnyObject. Any refers to an instance of any type at all, not including function types. AnyObject refers to an instance of any class type. We discuss Any and AnyObject more in Hour 15, "Adding Advanced Type Functionality."

Initializing Dictionaries

As mentioned already, instances of all types in Swift must be initialized first before use with at least a zero value or empty array or dictionary. There are two ways to declare an empty Dictionary in Swift for easy initialization. The following four lines are functionally the same, just written differently to illustrate the differences in how you can initialize a Dictionary instance.

```
var newDictionary = Dictionary<String, String>()
var newDictionary: Dictionary<String, String> = [:]
var newDictionary = [String : String]()
var newDictionary: [String : String] = [:]
```

The first line uses the open- and closed-parentheses to tell Swift to use Dictionary's default init() method, which returns an empty instance of a Dictionary<String, String> structure. The second line initializes a Dictionary<String, String> instance by giving it an empty dictionary literal ([:]). The third line uses short-hand syntax for declaring a Dictionary of type [String : String], similar to Array short-hand, and uses open- and closed-parentheses to initialize. The fourth line uses short-hand syntax again and then assigns an empty dictionary literal. Any of these methods of initialization is correct and acceptable. Here we make the dictionary a var because if we declare a constant dictionary with let, it won't allow us to modify it in the future.

NOTE

Best Practice for Declaring Instances of `Dictionary`

The suggested best practice for declaring instances of `Dictionary` is to use the short-hand syntax from the third and fourth lines of the previous example. This is for consistency and readability, as it visually models the structure of a `Dictionary` better than `Dictionary<KeyType, ValueType>`.

Type Inference with Dictionaries

Swift can also infer the types of the keys and values of dictionaries by the types of the values given during initialization. Listing 4.4 shows how to explicitly declare a dictionary with typed keys and values, and then also by using Swift's type inference.

LISTING 4.4   Using Type Inference to Reduce Code

```
// First, declare a Dictionary with explicit types
var myDictionary: [String : Double] = [ "pi" : 3.14 ]
// Next, we'll declare the same Dictionary using type inference
var myDictionary = [ "pi" : 3.14 ]
```

As you can see, not only did Swift infer that `myDictionary` is a `Dictionary` based on the provided dictionary literal, but it also inferred the types of the keys and values inside the dictionary. That is powerful! In addition to Swift's type inference saving us some time typing, type inference also greatly reduces the risk of errors occurring down the road, because Swift is checking for type safety any time your variable or constant is used.

Adding Data to Dictionaries

As seen previously, you can initialize dictionaries with dictionary literals, such as `[ "pi" : 3.14 ]`. You can provide more than one key-value pair in a literal by separating each pair with a comma. For instance, Listing 4.5 initializes a dictionary with two key-value pairs.

LISTING 4.5   Initializing a Dictionary with Multiple Key-Value Pairs

```
var specialNumbers = [ "pi" : 3.14, "gravity" : 9.8 ]
```

The `Dictionary` instance from Listing 4.5 now holds two key-value pairs and can be visualized abstractly in Table 4.3, much like we did previously with arrays.

TABLE 4.3 Dictionary Visualization

Key	Value
"pi"	3.14
"gravity"	9.8

Rarely will you ever have all the data you need upon initialization, so we need a way to later add data to the dictionary variable after it's been initialized. Swift provides two ways for us to add data to a dictionary: use the updateValue(value:, forKey:) method or use subscript syntax. The updateValue(value:, forKey:) method syntax looks a little intimidating if you haven't seen Objective-C's method names before, and we cover functions and methods in more detail in Hour 8, "Using Functions to Perform Actions." Dictionaries in Swift, unlike arrays, can create a key-value pair simply by using subscript syntax to add a value for a given key, even if the key doesn't exist yet. Swift adds the key-value pair when you reference a key that doesn't exist, when using the assignment operator (=). Listing 4.6 builds upon Listing 4.5 by adding a new key-value pair to the existing dictionary.

LISTING 4.6 Adding a New Key-Value Pair

```
01:  specialNumbers["this year"] = 2014  // adds 2014.0 for key "this year".
02:  specialNumbers.updateValue(2013, forKey: last year)  // adds 2013.0 for
➥key "last year"
```

Did you see how Swift automatically adds the .0 to the end of both 2014 and 2013? That's because the specialNumbers dictionary holds Doubles for its values. Even though we entered integer values, Swift converted them to Double values to satisfy its type safety requirement.

In Listing 4.6, Line 1 used subscript syntax, and Line 2 used the updateValue(value:, forKey:) method to illustrate another way to add data to a dictionary. Both lines are functionally the same. However, the updateValue(value:, forKey:) method returns the previous value for the specified key, if any. This can be helpful if you want to verify that an update actually took place. If there were no existing key-value pair, updateValue(value:, forKey:) returns nil, which we discuss more in Hour 5, "Understanding Optional Values."

Despite the intimidating syntax, updateValue(value:, forKey:) should be read aloud as plain English and maybe it will make sense: "Update value 2013 for key 'last year'." The difference here over what you may have seen in C, C#, or another language is that instead of placing parameters inside parentheses one after another, Swift shares some commonality with Objective-C by placing parameter names as part of the method signature to make the code more readable and to make how parameters are used more understandable.

Removing Pairs from Dictionaries

Since dictionaries are unordered lists, no index-shifting needs to happen when removing items from a Dictionary instance. There are two ways to remove items from a dictionary: subscript syntax or the `removeValueForKey(key:)` method. Listing 4.7 illustrates both ways of removing items from our dictionary, building upon Listing 4.6.

LISTING 4.7 Removing Pairs from Dictionaries

```
specialNumbers["this year"] = nil  // setting a key's value to nil removes the pair
specialNumbers.removeValueForKey("last year")  // removes the pair
➥where key = "last year"
```

Common Dictionary Methods and Properties

As with arrays, a variety of properties and methods is available for dictionaries as well. The `count` property exists on `Dictionary` also, which returns the number of key-value pairs inside. You can also retrieve an `Array` instance of just the `Dictionary`'s keys or values, by using the `myDictionary.keys` property or `myDictionary.values` property, which can be helpful when using iteration loops. As mentioned earlier with arrays, you can Command-click the `Dictionary` type wherever you have it in Xcode to be taken directly to the `Dictionary` struct's definition for more information.

Tuples

Tuples are a feature of Swift that is new to most C and Objective-C programmers. Tuples are an interesting case in Swift in that they represent a grouping of values as a compound value, but Tuple itself is not a type you can declare like you can an `Array` or `Dictionary`. Tuples can be used to extract the index and value from an `Array` item, or the key and value from a `Dictionary` item, as a pair that can extract those values to individual temporary values. Tuples are often used in `for-in` loops, and Listing 4.8 illustrates using tuples for arrays and dictionaries.

LISTING 4.8 Using Tuples with Arrays and Dictionaries

```
let anArray = ["Mary", "had", "a", "little", "lamb"]
let aDictionary = ["fleece color" : "white as snow",
            "Mary's location" : "lamb was sure to go"]
// first use tuples in anArray
for (index, value) in enumerate(anArray) {
    println("Index: \(index), value: \(value)")
}
```

```
// next, use tuples in aDictionary
for (key, value) in aDictionary {
    println("Key: \(key), value: \(value)")
}
```

In Listing 4.8, we use tuples for iterating over both an array and a dictionary. Notice that we write `enumerate(anArray)` for the array, versus just the name `anArray`. If we had just written `anArray` to iterate over, Swift would require us to not use a tuple but rather just a `String` type since `anArray` is of type `[String]` by inference.

Iterating over the dictionary is a little more straightforward, as we just reference the dictionary by name. In both cases, we create a tuple inside the parentheses to be used temporarily, and the tuple consists of the values named inside the parentheses. The values' types are inferred by Swift; for `anArray`, index is of type `Int`, and value is of type `String`, and these are the temporary values Swift creates for us as part of the tuple to extract from the array. As you work through this book and more code of your own, you'll find that this is a powerful and useful feature.

Summary

In this hour we learned a lot about arrays and dictionaries in Swift, how they are stored, referenced, indexed, initialized, and how to perform actions or get information about them. We also learned about tuples and the role they play with arrays and dictionaries.

In the next hour, we explore the concept of optional values in Swift, which are a terrific feature of the language to help ensure the safety of values.

Q&A

Q. Arrays and dictionaries seem similar. What is the difference?

A. Arrays involve a set of data objects with random access to those objects. Dictionaries store pairs of the objects. This makes dictionaries a better choice when storing relationships between objects.

Q. Can an array contain values with differing data types?

A. No. Array elements must be of the same type.

Q. Are there performance differences between using an array, dictionary, or tuple?

A. This is best answered on a case-by-case basis. The best practice is to create concise code to best fit the application. Always avoid code bloat, and then run performance tests on your application to increase speed.

Workshop

The workshop contains quiz questions and exercises to help you solidify your understanding of the material covered. Try to answer all questions before looking at the answers that follow.

Quiz

1. How can you find the total number of items in an array in Swift?

2. In the following code, what is the value of `petArray[0]`?

    ```
    var petArray = ["Dog",  "Cat", "Bird", "Fish"]
    ```

3. What is wrong with the following code?

    ```
    let petArray = ["Dog", "Cat", "Bird", "Fish"]
    petArray.append("Fish")
    ```

4. Given the following code, how could you update Player One's score to 125.0?

    ```
    var highScore = [ "Player One" : 99.0, "Player Two" : 99.7 ]
    ```

5. How could you correct the following code?

    ```
    var avgMileage = [ "To Work" : 32, "To School" : 20, "To Work":18 ]
    ```

Answers

1. `count` returns the number of elements in an array.

2. The value of `petArray[0]` is `Dog`.

3. You cannot add or remove elements to array constants.

4. You could update it like this:

    ```
    highScore.updateValue(125.0, forKey: "Player One")
    ```

5. Dictionary keys must be unique:

    ```
    var avgMileage = ["To Work" : 32, "To School" : 20, "Return To Work":18 ]
    ```

Exercise

Create a new playground. Create an array that contains your first and last name as values. Create a variable that points to the same array to make a copy. Add, remove, and alter values in each array and observe the results.

Now use the same values in a dictionary. Attempt to add and remove items from the array and dictionary.

Understanding Optional Values

What You'll Learn in This Hour:

▶ What are optional values

▶ Why optionals were introduced in Swift

▶ How optionals assist with type safety

▶ How to declare a variable as optional

▶ What nil values are, and how to handle nil

This hour we discuss a new concept that is not yet in most programming languages called optional values. We have learned so far about Swift's type safety and how Swift requires variables and constants to have a data type, whether explicitly annotated or inferred, and also be initialized with a value. Optionals in Swift are a way to handle the absence of a value, which can and does happen in many cases. Let's dive in to discuss what that means.

What Are Optional Values?

Optionals in Swift are instances that may or may not have a value. Swift's idea of an optional value is to help prevent you from writing code that could reference the absence of any value, which is denoted by a keyword called **nil**, when you meant to reference an actual value. nil is a familiar concept if you come from the Objective-C world, where nil is a pointer to an empty object. In Objective-C, you could use nil to your advantage; if an object were nil and you sent it a message (such as asking for its array contents in reverse order), nil would just stifle the message sent. Then, you could check for nil in your code and assume that if nothing happened or you received no array the object was nil. Then you go on your merry way by creating an instance of that object yourself.

In Swift, however, nil is handled a little differently. nil is still the absence of a value, but because Swift variables and constants must have an initialized value (in other words, a non-nil value), variables and constants cannot be nil in Swift. Also, in Swift, nil can apply to any data type, not just reference types, like the way Objective-C used nil. Think of it this way: Let's say you have two variables, a and b, where a equals 5 and b is nil. You try to create c = a + b, but since b happens to be nil, the app would crash because nil is the *absence* of a value, not just 0.

To create a safeguard around the issue of nil values, Swift uses optionals. Anytime you have a variable that you know could have a nil value, you designate the variable to be an optional variable, and what Swift does is create a **wrapper** around the variable's value, just in case it may be nil. If the value is nil, you are protected from runtime errors that would crash your app by otherwise directly accessing nil.

How to Designate a Variable as Optional

The Swift syntax for designating a variable as optional is simply appending the question mark character (?) to the end of the variable's type in its declaration. The following code declares a variable as an optional String.

```
var myOptionalString: String?
```

Because we are not initializing myOptionalString with any value, it contains nil. But, since String values cannot be nil (nor can any other value of any type, for that matter), we tell Swift that it is optional with the question mark character after the type. Swift's compiler recognizes this and knows that myOptionalString must use special operations to **unwrap** it before use.

NOTE

Optionals Can Only Be Variables

As a general best practice, it is suggested that you use the let introducer to create constants as often as possible where necessary in your code as an optimization feature, and, of course, for safety. Optionals, however, cannot be constants and *must* be variables. The reason for this is that an optional may or may not be nil, and it may change to or from nil later, so it must be a variable with its chance of change.

Wrapping and Unwrapping Optional Variables

These terms are not uncommon to most programmers, as often a particular app or framework requires you to wrap a value or object inside another object to be passed around to another function or method, or for storage. Apple's Foundation framework includes data types such as the NSArray and NSDictionary classes, which are similar to Swift's Array and Dictionary structures. A big difference, though, is that NSArray and NSDictionary store their values as type id, which is a pointer to any type of *object*. This means that to store a value, let's say the integer 6, into an NSArray or NSDictionary, you have to wrap it into an NSNumber object. Then, to get the value out to use it, `NSArray` and `NSDictionary` would return the object of type `id`, so you would have to explicitly unwrap, or *cast down* to the desired type—in this case `int`. (Note the lowercase `int`. In C, scalar types are lowercase. In Swift, the equivalent is `Int`.)

Wrapping and unwrapping in Swift work similarly, except that with optionals you aren't converting the type to another, per se. A better way to think about optionals is to think about your variable in front of you and then imagine a big box around it, keeping it safe from the elements. There may be something inside the box, or there may be nothing inside the box. But Swift allows the box to represent your value as it exists in your app and gets used and passed around. When you need to access the value, you unwrap (or, in this analogy, unbox) the value and access it directly.

Optional values are wrapped by default, so you don't need to explicitly wrap them. To unwrap, however, you can do that several different ways. Let's discuss what those methods of unwrapping are and what would be the best cases in which to use them.

Forced Unwrapping with the Unwrap Operator

First and foremost, Swift provides an **unwrap operator**. We didn't discuss this in Hour 3, "Using Operators in Swift," because it wouldn't have made any sense to you yet, having not learned about optionals at that point. The unwrap operator is simply the exclamation point (`!`) character immediately following the optional variable's name in code. This is called **forced unwrapping**. Listing 5.1 shows the declaration of an optional `String` variable and then using it in code.

LISTING 5.1 Declaring and Unwrapping Optional Values

```
var optStr: String?  // declares optStr as an optional String, value of nil
optStr = "I'm an optional string"
let unwrappedString = optStr!  // unwraps and assigns the actual string value
println(unwrappedString)  // prints "I'm an optional string" to the console
```

As you can see from Listing 5.1, declaring, assigning, and unwrapping optional values do not look too daunting. It's a nice safety measure that Swift implements to reduce the potential for apps to crash by accessing `nil`.

CAUTION

Ensure You Don't Forcibly Unwrap a Nil Value

The unwrap operator forcibly unwraps an optional variable and should only be used when you know that the variable contains a value. If you unwrap an optional variable that contains `nil`, your app will crash at runtime, logging the message "Fatal error: Unexpectedly found nil value while unwrapping an Optional value."

Forced unwrapping is handy and easy to do when you know that the variable contains a non-nil value. But what if you aren't sure that the value isn't nil? We can use **optional binding** to check the variable's value first before using it.

Optional Binding to Unwrap Variables

Because we may not know the inner value of a wrapped optional value at the time we receive it, we cannot always use the force unwrap operator to get at the value inside, because it may be nil. Swift has a mechanism called optional binding, used in an if let statement, to help us both unwrap a value and test it for validity before using it. Optional binding is useful because it assigns the unwrapped value to a temporary constant for use within the scope of the if let statement. (For more discussion on conditional syntax with if statements, see Hour 6, "Controlling Program Flow with Conditionals.")

Listing 5.2 shows an example of how to use optional binding in an if let block to illustrate how, depending on whether the value inside the optional wrapper is nil, different statements or expressions will be executed.

LISTING 5.2   Using Optional Binding to Unwrap and Use Optional Values

```
var optionalString: String? = "I am a string."
if let unwrappedString = optionalString {
    println("unwrappedString is not nil, and equals \(unwrappedString)")
} else {
    println("optionalString contains nil")
}
```

Using optional binding, we were able to assign the unwrapped value inside optionalString to unwrappedString, if it is not nil. If optionalString's value is nil, then the else block executes and prints "optionalString contains nil". If you were following along and typing the code here, did you find the same results, giving optionalString a string value or nil?

NOTE

Optionally Bound Values Live Only in their Declared Scope

Keep in mind that when using optional binding, the variable or constant declared in the if let (or if var for a bound variable) statement is used for only the life of the if block. Once execution passes outside the last curly brace, be it for the first if block, an else if block, or an else block, the variable or constant is deallocated and you cannot use it any longer. Attempting to use the constant or variable outside of its declared scope will result in a compiler error about use of undeclared variables.

Implicitly Unwrapped Optionals

Swift has a concept called **implicitly unwrapped optionals**, wherein you declare a variable as an optional, but with the intention that it won't have a `nil` value any time after it gets initialized with a value. To declare a variable as an implicitly unwrapped optional, you use the exclamation point character (`!`) immediately following the type name, rather than the question mark character (`?`). Here is what an implicitly unwrapped optional variable's declaration looks like.

```
var implicitInt = Int!
```

No initial value is given, but when it is initialized with a value (such as in an `init()` method, which we discuss in more depth in Hour 13, "Customizing Initializers of Classes, Structs, and Enums"), it will be known to have a value always, until it is deallocated from memory. This also means that you cannot assign `nil` to the implicitly unwrapped variable after it has been initialized with a valid value.

There are several benefits to using implicitly unwrapped optionals. First, sending known good input to a class that returns an optional value would normally mean a lot of checking for a value inside the optional variable, when you know that the returned value is a valid value inside the optional. Second, implicitly unwrapped optionals remove the need to use the force unwrap operator on optional variables before accessing the value or calling methods on the variable. This leads to cleaner and more easily readable code and less confusion about accidentally calling methods directly to an optional versus the underlying value.

CAUTION

Implicitly Unwrapped Optionals Are Still Optionals

Even though Swift handles the unwrapping of implicitly unwrapped optionals without you needing to, if the optional value is `nil` you will still have a runtime error and the app will crash. Make sure the value has been initialized to a non-`nil` value before use.

Listing 5.3 illustrates implicitly unwrapped optionals, including declaration, receiving optional return values, and usage in the app. The listing uses a method on `Dictionary` that we discussed earlier, `updateValue(value:, forKey:)`, which returns the old value after successfully updating, or `nil` if the key-value pair did not exist prior. Since it could return `nil`, `updateValue(value:, forKey:)` returns an optional value of the same type as the value we updated.

LISTING 5.3   Using Implicitly Unwrapped Optionals

```
var optionalInt: Int!  // optionalInt is an implicitly unwrapped optional
var myDictionary = ["life" : 32]  // myDictionary is a mutable Dictionary
optionalInt = myDictionary.updateValue(42, forKey:"life")  // updates value for
➡key and returns 32 to optionalInt
println(optionalInt)  // we can use optionalInt normally, without forced unwrapping
```

Nil Coalescing Operator

Another new operator to discuss is the **nil coalescing operator**. The nil coalescing operator is an infix operator and is denoted with two question marks (??) in between two values. The left-hand operand is an optional value, and the right-hand operand is any non-nil value. The operator returns an unwrapped value of the optional if one exists or the operand on the right if the left-hand optional is nil. Here is an example of the nil coalescing operator.

```
let result = optionalString ?? "No value"
```

In the preceding example, if optionalString is nil, then "No value" is assigned to result. Otherwise, the unwrapped optionalString value is assigned to result.

Use Case for Optionals

A real-world situation where you would use optional variables would be something like writing an iOS app that tracks your vehicle's mileage statistics when you pump fuel. You would have several data points to enter each time: the current odometer at fill-up, the cost-per-gallon or liter, and the number of gallons or liters you purchased. These would all be numbers entered into the app's input view into an object called UITextField (or a subclass thereof), with a property named *text*. To get the odometer reading from the user, you would access that data by creating a constant of type String, since text fields are always strings, and using the assignment operator (=) to set the text field's text property value to your constant.

```
let odometerReading = odometerField.text
```

You would do the same for the cost-per-gallon or liter, and the number of gallons or liters purchased. Now that you have the odometer reading, you need to convert that string data to an Int so that you can calculate different metrics, such as distance driven between fill-ups, average miles-per-gallon or kilometers-per-liter, and anything else your users might find useful about their vehicle. The String structure provides a method called toInt(), which converts a String instance to an Int instance, and returns an optional Int. Why does it return an optional Int? Because if the user was cheeky and entered "two thousand five hundred sixty four" instead of "2564" for the odometer reading, "two thousand five hundred sixty four" cannot be converted to an Int type, and thus would return nil.

Let's try this out in an exercise. At this point, we aren't using Interface Builder (the built-in visual interface design component to Xcode) to build an interface where we would have a UITextField, but Xcode 6's playgrounds are sophisticated enough to let us use them in code as actual workable and testable objects, so let's do that.

Simulate Getting Input from a User and Unwrapping the Data

Walk through an example using Xcode 6 playground to understand receiving user data, convert strings to integers, and handle optionals appropriately. (Note: There is probably a more efficient way to perform the steps provided here, but it is laid out this way to help you really grasp the concepts discussed in the book thus far in a combined program.)

1. Open Xcode 6 and create a new iOS playground. Clear the contents of the playground file.

2. To use `UITextField` objects in our code, we need to import the `UIKit` framework. Add the `import UIKit` statement at the top of our playground, if not already added.

   ```
   import UIKit
   ```

3. Declare three constant instances of `UITextField` objects. The syntax is similar to that of what we have done with other types thus far, just add an open and closed parentheses after `UITextField`. One will be for the current odometer reading, one for the last odometer reading, and one for number of gallons purchased. Also, make two `UILabel` objects, for simulating displaying the results to the user.

   ```
   let odometerField = UITextField()     // input field
   let lastOdometerField = UITextField() // input field
   let gallonsField = UITextField()      // input field
   let avgMPGLabel = UILabel()           // output label
   let distanceLabel = UILabel()         // output label
   ```

4. Now that we have instances of `UITextField`, we can adjust their properties, and this is where we simulate the user entering the mileage.

   ```
   odometerField.text = "2564"  // simulating user entering their current
   ➥odometer
   lastOdometerField.text = "2114"  // simulating user entering last odometer
   gallonsField.text = "16"  // simulating user entering gallons purchased
   ```

5. Next, we want to store the user input into constants of our own. (These constant names have "`String`" at the end of each one, but you may choose other names; I chose these to illustrate their types, as they are inferred by Swift.)

   ```
   let odometerString = odometerField.text
   let lastOdometerString = lastOdometerField.text
   let gallonsString = gallonsField.text
   ```

6. Declare the variables that we will work with as `Double` types. These store the data that get sent back to the user interface for metrics about the vehicle's fuel performance.

```
var avgMilesPerGallonDouble = 0.0  // Swift infers the Double type
var distanceDouble = 0.0
var gallonsDouble = 0.0
```

7. Use optional binding to unwrap values, if they exist, and store them into temporary constants. Use the constants in your equations to calculate the metrics.

```
if let odometerInt = odometerString.toInt() {
    distanceDouble = Double(odometerInt)
}
if let lastOdometerInt = lastOdometerString.toInt() {
    distanceDouble -= Double(lastOdometerInt)
}
if let gallonsInt = gallonsString.toInt() {
    gallonsDouble = Double(gallonsInt)
    avgMilesPerGallonDouble = distanceDouble / gallonsDouble
}
```

8. For completeness, assign the calculated values to user interface fields to display these calculated metrics to the user. (Since we do not have an interface, the playground simulates that for us. You would do this in your real app's code, but here you may not get the appropriate feedback that your calculations worked. Simply type the variable names on a line of code if you want to see your results.)

```
avgMPGLabel.text = "\(avgMilesPerGallonDouble) MPG"
distanceLabel.text = "\(distanceDouble) miles per fill-up"
// or to get console output feedback, use the following two lines of code
avgMilesPerGallonDouble
distanceDouble
```

Congratulations are in order if you stuck with it and finished the Try It Yourself example and got the expected results! This was a long example, and it utilized not only optional binding to unwrap optional values but was a good refresher for concepts learned in previous hours. Figure 5.1 shows the completed Try It Yourself example for you to compare results.

```
● ● ●                  🎬 Ch05 Optionals TIY.playground
🔡 | ‹  › | 🎬 Ch05 Optionals TIY.playground › No Selection
 1  import UIKit
 2
 3  let odometerField = UITextField()                    UITextField
 4  let lastOdometerField = UITextField()                UITextField
 5  let gallonsField = UITextField()                     UITextField
 6  let avgMPGLabel = UILabel()                          UILabel
 7  let distanceLabel = UILabel()                        UILabel
 8
 9  odometerField.text = "2564"                          UITextField
10  lastOdometerField.text = "2114"                      UITextField
11  gallonsField.text = "16"                             UITextField
12
13  let odometerString = odometerField.text              "2564"
14  let lastOdometerString = lastOdometerField.text      "2114"
15  let gallonsString = gallonsField.text                "16"
16
17  var avgMilesPerGallonDouble = 0.0                    0.0
18  var distanceDouble = 0.0                             0.0
19  var gallonsDouble = 0.0                              0.0
20
21  if let odometerInt = odometerString.toInt() {
22      distanceDouble = Double(odometerInt)             2,564.0
23  }
24  if let lastOdometerInt = lastOdometerString.toInt() {
25      distanceDouble -= Double(lastOdometerInt)        450.0
26  }
27  if let gallonsInt = gallonsString.toInt() {
28      gallonsDouble = Double(gallonsInt)               16.0
29      avgMilesPerGallonDouble = distanceDouble / gallonsDouble   28.125
30  }
31
32  avgMPGLabel.text = "\(avgMilesPerGallonDouble) MPG"  UILabel
33  distanceLabel.text = "\(distanceDouble) miles per fill-up"  UILabel
34  avgMilesPerGallonDouble                              28.125
35  distanceDouble                                       450.0
36
```

FIGURE 5.1
The completed Try It Yourself example with optional binding to unwrap optionals.

There is a lot more to optionals in Swift, but we need to cover a few more concepts first. We return to optionals in Hour 19, "Working with Optional Chaining." Optional chaining is a powerful feature in Swift that enables you to traverse object hierarchies of optional values in one line of code without having separate checking mechanisms for each optional value. For now, let's move on to Hour 6.

Summary

This hour introduced optional variables, a relatively new concept not yet implemented in many programming languages, as a way to better safeguard variables from being accessed while containing nil. This is a major player in Swift's language, and you will find yourself regularly using optional values.

You learned how to declare a variable as an optional with the optional declaration operator (?), and what being an optional variable means. You also learned several different methods for unwrapping: forced unwrapping by using the force unwrap operator (!); implicit unwrapping by declaring an optional variable with the implicit optional operator (!) immediately following the variable's type; and `if let` statements, which both unwrap and compare the unwrapped value against `nil` to determine whether a value exists and executes the appropriate section of code.

Q&A

Q. What are some differences between using `nil` in Objective-C and optionals in Swift?

A. Objective-C uses `nil` with pointers. Optionals in Swift work for all types, while `nil` in Objective-C works only with classes. As we learned, optionals are safer in Swift when coupled with the built-in unwrap operator.

Q. Wait a minute. `nil` exists in Swift, and `nil` also exists in Objective-C. What is the difference between `nil` in each?

A. Swift's `nil` is different from `nil` in Objective-C. In Objective-C, `nil` acts as a pointer to an object that does not exist. `nil` is not a pointer in Swift; it simply means that a value of a certain type is missing.

Q. Will a `nil` optional that is force unwrapped give a compile-time error?

A. No. The compiler assumes that the optional does indeed have a value since forced unwrapping was used. The error occurs when the app is run.

Workshop

The workshop contains quiz questions and exercises to help you solidify your understanding of the material covered. Try to answer all questions before looking at the answers that follow.

Quiz

1. A variable that holds a phone number in an app may contain a value or it may not. The following code snippet was used, but it is incorrect. How would you correct it?

```
var phoneNumber:String = nil
```

2. How do you use forced unwrapping of optionals in Swift?

3. What is optional binding in Swift?

4. Create an implicitly unwrapped optional that contains a user's score in a game.

5. Can an optional be a constant?

Answers

1. An optional should be used instead: `var phoneNumber:String?`

2. Forced unwrapping can be completed by adding an exclamation point (`!`) character immediately following the optional variable's name:

    ```
    var phoneNumber: String?
    phoneNumber = "555-555-5555"
    let unwrappedPhoneNumber = phoneNumber!
    ```

3. When used in an `if let` statement, optional unbinding unwraps a value and tests it for validity before using it.

4. Implicitly unwrapped optionals can be created by adding an exclamation point (`!`) instead of the question mark (`?`) immediately following the type name:

    ```
    var userScore: Int!
    userScore = 100
    ```

5. No. An optional may change to or from `nil` so it must be a variable since the value can change.

Exercise

Create a new iOS playground. Create a string optional that can hold a value for user feedback in a game app. Practice assigning a value to the optional and using forced unwrapping. Next, use optional binding to unwrap and use the optional value. Finally, rewrite the optional as an implicitly unwrapped optional.

HOUR 6

Controlling Program Flow with Conditionals

What You'll Learn in This Hour:

▶ How to use `if` statements to control logic
▶ How to use `switch` statements to control logic
▶ How to use range and tuple matching for controlling flow
▶ How to transfer control of code execution

In programming, you often need to make decisions in code based on the state of a value, what type of device is being used, what screen is presented, or any of a multitude of other decision points. These decision points are called **conditions**, and based on the value of a condition (whether true or false), a particular path of logic is then executed in code.

In this hour, we discuss how Swift uses conditional operations to enable you to modify the path of code executed and customize application flow. The two conditional operations provided in Swift are the **if** statement and the **switch** statement. Both make possible conditional branching of code, or put differently, they make possible execution of different expressions, behaviors, or code paths based on a given set of criteria.

The `if` Statement

The first method of using conditional programming in Swift is by using the `if` statement. The `if` statement is perhaps the most common and simple conditional logic checking paradigm in computer programming. We have already seen the `if` statement utilized a few times throughout this book so far in simple use cases, and you probably have an idea of how to use a basic `if` statement just by context. Let's discuss the syntax a little more here and get a better feel for what you can do with `if` statements, and when they are appropriate to use.

If you are coming from the C or Objective-C world, you are accustomed perhaps to the syntax looking something like the code in Listing 6.1.

LISTING 6.1 The `if` Statement in C/Objective-C

```
BOOL valueToCheck = YES;
if (valueToCheck == YES) {
    // code to execute if valueToCheck is true
}
```

The `==` `YES` is redundant, as is `==` `true` in Swift, and can be removed. Next, Listing 6.2 shows how the same section of code looks in Swift.

LISTING 6.2 The `if` Statement in Swift

```
let valueToCheck = true
if valueToCheck {
    // code to execute if valueToCheck is true
}
```

The thing to notice here is that C and Objective-C require parentheses around the condition being checked, and Swift does not require it, although you can insert parentheses if it assists with readability.

Although there is that slight difference in syntax between Swift and C/Objective-C, they behave exactly the same way as with pretty much most any other programming language. The `if` statement has been around for a long time in many programming languages.

The basic `if` statement that we covered only executes code inside its curly braces if the condition is true. But what if we want an alternate expression to execute if the statement is false? Swift, as with most every other language, provides an **else** clause, which executes code inside a different set of curly braces when the condition is false. Since the syntax is exactly the same as C and Objective-C, minus the parentheses around the conditions, I won't have separate listings describing the differences; Listing 6.3 shows the same logic check as Listing 6.2, but this time adds the `else` clause.

LISTING 6.3 Using an `if-else` Statement in Swift

```
let valueToCheck = true
if valueToCheck {
    println("valueToCheck is true")
} else {
    println("valueToCheck is false")
}
```

Adding an `else` clause to execute code based on a false condition is done simply just by adding `else { ... }` immediately after the closing brace of the true block. If read aloud, this code could be dictated as "If valueToCheck is true, then execute the first block of code. Else, execute the second block of code." The else clause acts as a way to catch any non-true condition and execute a certain block of code, when all else fails.

To add more potential paths of execution to an `if` statement, you use the **`else if`** syntax. The `else if` syntax simply gives you more chances to verify a true value and execute a particular block of code before resuming execution of code or having an `else` clause catch any non-true condition. Listing 6.4 illustrates the `else if` syntax.

LISTING 6.4 Using `else-if` Syntax

```
let myColor = "blue"
if myColor == "red" {
    println("Stop signs are red")
} else if myColor == "blue" {
    println("The sky is blue in Ohio...sometimes")
} else {
    println("I don't know what color myColor is")
}
```

The `if`, `else-if`, and `else` syntax in Swift is straightforward. The condition being tested must evaluate to either true or false, and depending on which operator and operands you use in your `if` or `else if` statements, the appropriate block of code is executed. You could test whether a number is greater than or equal to another number, check strings for equality, verify whether a certain character is in a string, or many other conditions, as long as they return a `Bool` value. Before we move on, let's work an example together. We use a Foundation function called `arc4random()` to generate a random integer for us and use the remainder operator (`%`) to keep the random number within a small range to check its values easily with an `if` statement.

TRY IT YOURSELF

Use `if`, `else-if`, `else` **Conditional Statements in Practice**

Write a random number generator and check the values using `if`, `else-if`, and `else`.

1. Open Xcode 6 and create a playground (Mac or iOS, it doesn't matter).

2. Remove all the existing code in the playground, and import the Foundation framework, so we can access the `arc4random()` function.

   ```
   import Foundation
   ```

3. Use the `arc4random()` function to create a random number and limit its scope to 0 - 9. Also, create an implicitly unwrapped string variable to hold our result.

```
let randomNumber = arc4random() % 10
var result: String!
```

4. First, check whether our `randomNumber` value is 0.

```
if randomNumber == 0 {
    result = "Zero is the first index in an array"
}
```

5. Next, check whether our `randomNumber` value is 1. (I'll include the closing brace from the initial if block, since the `else if` command belongs on the same line.)

```
} else if randomNumber == 1 {
    result = "One is the loneliest number..."
}
```

6. Add an `else` block to act as a default block of code to run, if none of our conditions are met. (Again, I'm including the final brace from the `else-if` block for continuity.)

```
} else {
    result = "Our random number is \(randomNumber)"
}
```

7. Finally, we can simply put the name of our result variable on a single line, and the playground displays its value in the results pane to the right.

```
result
```

You might have seen that the value of our random variable was shown in the Xcode playground's results pane, so this test may seem frivolous. However, the point of this example was to get you familiar with the structure of using if, else if, and else statements to execute code based on meeting certain conditions.

Try your code against different random values generated by re-executing the playground (click the Editor menu, and then click Execute Playground). You see the random number change, and the result variable should adjust accordingly. Figure 6.1 shows what the playground should look like upon completion.

FIGURE 6.1
The completed Try It Yourself example for if statements in a playground.

Ternary Conditional Operators

Hour 3, "Using Operators in Swift," discussed unary and binary operators, but there is a third type of operator in Swift that returns values based on a conditional check, called a **ternary conditional operator**. Swift has only one ternary conditional operator, and it is written as short-hand for a longer if-else expression that checks a particular case or condition and provides a value for the true branch and another value for the false branch. Let's take a look at a common if block to show how a regular if-else conditional block would look as a ternary operation in Listing 6.5.

LISTING 6.5 **Using Ternary Conditional Operators**

```
01:  let salary = 50000
02:  let bonus = 10000
03:  var totalPay = 0
04:  let employeeShouldReceiveABonus = true
05:
06:  // the following code is a traditional if block
07:  if employeeShouldReceiveABonus {
08:      totalPay = salary + bonus
09:  } else {
10:      totalPay = salary
11:  }
12:
13:  // the following code is a ternary conditional operation replacing lines 7-11
➥above
14:  totalPay = (employeeShouldReceiveABonus) ? salary + bonus : salary
```

As you can see, the ternary conditional operator succinctly interprets the Boolean value employeeShouldReceiveABonus and based on its value (true or false) returns salary + bonus if true or just salary if false. The code on line 14 is exactly the same as the code in lines 7 through 11. The ternary conditional operator can easily become difficult to read, so be sure to use concise variable or constant names, but make sure they are still descriptive enough to get the point across as to what the code is performing and returning.

NOTE

Parentheses Are Optional

Remember that in `if` statements, using parentheses is optional. This is also the case for ternary conditional operators. Line 14 in Listing 6.5 included parentheses, as sometimes it helps readability or knowing what is being evaluated, but in this case I could have left them out.

The `switch` **Statement**

Swift also provides another condition checking mechanism, and that is the `switch` statement. The `switch` statement compares a value against a set of possible matching patterns. Not only is the syntax structured a little differently than an `if` statement, the way you can match values is also different.

The `switch` statement compares different **cases**, in which each case is a value or pattern to compare against the value being considered in the `switch` statement itself. If a match is found, the block of code corresponding to the matched case is executed. Switch cases are checked in sequential order, meaning that the first is checked, then second, and so on. If two cases provide a positive match, be sure to structure your `switch` cases in the order you prefer.

Every `switch` statement must be **exhaustive**, meaning that you must either provide a case clause and a subsequent block of code to execute for every value or pattern to match, or provide a **default case**. The default case is much like the `else` block in an `if` statement, in which if no condition or pattern match is met, the default block of code is executed. Let's rewrite the random number example from earlier in this hour with a `switch` statement in Listing 6.6. Note: if you're following along with your own playground, either an iOS or Mac playground will work with this example.

LISTING 6.6   Using the `switch` Statement

```
01:   import Foundation
02:
03:   let randomNumber = arc4random() % 10
04:   var result: String!
05:
06:   switch randomNumber {
07:   case 0:
08:       result = "Zero is the first index in an array"
09:   case 1:
```

```
10:      result = "One is the loneliest number..."
11:  default:
12:      result = "Our random number is \(randomNumber)"
13:  }
14:
15:  result
```

The syntax is a little different, but the concept is the same for this example. In fact, the length of the program increased by one line. So why would we use `switch` statements when we could use `if` statements? You may not always need to, but `switch` statements can do a lot more advanced pattern matching than `if` statements can. Let's start by discussing what can be matched in `switch` statements.

Match More Than Just `Int` Values

Switch statements in other languages, such as C and Objective-C, require the value to be compared to be an integer. C and Objective-C also require a **break** keyword at the end of every case block, because program execution would go to the next case (which may also be true but not desired) and inadvertently execute code you don't want executed. In Swift, `switch` cases can match many more types than just integers, such as strings, characters, doubles, floats, Boolean values, ranges, and tuples. You can even match multiple values with one case statement, rather than needing a case statement for each value to match. Also, `switch` statements do not **fall through**, which means that once the code in a specified case executes, code execution does not fall to the next case in the absence of a break command; rather, execution leaves the entire `switch` block.

NOTE

Explicit Break or Fall Through in `switch` Cases

Although Swift does not require an explicit `break` command at the end of every case block, you can add the `break` statement for clarity or to show specific intent. If, on the other hand, you want to opt in to fall-through behavior, you can add the **fallthrough** statement to the end of a case block, and program flow continues executing the next case if it matches or default case, if one exists.

Listing 6.7 illustrates how to use Swift's `switch` statement to match against multiple values with a single case statement. This can be useful for when you want the same block of code to be executed if more than one value could satisfy the match.

LISTING 6.7   Matching Multiple Values in a Single Case

```
let farmAnimal = "chicken"
switch farmAnimal {
case "cow", "pig", "goat":
```

```
    println("cow, pig, or goat was matched")
case "chicken", "rooster":
    println("chicken or rooster was matched")
default:
    println("unrecognized farm animal")
}
```

Switch Range Matching

switch statements in Swift can also match cases using range operators, discussed in Hour 3. This enables you to compare a value to check whether it is between a specified range of values, and if so, execute the first case block that satisfies the match. Say, for example, that you are writing an app that compares a student's exam score to the A-B-C-D-F grading scale, where an A is 90 to 100, a B is 80 to 89, a C is 70 to 79, a D is 60 to 69, and an F is below 60. Since you are already familiar with using the half-closed range and closed range operators, let's walk through this together in the following Try It Yourself section.

▼ TRY IT YOURSELF

Determine a Student's Grade Letter

Use a switch statement and range matching cases to determine a student's grade letter.

1. Open Xcode 6 and create a new playground. (Either iOS or Mac playground will work.)

2. Remove all the existing code in the playground and import the Foundation framework, so we can access the arc4random() function.

   ```
   import Foundation
   ```

3. Use the arc4random() function to create a random number and limit its scope to 0 - 100. Also, create an implicitly unwrapped string variable to hold our grade.

   ```
   let examScore = arc4random() % 101  // generates random number between 0-100,
   ➥inclusive
   var grade: String!
   ```

4. Begin the switch statement by comparing examScore's value. Xcode automatically adds a closing curly brace after pressing Return.

   ```
   switch examScore {
   ```

5. Place the cursor on the line in between the curly braces and add a case statement for the closed range of 90 to 100, followed by a colon (:). On the next line, set the grade to "A".

   ```
   case 90...100:
       grade = "A"
   ```

6. On the next line, add a case statement for the half-closed range of 80 to 90, followed by a colon. Then set the grade to "B".

```
case 80..<90:  // this could have also been 80...89
    grade = "B"
```

7. Repeat step 6 for "C" (half-closed range of 70 to 80), and "D" (half-closed range of 60 to 70).

```
case 70..<80:
    grade = "C"
case 60..<70:
    grade = "D"
```

8. To finish the `switch` statement, add a default clause, where the grade will be "F". Here, the closing curly brace of the `switch` statement is shown.

```
default:
    grade = "F"
}
```

9. Display a string in the playground using string interpolation to display a message and what grade the student earned. This is sometimes quicker in playgrounds than using `println(...)`.

```
"Student received: \(grade)"
```

If you followed the Try It Yourself example, your code should look like Figure 6.2.

```
 1  import Foundation
 2
 3  let examScore = arc4random() % 101          98
 4  var grade: String!                          nil
 5
 6  switch examScore {
 7  case 90...100:
 8      grade = "A"                             "A"
 9  case 80..<90:
10      grade = "B"
11  case 70..<80:
12      grade = "C"
13  case 60..<70:
14      grade = "D"
15  default:
16      grade = "F"
17  }
18
19  "Student received: \(grade)"                "Student received: A"
20
```

FIGURE 6.2
The completed Try It Yourself example for `switch` statements using range matching.

Switch Tuple Matching

As you saw in Hour 4, "Working with Collection Types," tuples are powerful and lightweight constructs. Tuples can be used in `switch` statement cases to match multiple values or even ranges of values. Some other tools available to you are **wildcards** and **value binding**. A wildcard, denoted by the underscore (_), means that any value in the considered value is a match for that place in the tuple. With value binding inside a tuple, you can declare a temporary constant or variable to the matched value in any place in the tuple. You can also reference values in the switch's considered value's tuple with dot syntax by appending a number corresponding to the place of the desired value in the tuple (tuples are zero-based like arrays). The example in Listing 6.8 illustrates some of the different ways you can match patterns, use wildcards or ranges, and even use value binding inside a tuple and switch case, and how to use the values inside a case's execution block.

LISTING 6.8   Using Tuples for Pattern Matching Inside Switch Cases

```
01:  let carInventory = ("Ford", 55)   // carInventory is a tuple of type (String,
➥Int)
02:
03:  switch carInventory {
04:  case (_, 50...100):
05:      "We have too many \(carInventory.0) cars. Sell! Sell! Sell!"
06:  case (let make, 0...20):
07:      "We are low on \(make). Buy more inventory."
08:  case ("Ford", let num):
09:      "We have \(num) Fords in stock."
10:  default:
11:      "Unrecognized make"
12:  }
```

In Listing 6.8, we declare a tuple of type (`String`, `Int`) in line 1 and assign it to `carInventory`. Line 2 is left blank for readability. In line 3, we begin our `switch` statement, considering the `carInventory` value. The first case, on line 4, compares a tuple with any kind of string as its first value (because of the underscore wildcard), and the closed range of 50 to 100. If that passes, then we use `carInventory.0` using dot syntax to display the first value in the `carInventory` tuple in line 5. In line 6, our case uses value binding to assign the constant `make` to whatever value is in the first field in the tuple, and then matches the number in inventory to the closed range of 0 to 20. If this case is true, then we can use `make` inside our code block because we temporarily bind the value to `make`. Here, value binding is just an explicit way to clearly outline in code our intention of using the value in code, rather than just using `carInventory.0`. Line 8 compares the string "Ford" directly and uses value binding for how many Fords it matches, and then uses the bound `num` in its resulting code branch. Finally, in line 10, we have our default case if no matches are made until this point, because switch statements must be exhaustive, and then close with the curly brace. Xcode warns you if you do not have an exhaustive switch statement, because Swift needs exhaustive checks to ensure safety.

Refining Switch Cases with the where Keyword

Swift's **where** keyword can be used in line with a case statement to refine the condition to be validated. Use the where keyword along with value binding into temporary constants, and you then can have dynamic value checking inside the case statement's conditional check. Listing 6.9 illustrates this, as it is much easier to see the where keyword in action, where we determine by the amount entered whether a word should be pluralized with an extremely generic use case. An actual pluralization implementation would have a more robust solution.

LISTING 6.9   Using the where Keyword in a Switch Case

```
01:   let wordTuple = ("car", 2)
02:
03:   switch wordTuple {
04:   case let (word, amount) where amount == 1:
05:       "You have \(amount) \(word)."   // if amount == 1, would print
➡"You have 1 car."
06:   case let (word, amount) where amount == 0:
07:       "You have no \(word)s."   // if amount -- 0, would print
➡"You have no cars."
08:   case let (word, amount):
09:       "You have \(amount) \(word)s."  // would print "You have 2 cars."
10:   }
```

A lot happens in these 10 lines of code, so let's break it down. In line 1, we create a simple tuple of type (String, Int) and assign it to wordTuple. Then in line 3, we consider wordTuple in the switch statement. Line 4 has the first case, where we use value binding to assign the (word, amount) tuple temporarily and extract individual values from it to compare the value of amount. It is obvious here that (word, amount) is equal to ("car", 2) because we declared that in line 1. However, there may be times when you're iterating over a list of items and you may not know the contents of the tuple, and this type of checking comes in handy. Line 5 uses the constants from the tuple with string interpolation to print the singular representation of word. Likewise, line 6 checks for amount == 0, which pluralizes word with a custom sentence. Finally, line 8 uses value binding to catch any value, so no default case is necessary, and makes the switch statement exhaustive. Line 9 assumes that any value other than 1 will be plural and appends an "s" to the end of the word constant.

NOTE

Tuples Can Hold More Than Two Values

Remember that tuples can be more than just a pair of values. Tuples can contain any number of items inside and can be used to quickly group together like objects or values. Tuples can even be used as return values for functions as a way to return more than one value or object from a function—something that wasn't available in C and Objective-C. We cover tuples as return types in Hour 8, "Using Functions to Perform Actions."

Transferring Control of Execution

In an effort to make code execution more efficient and flexible, Swift has four ways to control program execution. Three of the methods are familiar if you are coming from a C or Objective-C background; **break**, **continue**, and **return** statements. The remaining method of control transfer is the `fallthrough` statement. Swift's execution flow with `switch` statements is similar to that of Pascal-based languages, where control of the program is transferred to the statement immediately following the closing curly brace of the entire `switch` statement. In contrast, C and Objective-C fall through to subsequent case statements and require a specific `break` statement at the end of each case, unless your program requires fall-through.

This hour discusses only the `break` and `fallthrough` statements, as they pertain to `switch` statements. The `continue` statement is discussed in Hour 7, "Iterating Code with Loops," and the `return` statement is discussed in Hour 8.

The `break` Statement

Although not specifically necessary in switch cases, the `break` statement can be useful in terms of efficiency. The `break` statement breaks execution of the current `switch` statement or enclosing loop and transfers control to the first line of code after the ending curly brace of the `switch` or `loop` statements. To use, simply insert a `break` statement after the last line of code you want executed before you want to break out.

In Swift, `break` is implied after each case statement's code has executed. The following snippet shows what a `break` statement looks like in code.

```
let someValue = 0
switch someValue {
case 0:
    "someValue is 0."
    break
default:
    break
}
"I am executed immediately following the break statement"
```

TIP

Use Break for Empty Cases

Because `switch` statements must be exhaustive and every case accounted for, `break` statements by themselves in a case block can be used to denote that no special code should execute for that case.

The `fallthrough` Statement

The `fallthrough` statement, as mentioned before, enables you to opt in to fall-through behavior in a `switch` statement. By nature, `switch` statements break their execution once they reach the end of a matching case's block, and control resumes after the `switch`'s ending curly brace. However, you can add the `fallthrough` statement at the end of a matching case's block to explicitly have your code's execution fall through to the next case, or the default case, whichever may match first. The following code snippet illustrates this behavior.

```
let anotherValue = 15
switch anotherValue {
case 0..<20:
    "\(anotherValue) is between 0 and 19"
    fallthrough
case 10..<20:
    "\(anotherValue) is between 10 and 19"
default:
    "default branch."
}
```

Here, we can see that the given value 15, stored in `anotherValue`, is within the half-closed range of 0 to 20 and is also within the half-closed range of 10 to 20. In a conventional Swift `switch` statement, switch cases are evaluated in sequence; the first case would execute and then immediately exit the `switch` statement entirely. However, we add the `fallthrough` statement, which means that since `anotherValue` is within the half-closed range of 10 to 20 also, that case's code also executes. Swift behaves this way for safety purposes so that you don't accidentally have other potentially passing cases execute inadvertently, and you must opt in to fall-through behavior if you want to have it.

Summary

This hour discussed both methods Swift uses to conditionally branch and execute different paths of code depending on evaluated criteria: the `if` statement and the `switch` statement. These statements are commonly used, so go back and reread any parts you may not feel completely comfortable with yet.

This hour also discussed the simplicity and power of pattern matching with `switch` statements, from matching ranges of values, tuples, and value binding. We also covered using the `where` statement to further refine switch cases by providing conditions that must be met to match that case. You also learned how to provide multiple matches for a single case statement, such as in the farm animal example, providing a way to reduce the amount of code needed to fulfill a specific purpose.

You also learned about controlling the transfer of execution by opting in to fall-through behavior with the `fallthrough` statement, as well as explicit breaking behavior with the `break` statement.

All these topics help equip you to better understand the upcoming hours, so let's move on to using loops to iterate expressions in code.

Q&A

Q. Is it better to use `else-if` or `switch`? They seem similar.

A. The `switch` and `else if` statements are similar, but as you saw in this hour, the syntax is different. This is another case where you should pick the one that works best for the context of the application that you are developing.

Q. Can you use nested `if`, `else if`, and `switch` statements in Swift?

A. You can use nested `if`, `else if`, and `switch` statements in Swift. Always be careful to ensure the readability of your code when using nested statements.

Q. Since `switch` statements must be exhaustive, what should I do if I do not want anything to happen in one of the cases?

A. This would be a perfect place to use `break`. The `break` statement enables you to declare that nothing should happen if the given case is true.

Workshop

The workshop contains quiz questions and exercises to help you solidify your understanding of the material covered. Try to answer all questions before looking at the answers that follow.

Quiz

1. Find the error and correct the code snippet:

```
let savingsAmount = 500
if (savingsAmount = 500) {
    println("Goal has been reached!")
}
```

2. What is the purpose of the default case in a `switch` statement?

3. What is `fallthrough` used for?

4. Create a constant named `x` with a value of 3. Create a `switch` statement to check whether the value of the constant `x` is between 1 and 4 or between 5 and 7. Nothing should happen if `x` is not in this range.

5. Create a constant to hold a student name and number. If the student number is equal to 1, display the text, "The first student name is `student name`". Do not display anything if the student number is not equal to 1.

Answers

1. The conditional must have two equal signs (`==`). Remember that one equal sign (`=`) denotes assignment while two equal signs (`==`) denotes equality comparison.

```
let savingsAmount = 500
if (savingsAmount == 500) {
    println("Goal has been reached!")
}
```

2. The default case handles what actions should occur if no other case in the `switch` is true. Swift case statements must be exhaustive, so the default case is helpful.

3. By default, Swift exits a `switch` statement if a case is true. The use of `fallthrough` allows execution to continue from one case to the next instead.

4. Solution:

```
let x = 3
switch x{
    case 1...4:
        println("The value is \(x). \(x) is between 1 and 4")
    case 5...7:
        println("The value is \(x). \(x) is between 5 and 7")`
    default:
        break
}
```

5. Solution:

```
let studentInformation = ("jDoe", 1)
switch studentInformation {
    case let (studentName, studentNumber) where studentNumber == 1:
        "The student name is \(studentName)"
    default:
        break
}
```

Exercise

Create a new OS X playground. Create a string that holds a student's first initial and last name (for example, "jDoe"). Write an `if-else` statement, and then a `switch` statement to check this value. If the name is equal to "jDoe" display the text, "You are student number 1". If the value is not equal to "jDoe" display the text, "You are not a registered student".

Iterating Code with Loops

What You'll Learn in This Hour:

▶ Why you want to use loops
▶ How to use for loops for counted iteration
▶ How to use for-in loops for fast enumeration
▶ How to use while and do-while loops for conditional looping
▶ How to iterate through arrays and dictionaries
▶ How to transfer control of execution with loops

In the last hour, we discussed controlling program flow with conditionals in which you can directly manipulate the path of execution of an app based on certain criteria. This hour also touches on controlling program flow, but in a different manner; we discuss how to loop certain blocks of code, expressions, and even iterate through items in arrays and dictionaries. Looping enables you to perform specific actions repeatedly or on each item in a collection. We also touch on transferring control of execution from within loops, much like we did with the break and fallthrough statements from last hour, but we discuss another control transfer statement and how each control statement behaves within loops.

Two Categories of Loops

Swift has two major categories of loops, often referred to as **while loops** and **for loops**. Many languages support both types of loops, and the concepts have been around for a long time. Having just discussed conditionals in the last hour, let's discuss while loops first, because they base their looping behavior only on a given condition.

While Loops

While loops will loop a set of statements until a certain condition is met. This is much like what we did in the last hour, where we used if and switch statements to check whether a condition was met to execute a certain set of statements. While loops are similar. However, they execute the given set of statements inside their block repeatedly until a condition is met.

Swift, like many other languages, has two types of while loops: **while loops** and **do-while loops**. The major difference is that while loops evaluate the condition at the beginning of the loop before the statements inside the block execute, and a do-while loop executes the first iteration automatically and then checks the condition at the end.

NOTE

How a While Loop Evaluates Conditions

While loops evaluate their conditions to ensure that they should execute the code within their block of statements or not. This means that while loops evaluate logical values just like `if` and `switch` statements do; if a condition is true, the set of statements gets executed. If a condition is false, the statements do not get executed. Loops determine whether a condition is true, and if so, execute the loop *one time*. Then, they re-evaluate the condition to see whether they should execute the loop again, and so on until the condition is met. Conditions are not limited to Boolean variables or constants. You can have a complex expression as your condition, as long as it evaluates to either true or false.

The While Loop

I hope I haven't confused you by saying that a while loop is a type of while loop. The while loop is like a song on an album of the same name. Programmers generally categorize both do-while and while loops as "while loops." With that distinction made, let's discuss the while loop, its syntax, and behavior.

As mentioned already, a while loop first checks its condition to see whether it should even execute the code inside its block. If the condition is true, the code inside the block executes once, and then the condition is checked again. If false, the statements inside the block do not execute, and program execution resumes on the next line after the while loop's ending curly brace. Listing 7.1 illustrates a simple while loop displaying 10 numbers in the console.

LISTING 7.1   While Loop Syntax

```
01:  var count = 0
02:  while count < 10 {
03:      println("count is \(count)")
04:      ++count
05:  }
```

In line 1 we create a simple `var`, `count`, of type `Int`, and set it to 0, as it will be used in the while loop's condition. Line 2 uses the `while` statement to begin the while loop and checks the condition first before any loop execution. In this case, 0 is less than 10, which returns true, so the program execution enters the loop. Line 3 simply prints a string showing the contents of `count`, and then line 4 increments `count` using the prefixed increment operator. When execution reaches the curly brace on line 5, the while loop *always* returns back to the line where it checks the condition (in this case, line 2). The reason that it always goes back to check the condition, even on the last iteration, is that the computer doesn't know it has reached the last iteration until its condition returns false. Once `count` is equal to 10, and the expression `while 10 < 10` is evaluated, the expression is false, and code would resume execution on line 6 (which is not shown here).

While loops are appropriate when the execution of statements inside the loop are strictly dependent upon a passing condition. In other words, the code inside a loop may never execute if the condition fails during its first validation. Be sure, however, that your while loops are structured in such a way that it will eventually evaluate to false and move on.

CAUTION

Be Aware of Infinite Loops

If you are not careful, you may experience what's called an **infinite loop**. An infinite loop can happen when the condition that gets evaluated each iteration is never false, so it just keeps going and going until the app either runs out of memory or is killed by some other means. Such an example would be if we never incremented `count` in the preceding example and it never was made equal to 10. Always be sure that your loop conditions will be met eventually.

The Do-While Loop

The do-while loop is similar to that of the while loop, with one small difference; the do-while loop performs the statements inside the loop exactly once before evaluating the loop's condition. If the condition is true, the statements inside the do-while loop are executed again. If the condition is false, control is transferred to the statement immediately following the while condition.

The do-while loop syntax has the condition at the end of the loop after the closing curly braces. Having the condition at the end of a do-while loop is nice, because not only does it make readability easier, but it also provides the visual validation that the statements inside the loop will run at least once until the condition is evaluated. Listing 7.2 rewrites Listing 7.1's code with a do-while loop instead of a while loop.

LISTING 7.2 Do-While Loop Syntax

```
01:  var count = 0
02:  do {
03:      println("count is \(count)")
04:      ++count
05:  } while count < 10
```

As you can see the general concepts of the do-while loop are the same as a while loop. But the biggest difference is that the do-while loop executes the statements inside the loop block *first*, denoted by the do statement on line 2, before evaluating the condition, whereas the while loops evaluates the condition first. You'll need to consider this knowledge when writing your own apps, as one loop is not better than another; rather, it depends on how you want the flow of your app to be.

▼ TRY IT YOURSELF

Use a Do-While Loop to Compare Values

Let's walk through an example and use random numbers to simulate rolling a pair of dice, to see how many times it takes for us to roll the same number on both dice.

1. Open Xcode 6 and create a new playground—either a Mac or an iOS playground is fine. Clear the contents of the playground.

2. Start by importing the Foundation framework, as we need that for the random number generator.

```
import Foundation
```

3. We need a few variables: two for the dice and one to count how many rolls it takes to get matching numbers.

```
var timesRolled = 0
var rollOne: Int
var rollTwo: Int
```

4. We can begin the do-while loop now, so write do and an open curly brace. (Note that when you type an open curly brace and press Return, Xcode automatically places a closing curly brace on the following line to help prevent you from accidentally forgetting to add it.)

```
do {

}
```

5. Inside the curly braces, generate two random numbers and assign them to our two roll variables. We use a different random number generator, which has a more uniform distribution. The arc4random_uniform(6) function generates a random number between 0 and 5. Then add 1 to make the final number between 1 and 6, such as the sides on a die.

```
rollOne = Int(arc4random_uniform(6)) + 1
rollTwo = Int(arc4random_uniform(6)) + 1
```

6. Here it is helpful to print each result so you can see the actual dice rolls, and then increment the `timesRolled` variable to denote that we rolled the dice.

```
println("one: \(rollOne), two: \(rollTwo)")
++timesRolled
```

7. That's all we need inside the do-while loop, so after the closing curly brace, add the `while` statement with the condition we need to evaluate.

```
} while rollOne != rollTwo
```

8. Print the final value of how many times we rolled the dice to get both dice equal.

```
println("You rolled the dice \(timesRolled) times to get
➥matching dice values.")
```

9. Hold the Command and Option keys together and press Return to show the Assistant Editor, where the results from the `println(...)` statements will display, showing your results.

NOTE

Differences in Random Number Generators

Notice in step 5 in the preceding Try It Yourself section that we use a new random number generator than the `arc4random()` `%` `x` expression we used previously. The `arc4random_ uniform(x)` function returns a random number using uniform distribution between 0 and x, and avoids **modulo bias**. Modulo bias can favor some remainders over others, depending on the "ceiling" number provided. Read more on modulo bias on Wikipedia at: http://en.wikipedia.org/wiki/ Fisher–Yates_shuffle#Modulo_bias.

This Try It Yourself example is perfect for the do-while loop because to find out whether our first roll has matching dice results, we need to roll at least once. The do-while loop lets us roll first before evaluating our condition. Remember, you can keep re-executing the playground to regenerate new random numbers to test your code by opening the Editor menu and then clicking Execute Playground. If you did everything correctly, your playground should look like Figure 7.1.

For Loops

The other type of loop in Swift is called a **for loop**. For loops iterate over statements of code a finite number of times, given in the syntax of the for statement. Like while loops, there are two types of for loops: the **for-condition-increment** loop (often just dubbed a for loop) and a **for-in** loop. Let's take a look at both for loops now.

FIGURE 7.1
The completed do-while loop example, with code and results.

The For-Condition-Increment Loop

The for-condition-increment loop, from here on out just called the for loop, is similar to the same loop in C, just with a small syntactic difference; Swift does not require any parentheses in the for loop, while C does.

The first thing a for loop does is initialize the variable that will serve as a counter; typically this is set to 0 or 1, or whatever counter number makes sense for your app. Then, a semicolon (;) is required to complete the second part of the for loop: the condition. The condition is much like what we have seen so far, where you must evaluate a condition to return true or false, so that the loop knows whether it should begin execution inside its loop or resume program flow after its final curly brace. After the condition is another semicolon, and then the incrementor. The incrementor could also be a decrementor, depending on the direction in which you are traversing numbers. You don't have to increment/decrement by 1, you could do so by 5, 17, or whatever number you need. All you're doing is telling the for loop how to change the counter variable once it has gone through an iteration of its loop.

Listing 7.3 illustrates both a for loop in C and a for loop in Swift, writing the same loop in both languages.

LISTING 7.3   For Loops in C and Swift

```
01:  // in C
02:  int result = 0;
03:  for (int count = 1; count <= 10; ++count) {
04:      result += count;
05:  }
06:  printf("%d", result);  // prints "55"
07:
08:  // in Swift
09:  var result = 0
```

```
10:  for var count = 0; count <= 10; ++count {
11:      result += count
12:  }
13:  println("\(result)")
```

In C, you can see in line 3 that the parentheses are required around the entire for statement, minus the keyword `for` itself, and ending before the starting curly brace. The only other differences are just the way that Swift and C declare variables differently, and also C uses `printf(...)` and Swift uses `println(...)` to print to the console.

Did you notice anything else? The for loop syntax reminds us a lot of the while loop from earlier in this hour. In fact, its behavior is identical to the while loop, in that there is an initialization, condition, statements to execute, and an increment. For these types of iterations, a for loop is many times preferred over a while loop, as its intent is clearer; the nature of a for loop is a known number of iterations, whereas while loops are designed to handle a variable number of iterations until a condition is met. In other words, while loops are not always dependent upon a counter that gets incremented. A while loop could have a condition to loop while `itemFound == false`, say for iterating over an array to find an element inside, which would then set the Boolean flag `itemFound` to true and exit the loop.

For loops are often used to iterate over a collection or list of items, such as arrays, because the count of arrays can always be retrieved by their `count` property. This way, you can easily access values at particular indexes, because your for loop counter will always be a valid index of the array. The following code snippet illustrates using a for loop over a collection of items:

```
let daysOfWeek = ["Mon", "Tue", "Wed", "Thu", "Fri", "Sat", "Sun"]
for var i = 0; i < daysOfWeek.count; ++i {
    // do something with the day
}
```

CAUTION

Stay In Bounds

Be careful while using for loops that you stay within the bounds of an array if you are iterating over one. Arrays are zero-based, which means their first index is zero, so your for loop should start at zero also and increment its way up (if working from the beginning to the end of the array). The for loop should always stop at `array.count - 1`, though, because `count - 1` is the last index of the array. Trying to access an element at index `count` in an array will throw an **out of bounds** exception, and your app will likely abort.

The For-In Loop

Another type of for loop is called the for-in loop. If you're coming from Objective-C, you may be familiar with the for-in loop already. The for-in loop is designed to iterate over every item in a collection, range, string, or progression made up of multiple items. The syntax of a for-in loop is more easily understood than that of a traditional for loop, in that it reads more closely like a sentence in the English language than a for loop. The make-up of a for-in loop looks like the following:

```
for item in items {
    // do something with item
}
```

The for-in loop also begins with the `for` keyword just like the for loop, but here you assign in-line a constant to work with (`item`), followed by the `in` keyword and then the collection, range, or progression to traverse (`items`). The `in` keyword denotes that we're going to inspect every item in the `items` collection. The for-in loop gives us a nicer way to iterate through an entire collection of items without having to know the count of how many objects are in the collection, keep a variable to count our current index, or worry about incrementing anything. This simplified behavior in a for-in loop is called **fast enumeration**. It enables us to quickly iterate over every item in a collection, range, or progression without having to write code to manage other parts of the loop.

NOTE

Scope and Declaration of For-In Loop Items

By including the name `item` in our previous example, Swift automatically declares `item` a constant of whatever type is held in the collection, range, or progression. Say you are using a for-in loop's fast enumeration to iterate over an array of `String` objects. Each instance of `item` is newly declared by Swift as a constant of type `String` and is only available within the braces of the for-in loop and disposed of at the end of each iteration. The `item` constant is not available outside the for-in loop.

Iterating Through Different Data Types with For-In Loops

Here is where some of Swift's power really shines. When iterating through different ranges, collections, progressions, and so on, Swift can automatically declare a constant of the necessary type by using type inference, including tuples of multiple types, for each item. Swift lets you use fast enumeration for any type or range that is a collection of something. The reason that Swift declares a constant is that the item evaluated should not be altered while using fast enumeration, because that would alter the sequence being enumerated.

Let's first discuss ranges. In Swift, you can use the for-in loop to iterate over a given range, using either the half-closed range or closed range operators. The item to be evaluated is a constant of type `Int`. Where we had incremented the `count` variable in the past, we cannot increment a constant value, so Swift discards the current item and creates a new one with a value one greater than the last value. The code in Listing 7.4 illustrates a for-in loop iterating over a closed range of numbers.

LISTING 7.4 **For-In Loop with Ranges**

```
01:   for count in -2...2 {
02:       println("count is \(count)")
03:   }
```

The code in Listing 7.4 should be pretty easy to understand by now. In line 1, we use a for-in loop, with the constant `count` to iterate through the given range. The range is a closed range, which consists of integer values `-2`, `-1`, `0`, `1`, `2`. Since each iteration assigns the next value to `count`, we can print the current value of `count` in a `println(...)` statement. If you're typing this as we go in a playground, remember to press Command-Option-Return to show the Assistant Editor, which shows the console output of your `println(...)` statements. A half-closed range would have worked here as well, but the loop would not have included the final `2` value.

Iterating over ranges is useful and less code to type than the traditional for loop, which can accomplish the same functionality. Sometimes you may just need to iterate over a collection a certain number of times, but you don't care for or need the counted value inside your loop. You can replace the constant `count` with the underscore (_), which lets Swift bypass storing the current count in a value usable by you and simply performs the iteration the given amount of times. This is useful if you need to perform an action using each item in a collection but don't care about the current count. The first line would look like `for _ in -2...2 {` in this case. In an actual program you may want to start at a sensible value such as 0 or 1 for your iteration, rather than -2; this was just for illustration.

Next, let's look at for-in loops for `Strings`. As we covered in Hour 2, "Learning Swift's Fundamental Data Types," `String` instances are actually made up of individual `Character` instances. This means that we can quickly and easily loop over every character in a string to do something with it. Listing 7.5 illustrates how to do this.

LISTING 7.5 **Using For-In Loops with Strings**

```
01:   let myWord = "Supercalifragilisticexpialidocious"
02:   var numberOfEsFound = 0
03:
04:   for eachChar in myWord {
```

```
05:        if eachChar == "e" {
06:            ++numberOfEsFound
07:        }
08:    }
09:    println("I found \(numberOfEsFound) e's in \(myWord)")
```

Iterating through `String` instances is pretty easy now that you know the basic syntax of for-in loops. In line 1, we declare a constant `String`, and in line 2 we declare a variable `Int` to keep track of how many instances of the letter e we would find in the given word. In line 4 we iterate over `myWord` by getting each character and storing it into `eachChar` at every iteration of the for-in loop. Lines 5-7 should be familiar to you from the previous hour, and then finally on line 9 we print the output.

Next, let's take a look at some more advanced types to iterate through with for-in loops, starting with the `Array` type. As we know, an array is a collection of items of the same type. So just like iterating over a `String`, which is a collection of objects of type `Character`, an `Array` of type `String` can be easily iterated through in a for-in loop in exactly the same way. Let's examine this type of iteration in a Try It Yourself example.

▼ TRY IT YOURSELF

Iterating Through Arrays with For-In Loops

Create an array and then iterate through each item using a for-in loop. Then use a `switch` statement to check each case for conditionally creating output.

1. Open Xcode 6 and create a new playground. Either a Mac or iOS playground will work.

2. Remove all the default contents inside the playground to start with a clean file.

3. Declare an array of `String` objects, and initialize it with an array literal.

   ```
   let bears = ["Papa bear", "Mama bear", "Baby bear"]
   // bears is of type [String]
   ```

4. Use the for-in loop to iterate over each bear string in the bears array.

   ```
   for bear in bears {
   ```

5. Use a `switch` statement to evaluate the `bear` constant and conditionally branch the code depending on which bear is the current bear. Depending on which bear is the current bear, the appropriate temperature of porridge should be printed to the console. Have a default case in the event that you don't know what bear is in the array. Don't forget the ending curly brace for the for-in loop.

```
switch bear {
    case "Papa bear":
        println("My porridge is too hot!")
    case "Mama bear":
        println("My porridge is too cold!")
    case "Baby bear":
        println("My porridge is just right!")
    default:
        println("Unrecognized bear. Intruder alert!")
    }
}
```

6. Hold the Command and Option keys and press Return to display the Assistant Editor. There, you'll see each line printed in the console, because we only supplied known bears to our array.

7. Add a different bear to the array, re-execute the playground (select the Editor menu, then click Execute Playground), and see what results you receive in the console in the Assistant Editor.

The completed Try It Yourself example should look like Figure 7.2.

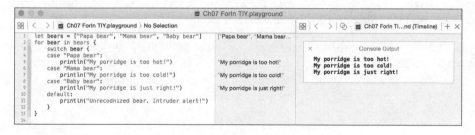

FIGURE 7.2
The completed Try It Yourself example for using for-in loops with an array.

Another facet of fast enumeration with for-in loops is iterating through dictionaries. The idea of iterating through dictionaries is similar to what we have discussed thus far, with one small difference; since dictionaries are built upon key-value pairs, we cannot just use a for-in statement such as `for item in myDictionary`. How would Swift know whether you mean the key or the value to assign to `item`?

Here is where we can use a tuple to iterate through a dictionary, by assigning temporary constants inside a tuple to both the key and the value at each iteration of the pairs in the dictionary. The syntax and an example are shown in Listing 7.6.

LISTING 7.6 Using For-In Loops with Dictionaries

```
01:  let retinaiPhonesAndYears = ["iPhone 4" : 2010,
                                  "iPhone 4S" : 2011,
                                   "iPhone 5" : 2012,
                                  "iPhone 5C" : 2013,
                                  "iPhone 5S" : 2013,
                                   "iPhone 6" : 2014,
                              "iPhone 6 Plus" : 2014]
02:  for (iPhone, year) in retinaiPhonesAndYears {
03:      println("The \(iPhone) was released in \(year).")
04:  }
// displays:
//   The iPhone 6 was released in 2014.
//   The iPhone 5C was released in 2013.
//   The iPhone 5S was released in 2013.
//   The iPhone 4 was released in 2010.
//   The iPhone 6 Plus was released in 2014.
//   The iPhone 5 was released in 2012.
//   The iPhone 4S was released in 2011.
```

Listing 7.6 shows how to use a tuple to extract the individual elements of a key-value pair in a dictionary and assign them to constants, as shown in line 2. The tuple (iPhone, year) is a tuple of type (String, Int), and through each iteration in the dictionary, those constants are assigned to the key and the value of the key-value pair, respectively.

I left the results in comments below the code to bring back up a point about dictionaries. Dictionaries are *unordered* lists of key-value pairs, and the order in which I received the output for this example may be different for you if you try Listing 7.6 in your own playground.

NOTE

Sorting Dictionary Key-Value Pairs

While dictionaries are inherently unordered, you can sort dictionaries before using them to get a sorted dictionary to work with. We cover sorting using the global sorted(...) function provided in Swift's standard library in Hour 24, "Learning Swift's Standard Library Functions."

Using tuples with for-in statements to iterate through dictionaries is useful. But there may be times when you don't need both items in a tuple, and maybe only need to iterate through just the keys or just the values. You can use the wildcard underscore (_) in place of a constant's name inside the tuple, and Swift ignores the value in place of the underscore. For instance with the iPhone release years in Listing 7.6, if you just need the year values to know how many releases there were per year, you could have a for-in loop that looks like this instead:

```
for (_, year) in retinaiPhonesAndYears {
    // do some calculation for the years, such as add how many released in 2013
}
```

One more example of using tuples in for-in loops is with arrays. It is possible to get the index and the item's value at the same time with fast enumeration, and that is by passing the collection name to the enumerate() function in-line in the for-in loop's statement. Listing 7.7 illustrates how this is done.

LISTING 7.7   Using For-In Loops with Enumerated Arrays

```
let beatles = ["Paul", "John", "Ringo", "George"]
var ringoIndex = 0
for (index, name) in enumerate(beatles) {
    if name == "Ringo" {
        ringoIndex = index
    }
}
println("Ringo is at index \(ringoIndex) in the beatles array.")
// Displays:
//   "Ringo is at index 2 in the beatles array."
```

Transferring Control in Loops

In the previous hour, we discussed methods of transferring control of your app's execution with the break and fallthrough statements, with regard to the conditional switch statement. Swift makes it possible to transfer control of execution from loops as well, and we discuss the two statements that enable you to do that: the **continue** and **break** statements. The continue and break statements can be used in both while loops and for loops.

Transferring Control with the continue Statement

Inserting the continue statement into a loop halts execution of the current loop's iteration, bypasses any remaining code in the loop, and resumes execution at the next iteration of the loop. The continue statement can be useful if you are checking a condition inside the loop, you know that no more execution needs to occur within this iteration, and you can safely move on to the next iteration. Any counter constant or temporary constant assigned as the current item in the iteration is discarded, and the counter is recreated with an incremented value, or the item points to the next item in the collection. Listing 7.8 shows a brief example of how a continue statement might be used.

LISTING 7.8   Using `continue` to Transfer Control

```
01:  var results = [Int]()  // creates an empty array of Ints
02:
03:  for count in 1...100 {
04:      let remainder = count % 7
05:      switch remainder {
06:      case 1...6:
07:          continue  // bypasses any further execution in this iteration
08:      default:
09:          results.append(count)
10:      }
11:      println("\(count) is divisible by 7")
12:  }
```

The code in Listing 7.8 should all be familiar to you, outside the `continue` statement in line 7. By placing the `continue` statement in the case matching any integer among 1 to 6, we tell the compiler to bypass any further code in the for-in block and resume at the next iteration. That means that line 11 will not execute unless `count` is divisible by 7.

Transferring Control with the `break` Statement

The `break` statement, when inserted inside a loop, terminates the current loop iteration and also ends the loop entirely, and resumes execution on the line after the loop's closing curly brace. This can be useful when you need to iterate over every item to check for a certain condition, or whether an item exists, and then exit the loop when the condition is found. Listing 7.9 illustrates an example of how you might use a `break` statement in a for-in loop.

LISTING 7.9   Using `break` to Transfer Control

```
let word = "Supercalifragilisticexpialidocious"
for eachChar in word {
    switch eachChar {
    case "x":
        println("\(word) contains an 'x'")
        break
    default:
        continue
    }
}
```

Our for-in loop in Listing 7.9 checks to see whether the letter "x" appears. If so, a message is displayed, and control is transferred out of the loop entirely. The reason is that once we've found the "x," we don't care about any further characters. You may run across many scenarios in your development career where you need to iterate through collections of some sort, and once you've found what you're looking for, there is no need for execution to continue. It is good to keep this in mind, because every line of execution means a little bit of your user's battery gets depleted, whether an iOS device or Macbook Pro/Air laptop. So be a good programming citizen, and don't needlessly execute code you don't have to.

Summary

In this hour, we covered many facets of Swift's two methods of iterating code: for loops and while loops. We also learned that for loops consist of for-condition-increment loops and for-in loops, and while loops consist of while loops and do-while loops, with examples of each type of loop.

We discussed different data types that could be iterated through, as well as how to handle iterating through collections with tuples to temporarily extract their values into constants to work with inside the loops.

Then we discussed transferring control of program execution with the `break` and `continue` statements. These statements assist in more efficient code execution, by bypassing unnecessary statements when the situation allows.

Q&A

Q. **Is it better to use for loops or while loops?**

A. While they seem similar, there is a big difference between for and while loops. A for loop is often used to iterate over arrays or where the end of the condition is known. A while loop is a little more flexible because you can add other data types to the condition. Carefully examining your need for a loop helps you determine the best type of loop to use in your program.

Q. **Is it possible to use a for loop without creating a new variable?**

A. Yes. It is not necessary to create a new variable when using a for loop, as you can reuse an existing variable if one has not yet been created. However, you will most likely want to reset the variable to a more sensible starting value.

Q. **Will I break anything if I accidentally create an infinite loop?**

A. An infinite loop can crash a program or an app or even lock up the user interface, depending on where you have created the infinite loop. You can quickly see an infinite loop in the playground, stop it, and correct the issue.

Workshop

The workshop contains quiz questions and exercises to help you solidify your understanding of the material covered. Try to answer all questions before looking at the answers that follow.

Quiz

1. Find the error and correct the code snippet so that output is displayed:

```
let count = 0
while count < 10 {
    println("count is \(count)")
    ++count
}
```

2. What is the purpose of the `break` statement inside a loop?

3. What is the best way to iterate over a collection of items, such as ranges and numbers?

4. Rewrite the following while loop as a for loop:

```
var count = 20
while count < 100 {
    println("first count is \(count)")
    count += 20
}
```

5. What is the purpose of the `continue` statement inside a loop?

Answers

1. The constant `count` should be a variable so that it can be incremented inside the loop.

```
var count = 0
while count < 10 {
    println("count is \(count)")
    ++count
}
```

2. When the `break` statement is used inside a loop it terminates the current loop iteration and also ends the loop entirely. Execution then continues on the line after the loop's closing curly brace.

3. The for-in loop is the best way to iterate over collections of items.

4. The `while` loop can be rewritten as a for loop as shown in the following code:

```
for var count = 20; count < 100; count += 20{
    println("count is \(count)")
}
```

5. Use the `continue` statement if you have a condition inside a loop that is found to be true and you know that no more execution needs to occur within this iteration. The code can now move on to the next iteration.

Exercise

Create a new OS X playground. Create a for loop that prints the 6 times table for numbers 1 through 100. Try to write this same code using a while loop instead of a for loop.

Using Functions to Perform Actions

What You'll Learn in This Hour:

▶ General syntax and structure of functions

▶ How to use parameters in functions

▶ How to use variadic parameters in functions

▶ How to return values from functions

▶ How to set external and internal parameters

▶ How to set default parameter values

▶ How to change values of parameters

So far in this book, you have learned some of the basic syntax of Swift, constants and variables of general data types in which we store values, and a fairly procedural approach to developing software. By procedural, I mean that our code starts running at line 1 and executes one line after another until the last line (with the exception of loops, which just reiterate the same lines of code until completion). In this hour, we take a look at **functions**, which are self-contained blocks of code designed to perform a specific task.

Functions are a bit of a stretch from what we've covered so far, but follow along closely and you should be okay. As you can see from the preceding "What You'll Learn in This Hour" list, we have a lot to cover. Some concepts of functions might be confusing, but it is appropriate to discuss functions now before we move any further in this book, as most every other hour relies heavily on functions.

Because functions are a key element of Swift programming and because they are used extensively throughout the remainder of this book, I suggest following along in your own playground or REPL in any listing or code snippet, in addition to the Try It Yourself sections, to get practice at typing functions. Truly, the more you do it, the more you will learn.

With that, let's start with a basic introduction to functions, their composition, and how to think about functions as more than they appear to be.

The Nature of Functions in Swift

As mentioned previously, functions are self-contained blocks of code designed to perform a specific task. The code inside a function can be similar to the examples we have done thus far in this book, such as iterating through collections to find a particular piece of data, use conditional switches and if statements to branch execution based on conditions, and so on. Functions can be as long or as short as they need to be to accomplish the task they are given.

NOTE

No Required Length of a Function

As noted, functions can be as long or as short as you need to perform the desired tasks. Many believe that functions should be less than 10 lines of code, no more than 4 lines of code, or what have you. The goal of a function is to accomplish a certain task, and if that task requires too many lines of code, you may want to investigate *refactoring* your code to isolate and extract parts that can be easily repeated, shortened, or even eliminated, all of which can help make your code cleaner, easier to read, and perhaps even more efficient.

The code inside a function, unlike code we have written so far, is not executed until it is **called**. To call a function, you simply call it by name and provide any parameters inside a pair of parentheses. You have already seen one function that fits this description—the `println()` function. It's a little easier to understand when you can see, so let's cover the syntax and structure of functions.

General Function Syntax and Structure

Functions in Swift follow a simple layout. All functions begin with the `func` keyword and then are given a name. After the name, a set of open and closed parentheses is required, inside which can be any number of parameters or values passed into the function to be used by the function. This is followed by the return type, the type of value the function returns. The function name, list of parameters, and return type all make up what is known as the function's **definition**. Finally, a pair of open and closed curly braces is required, inside which is the code your function performs when called. Figure 8.1 illustrates the syntax breakdown of a function.

```
func  funcName ( param1 : Type ,  param2 : AnotherType ,..) ->  ReturnType  {
    return  someValue
}
```

FIGURE 8.1
The syntactic structure of a function in Swift.

The syntax can be broken down as follows:

▶ **funcName**: This is the name of the function. Swift functions generally begin with a lowercase letter then capitalize every word thereafter and contain no spaces, such as `addTheseTwoNumbers` or `findMeanMedianAndMode`. Function names should be descriptive as to what the function does.

▶ **param1:Type, param2:AnotherType,..**: This syntax should be familiar to you; the only nuance is that each parameter is separated by a comma. Parameters are values sent into a function by the caller. Not all functions have, or even need, parameters. Each parameter looks like a typical Swift variable declaration, just without the `let` or `var` introducer, in that you name the parameter, enter a colon (`:`), and then provide that parameter's type. Finally, the trailing `..` signifies that there may be more parameters.

▶ **-> ReturnType**: This is the type of value that the function returns. The `->` symbol (a dash followed by the right angle bracket), indicates "this function returns data of type ReturnType." `ReturnType` could be `Int`, `String`, `Bool`, `Char`, and so on, or even a custom type that you create.

▶ **{ and }**: These curly braces indicate the beginning and the end of a function. This is exactly the same as the curly braces you are familiar with from such statements as `switch` and `if`, and `for` and `while` loops. Once execution reaches the ending curly brace, the function is done, and execution resumes on the next line, or the next line after the caller.

▶ **return someValue**: In a function that indicates a return type (with `-> ReturnType`), you must have a `return` statement, followed by a value of type `ReturnType` to return. This value gets passed back to the line of code that called the function. If the function does not have a return type indicated, you do not need to write an explicit return statement. You learn more about returning values later in the hour.

The structure of a function in Swift is a little different than you might be used to if you are coming from a C or Objective-C background. Having the return type at the end certainly takes some getting used to. However, Swift's function syntax does make it more clear what the intent is, that it is indeed a function, what its parameters are, and what it will ultimately return. To me, it reads more like a sentence: "This function is named addTwoNumbers, it takes two numbers of type Int as parameters, and it returns a value of type Int."

Now that we understand the syntactic structure of a function, let's examine functions at an easy level and move our way up. As mentioned earlier, you see a lot of code in this hour, so get your playground or REPL ready, and let's get going.

Functions with No Parameters and No Return Type

The most basic function accepts no parameters and returns nothing. The function definition is short and only contains the function name and an empty set of parentheses. Listing 8.1 illustrates a function with no parameters and no return type, which simply prints a line inside its curly braces.

LISTING 8.1   A Function with No Parameters and No Return Type

```
01:   func printHelloWorld() {
02:       println("Hello, world!")
03:   }
```

The function in Listing 8.1 should be easy to understand. In line 1, we see the `func` keyword, followed by the name of the function, `printHelloWorld`. Then, we see the empty set of parentheses indicating there are no parameters, followed by the open curly brace, signifying the beginning of the code inside the function. Line 2 simply prints "Hello, world!", as any good sample app should. Line 3 closes the curly brace for the function, indicating the end of the function.

If you typed this into your playground, or the Swift REPL, you notice that nothing printed to the console output window. Why not? We never *called* the function. Here's how we call our `printHelloWorld` function:

```
printHelloWorld()
```

That's it. Now, you should see "Hello, world!" in the console output in Xcode's Assistant Editor or in the console output of the Swift REPL.

The Type of a Function

Before we go any further, an important piece to discuss about functions is that they have a type, consisting of the parameter types and the return type. For instance, let's say we have the `printHelloWorld` function from Listing 8.1. The type of this function is `() -> ()`. This literally means "a function that takes no parameters and returns an empty tuple." When a function returns an empty tuple (also known as a type called `Void`, which is the same as saying the function returns nothing), we don't write the `-> ()` because it's redundant and unnecessary, but under the hood that's part of the type. It is important to know the type of a function, and throughout this hour I make a note of the type of a function whenever it is necessary. In the next hour we discuss some advanced function topics, such as passing functions as function parameters, in which you need to know the function type.

Because a function has a type, just like `String` or `Int` are types, it is helpful to think about functions as first-class objects, too. The syntax can get a little difficult to understand, but as long as you understand this point about function types, you should have no problem later.

Functions with Parameters

As we've seen in the function structure example in Figure 8.1, you can place parameters inside the parentheses of a function. This enables you to send values to a function and have that function work with or manipulate those values as part of its greater task. A function can have as many or as few parameters as necessary, if any, to accomplish its task. However, having too many parameters may indicate that your function could be trying to do too much, and you may need to refactor into smaller, more manageable functions.

Let's take a look at a function that takes a single parameter, of type `Int`, and prints a line of output as many times as the parameter tells. For instance, if the parameter is equal to the number 3, it prints out 3 lines of input. Listing 8.2 shows us how to do that.

LISTING 8.2   A Function with One Parameter

```
01:  func printHelloTimes(times: Int) {
02:      for _ in 1...times {
03:          println("Hello to you!")
04:      }
05:  }
06:
07:  printHelloTimes(3)
// Displays the following output:
//  Hello to you!
//  Hello to you!
//  Hello to you!
```

The declaration of the function in line 1 should be well-understood by this point. We declare the function with the `func` keyword, give it a name (in this case `printHelloTimes`), and then inside the parentheses we provide a parameter with an associated type, `times: Int`. `times` is known to the function as an **internal parameter**, or **local parameter**, in that `times` can only be used inside the **scope** of the function.

NOTE

Scope of Variables and Constants

A scope is a defining context inside which a variable or constant lives. In Listing 8.2, the scope of the parameter `times` is considered only to be inside the function because it is defined in the function's parameter list. The scope of a variable or constant defines what elements can and can't access it. In other words, because the `times` parameter is scoped to the `printHelloTimes` function, it cannot be used or accessed outside of that function.

`times` is also a constant. If you try to modify `times` inside the function, you receive a compiler error. To change the value of a parameter inside the function, use the `var` introducer before the parameter name inside the parentheses, as shown in the following function definition snippet:

```
func functionWithVariableParameter(var name: String) {
```

Finally, line 7 calls our `printHelloTimes` function and provides the number 3 as an **argument**. An argument to a function is the value you give to a parameter. If a function has required parameters, you must supply valid arguments to it.

If you remember from Figure 8.1, to have multiple parameters in a function, you separate the parameters and types by a comma. Listing 8.3 is a modified version of the function in Listing 8.2, adding a second parameter and using both parameters inside the function.

LISTING 8.3   Using Multiple Parameters Inside a Function

```
func printWord(word: String, numberOfTimes: Int) {
    for _ in 1...numberOfTimes {
        println("Hello \(word)")
    }
}
printWord("wonderful person reading this book", 4)
```

The function in Listing 8.3 takes two parameters; one `String` and one `Int`, separated by a comma. Notice how the names of the parameters, along with the name of the function, help describe what the function is and does. If you come from Objective-C, you're probably familiar with that naming convention, as parameters to methods extended the name of the method and combined made it easy to read and understand what the method was intended to do, return, or both.

NOTE

Argument Validation

In the interest of keeping these examples brief and explanatory, I left out value validation. If, for instance, I had entered -4 instead of 4 as the argument to `printWord(word:` `numberOfTimes:)`, I would not have gotten the intended results at all. We won't cover validation in this book, but to validate values you can simply check to make sure values fit a certain criteria before using them, with if statements, switch statements, and the like.

Functions with Variadic Parameters

Now that we've discussed using parameters inside function definitions, Swift offers us another way to add parameters but of an unknown length. **Variadic parameters** are parameters that can have an unknown number of elements, and when the function is called, the variadic parameters are stored in an array with a length equal to the number of arguments sent from the caller. The syntax for variadic parameters is simple: Just append three dots (...) to the end of the type of the parameter, such as (`numbers: Int...`). Of course, for consistency and readability, it may behoove you to name the parameter with a plural name to indicate that it can take many values as arguments.

Variadic parameters must be the last parameter in a list of parameters, if there are multiple parameters in a function definition. Typically there will not be a need for more than one variadic parameter per function.

Variadic parameters can also take zero elements, at which time the function creates an array with zero elements, or in other words, an empty array. This can be used to our advantage, without having to use any special code to check for nil or whether any arguments were passed at all, although you could check whether an array is empty with the `.isEmpty` property if your app logic required. Listing 8.4 details the use of variadic parameters by adding all the numbers passed in as arguments to the function.

LISTING 8.4 Using Variadic Parameters in Functions

```
01:   func addVariadicNumbers(numbers: Int...) {
02:       var result = 0
03:       for eachNum in numbers {
04:           result += eachNum
05:       }
06:       println("Sum total of numbers: \(result)")
07:   }
08:
09:   addVariadicNumbers(1, 2, 3, 4, 5)
```

```
10:   addVariadicNumbers(4)
11:   addVariadicNumbers()
// Displays:
//   Sum total of numbers: 15
//   Sum total of numbers: 4
//   Sum total of numbers: 0
```

Right in Line 1 we see the use of the variadic parameter inside the parentheses. Since Swift translates all the arguments provided into an array at runtime, we can use numbers as an array, so we use fast enumeration with a for-in loop (lines 3 through 5) to quickly add all the values into a results variable and then print the result. Lines 9 through 11 show different ways to call the function with variadic parameters, the first with many arguments, then one argument, and no argument.

NOTE

Arguments Can Be Constants or Variables

In these examples we used Int literals as arguments passed to functions. Don't forget that you can pass constants or variables too, as long as they are the same type as the receiving parameter.

After seeing a function like the one in Listing 8.4 performing an arithmetic task, it would be nice if we could return the value to the caller so that further processing could take place, or even display a value to the user on the screen. Good news, Swift provides a return statement that we can use to return a value, object, tuple, or even another function back to the caller. Let's discuss returning variables next in a basic context and work our way up to more complex scenarios.

Functions with Return Types

So far our examples of functions have only printed out lines of text to the console. While it's helpful to see them while learning the structure and usage of functions, it really doesn't help you with anything much applicable to solving real problems with code. Some of the power of functions comes in their capability to return data to their caller to be used after the function has finished execution, and that is by using the return statement.

If you recall from Figure 8.1, the return type of a function is introduced with the -> symbol, followed by the return type itself. You do not provide a return name, just a type. If we take the example in Listing 8.4 and change the function to return a value instead of just printing it, the example looks like the following in Listing 8.5.

LISTING 8.5   Returning Values from Functions

```
01:  func addVariadicNumbers(numbers: Int...) -> Int {
02:      var result = 0
03:      for eachNum in numbers {
04:          result += eachNum
05:      }
06:      return result
07:  }
08:
09:  let sum = addVariadicNumbers(7, 4, 9)
// sum is a constant Int, and is equal to 20
```

The major changes in Listing 8.5 from Listing 8.4 are that line 1 adds an `Int` return type, and line 6 uses the `return` statement, rather than just printing with `println`, to return the results variable. This satisfies the function's return type of `Int`. Then, in line 9, we assign the returned value to a constant `Int` named `sum`.

NOTE

Use Return to Transfer Control

If you remember from Hour 6, "Controlling Program Flow with Conditionals," and Hour 7, "Iterating Code with Loops," regarding control flow with conditionals and loops, we discussed four statements that Swift uses to transfer control of execution: `break`, `continue`, `fallthrough`, and `return`. `return` is the last one, and we had not yet talked about it until now, because it didn't then make sense outside the context of functions. The `return` statement ends execution in a function, and returns a value specified (or no value if `return` is used by itself in a function without a return type). You are not limited to one `return` statement inside a function; rather, you can have as many as makes sense for your purposes, such as inside cases in a `switch` statement. Keep in mind, though, that once the `return` statement is executed, no more code inside the function will be executed.

A feature native to Swift, but new to C and Objective-C developers, is the concept of returning multiple values from functions. This is accomplished using tuples, and the syntax looks identical to how you define parameters for a function. To define a tuple of values as the return type, you put the values and return types inside parentheses, as usual. The values are in the format `(value1: Type, value2: AnotherType, ...)`. When you have a tuple as the return type, the return statement must also return a valid tuple, matching the types in the function's definition. To illustrate this, examine the following code snippet to inspect the syntax for defining a tuple return type and returning a tuple.

```
func thisFuncReturnsATuple() -> (a : Int, b : Int, c : Int) {
    return (1, 2, 3)
}
```

The code snippet uses named parameters inside the tuple. You can also create an **anonymous tuple**, which would look like `(Int, Int, Int)`, but having names in the tuple makes extracting values a bit more obvious if you need to do so.

Let's walk through an example of a function returning a tuple in this next Try It Yourself section.

▼ TRY IT YOURSELF

Create a Function to Return Mean, Median, Mode

We take everything you've learned up to now about functions and combine them in this example. Write a function that accepts a variadic parameter of integers and returns the mean, median, and mode.

1. Open Xcode 6 and create a new playground. Either an iOS or Mac playground will work.

2. Clear the playground's existing code and declare a function named `meanMedianMode` that takes a variadic parameter of integers and returns a tuple of a `Double` and two `Int`s named mean, median, and mode. Don't forget the opening curly brace for the function.

```
func meanMedianMode(numbers: Int...) -> (mean: Double, median:
➥Int, mode: Int) {
```

3. Find the mean by finding the sum of all numbers in the variadic parameter, and then dividing by the total number of arguments. We have to cast `number` and `numbers.count` to type `Double`, because our average could contain a decimal value.

```
// find mean
var sum = 0.0
for number in numbers {
    sum += Double(number)
}
let mean = sum / Double(numbers.count)
```

4. Find the median by sorting the array of numbers and then finding the item in the middle of the array. (Note: this step uses something called a closure, which we discuss in detail in Hour 9, "Understanding Higher Order Functions and Closures." The syntax may look scary, so for now, just type the code and know that it sorts the array.). For simplicity, this function rounds up the `midIndex` for arrays with an even number of elements, although actual median calculations might average the middle two elements or round the index down.

```
// find median
let sortedNumbers = numbers.sorted({ num1, num2 in
    return num1 < num2 })
let midIndex = numbers.count / 2
let median = sortedNumbers[midIndex]
```

5. Finding the mode is a bit more complicated, so we split into multiple steps. First, declare an empty dictionary of type `[ Int : Int ]`. This stores each number in numbers as a key and the number of times that number is in the numbers array as the value.

```
// find mode
var occurrences: [Int : Int] = [:]
```

6. Iterate through each number in the numbers array and increment its associated value in the occurrences dictionary or set a new value of 1 for that key.

```
for number in numbers {
    if var value = occurrences[number] {
        occurrences[number] = ++value
    } else {
        occurrences[number] = 1
    }
}
```

7. Now we have a dictionary that holds each number as a key and how many times that number appears in numbers as that key's value. Declare a variable tuple to store the highest pair, iterate through the occurrences dictionary to find the highest value, and assign that pair to the highest pair tuple. Assign a constant for mode equal to the highest pair's key.

```
var highestPair: (key: Int, value: Int) = (0, 0)
for (key, value) in occurrences {
    highestPair = (value > highestPair.value) ? (key, value) :
highestPair
}
let mode = highestPair.key
```

8. Now that we have all three values, we can return them in a tuple. Close the curly brace of the function.

```
// return tuple of results
return (mean, median, mode)
}
```

9. Assign a constant to the returned value of `meanMedianMode(1, 1, 2, 3, 5, 8, 13)`.

```
let mmm = meanMedianMode(1, 1, 2, 3, 5, 8, 13)
```

10. View the values of each member in the tuple by using dot-notation.

```
mmm.mean    // displays 4.7142857142857...
mmm.median  // displays 3
mmm.mode    // 8
```

This Try It Yourself section contains a lot of code, but you should be familiar with all the code used in it, outside the closure in step 4. The completed playground should look like the image in Figure 8.2. Check your results against the results in the image to make sure you got it all right. If you are an experienced developer, you may be looking at that code and thinking that it is horribly inefficient. Yes, it can be refactored and reduced, and by the end of this hour and next, we reduce most of these chunks of code down to one line each. We are just scratching the surface so far concerning how powerful Swift can be with regard to functions.

```
1    //
2    // Find mean, median, and mode of a set of numbers
3    //
4
5    func meanMedianMode(numbers: Int...) -> (mean: Double, median: Int, mode: Int) {
6        // find mean
7        var sum = 0.0                                              0.0
8        for number in numbers {
9            sum += Double(number)                                 (7 times)
10       }
11       let mean = sum / Double(numbers.count)                     4.71428571428571
12
13       // find median
14       let sortedNumbers = numbers.sorted({ num1, num2 in         [1, 1, 2, 3, 5, 8, 13]
15           return num1 < num2 })                                 (6 times)
16       let midIndex = numbers.count / 2                           3
17       let median = sortedNumbers[midIndex]                       3
18
19       // find mode
20       var occurrences: [Int : Int] = [:]                         0 key/value pairs
21       for number in numbers {
22           if var value = occurrences[number] {
23               occurrences[number] = ++value                     [Some 2]
24           } else {
25               occurrences[number] = 1                           (6 times)
26           }
27       }
28       var highestPair: (key: Int, value: Int) = (0, 0)           (.0 0, .1 0)
29       for (key, value) in occurrences {
30           highestPair = (value > highestPair.value) ? (key, value) : highestPair    (6 times)
31       }
32       let mode = highestPair.key                                 1
33
34       // return tuple of results
35       return (mean, median, mode)                                (.0 4.71428571428571, .1 3, .2 1)
36   }
37
38   let mmm = meanMedianMode(1, 1, 2, 3, 5, 8, 13)                (.0 4.71428571428571, .1 3, .2 1)
39   mmm.mean                                                      4.71428571428571
40   mmm.median                                                    3
41   mmm.mode                                                      1
42
```

FIGURE 8.2
The completed playground for the Mean, Median, Mode function.

NOTE

Return Values Can Be Ignored

The returned values from functions can also be ignored if you don't need their data. Sometimes you just need to call a function to perform a particular task, but you don't care about its return value. In that case, you would just not assign a variable or constant to the returned value and just call the function directly.

External Parameter Names

So far we have only discussed internal parameter names in functions. This means that the function can use the parameters by name inside the function, but the caller has no reference to the name of the parameter when calling the function. This can sometimes be confusing when multiple parameters are required, but the order is important.

Swift provides a way to specify external parameter names when declaring function definitions, which helps make coding easier for three reasons: First, the caller has a better frame of reference for which argument is necessary and in which order. Second, it can help shorten the internal parameter to be used within the function, saving time by not having to type perhaps verbose parameter names every time you need to reference that parameter. Finally, it helps the definition of the function read more like a sentence, giving a better understanding of what the function's purpose is.

The way to make an external parameter is to provide an external name, a space, then the internal name, a colon (:), and then the type, such as (externalName name: String). For example, see Listing 8.6 to see how using external parameters can be used to benefit the function and the caller.

LISTING 8.6 Using External Parameter Names

```
func multiply(thisNumber num1: Int, byAnotherNumber num2: Int) -> Int {
    return num1 * num2
}
let result = multiply(thisNumber: 6, byAnotherNumber: 7)
// result is equal to 42
```

Reading the function definition aloud sounds like "multiply this number by another number and return a value of type Int." It is also clearer to the caller just what the intention of the function is and what each argument is for. Internal to the function, we simply just use num1 and num2, saving ourselves some keystrokes.

Functions do not always need external parameters. In fact, if you choose the naming of your function well, you can use an internal name for the first parameter and external names for a better description with the remaining parameters. A rewritten function definition from Listing 8.6 could look like the following snippet:

```
func multiplyThisNumber(num1: Int, byAnotherNumber num2: Int) -> Int {
```

Calling this method now reads more like a sentence:

```
multiplyThisNumber(3, byAnotherNumber: 7)
```

If your internal parameter name is sufficient for use inside and outside a function, and you don't want or need to specify an explicit external parameter name, you can use the hash symbol (#) before the internal parameter name. This tells Swift that the caller must use the parameter name, and the function can use the same parameter name. Listing 8.7 illustrates this parameter shorthand syntax.

LISTING 8.7   Using External Parameter Shorthand Syntax

```
func append(#lastName: String, toFirstName firstName: String) -> String {
    return firstName + " " + lastName
}
let fullName = append(lastName: "Miller" toFirstName: "BJ")
// fullName is equal to "BJ Miller"
```

Default Parameter Values

A nice feature of Swift is that you can provide default values for parameters in functions, and thus remove that argument from the function call if you decide to use the default value. Assigning a default value in a function definition is as easy as assigning the value directly in line with the declaration, just as you normally would with any variable or constant. Listing 8.8 illustrates how to use default parameter values.

LISTING 8.8   Using Default Parameter Values

```
func addExercise(exercise: String, withDuration duration: Int = 20) {
    println("You did \(exercise) for \(duration) minutes.")
}
addExercise("walking")
addExercise("cycling", 30)
// Displays:
//   You did walking for 20 minutes.
//   You did cycling for 30 minutes.
```

Change Argument Values with In-Out Parameters

Earlier in this hour we discussed briefly how to make a parameter into a variable instead of a constant, to be used inside a function. Making a parameter a variable works only within the scope of the function and does not impact the arguments supplied to the function from the caller. You may need to swap the values of two variables or sometimes even get valuable error data if something goes wrong, and often it is easier to use **in-out** parameters instead of a return value. In-out parameters actually change the value of the variable such that it is retrievable from outside the function.

To declare a parameter as an in-out parameter, simply add the `inout` keyword before the parameter name inside the function's description parentheses. Then, to call a function with in-out parameters, you must place the ampersand operator (`&`) immediately prefixing the name of the variable. The ampersand tells the compiler that the function can directly change the value of the variable. Let's take a look at Listing 8.9 to see how in-out parameters work and can be beneficial.

LISTING 8.9   Using In-Out Parameters

```
func reverseWords(inout firstWord: String, inout secondWord: String) {
    var tempWord = firstWord
    firstWord = secondWord
    secondWord = tempWord
}
var first = "I am first"
var second = "I am second"
reverseWords(&first, &second)
println(first)    // displays "I am second"
println(second)   // displays "I am first"
```

Objective-C did not have the ability to return multiple values inside a return type like Swift can with tuples. To get around that, Objective-C utilized in-out parameters (with slightly different syntax) to accomplish this goal. In-out parameters are useful but are not as obvious as a function having a return type and a return statement. In-out parameters should be used when you want changes to a variable to persist after a function has manipulated it, rather than returning a value and storing the result in a new variable or constant.

Summary

This hour provided a lot of information, and some concepts about functions are difficult to understand if you've not worked with them in the past. Go back over this hour again if you feel you need to rehash any of the information. Over the next hours, we use functions a lot more, so it is important to understand their structure, syntax, and use.

We discussed the basic structure and syntax of a function in Swift, how to use parameters with functions, and how to return values from functions. We also discussed how to identify the type of function, which is important to know when working with functions, parameters, and return types. As for parameters, we discussed how to use variadic parameters to pass in an unknown amount of arguments at once and convert it to an array, as well as using internal and external names for function parameters. After that, we discussed changing variable values externally with in-out parameters and prepopulating parameters with default parameters.

We aren't done with functions yet. In the next hour we discuss higher order functions, as well as closures, which are a special type of function and are a powerful feature of Swift.

Q&A

Q. Why would you need to use default parameters?

A. Default parameters are handy for developers. If you have existing functions and find that you need to add another parameter to the function, a default parameter could prevent your function from breaking your current code base. If you set a default parameter value, all existing function calls will still function normally.

Q. What are the naming rules for creating function names in Swift?

A. You want to avoid using any function names that are built into Swift. Functions must start with a letter and cannot contain spaces. It is also a generally accepted practice to use lower camel case for function names.

Q. Can a function have more than one variadic parameter?

A. No, a function can have at most one variadic parameter. If other parameters are used in the function, the variadic parameter must appear last in the parameter list to avoid confusion and errors.

Workshop

The workshop contains quiz questions and exercises to help you solidify your understanding of the material covered. Try to answer all questions before looking at the answers that follow.

Quiz

1. What is wrong with this code?

```
func showUserID() -> Int {
    println("Hello there!")
    return 5
    return 6
}
```

2. When using short-hand external parameters, the external and internal names are the same. What symbol can you use to tell Swift that the caller must use the parameter name, and the function can use the same parameter name?

3. By default, are all parameters constants or variables?

4. If you want to modify a variable inside the body but you want the changes to persist outside the body, what can you use?

5. What is wrong with the following code?

```
func welcomeUser(userName: String, withEmail: String = " ", userID: Int) {
    println(userName)
}
```

Answers

1. Once the return statement is called, no other values can be returned.

```
func showUserID() -> Int {
    println("Hello there!")
    return 5
}
```

2. You can use the (#) symbol to tell Swift that the caller must use the parameter name, and the function can use the same parameter name.

3. By default, all the function parameters are constants in Swift.

4. If you want to modify a variable inside the body but you want the changes to persist outside the body, you can define the parameter as an in-out parameter. This is also known as a pass-by-reference.

5. The parameter with a default value should occur last in the parameter list.

Exercise

Create a new OS X playground. Create a function that displays the current stock name and price for multiple stocks. Practice using default parameter values, variadic parameters, and different return values.

Understanding Higher Order Functions and Closures

What You'll Learn in This Hour:

- ► What higher order functions are
- ► How to accept functions as parameters and return functions
- ► How to nest functions
- ► What a closure is
- ► How to use reduce code with closures

The last hour introduced and discussed functions in Swift in great detail, from the general structure of a function to the different ways to add parameters and return values of different types. This hour we dive even deeper into functions with higher order functions and add a new term to our vocabulary: **closures**. Grasping the concepts and really understanding the syntax of functions from the last hour is important to moving forward this hour, so if you feel you still need to strengthen your skills with functions, take the time to reread or practice the code samples again.

Let's begin this hour by continuing our discussion of functions with higher order functions.

Higher Order Functions

While Swift is not a full-fledged functional programming language, it does have some functional aspects to it that are helpful. Swift utilizes **higher order functions**, which is just another way of saying that functions in Swift can take functions as parameters—or even return functions.

NOTE

Functional Programming

Wikipedia describes functional programming as "a programming paradigm, a style of building the structure and elements of computer programs that treats computation as the evaluation of mathematical functions and avoids state and mutable data." Further, "the output value of a function depends only on the arguments that are input to the function." Functional programming deserves an entire book devoted to it (and several have been written already), so we won't dig too deeply into the topic, and it doesn't require you to do anything specific in your code; I merely point this out as information about the kind of code we are writing here.

Returning Function Types

Since functions have a type, just as a variable could be a String, Bool, Int, or what have you, a variable can be of a function type. That means that we can store references to functions in local variables or constants, make a function be parameters of a function, or have a function's type be the return type of a function. Using functions as return types is easy in Swift; simply put the type of the function you'll be returning after the -> symbol in the function definition. Function syntax can get a little tricky to read once you start returning functions, but this is yet another reason why it makes sense to have return types at the end of a function definition, instead of at the beginning as in C and Objective-C; the structure still has a readable flow. To return a function that takes an Int and returns a String looks something like the following code snippet.

```
func someFunc() -> (Int) -> String
```

This function reads aloud as "A function named someFunc that takes no parameters, and returns a function that takes a single Int parameter and returns a String."

In Listing 9.1 I'll rewrite the meanMedianMode function from Hour 8, "Using Functions to Perform Actions," to separate out each average into its own function with its own return type. Then I'll have a central function that receives a string as a parameter and returns one of the average functions. Note that the median function rounds midIndex up for an array with an even count, which is fine for the purposes of this example. If you are following along on your own, feel free to alter the median function to calculate a true median by finding the middle two values, adding them together, and then dividing by two. Also note that I have changed the variadic parameters to arrays.

LISTING 9.1   Returning Function Types from Functions

```
01:   func mean(numbers: [Int]) -> Double {
02:       var sum = 0.0
03:       for number in numbers {
04:           sum += Double(number)
```

```
05:      }
06:      let mean = sum / Double(numbers.count)
07:      return mean
08: }
09:
10: func median(numbers: [Int]) -> Double {
11:      let sortedNumbers = numbers.sorted({ (num1: Int, num2: Int) -> Bool in
12:          return num1 < num2
13:      })
14:      let midIndex = numbers.count / 2
15:      let median = Double(sortedNumbers[midIndex])
16:      return median
17: }
18:
19: func mode(numbers: [Int]) -> Double {
20:      var occurrences: [Int : Int] = [:]
21:      for number in numbers {
22:          if var value = occurrences[number] {
23:              occurrences[number] = ++value
24:          } else {
25:              occurrences[number] = 1
26:          }
27:      }
28:      var highestPair: (key: Int, value: Int) = (0, 0)
29:      for (key, value) in occurrences {
30:          highestPair = (value > highestPair.value) ? (key, value) : highestPair
31:      }
32:      return Double(highestPair.key)
33: }
34:
35: func performMathAverage(mathFunc: String) -> ([Int]) -> Double {
36:      switch mathFunc {
37:          case "mean":
38:              return mean
39:          case "median":
40:              return median
41:          default:
42:              return mode
43:      }
44: }
45:
46: var mathFunc = performMathAverage("mean")
47: mathFunc([1, 1, 2, 3, 5, 8, 13])                    // 4.714285714285...
48: mathFunc = performMathAverage("median")
49: mathFunc([4, 5, 6])                                 // 5.0
50: mathFunc = performMathAverage("mode or not mode")
51: mathFunc([1, 1, 2, 3, 5, 8, 13])                    // 1.0
```

The first thing to notice is that all three averaging functions share the same types for parameters and return types in lines 1, 10, and 19. This becomes useful later when we call those functions. The code for the mean, median, and mode calculations is the same; they're just now inside their own respective functions, of type `([Int]) -> Double`. In line 35, we create a new function called `performMathAverage`, which takes one parameter, of type `String`, and returns a function of type `([Int]) -> Double`. Since our averaging functions all are of type `([Int]) -> Double`, our `performMathAverage` function can return any of our averaging functions as its return value. Line 46 then stores a returned function from `performMathAverage` based on what string we provide as an argument, which is `"mean"`. Now `mathFunc` is a variable of type `([Int]) -> Double`. See how that works? If `mathFunc` is a variable of type `([Int]) -> Double`, we can call it with an array of `Int`s and it should provide us with a `Double`. And line 47 verifies our assumption, by returning 4.714285714285. Then in line 48 we reassign `mathFunc` to the median function and send it a new array of `Int`s on line 49, resulting in 5.0 being returned. I agree that if this is new to you, the syntax is a little difficult to understand, but the more you practice it, the more fluent you'll become with Swift functions.

NOTE

Syntax for Returning Functions

Notice in `performMathAverage`, inside the switch cases, we return either `mean`, `median`, or `mode`, and not `mean()`, `median()`, or `mode()`. This is because we are not *calling* the methods, rather we are returning a *reference* to it, much like function pointers in C. When the function is actually called to get a value you add the parentheses suffixed to the function name.

Notice, too, that any of the average functions could be called independently without the use of the `performMathAverage` function. This is because `mean`, `median`, and `mode` are called **global functions**. If we want to hide functions from the global scope so that only our `performMathAverage` function (or whatever containing function you might be using at the time) can access particular functions, we can use **nested functions**.

Nesting Functions Within Functions

It shouldn't surprise you, with as powerful and flexible as Swift is, that we can nest functions within functions. Nested functions are simply written inside a containing function, and therefore are only accessible within the containing function, not globally like standard functions. This can be useful for providing a layer of abstraction or privacy when necessary, to avoid certain functions from being called directly, or to be returned from a containing function when a particular criterion has been met. The `mean`, `median`, and `mode` functions in Listing 9.1 could be nested inside `performMathAverage`, and the example would behave the same.

Nested functions also have access to constants and variables from the containing function's scope. This means that if we declare a function, and directly inside that function we declare a sum variable equal to 0.0, we could then create a function inside the first function, where we would be able to access sum without any issue. If we alter the sum value inside the nested function, Swift creates a *reference* to that value so that we can modify sum's value directly. If we do not alter sum inside the nested function, but rather just use it for its value, Swift creates a *copy* of the value to be used in our nested function.

CAUTION

References Versus Values in Nested Functions

As mentioned earlier, if a nested function accesses a property (a variable or constant) of the containing function's scope, Swift either makes a reference to or a copy of the value. Accessing by reference means that you are directly accessing or modifying the contents of the variable at that location in memory. Accessing by value means that Swift creates a copy of the value for you to use without modifying the original. Swift does this because you may have two nested functions that both need access to a property in the containing function's scope. One function needs to modify the value, but the other function needs to have a copy of the property's original value. If both nested functions used a reference to the property's value, the function that needed the unchanged value would now have the changed value, and your app could experience unwanted behavior.

Let's rewrite the mean, median, and mode average functions to be nested functions inside the performMathAverage function. This makes it possible for us to publicly declare a variable of type ([Int]) -> Double, which enables us to have that variable change to any average function we want. Listing 9.2 illustrates our performMathAverage function with nested functions. For brevity, I have commented out the code inside the median and mode functions as it is the same as Listing 9.1.

LISTING 9.2 Nested Functions

```
01:   func performMathAverage(mathFunc: String) -> ([Int]) -> Double {
02:       var sum = 0.0
03:       func mean(numbers: [Int]) -> Double {
04:           for number in numbers {
05:               sum += Double(number)
06:           }
07:           return sum / Double(numbers.count)
08:       }
09:
10:       func median(numbers: [Int]) -> Double {
11:           // insert median code here
12:       }
13:
14:       func mode(numbers: [Int]) -> Double {
```

```
15:            // insert mode code here
16:        }
17:
18:        switch mathFunc {
19:            case "mean":
20:                return mean
21:            case "median":
22:                return median
23:            default:
24:                return mode
25:        }
26:    }
27:    var mathFunc = performMathAverage("mean")
28:    mathFunc([10, 11, 10, 12, 10, 13])  // displays 11.0
29:    mathFunc = performMathAverage("median")
30:    mathFunc([10, 11, 10, 12, 10, 13])  // displays 11.0
31:    mathFunc = performMathAverage("mode")
32:    mathFunc([10, 11, 10, 12, 10, 13])  // displays 10.0
```

This example shows you how functions can be nested but still be accessible outside the scope of their containing function by returning a reference to them. Notice also in line 2 that sum is a variable scoped to the performMathAverage function, but it is still accessible inside the mean function. If you tried to assign mathFunc = mean, you would get a compiler error, "Use of unresolved identifier 'mean'". In line 27 we assign performMathAverage("mean") to mathFunc, which is of type ([Int]) -> Double, and refers to the mean function. Since mathFunc is a variable of type ([Int]) -> Double, we can also use performMathAverage to assign different returned functions to it of that same type, which is what we do in lines 29 and 31. Lines 28, 30, and 32 all send integer array literals as arguments to the function that mathFunc refers to at that time and receive the respective output.

Using Functions as Function Parameters

Just as you would specify the function type as a return value, using functions as parameters to functions is similar. The only difference, however, is that you name the parameter to be of a function type, rather than just specifying the type when returning. Figure 9.1 illustrates the syntax of using functions as parameters in a function definition.

```
func someFunc(externalParamName internalParamName: ( FuncParamType ) -> FuncReturnType ) -> ReturnType {
    // write some code...
    return someValue
}
```

FIGURE 9.1
The structure of a function definition with a function as a parameter.

So why would you want to send functions as arguments to functions? Perhaps you want to perform a particular function upon a particular piece of data, and you can send both as arguments to a function that will perform that task.

Now, let's do a Try It Yourself, using a function as parameters to a function.

Perform a Function on Each Member of an Array

Create a function that takes an integer array and a function, and returns a new array with the elements modified by the function argument.

1. Open Xcode 6 and create a new playground. Either a Mac or an iOS playground will work. Clear the contents of the playground.

2. Create a function that simply squares a number given to it. We use this as the function to pass as an argument later. Make it simple; just require the function to take an Int parameter and return an Int.

```
func square(num: Int) -> Int {
    return num * num
}
```

3. Create a function to iterate over each element in an array of integers and then call the supplied function with the array element as its argument. Then, return the new array.

```
func mapEachElement(inArray arr: [Int], withFunc aFunc: (Int) -> Int) ->
➡[Int] {
    var returnArray = [Int]()
    for num in arr {
        returnArray.append(aFunc(num))
    }
    return returnArray
}
```

4. With the functions built, create an array to pass in to mapEachElement as an argument.

```
let firstArray = [1, 2, 3, 4, 5]
```

5. Assign a new array to the result of calling mapEachElement with firstArray and the square function.

```
let squareArray = mapEachElement(inArray: firstArray, withFunc: square)
```

Hopefully that wasn't too bad, and you're getting the hang of functions. If you followed along and did the example correctly, your playground should look like Figure 9.2. Incidentally, with this example, you've just written a modified version of a Swift standard library function called **map**. The map function is powerful, and we further explore it later in this book.

```
1   //
2   // Ch09 Map Each Element Try-It-Yourself example
3   //
4
5   func square(num:Int) -> Int {
6       return num * num                                        (5 times)
7   }
8
9   func mapEachElement(inArray arr: [Int], withFunc aFunc: (Int) -> Int) -> [Int] {
10      var returnArray = [Int]()                               0 elements
11      for num in arr {
12          returnArray.append(aFunc(num))
13      }
14      return returnArray                                      [1, 4, 9, 16, 25]
15  }
16
17  let firstArray = [1, 2, 3, 4, 5]                            [1, 2, 3, 4, 5]
18  let squareArray = mapEachElement(inArray: firstArray, withFunc: square)    [1, 4, 9, 16, 25]
19
```

FIGURE 9.2
The completed playground for the `mapEachElement` exercise.

Closures

Closures are self-contained chunks of code. They resemble functions in that the code inside their curly braces is only executed when acted upon or called, but the biggest difference is they can be anonymous. Some closures don't have a name, so you can't just arbitrarily call a closure to be executed. You see how they are executed shortly, but first let's cover some definitions.

There are three types of closures in Swift, and we've already discussed two of them: global functions and nested functions. Global functions are really closures that are named but do not capture any values from a containing context. Nested functions are named closures and can capture values from their containing function. The last type of closure, **closure expressions**, do not have a name but can capture values from their containing context. The act of capturing outside values and references to be used inside a closure is called **closing**, hence the name closure.

Since we already covered global functions and nested functions, let's take a few minutes to examine closure expressions, their syntax and structure, and walk through some of their powerful capabilities to express code quickly and succinctly without losing clarity or readability.

Structure of Closure Expressions

Closure expressions in Swift follow the general syntactical structure illustrated in Figure 9.3.

```
{ ( param : ParamType , paramTwo : AnotherType ,..) -> ReturnType in
    // code inside closure goes here
    return someValue
}
```

FIGURE 9.3
The structure and syntax of a closure expression in Swift.

Inside the curly braces (because, remember, closure expressions do not have names), you define the parameters and their types inside parentheses like you would a global or nested function, and then provide the return symbol (->) and a return type. Immediately following the return type is the keyword in, which denotes the separation of the closure's definition from the code to execute. After the in keyword, you write the code to execute inside the closure expression, and then end the closure expression with the ending curly brace, just like any other function.

This seems straightforward, considering it is reasonably similar to the structure of global or nested functions. However, wouldn't it be nice if we could shorten the syntax to be a little less verbose and a little more powerful? It turns out we can, and over the next several examples we reduce the size of a function by utilizing Swift's powers of type inference, implicit returns, short-hand syntax, and **trailing closures**. These make it clearer in one to two lines of code what we are accomplishing, rather than five lines of standard for loops to manipulate the return value.

Let's take a look at how we start accomplishing this goal in Listing 9.3, by using the mean function from Listing 9.1. We use an **instance method** on Array called **reduce**, since our input parameter is an array of integers. The reduce function iterates through each item in the array and recursively builds a return value based on the function operation in the closure expression.

NOTE

Instance Methods

Instance methods are functions that can be called on an instance of a class, struct, or enum, rather than on the type itself. We discuss instance methods and type methods more in Hour 10, "Learning About Structs and Classes," Hour 11, "Implementing Class Inheritance," and Hour 12, "Harnessing the Power of Enums."

Before starting Listing 9.3, let's quickly look at the syntax of the reduce instance method. The syntax is a little strange, so examine Figure 9.4.

```
func mean2(numbers: [Int]) -> Double {
    sum = numbers.reduce( initial: U , combine: (U, Int) -> U )
}
          M  U reduce(initial: U, combine: (U, Int) -> U(U, Int) -> U)
```

FIGURE 9.4
Xcode's auto-complete feature displaying the syntax for the reduce instance method.

What's with the letter U? In Swift, the letters T, U, or any other single capital letter are commonly used to denote a **placeholder type**, which means that you can use any type you want, as long as wherever else you see a T or U (or whatever other letter is assigned), you must use that same type. So for instance, if we set a variable of type Double to the initial parameter, we would also have to use a Double as the first parameter and the return type inside the function for the combine parameter.

LISTING 9.3   Using `reduce` Function on an Array

```
01:  func mean2(numbers: [Int]) -> Double {
02:      var sum = 0
03:      func meanCombine(num1: Int, num2: Int) -> Int {
04:          return num1 + num2
05:      }
06:      sum = numbers.reduce(0, combine: meanCombine)
07:      return Double(sum) / Double(numbers.count)
08:  }
09:  mean2([5, 6, 7])   // displays 6.0
```

In the reduce function, the second parameter is a function that takes a parameter of any type (U) and another of type Int, and returns a value of type U. So, on line 3, we created a nested function that takes two Int parameters and returns an Int. The nested function returns the two parameters added together. Line 6 is the call to the reduce function itself, but notice that we don't have the parentheses after meanCombine for the combine parameter in the reduce function. Do you know why? We are passing in a *reference* to the meanCombine function, not *calling* it directly; the reduce function calls meanCombine during its execution, so for now reduce just needs to know what chunk of code to execute. The reduce function automatically passes in the necessary arguments to the meanCombine function for us when it calls meanCombine from its execution. Finally, line 9 shows that when we call mean2 with an array of Ints, it returns the appropriate result.

Great, you're learning about the reduce function and how to use a closure as one of the arguments to pass in to it. But this looks like a lot of work compared to the simple, straightforward approach to the mean function in Listing 9.1 Let's take a look at how to simplify this by removing the line that initializes sum to 0, because we can just assign it to the returned value of the reduce function. In addition to that, let's remove the nested `meanCombine` function and use a closure expression instead. Listing 9.4 illustrates how we accomplish these objectives.

LISTING 9.4   Using Closure Expressions as Parameters

```
01:   func mean3(numbers: [Int]) -> Double {
02:       let sum = numbers.reduce(0, combine: { (num1: Int, num2: Int) -> Int in
03:           return num1 + num2
04:       })
05:       return Double(sum) / Double(numbers.count)
06:   }
07:   mean3([2, 3, 4, 5, 6, 7])   // displays 4.5
```

This is looking better, and we reduced our function by 2 lines to 4. Take a look at line 2, where we declare the closure expression's parameters and return type. We know that Swift is powerful when it comes to type inference, so can't we use type inference here? Yes! Listing 9.5 reduces the size of the closure by removing the types, because they are implied by the `combine` parameter, simplifying the closure expression's structure.

LISTING 9.5   Using Type Inference in Closure Expression Definitions

```
01:   func mean4(numbers: [Int]) -> Double {
02:       let sum = numbers.reduce(0, combine: { num1, num2 in
03:           return num1 + num2
04:       })
05:       return Double(sum) / Double(numbers.count)
06:   }
07:   mean4([1, 1, 2, 3])   // displays 1.75
```

Our function is looking easier to read without the extra type information in the closure expression's definition, letting us clearly see the parameter names and closure structure without distraction. We even dropped the parentheses around num1 and num2.

Our function didn't reduce any lines of code, though. Let's further refine our example by utilizing a feature in Swift called **implicit returns**. Since our closure expression really only calculates the addition of two numbers, it is referred to as a **single-expression closure**, and therefore the return can be implied. Listing 9.6 shows how this is done.

LISTING 9.6   Using Implicit Return Statements in a Closure Expression

```
01:   func mean5(numbers: [Int]) -> Double {
02:       let sum = numbers.reduce(0, combine: { num1, num2 in num1 + num2 })
03:       return Double(sum) / Double(numbers.count)
04:   }
05:   mean5([7, 7, 11])   // displays 8.3333
```

We have no more return statement inside the closure expression since it is implied, and the closure expression is still readable and understandable. We also reduced the length of the function down to two lines. But why stop now?

Swift provides **shorthand argument names** when used inline inside closures, which is denoted by the dollar sign ($) and the number of the argument, starting with zero (0). For instance, the first parameter could be referenced as $0, the next as $1, and so on. Using shorthand argument names enables you to remove the closure expression's argument list, as well as the `in` keyword since all that is left is the body of the closure, further reducing the code needed to cleanly express our intent with the operation and return value of the closure. Listing 9.7 illustrates using shorthand argument names in our function.

LISTING 9.7   **Using Shorthand Argument Names**

```
01:   func mean6(numbers: [Int]) -> Double {
02:       let sum = numbers.reduce(0, combine: {$0 + $1})
03:       return Double(sum) / Double(numbers.count)
04:   }
05:   mean6([10, 11, 12])   // displays 11.0
```

This is really getting fun! Because of our need to return a value of type `Double`, we still have to cast `sum` to be of type `Double`, but isn't this much clearer? Let's take this another step closer to being as concise and clear as possible.

As a good rule of practice, functions in Swift should typically have any function parameters as the last parameter in the list of parameters. When a function has a function parameter as its last parameter, you may use a **trailing closure** for the final argument. This places the closure *outside* the ending parenthesis and is useful if the closure expression is long. But if we use a trailing closure, what happens to the `combine` parameter name? You got it—it's gone too. Listing 9.8 illustrates our mean function with a trailing closure and then simplifies it one more step with another iteration of the function, which makes the function one simple line.

LISTING 9.8   **Using Trailing Closures**

```
01:   func mean7(numbers: [Int]) -> Double {
02:       let sum = numbers.reduce(0) {$0 + $1}
03:       return Double(sum) / Double(numbers.count)
04:   }
05:
06:   func mean8(numbers: [Int]) -> Double {
07:       return Double(numbers.reduce(0) {$0 + $1}) / Double(numbers.count)
08:   }
```

In line 2 you can see the use of the trailing closure, which is really the final argument to the `reduce` function. Isn't this so much clearer? Line 3 has come along with us as the final line since Listing 9.3, so in the second function (`mean8`), we bring up the division statement to the end of the line and return the final value on line 7.

Thanks to the power of Swift's capabilities for type inference, implicit returns, shorthand syntax, and trailing closures, we simplified our `mean` function from 6 lines to 1, and kept the clarity and readability.

Some closure expressions in Swift require a Boolean return value, such as with sorting. Using **operator functions**, you can reduce a final parameter to just an operator, such as < or > for sorting, as shown in the following snippet:

```
let a = [5, 4, 1, 3, 2]
let b = a.sorted(<)   // b is equal to [1, 2, 3, 4, 5]
```

Also, if a function only requires one parameter, and it is of a function type, you can supply the trailing closure to the function as its only argument, and you may remove the parentheses completely. The parentheses would not be necessary since the argument to the function is the trailing closure.

I hope you're really grasping the power of closures in Swift and getting comfortable writing them in concise syntax that still makes sense to you. Take a few minutes to let these concepts sink in and repeat any material you may not have understood. When you're ready, let's walk through an example in this next Try It Yourself section.

TRY IT YOURSELF ▼

Rewriting the `median` Function

Rewrite the `median` function to be as concise as possible, while still being clear in intent and readable. Change the function to return an `Int`, as it only receives `Int` values, and our median function returns the value at the middle of the array. This would break the ability to return `median` from `performMathAverage`, as its definition would change, but that's okay for this example since this will be a new playground. Again, this is not the mathematically precise median average for arrays with an even number of elements; feel free to adjust this example to calculate the true median by averaging the two middle values of an array with an even number of elements. The goal of this exercise is to understand using functions to simplify code.

1. Open Xcode 6 and create a new playground. Either a Mac or iOS playground will work. Clear the contents of the playground.

2. Write the entire `median` function, as it was in Listing 9.1, but change the return type to `Int` from `Double`.

```
func median(numbers: [Int]) -> Int {
    let sortedNumbers = numbers.sorted({ (num1: Int, num2: Int) -> Bool in
        return num1 < num2
    })
    let midIndex = numbers.count / 2
    return sortedNumbers[midIndex]
}
```

3. Use type inference to remove the parameter types and return type from the closure expression.

```
func median(numbers: [Int]) -> Int {
    let sortedNumbers = numbers.sorted({ num1, num2 in
        return num1 < num2
    })
    let midIndex = numbers.count / 2
    return sortedNumbers[midIndex]
}
```

4. Use implicit return syntax to remove the return statement.

```
func median(numbers: [Int]) -> Int {
    let sortedNumbers = numbers.sorted({ num1, num2 in num1 < num2 })
    let midIndex = numbers.count / 2
    return sortedNumbers[midIndex]
}
```

5. Use shorthand argument names to shorten the single-expression closure.

```
func median(numbers: [Int]) -> Int {
    let sortedNumbers = numbers.sorted({ $0 < $1 })
    let midIndex = numbers.count / 2
    return sortedNumbers[midIndex]
}
```

6. Use trailing closure syntax to clarify that the closure is the only argument to the sorted instance method. The parentheses are not necessary when calling the sorted function because the only argument is the trailing closure.

```
func median(numbers: [Int]) -> Int {
    let sortedNumbers = numbers.sorted { $0 < $1 }
    let midIndex = numbers.count / 2
    return sortedNumbers[midIndex]
}
```

7. Use an operator function to remove the shorthand argument names and reduce the closure expression even further.

```
func median(numbers: [Int]) -> Int {
    let sortedNumbers = numbers.sorted(<)
    let midIndex = numbers.count / 2
    return sortedNumbers[midIndex]
}
```

8. Reduce the entire `median` function to a single line.

```
func median(numbers: [Int]) -> Int {
    return numbers.sorted(<)[numbers.count / 2]
}
```

Upon completion, your playground should look like the playground in Figure 9.5. The playground in Figure 9.5 has different function names for each step in the Try It Yourself section, to prevent name conflicts.

```
     Ch09 Median Rewrite TIY.playground

     Ch09 Median Rewrite TIY.playground ⟩ No Selection

1    //
2    // Ch09 Try It Yourself - median function re-write
3    //    Each function here has a new name to allow us to visualize each step
          in the TIY section without name conflict here in the Playground.
4    //
5    func median(numbers: [Int]) -> Int {
6        let sortedNumbers = numbers.sorted({ (num1: Int, num2: Int) -> Bool in    [1, 2, 3, 4, 5]
7            return num1 < num2                                                     (4 times)
8        })
9        let midIndex = numbers.count / 2                                           2
10       return sortedNumbers[midIndex]                                             3
11   }
12
13   func median2(numbers: [Int]) -> Int {
14       let sortedNumbers = numbers.sorted({ num1, num2 in                         [1, 2, 3, 4, 5]
15           return num1 < num2                                                     (4 times)
16       })
17       let midIndex = numbers.count / 2                                           2
18       return sortedNumbers[midIndex]                                             3
19   }
20
21   func median3(numbers: [Int]) -> Int {
22       let sortedNumbers = numbers.sorted({ num1, num2 in num1 < num2 })          (5 times)
23       let midIndex = numbers.count / 2                                           2
24       return sortedNumbers[midIndex]                                             3
25   }
26
27   func median4(numbers: [Int]) -> Int {
28       let sortedNumbers = numbers.sorted({ $0 < $1 })                            (5 times)
29       let midIndex = numbers.count / 2                                           2
30       return sortedNumbers[midIndex]                                             3
31   }
32
33   func median5(numbers: [Int]) -> Int {
34       let sortedNumbers = numbers.sorted { $0 < $1 }                             (5 times)
35       let midIndex = numbers.count / 2                                           2
36       return sortedNumbers[midIndex]                                             3
37   }
38
39   func median6(numbers: [Int]) -> Int {
40       let sortedNumbers = numbers.sorted(<)                                      [1, 2, 3, 4, 5]
41       let midIndex = numbers.count / 2                                           2
42       return sortedNumbers[midIndex]                                             3
43   }
44
45   func median7(numbers: [Int]) -> Int {
46       return numbers.sorted(<)[numbers.count / 2]                                3
47   }
48
49   median([1, 2, 3, 4, 5])                                                        3
50   median2([1, 2, 3, 4, 5])                                                       3
51   median3([1, 2, 3, 4, 5])                                                       3
52   median4([1, 2, 3, 4, 5])                                                       3
53   median5([1, 2, 3, 4, 5])                                                       3
54   median6([1, 2, 3, 4, 5])                                                       3
55   median7([1, 2, 3, 4, 5])                                                       3
56
```

FIGURE 9.5
The completed playground for the median rewrite Try It Yourself section.

Summary

Hopefully by now you are becoming familiar with functions and closures, and the structure and syntax are becoming easier to understand. We use them frequently throughout the remainder of this book, so if you don't understand anything regarding functions or closures, I suggest reviewing the previous hour and this current hour to really get a good grasp on the concepts and syntax.

In this hour, we continued Hour 8's discussion on functions by introducing higher order functions. Higher order functions can accept functions as parameters or return functions. Then we discussed nested functions as a way to create functions for use within a containing function but which are not available globally. To use a nested function globally, we introduced a way to return a reference to the nested function from the global function and store the reference in a variable. Sending arguments to the variable executed the nested function with those arguments.

Then we discussed in great detail closures in Swift. Closures are a powerful feature, enabling you to send a closure as an argument to a function and drastically reduce the amount of code needed to not only complete the task but also clearly describe what the code should be doing in the closure expression. Swift closures can be reduced in length but retain their clarity with the use of five key features: type inference, implicit returns, shorthand argument names, trailing closures, and operator functions.

In the next hour, we discuss two Swift building blocks, structs and classes, and how you can build your own custom data types.

Q&A

Q. What are higher order functions?

A. Higher order functions are functions that can take functions as parameters or return functions.

Q. How are nested functions and global functions different?

A. Nested functions are defined inside other functions and are only accessible from within the containing function. They also have access to constants and variables found in the containing function's scope. Global functions are accessible from anywhere in our program.

Q. Is it better to use named parameters or shorthand argument names inside inline closures?

A. The answer to the question depends on your code. You should choose whichever style makes your code clearer and easier to understand.

Workshop

The workshop contains quiz questions and exercises to help you solidify your understanding of the material covered. Try to answer all questions before looking at the answers that follow.

Quiz

1. At the end of the following code snippet, what are the values of `firstHello` and `secondHello`?

```
func sayHello() -> String {
   return "Hello!"
}
let firstHello = sayHello()
let secondHello = sayHello
```

2. What are the three types of closures discussed in this hour?

3. What does the following function do?

```
func someFunction( x: Int, y: Int, f: (Int, Int) -> Int ) -> Int {
   return f(x,y)
}
```

4. If you use the function `someFunc` from the previous question in the following expression, what value will be assigned to `result`?

```
let result = someFunction( 2, 3, { (a, b) -> Int in return a * b})
```

Answers

1. `firstHello` contains the string "Hello!", but `secondHello` is a reference to the function `sayHello()`.

2. Global functions, nested functions, and closure expressions.

3. The function `someFunc()` takes three arguments and returns an integer. The first two arguments are integers `x` and `y`. The final argument is a reference to a function that accepts two integers as arguments and returns an integer.

   When provided with two integers `x` and `y` and a function `f`, `someFunc(x,y,f)` will call `f`, with arguments `x` and `y` and return the result.

4. The arguments to `someFunc()` are the integers 2 and 3 and a function that multiplies two integers together. The result of the function is therefore 6.

Exercise

Create a new OS X playground. We're going to practice passing functions as arguments to other functions.

Write a function min that finds the minimum value in an array of integers and returns it and a function max that finds the maximum value in an array of integers and returns it. Test your functions to make sure they work as expected.

Next, create a function that returns an integer and takes an array of integers and a reference to a function as arguments. This new function should apply the supplied function to the array and return the result. Now, pass an array of integers and a reference to min and make sure that you get the correct value back. Repeat the process with max.

Learning About Structs and Classes

What You'll Learn in This Hour:

▶ How to define and create structs and classes
▶ How to declare properties in structs and classes
▶ How to create methods in structs and classes
▶ How Swift handles value and reference types
▶ How to inherit properties and methods from superclasses
▶ How to use memberwise initializers in structs
▶ How to specify security through access controls

In this hour, we discuss two building blocks in Swift that you have seen previously in this book but haven't really examined until now: structures (called **structs**) and **classes**. Structs and classes are flexible constructs that allow you to easily and quickly create custom types for storing, manipulating, and returning data. By using instances of these constructs, and making them interoperate with instances of other types, we form entire apps. We discuss structs and classes together in this hour because, in Swift, the lines delineating the two constructs are somewhat blurred as compared to what you may find in other languages. Once you learn about structs and classes, object-oriented programming becomes much easier, and the concepts discussed in this book thus far become far more applicable.

Overview of Structs and Classes in Swift

Structs and classes are blueprints to data types that you can create and that are already provided in Swift. Some structs that you have already seen are the data types `String`, `Int`, `Bool`, `Array`, and `Dictionary`, to name a few.

Before we get into how structs and classes are structured and the syntax of creating and using them, let's take a look at some delineating definitions of both structures.

Swift structs are value types with which you can create properties (either variables or constants) to save data about a struct instance and create functions (called **methods**) to add functionality to that instance.

Swift classes are reference types with which you can create properties (either variables or constants) to save data about a class instance and create functions (called methods) to add functionality to that instance.

Those two definitions look awfully similar. In fact, they are identical except for one big difference: Structs are **value types** and classes are **reference types**. Obviously, these are oversimplified definitions, and we discuss more differences throughout this and future hours, but the type difference is important. Being a value type, a struct is *passed by value*, meaning that any time you need to send a struct to a function or even create another variable or constant of an existing struct, a complete copy is made of the struct and the new copy is used in the new variable or constant. This means that the original struct property is kept intact, even if the copy changes.

Classes, however, behave differently. Because classes are reference types, this means that instead of a copy being created and manipulated, a reference to the actual sole instance is passed around and/or used and can be modified directly by a second variable assigned to that reference. To visualize the differences between structs as value types and classes as reference types, see Figure 10.1.

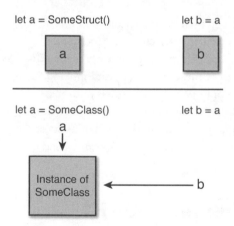

FIGURE 10.1
Diagram illustrating the differences between value types and reference types in memory.

In Figure 10.1, the top half of the diagram illustrates declaring a to equal an instance of SomeStruct and assigning b to be equal to a. When you use assignment with value types, a copy is made, and this is denoted by b having its own unique instance; it just happens that all of b's properties and methods start out the same as a's, and they are of the same type from the assignment.

In the lower half of the illustration, a is assigned a reference to an instance of SomeClass, hence the letter a being above the instance's shape and pointing to the instance, rather than inside the shape like the a struct value. Then b is assigned a reference to the same instance that a references, so b doesn't actually get its own instance like the struct example; b receives a reference to the existing instance of SomeClass that a also references.

That's enough for now in terms of differences between classes and structs. Let's now take a look at their similarities and begin creating classes and structs in code.

What Swift Structs and Classes Have in Common

Classes and structs in Swift share a few common features. The basic syntax structure is also identical outside the initial keyword class or struct for defining a class or a struct, respectively. Both can define variables and constants (called **properties**) that can be used to store values, and both can define functions (called methods) that can be used to add functionality to their structures. We cover these concepts in detail this hour. There are other similarities that both classes and structs share, such as custom subscripts, custom initializers, extensions, and conformance to protocols, but we discuss those in later hours.

Before we dive into defining methods and properties in our classes and structs, let's first examine the syntax of both constructs. See Figure 10.2 for an example of what each definition looks like in code.

```
struct MyCustomStruct {

}
class MyCustomClass {

}
```

FIGURE 10.2
The syntax for creating structs and classes is nearly identical, with the exception of their keywords.

As you can see in Figure 10.2, to create a struct, you use the `struct` keyword, and to create a class, you use the `class` keyword. Then you name the structure and provide the open and closed curly braces, where the body of the structure will go.

NOTE

Naming Conventions

There are no laws, per se, for how you should name classes and structs and their corresponding properties and methods. There are, however, widely accepted naming conventions, and it is highly suggested that you follow these conventions for consistency. Swift types should use **upper camel case**, such as `MyDataType`. Swift properties and methods, as well as instances of types, should use **lower camel case**, such as `myStringInstance`.

Defining Properties

One of the basic ideas behind structs and classes is that you can create **properties** to store data in an instance of a struct or class. Properties can be either constants or variables, declared with the `let` or `var` introducers, respectively, just as we've seen earlier in this book.

Let's take a look at how to declare variable and constant properties inside a struct. We start by creating a point on a coordinate system, which is a common use for structs in many languages. The `Point` struct should have an `x` and `y` coordinate, so let's make those of type `Double`. Listing 10.1 illustrates creating our `Point` struct.

LISTING 10.1 Creating a Point Struct

```
struct Point {
    var x: Double
    var y: Double
}
```

Because the `x` and `y` properties store data directly without any sort of calculation, they are referred to as **stored properties**. We cover computed properties in Hour 14, "Digging Deeper with Properties."

Creating a struct in Swift is simple. Structs are great data types when you need a small structure to hold values and perhaps a little extra functionality by adding methods. We add methods shortly, but first, let's declare an instance of our `Point` struct. Listing 10.2 shows how to declare a couple instances of `Point`.

LISTING 10.2   **Creating an Instance of the Point Struct**

```
let pointA = Point(x: 1.0, y: 2.0)    // displays {x 1.0, y 2.0}
let pointB = Point(x: 4.0, y: 6.0)    // displays {x 4.0, y 6.0}
pointB.x                              // displays 4.0
```

Notice when we declare our instances, Xcode forces us to include the x and y parameter names and arguments inside the parentheses. In Swift, this is called a **memberwise initializer**. Because there is no specific initializer method inside the struct, and all Swift variables and constants need to be initialized with a value before use, Swift requires us to set values upon instantiation. This is not only for safety, but this is also a pretty nice convenience. It suggests to you, the developer, that there are properties that need values, their type, and how many properties there are. Memberwise initializers are specific to structs; classes do not have memberwise initializers.

TIP

Initializing Properties in Structs

To avoid requiring the memberwise initializer for your struct, you can initialize your properties to have a value when you define them. This is done exactly the way you have done in the past by typing something such as `var x: Double = 0.0`, or more simply `var x = 0.0`. Then to declare an instance of `Point`, you can simply type `var pointC = Point()`. This only applies if all properties in the struct are given initial values when defined.

We declared these instances as constants, because for now we do not need them to change. But what if our struct instances are constants but our struct's instance properties are variables? If our struct instance is a constant, we cannot change any of its properties; even if they are variable properties, our struct instance is constant.

In the third line, we typed `pointB.x`. This gets the x property's value from the `pointB` instance. Using the instance name, a dot, and then the property name is known as using **dot syntax**. Dot syntax is a simple and powerful way to access properties and methods on an instance, and even properties on instances inside instances, and so on. You will see a lot more of dot syntax throughout this book, as you will use it daily in your Swift programming life.

Instance Methods

Let's continue this example by adding a function, called an **instance method**, to our Point struct. Say we want to find the distance to any arbitrary coordinate. This functionality is a perfect task for an instance method.

To accomplish this calculation, we need the Pythagorean Theorem. If I just gave you bad memories of high school, my sincere apologies. The Pythagorean Theorem states that given a right triangle with a known base and height, we can calculate the length of the side opposite the right angle, in a formula well-known as $a^2 + b^2 = c^2$. Let's do this in the next Try It Yourself section. You need to import the Foundation framework to be able to access some built-in math capabilities (such as absolute value and square root) and add an instance method called `distanceTo(point:)`. This is just like creating a function as we did in Hour 8, "Using Functions to Perform Actions," and Hour 9, "Understanding Higher Order Functions and Closures," so you should be able to follow along just fine.

▼ TRY IT YOURSELF

Adding an Instance Method to a Struct

Create the Point struct here and add an instance method to the struct that calculates the distance to another point using the Pythagorean Theorem.

1. Open Xcode 6 and create a new playground. Either a Mac or iOS playground will work. Clear the contents of the playground.

2. Begin by importing the Foundation framework.

   ```
   import Foundation
   ```

3. Define the `Point` struct.

   ```
   struct Point {

   }
   ```

4. Add two properties of type `Double` for the x and y coordinates inside the curly braces.

   ```
   var x: Double
   var y: Double
   ```

5. Define the `distanceTo(point:)` method, which takes a parameter of type `Point` and returns a `Double`. Use shorthand syntax, the hash sign (#), for making the internal parameter name the same as the external parameter name, as it makes calling the method more readable.

   ```
   func distanceTo(#point: Point) -> Double {

   }
   ```

6. Inside the `distanceTo(point:)` method, calculate sides a and b of the right triangle by finding the absolute value difference between the x values and y values.

   ```
   let a = abs(self.x - point.x)
   let b = abs(self.y - point.y)
   ```

7. After assigning values to a and b, we can now calculate c. Return c. (Note: We could just return the calculated value without assigning to c, but creating c fulfilled the Pythagorean Theorem of $a^2 + b^2 = c^2$.)

```
let c = sqrt(a * a + b * b)
return c
```

8. That's all for the method, and that's all for the struct. Create two instances of the struct now, outside the struct's curly braces.

```
let pointA = Point(x: 1.0, y: 2.0)
let pointB = Point(x: 4.0, y: 6.0)
```

9. Now that we have two points, calculate the distance between them by using our new instance method.

```
let distance = pointA.distanceTo(point: pointB)    // displays 5.0
```

NOTE

The `self` Keyword

Notice in Step 6 that we use `self.x` and `self.y`. While not completely necessary to use in the preceding example (Swift infers that you mean to use `x` and `y` instance properties), it sometimes helps readability to be explicit about which properties you are using in an expression. The `self` keyword refers to the instance currently being operated on. There are some times when the `self` keyword is necessary, such as inside closures or to remove ambiguity between input parameter names and instance property names. We discuss using `self` inside closures in Hour 16, "Understanding Memory Allocation and References," and using `self` to remove ambiguity inside initializers in Hour 13, "Customizing Initializers of Classes, Structs, and Enums."

In step 5, you add the `distanceTo(point:)` instance method to our `Point` struct, which should be familiar to you by now. Step 6 uses the Foundation function `abs(x: T)` to find the absolute value (which returns a non-negative number) of a number or equation, and then step 7 calculates the distance by taking the square root (using the `sqrt(x: Double)` Foundation function) of $a^2 + b^2$.

Upon completion of the Try It Yourself section, your code should look similar to that in Figure 10.3.

The only difference between functions as we've known them and instance methods is that we don't call the instance methods directly in the Try It Yourself example; we call them with dot syntax as part of our instance. We can, however, call instance methods from within other instance methods in a class or struct, and calling a function is as simple as calling it as we did in Hours 8 and 9—directly and providing any arguments if necessary.

```
●●●              ▣ Ch10 TIY Adding Instance Method to Struct.playground
🔳 | ⟨  ⟩ | ▣ Ch10 TIY Adding Instance Method to Struct.playground ⟩ No Selection
 1   import Foundation
 2
 3   // Try It Yourself — Adding an Instance Method to a Struct
 4   struct Point {
 5       var x: Double
 6       var y: Double
 7
 8       func distanctTo(#point: Point) -> Double {
 9           let a = abs(self.x - point.x)          3.0
10           let b = abs(self.y - point.y)          4.0
11           let c = sqrt(a * a + b * b)            5.0
12           return c                               5.0
13       }
14
15   }
16
17   let pointA = Point(x: 1.0, y: 2.0)             {x 1.0, y 2.0}
18   let pointB = Point(x: 4.0, y: 6.0)             {x 4.0, y 6.0}
19   let distance = pointA.distanctTo(point: pointB) 5.0
20
```

FIGURE 10.3
The completed Try It Yourself example, adding an instance method to the Point struct.

Let's say we want to have a method to return half the calculated distance. We can call the distanceTo(point:) instance method from within another instance method to assist in calculating the value. Listing 10.3 illustrates how to call an instance method from another instance method.

LISTING 10.3 Calling Instance Methods From Instance Methods

```
01:   struct Point {
02:       // properties go here
03:       func distanceTo(#point: Point) -> Double {
04:           // Pythagorean calculation here
05:       }
06:       func halfDistanceTo(#point: Point) -> Double {
07:           return distanceTo(point: point) / 2.0
08:       }
09:   }
10:   let halfDistance = pointA.halfDistanceTo(pointB)
```

The major difference here is that on line 6 we add the instance method halfDistanceTo(point:), which simply gets the distance from the distanceTo(point:) method by passing a copy of the point value, and then divide by 2.0. I divided by 2.0 for consistency; Swift can infer that I want to return a Double, but sometimes it helps code readability to be explicit with literals.

Armed with your knowledge of functions from the previous two hours, you should be familiar with the syntax of creating a function with a parameter and calling it with an argument. The exact same thing is happening here; the difference is that our function belongs to our instance of the `Point` struct, so we must call the instance method as part of the `point` instance.

Struct and Class Similarities

So far this hour, almost everything discussed with structs and shown in examples can be done with classes too, the only exception being that structs can use memberwise initialization as default behavior without you needing to provide an initializer. The syntax is identical (except you'd use `class` instead of `struct` to define a class); you can use properties to store data and methods to perform tasks and return values. In fact, to illustrate these points about classes, let's walk through an example in the following Try It Yourself section.

NOTE

Memberwise Initialization Is Only for Structs

Although we were discussing the similarities of structs and classes, the only difference in code we saw, other than the `struct` or `class` keyword, is that structs use memberwise initialization. This method of initialization is Swift's way of ensuring that all non-optional properties have a value. You can create your own initializers for structs, but we cover that in Hour 13.

TRY IT YOURSELF ▼

Define a Class with Properties and Methods

Now that we've defined a struct with properties and methods, let's make a class that has properties and instance methods.

1. Open Xcode 6 and create a new playground. Either a Mac or iOS playground will work. Clear the contents of the playground.

2. Import the Foundation framework to gain access to standard math functions and create a class called `Circle`.

```
import Foundation
class Circle {


}
```

3. Inside the curly braces of the class, create a variable of type `Double`, named `radius`, and initialize it to 0.0.

```
var radius = 0.0
```

4. Create a function that returns the diameter of the circle.

```
func diameter() -> Double {
    return 2 * radius
}
```

5. Create a function that returns the area of the circle.

```
func area() -> Double {
    return M_PI * radius * radius
}
```

6. With your property and two methods inside the class's curly braces, our class is finished. After the closing curly brace, create an instance of the `Circle` class, as a constant.

```
var circle = Circle()
```

7. Assign your circle instance a radius of 5.0.

```
circle.radius = 5.0
```

8. Call your circle instance's methods to find the diameter and area of your circle.

```
"Circle diameter: \(circle.diameter()), area: \(circle.area())"
```

This Try It Yourself section walked you through creating a class named `Circle`, creating a `radius` property inside it, and two instance methods that returned calculations for the area and diameter of a circle. When finished, your code should look like the code in Figure 10.4.

FIGURE 10.4
The completed Try It Yourself section for creating a `Circle` class with properties and instance methods.

Differences Between Structs and Classes

Structs and classes also have their fair share of differences. For instance, as mentioned earlier, classes are reference types and structs are value types. To get a quick glimpse at what this actually means, open the playground you just worked in where you created a `Circle` class and modify the declaration of your circle variable to the following:

```
let circle = Circle()
```

Did you notice that you don't get any compiler errors about modifying a constant? That's because classes are reference types. Swift retains a constant pointer to the `Circle` instance, and that's what is constant, not the values of the properties inside (unless the properties themselves were declared as constants). If you declare a constant struct, the struct is immutable and so are its values even if they were defined as variable properties, because structs are value types. You've been doing this all along, as `Int`, `String`, `Bool`, `Array`, `Dictionary`, and several others we've used are structs.

Listing 10.4 illustrates what happens when you make copies of struct and class instances and how modifying the copy impacts the original, if at all. We reuse the `Point` struct and `Circle` class from previous examples for brevity.

LISTING 10.4 Copying Struct and Class Instances

```
01:    var newPoint = Point(x: 4.0, y: 3.0)
02:    var newPointCopy = newPoint
03:    newPointCopy.y = 17.4
04:    newPoint                         // displays {x 4.0, y 3.0}
05:    newPointCopy                     // displays {x 4.0, y 17.4}
06:
07:    var newCircle = Circle()
08:    circle.radius = 3.0
09:    var newCircleCopy = newCircle
10:    newCircleCopy.radius = 7.5
11:    newCircle                        // displays {radius 7.5}
12:    newCircleCopy                    // displays {radius 7.5}
```

As you can see in Listing 10.4, line 1 creates an instance of `Point`, and then line 2 creates a copy of the `newPoint` instance. What Swift effectively does is create a new variable in memory to hold `newPointCopy` with its own properties and instance methods, with starting values given from `newPoint` (so `newPointCopy`'s initial x and y values are 4.0 and 3.0, respectively). Changing any property in `newPointCopy` has no impact on `newPoint`'s properties, since they are separate values.

The Circle instance, however, behaves differently. Being a reference type, when we created a new Circle instance in line 7 and set its radius property in line 8, Swift created a space in memory for the newCircle instance, just like it does for a struct. The difference comes when we create a new variable, newCircleCopy, and assign it to newCircle in line 9. Swift actually gives newCircleCopy a reference to the same instance newCircle refers to, so now two variables point to the same instance of Circle. This means that newCircle is a reference to a Circle instance just as newCircleCopy is a reference to the same Circle instance. In C and Objective-C, variables of a reference type are called **pointers**, and your pointer actually pointed to the physical memory address where the instance was stored. Swift instead, in the name of safety, does not let you alter that memory location directly, but still gives you the capability to use reference types to have multiple variables or constants pointing to the same instance.

NOTE

Efficient Copying

With regard to copying value types, Swift is actually optimized to only copy values when necessary. This means that when you set a new struct instance to equal another, Swift waits to physically copy the data into a brand new instance until the point where any values change and it becomes necessary to have two separate instances in memory. This is an optimization to decrease the amount of memory your app consumes.

Let's take a look at some more differences, starting with structs.

Mutating Struct Properties

Swift structs can have instance methods, but those instance methods cannot mutate the properties inside a struct by default. To allow them to do so, add the **mutating** keyword before the func keyword of the instance method that you want to have change one or more property values. Listing 10.5 illustrates how this can be done. Also, I omitted the distanceTo(point:) function for brevity.

LISTING 10.5 Mutating Struct Properties from Instance Methods

```
01:   struct Point {
02:       var x: Double
03:       var y: Double
04:
05:       mutating func moveToZero() {
06:           self.x = 0.0
07:           self.y = 0.0
08:       }
09:   }
10:   var point = Point(x: 3.5, y: 6.0)
11:   point.moveToZero()              // x is now 0.0, y is now 0.0
```

Swift classes do not require you to prefix the `mutating` keyword before a method definition because class instance methods can alter properties as part of their normal behavior.

Comparing Class Reference Equality

There will be times when you need to compare two class instances. To compare class equality, we use the *identical to* operator (`===`), which is used to compare class instance references to determine whether they point to the same instance. Likewise, we can use the *not identical to* operator (`!==`) for class instances. Listing 10.6 illustrates using the equal to and identical to operators for classes in simple `if` statements.

LISTING 10.6   Using Identical To Operator

```
01:  let circleOne = Circle()
02:  circleOne.radius = 5.0
03:  let circleTwo = Circle()
04:  circleTwo.radius = 5.0
05:  let circleThree = circleOne
06:
07:  if circleOne === circleTwo {
08:      "circleOne is identical to circleTwo"
09:  } else {
10:      "circleOne is not identical to circleTwo"
11:  }
12:
13:  if circleOne !== circleThree {
14:      "circleOne is not identical to circleThree"
15:  } else {
16:      "circleOne is identical to circleThree"
17:  }

// displays "circleOne is identical to circleThree"
```

Despite `circleOne` and `circleTwo` both having `radius` values of 5.0, they are not identical instances. `circleOne` and `circleThree`, however, are identical instances, because we assigned `circleOne`'s reference to `circleThree` in line 5. See Figure 10.5 for a visual representation of the instance assignments in Listing 10.6.

In Swift, when we declare a struct or class and use the `TypeName()` syntax, we initialize a new instance of that type. This is why `circleOne` and `circleTwo` are not identical, even though they both have a `radius` value of 5.0. They are two separate instances in memory.

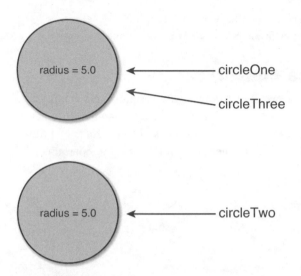

FIGURE 10.5
The align attribute enables you to left justify, right justify, and center text.

Comparing Instance Equality

Comparing class and struct equality is not as easy. To check equality, we would have to provide our own mechanism for validating two struct instances or two class instances are equal, because Swift cannot infer what makes a custom struct or class equal, and we may have our own definition for equality. We discuss how to create custom equality functions in Hour 18, "Using Extensions to Add Type Functionality."

When to Use a Class or a Struct

Classes and structs are similar, so when do you use a class and when do you use a struct? Here are some general guidelines, but each case will be different and depending on your code; you may need to choose one or the other for different reasons.

A struct is good for when you need to encapsulate small, simple data values, when you want values copied rather than passed by reference, and/or when you know that there is no need to inherit from another type. Some examples of structs are the common data types you're familiar with such as `Int`, `Double`, `Bool`, `Array`, and `Dictionary` to name a few. You may also want a struct for 2D or 3D coordinate instances, geometric shape instances, or other simple structures that are value based.

A class is a good choice for when you need to pass a construct by reference, inherit functionality from a parent class, or have a larger structure to manage than just holding simple data structures. Often you will find yourself creating classes, but structs do serve their purpose in Swift, so think carefully about what type of structure your data types need to be when creating them. Currently Apple suggests using structs until the need for class behavior arises, but because Swift is such a new language, this guidance could change.

Summary

This hour introduced constructs known as structs and classes and examined the similarities of and differences between each. In Swift, the functionality of the two is much closer than what some programmers may have experienced in other languages.

We explored what it means when we say structs are value types and classes are reference types. You also learned the basic structure of both classes and structs, by adding properties and instance methods to add stored data and functionality to the constructs. These concepts were discussed and even visualized with diagrams illustrating what is actually happening in memory when we allocate new classes or structs and also when we copy them.

Throughout the remainder of this book, we explore more functionality available to structs and classes, as well as a new value type, called an **enum**, discussed in Hour 12, "Harnessing the Power of Enums." There are more differences and more similarities to cover, and each deserves its own hour.

Q&A

Q. What is a reference type?

A. The most important thing to remember is that when you copy a reference type, by passing it as an argument, initializing it, or assigning to it, you are actually creating a new reference to the existing instance. This means that if you make changes to the copy, you'll be changing your original instance too.

Q. What is a value type?

A. Unlike reference types, when you copy a value type you are creating a unique instance of the variable. This means that changes in the copy won't be reflected in the original.

Q. How do I know if I should use a class or a struct?

A. The answer isn't always clear, but in general you should use structs if you have small, simple data values and you want to be able to make copies with independent state. You should use classes when dealing with larger, more complex structures. In the next hour you'll learn about class inheritance, which gives you a better understanding of when to prefer classes to structs.

Q. What does the identical to operator (===) do?

A. The === operator compares two references (variable or constant) and evaluates to true if they reference the same instance, and evaluates to false if they do not reference the same instance. This means that two structs will never be identical to (===) one another, even if one is a direct copy of the other.

Workshop

The workshop contains quiz questions and exercises to help you solidify your understanding of the material covered. Try to answer all questions before looking at the answers that follow.

Quiz

1. Are classes value types or reference types? How about structs?

2. What model is `newCar` after we run the following code? What model is `usedCar`?

   ```
   struct Car {
     var make: String
     var model: String
   }
   var newCar = Car(make: "Ford", model: "Explorer")
   var usedCar = newCar
   usedCar.model = "Focus"
   ```

3. What's wrong with the following code?

   ```
   class Car {
     var make: String
     var model: String
   }
   var newCar = Car(make: "Ford", model: "Explorer")
   ```

4. What does the `mutating` keyword do?

Answers

1. Classes are reference types; structs are value types.

2. Structs are value types, so when we set `usedCar` equal to `newCar`, we create a whole new copy of the object. So when we change the model of `usedCar`, we don't change anything about `newCar` meaning that at `usedCar.model` is "Focus" but `newCar.model` is still "Explorer."

3. Classes do not provide memberwise initializers by default. If this were a struct instead of a class, the code would work.

4. The `mutating` keyword enables a member function in a struct to change the values of that struct's properties.

Exercise

Create a new OS X playground. Create a struct called `Person` with properties `firstName`, `lastName`, and `age` of appropriate data types. Add a method that allows you to change a person's last name. Create an instance of `Person` with your information and test your method to make sure it works.

Now, change `Person` to a class and repeat the process. Notice the differences in the initializer and in the name changing method.

HOUR 11
Implementing Class Inheritance

What You'll Learn in This Hour:

- ▶ What is class inheritance
- ▶ How to create subclasses from base classes
- ▶ How to build a class hierarchy
- ▶ How to access properties and methods in a superclass
- ▶ How to override methods in a subclass
- ▶ How to prevent overriding
- ▶ What class identity is

In the last hour we discussed both classes and structs as blueprints for creating instances of data. This hour focuses solely on classes, and some of the extra functionality available in Swift, called **inheritance**. Class inheritance is a concept that has been around for a long time in many object-oriented languages, so if you are familiar with inheritance, you should follow along easily. If you aren't familiar with inheritance, fear not. We discuss the many aspect of inheritance as it relates to Swift and emphasize your learning with examples you can follow. Let's start by defining what inheritance is and why you may want to use it in your apps.

What Is Inheritance?

As mentioned, inheritance is a concept that has been a part of many object-oriented languages for a long time. Inheritance is the practice of inheriting characteristics from another class, in terms of properties, methods, and subscripts. This enables you to create a hierarchy of classes that more appropriately define what an instance of a class should look like, clearly outline responsibilities of a class at a particular level, as well as keep classes small and manageable.

NOTE

Class Subscripts

Although we haven't yet discussed subscripts, class inheritance can inherit custom subscripts you create that help you access data in your class instance easily. We discuss subscripts in greater detail in Hour 15, "Adding Advanced Type Functionality."

You may want to inherit functionality of a class so that you can customize its behavior or further refine the type of object you are dealing with. For instance, let's say you are working with instances of musical instruments. There are many categories of musical instruments, but ones of note (pun intended) are percussion, winds, and strings. Winds can be broken down into woodwinds and brass. I'm sure there are many other further classifications we could identify, but I think you get the idea. There are common functionalities of all musical instruments and some that are particular to percussion, some to strings, and some to winds. This type of analysis on objects is how we identify relationships and realize how to use class inheritance to our advantage when writing software. But how do we find a good starting point?

Identifying a Base Class

A **base class** acts as the root object of a hierarchy. Base classes do not inherit from any other class; they serve as the class from which other classes inherit functionality. In Swift, unlike Objective-C, you do not need to inherit from a base class, either directly or indirectly, for every class you create. Objective-C classes have to inherit from a base class, most commonly `NSObject`, to provide mechanisms for allocating memory and initializing the instance and for providing many standard properties and methods, such as a printable description of the object and a hash value. Swift does not require a base class, which is nice because your class instances now do not come with a lot of extra baggage that you may not need, keeping your instances leaner.

Not every app needs a robust hierarchy to describe the required model instances, but the musical instrument example is a good illustration of how to start with a somewhat generic base class, and through each subclass in the hierarchy, start to implement functionality particular to that class. The hierarchy idea is similar to the biological classification system of life, domain, kingdom, phylum, class, order, family, genus, and species. Each level of the classification gets more specific and shares commonalities between ancestors. Figure 11.1 illustrates what our `MusicalInstrument` class hierarchy might look like, with `MusicalInstrument` being our base class.

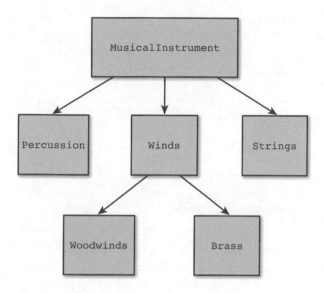

FIGURE 11.1
The MusicalInstrument base class with more specific subclasses inheriting from superclasses in a class hierarchy.

As a best practice, you may want to keep your base classes small, but be sure to put as much functionality inside that is common to all classes that inherit from the base class. Our MusicalInstrument base class may only have one method, called makeSound, but that may be all we need in the base class, the act of making a sound. Every subclass can modify that method, or *override* that method, to customize its own particular sound.

Creating a Subclass

What makes a class a base class is the fact that you designate other classes to inherit from it. This begins a hierarchical relationship between the two classes in which the class being inherited from is called the **superclass**, and the class inheriting from a superclass is called a **subclass**. A subclass is simply a class composed of everything it directly implements plus everything it inherits. A subclass inherits properties, methods, and subscripts from not only its direct superclass, but everything up the hierarchy chain up to and including the base class.

NOTE

Other Terminology for Superclass and Subclass

Sometimes superclasses and subclasses are called **parent** and **child** classes because of their relationship to each other, but throughout this book we call them superclasses and subclasses.

There is no special syntax to defining a base class; you simply create a class as you normally would. Creating a subclass has one small syntactical difference from a normal class declaration: After the class name, append a colon (:) and then the class name from which you want to inherit. Figure 11.2 shows sample syntax of a class inheriting from another class.

```
class SomeClass : SomeOtherClass {
}
```

FIGURE 11.2
The syntactical structure of defining a subclass to inherit from a superclass.

In Figure 11.2, we see the class SomeClass inheriting from SomeOtherClass. This is great for an example, but let's take a look at how we might implement our own classes and take advantage of inheritance. Listing 11.1 illustrates how we would implement a base MusicalInstrument class and then create the three types of instrument classes from the base class. For now, the subclasses do not have anything in them.

LISTING 11.1   Creating a Base Class and Subclasses

```
class MusicalInstrument {
    func makeSound() -> String {
        return "I make no sound yet."
    }
}

class Percussion : MusicalInstrument {
}
class StringedInstrument: MusicalInstrument {
}
class WindInstrument: MusicalInstrument {
}
```

I chose StringedInstrument instead of String, because String is already the name of a Swift struct, and followed suit with WindInstrument. Right now our subclasses don't do anything. However, since our subclasses are composed of everything they directly declare, plus what they inherit, what would happen if we tried to call makeSound() on an instance of WindInstrument? Let's find out in Listing 11.2.

LISTING 11.2   Declaring an Instance of a Subclass and Calling Inherited Methods

```
let clarinet = WindInstrument()
clarinet.makeSound()   // displays "I make no sound yet."
```

Well, this clarinet is no good! It doesn't make any sound yet. How can we change inherited behavior in our subclasses? We use **overriding**.

Overriding Inherited Methods

Overriding is a concept that enables you to replace the functionality of an inherited property, method, or subscript, to be tailored to the responsibility of the class. It is common when overriding to call the superclass's implementation of the characteristic being overridden, to add your own functionality to the existing functionality. We see an example of that later in this hour.

To override a method inherited from a superclass, you redeclare the method with the same definition but add the `override` keyword at the beginning of the line, before the `func` keyword. Listing 11.3 illustrates just the `WindInstrument` class, to keep the example brief; if you are following along with your own REPL or playground, feel free to override the `makeSound()` function in the other subclasses.

NOTE

Xcode Provides Help with Overriding

Overriding characteristics of a superclass in your custom subclass must be done properly. In other words, you cannot override a method that is not defined in your superclass, and you cannot redefine a method in a subclass that is defined in the superclass without using the override keyword. Xcode's compiler will catch these issues and will actually offer to use the override keyword in its auto-complete feature or warn you that you cannot override a nonexistent method.

LISTING 11.3   Overriding an Inherited Method

```
01:  class WindInstrument : MusicalInstrument {
02:      override func makeSound() -> String {
03:          return "I use a mouthpiece and make a beautiful sound."
04:      }
05:  }
```

On line 2, you can see that we use the `override` keyword to declare that we are modifying the inherited method. Then, in line 3, we return a different string to refine our `makeSound()` method's return value. Now, calling `clarinet.makeSound()` displays our new return value.

Let's take a look at another implementation of inheritance in this Try It Yourself section. You create a base class of a generic Shape with a few properties and a function to calculate the area. Then, you subclass the Shape class to a more specific shape and override its area() method to make it return the calculated value of the area of that shape since area formulas are different for different shapes.

▼ TRY IT YOURSELF

Creating a Base Class and a Subclass and Overriding an Instance Method

Utilize what you've learned so far to create a base class and a subclass and override an instance method.

1. Open Xcode 6 and create a new playground. Either a Mac or an iOS playground will work. Clear the contents of the playground.

2. Create your base class, called Shape.

   ```
   class Shape {

   }
   ```

3. Declare a variable named title and give it an initial value of "shape". Place this inside the Shape class's curly braces.

   ```
   var title = "shape"
   ```

4. Define the area() function, but since we don't know what type of shape this generic shape is, simply return 0.0 for now.

   ```
   func area() -> Double {
       return 0.0
   }
   ```

5. Next, define a method called description(), and it will serve as a verbose description of our Shape instance.

   ```
   func description() -> String {
       return "I am a \(title). My area is \(area())."
   }
   ```

6. That's all for our Shape base class. Next, define a subclass of Shape called Square.

   ```
   class Square : Shape {

   }
   ```

7. Our `Square` class needs to have measurements for its `sideLength`, so make that variable initialized to 0.0, so Swift infers it to be of type `Double`.

```
var sideLength = 0.0
```

8. Now that we know we are a `Square`, with a proper `sideLength` length, we can override the `area()` method to provide a valid calculation for the area of a square.

```
override func area() -> Double {
    return sideLength * sideLength
}
```

9. Now that we have both classes created, declare constant instances of `Shape` and `Square`, and call their `area()` and `description()` methods.

```
let shape = Shape()
let square = Square()
shape.area()
shape.description()
square.area()
square.description()
```

10. Notice that you can call the `area()` and `description()` methods on `square`, although they aren't directly defined in our `Square` class, because they are inherited. Set the `sideLength` and `title` properties of the `square` instance.

```
square.sideLength = 4
square.title = "SQUARE"
```

11. After modifying the square instance, compare it with the shape instance by calling the `area()` and `description()` methods again. Notice that although `Square` is a subclass of `Shape`, the instances are separate instances, and modifying one does not impact the other.

```
shape.area()
shape.description()
square.area()
square.description()
```

When you've finished this Try It Yourself section, your code should look like the code in Figure 11.3.

`Square` is a class just like any other class, and even though it inherits from the `Shape` class, it does not have to override any methods if it is not necessary but can happily use them. Also, you could implement any new methods on `Square` that are not a part of `Shape`, as well as properties or subscripts.

```
     ●  ●  ●              ⚉ Ch11 TIY Shape Square.playground
    ⊞⊞  <   >  | ⚉ Ch11 TIY Shape Square.playground ⟩ No Selection
     1    class Shape {
     2        var title = "shape"
     3        func area() -> Double {
     4            return 0.0                                    (4 times)
     5        }
     6
     7        func description() -> String {
     8            return "I am a \(title). My area is \(area())".   (4 times)
     9        }
    10    }
    11
    12    class Square : Shape {
    13        var sideLength = 0.0
    14
    15        override func area() -> Double {
    16            return sideLength * sideLength                (4 times)
    17        }
    18    }
    19
    20    let shape = Shape()                                   {title "shape"}
    21    let square = Square()                                 {{title "shape"} sideLength 0.0}
    22    shape.area()                                          0.0
    23    shape.description()                                   "I am a shape. My area is 0.0"
    24    square.area()                                         0.0
    25    square.description()                                  "I am a shape. My area is 0.0"
    26
    27    square.sideLength = 4                                 {{title "shape"} sideLength 4.0}
    28    square.title = "SQUARE"                               {{title "SQUARE"} sideLength 4.0}
    29
    30    shape.area()                                          0.0
    31    shape.description()                                   "I am a shape. My area is 0.0"
    32    square.area()                                         16.0
    33    square.description()                                  "I am a SQUARE. My area is 16.0"
    34
```

FIGURE 11.3
The completed Try It Yourself section for creating the `Shape` base class and `Square` subclass.

Accessing `super`

You may have methods in your superclass that are not overridden in your subclass, or you have methods in your subclass that might be appending behavior to the superclass's implementation, and you need to access the superclass's methods, properties, or subscripts. To do this, you use the `super` keyword to access the current subclass instance's superclass functionality. Swift is a **single inheritance** language, meaning that any given class can have no greater than one immediate superclass. In future hours we discuss how to obtain functionality from different sources other than a superclass, but for now, we focus on inheriting from one single superclass.

The `super` keyword in your subclass is used just as if it were an instance itself. You can call any attribute of the superclass with dot syntax, just as you would a normal instance of any class. To illustrate this more visually in code, take a look at Listing 11.4.

LISTING 11.4   Accessing super from a Subclass

```
import Foundation
class Shape {
    var title = "shape"
    func area() -> Double {
        return 0.0
    }
    func description() -> String {
        return "I am a \(title). My area is \(area())"
    }
}

class Circle : Shape {
    var radius = 0.0
    override func area() -> Double {
        return M_PI * radius * radius
    }
}

class Sphere: Circle {
    override func description() -> String {
        return super.description() + ". My volume is \(volume())"
    }
    func volume() -> Double {
        return (4.0 * super.area() * radius) / 3.0
    }
}

let sphere = Sphere()
sphere.title = "SPHERE"
sphere.radius = 2.0
sphere.area()  // which doesn't really make sense for a sphere, but shows that
➥Sphere still inherits this method
sphere.volume()        // displays 33.51...
sphere.description()  // displays "I am a SPHERE. My area is 12.56... My volume is
➥33.51..."
```

In Listing 11.4, we see a similar structure as the Try It Yourself section, including creation of a `Circle` subclass. However, this time we go one subclass further and create a `Sphere` class, inheriting from `Circle`. So now the chain of inheritance goes `Shape` => `Circle` => `Sphere`. This means that `Sphere` inherits everything not only from `Circle`, but also `Shape`. The `Sphere` class overrides the `description()` method but appends a string to `super.description()`. Looking at the playground result output, it's easy to understand what impact calling `super.description()` has. Then in the `volume()` function, `Sphere` calls `super.area()`

to get the value of the area of a circle, because the area (pi * r^2) can be used as part of the volume equation (4/3 * pi * r^3).

You will find that calling `super.method()` or `super.property` will be a fairly common occurrence for you, especially in the Cocoa and Cocoa Touch frameworks. As you become more familiar with creating apps, you'll discover something called view controller lifecycles, for example. In an iOS app, each time a view comes onscreen, it is controlled by a **view controller**, and each view controller has methods you can implement to customize the behavior of the class at certain points in time of the view controller's lifecycle. For instance, when a view controller is instantiated and a view comes onscreen, a method called `viewDidLoad()` is called right before the view is shown onscreen. It is a common practice to perform actions in this method and then call `super.viewDidLoad()` to ensure that the view controller's superclass has a chance to execute its implementation of `viewDidLoad()` and so on up the inheritance chain.

Preventing Overrides

There may be times when you want or need specific attributes of a class to not be overridden. To prevent overriding of any property, method, subscript, or even prevent a class from being subclassed, prefix the declaration with the `final` keyword. This tells the Swift compiler that any subclass that inherits from the current class can still access the current superclass implementation but should not be able to provide its own custom implementation. Let's go through preventing overriding a method in this next Try It Yourself section.

▼ TRY IT YOURSELF

Prevent Overriding a Superclass Method

Spheres don't have an area like a circle does, but they can have a surface area, which is a completely different attribute, as well as calculation. Prevent overriding the `area()` method in `Circle` to avoid an ambiguous definition of area and provide a surface area function for clarity.

1. Open Xcode 6 and create a new playground. Either a Mac or an iOS playground will work. Clear the contents of the playground.

2. Add the `Shape`, `Circle`, and `Sphere` classes, as in Listing 11.4.

```
import Foundation
class Shape {
    var title = "shape"
    func area() -> Double {
        return 0.0
    }
}
```

```
        func description() -> String {
            return "I am a \(title). My area is \(area())"
        }
    }
    class Circle : Shape {
        var radius = 0.0
        override func area() -> Double {
            return M_PI * radius * radius
        }
    }
    class Sphere : Circle {
        override func description() -> String {
            return super.description() + ". My volume is \(volume())"
        }
        func volume() -> Double {
            return (4.0 * super.area() * radius) / 3.0
        }
    }
```

3. Modify the `Circle` class implementation to prevent the `area()` method from being overridden.

```
class Circle : Shape {
    var radius = 0.0
    final override func area() -> Double {
        return M_PI * radius * radius
    }
}
```

4. Modify the `Sphere` class implementation to add the `surfaceArea()` method.

```
class Sphere : Circle {
    override func description() -> {
        return super.description() + ". My volume is \(volume())"
    }
    func volume() -> Double {
        return (4.0 * super.area() * radius) / 3.0
    }
    func surfaceArea() -> Double {
        return 4.0 * M_PI * radius * radius
    }
}
```

5. Now that `Circle`'s implementation of `area()` is final, try to override the `area()` method in the `Sphere` class. What compiler error do you receive?

```
override func area() -> Double {    // Error!
```

As you can see in step 4 of the Try It Yourself section, we can still access and retrieve a return value from the `area()` method from step 3. This is because even though the `area()` method is marked as `final`, we can still access it and retrieve its return value. We just cannot override the method to provide our own implementation of it, as you can see in step 5. The completed code, as well as the compiler error, should look identical to Figure 11.4.

```swift
import Foundation

class Shape {
    var title = "shape"
    func area() -> Double {
        return 0.0
    }

    func description() -> String {
        return "I am a \(title). My area is \(area())"
    }
}

class Circle : Shape {
    var radius = 0.0
    final override func area() -> Double {
        return M_PI * radius * radius
    }
}

class Sphere : Circle {
    override func description() -> String {
        return super.description() + ". My volume is \(volume())"
    }
    func volume() -> Double {
        return (4.0 * super.area() * radius) / 3.0
    }
    override func area() -> Double {          // Instance method overrides a 'final' instance method

    }
    func surfaceArea() -> Double {
        return 4.0 * M_PI * radius * radius
    }
}
```

FIGURE 11.4
The completed Try It Yourself section, preventing overriding the `area()` method.

Class Identity

At first sight, subclassing may seem understandable and a fairly easy concept to learn. But it may leave you wondering, "Why would I need to do this?" In Objective-C, each class had an **isa pointer** inside it for identity. It basically said "this class *is a* <insert class name here>". This means, using the same *isa* terminology, that an instance of our `Sphere` class *is a* `Shape`, too, because it inherits from `Shape`. Often, to keep functions or other sections of code generic enough to handle multiple kinds of types for a single argument, you could set the parameter type to the most generic superclass; that way your function could accept any instance of that class or a subclass thereof.

Let's take a look at this in Listing 11.5. We create a generic function that takes a parameter of type Shape. Look what happens when we send the function different instances of different subclasses of Shape. The class definitions have been omitted for brevity, as nothing in them changes for this example.

LISTING 11.5   **Class Identity**

```
func printDescriptionForShape(shape: Shape) {
    println(shape.description())
}

let sphere = Sphere()
sphere.title = "SPHERE"
sphere.radius = 4.0

let square = Square()
square.title = "SQUARE"
square.sideLength = 5.0

printDescriptionForShape(sphere)   // displays "I am a SPHERE. My area is
➥50.265... My volume is 268.082..."
printDescriptionForShape(square)   // displays "I am a SQUARE. My area is
➥25.0"
```

Notice how calling the description() method for each instance called that respective instance's description() implementation and not the Shape class's description() method. Structuring your code this way can be beneficial, as you can see from Listing 11.5. We do not need to create two different functions, printDescriptionForShape and printDescriptionForSquare, as well as for our other shapes, because any class instance that is a Shape can be passed in as our argument and satisfies Swift's type safety requirement.

Summary

In this hour, we discussed the concept of inheritance. Inheritance is simply the act of creating a subclass from another class in which the subclass is a composition of everything it implements directly as well as everything from the superclass. Subclassing is important in object-oriented programming, and it is something you will find yourself doing frequently in your career as a software developer.

Once you understood base classes, superclasses, and subclasses, we examined a process called overriding. Overriding enables you to customize the implementation of whatever attribute you are overriding. You can also call the superclass's implementation inside your overriding method by using the `super` keyword.

You then learned how to prevent a subclass from overriding particular attributes by prefixing the `final` keyword to a method, property, or subclass declaration. This leaves the attribute still accessible by a subclass, but the compiler marks the attribute as unable to be overridden.

Finally, you learned about class identity, meaning that any subclass of a given class is a class of the superclass's type too. This can help reduce the amount of code needed to accomplish tasks and makes code more reusable.

In the next hour, we dive into enumerations. Enumerations are value types just like structs, but they have a wildly different implementation than in other languages, so we're in for some fun next hour.

Q&A

Q. Does every Swift class have a superclass?

A. No. Classes in Swift do not have to inherit from a superclass.

Q. Why would I ever need to create a subclass?

A. Subclassing enables you to inherit the behaviors of a superclass and then refine them to better suit your needs. By creating a subclass instead of starting from scratch with a new class, you can save yourself a lot of work, and finding bugs will be easier because you'll have less code to look through.

Q. Can a Swift class inherit from more than one superclass?

A. No. Swift is a single inheritance language, which means that a class can inherit from at most one superclass. Swift does support similar functionality with a feature called protocols, which is covered in Hour 17, "Using Protocols to Define Behavior."

Q. Can a Swift class have more than one subclass?

A. Yes, a class can have as many subclasses as you want. Single inheritance in Swift means that a class can't have more than one superclass but does not restrict the number of subclasses you can create.

Workshop

The workshop contains quiz questions and exercises to help you solidify your understanding of the material covered. Try to answer all questions before looking at the answers that follow.

Quiz

1. When writing a new subclass, how do you change the behavior of a method that already exists in your superclass?

2. Can you create a class that can never have subclasses?

3. What's wrong with the following code?

```
class Vehicle {
  var speed: Double = 0
}

class Car : Vehicle {
  var wheels: Int = 4
}

func showVehicleInfo(vehicle: Vehicle) {
  println("My current speed is \(vehicle.speed).")
}

func showCarInfo(car: Car) {
  println("I have \(car.wheels) wheels");
}

var myCar = Car()
var myVehicle = Vehicle()

showCarInfo(myVehicle)
showVehicleInfo(myCar)
```

4. True or false? If my class overrides a method defined by its superclass, my class can never access the superclass's implementation of the method.

Answers

1. Write the method as you normally would, but prefix the method definition with the `override` keyword. Make sure your new method has the same signature as the one you're replacing, or you'll end up overloading the method instead of redefining it.

2. Yes! The `final` keyword can be used on classes, properties, subscripts, and methods. If you prefix your class definition with `final`, then no other class can ever inherit from it.

3. The function `showCarInfo()` takes an object of type `Car` as an argument, but we're trying to pass it an object of type `Vehicle`, which is an error. Notice that `showVehicleInfo(myCar)` is just fine because `Car` is a subclass of `Vehicle`, so `myCar` is a vehicle as far as our program is concerned.

4. False. A subclass can access a superclass's implementation of an overridden method by using the `super` keyword. For example, `super.description()` would call the description method in the parent class, not the version defined in the current class.

Exercise

Create a new OS X playground. Create a `Building` class that has properties that hold the number of floors in the building and the building's address. Create a subclass of `Building` called `House` that has properties for the number of bedrooms and the number of bathrooms in the house. Create a second subclass of `Building` called `Store` that contains the name of the store and the name of the store manager.

Add description methods to all three of your classes. These methods should display all the information about the class. Remember that stores and houses are both buildings, so they should show address and number of floors as part of their descriptions.

Finally, write a function that takes any kind of building and prints out that building's address.

Harnessing the Power of Enums

What You'll Learn in This Hour:

- ▶ What an enumeration is
- ▶ How to use enums to group related items
- ▶ How to access enum raw values
- ▶ How to use associated values
- ▶ How to use `switch` statements with enums
- ▶ How to add methods to enums

Enumerators are simply a structure of data that groups together related values. By that definition, it may not seem much different from any other topic we've talked about thus far, namely, structs, classes, dictionaries, arrays, and tuples. Swift enumerators, called **enums**, are a special kind of grouping structure in that they can keep a logical list of items, either with an ordered or unordered backing value, and are incredibly useful when working with items that can have only one option selected. Swift enums are a lot different than enums from other languages, as can be seen in the preceding list of topics. So let's get started and dive into what makes enums so special and powerful in Swift.

Understanding Swift Enums

If you come from a C background, you may be familiar with enums. C enums are integer-based. They are used to give a more meaningful representation to a numeric list of values, such as the colors of the rainbow. Consider the following scenario: We want to easily store the colors of the rainbow with a corresponding integer, so that we can have the user enter a number 1 through 7 and get a color in return. In C we would either have to define seven #define statements, assigning each color an integer, or seven `const int` values each with a color being assigned an integer value. Using these in code would cause a lot of extra effort to ensure that each matched the same type, and each value was sequential (versus accidently giving two colors the number 6, for example).

Enums solve that problem nicely. In C, an enum might look like the following code snippet:

```
// enums in C
enum ColorsOfRainbow {
    red,
    orange,
    yellow,
    green,
    blue,
    indigo,
    violet
};

// how to use the enum in code
enum ColorsOfRainbow myColor = green;   // myColor is equal to 3
```

Here, we create an enum called `ColorsOfRainbow` and provide it with the seven colors in a rainbow. Each color is implicitly assigned an integer value, starting with zero (0), because enums by default are zero-based. If you want different values, you could assign each one its own value, or if you want to start the enumeration at 1, you could just assign `red = 1`, and it would adjust each enum member value accordingly, so `orange` would equal 2, and so on.

But that's about all you can do with enums in C.

Swift enums are value types just like structs and are first-class types. In addition to storing enumerated values like C enums, they can be extended with properties, methods, and more. Let's cover the structure of a Swift enum.

NOTE

First-Class Types

Being a first-class type means that instances of that type can do all the following: be passed as an argument to a function or subroutine, be returned from a function or subroutine, and be assigned to a variable or constant.

Swift Enum Structure

Enums in Swift do not always have to be integer-based. In fact, by default, each enum member is a full-fledged value with its type explicitly defined by the enum. The syntax for enums in Swift is a little different; not only do you not need the trailing semicolon (`;`), but each member must be prefixed with the `case` keyword, unless members are declared on a single line separated by commas. Figure 12.1 illustrates how to declare enums in Swift with multiple members per line, or on a single line.

```
enum EnumTypeName {
    case MemberOne , MemberTwo , MemberThree
    case MemberFour , MemberFive
    case MemberSix
}
```

FIGURE 12.1
The basic structure of an enum in Swift with various ways to declare members.

Figure 12.1 shows the basic structure of a Swift enum declaration, before we get into more advanced ways to empower enums. Basically, a Swift enum has a name and one or more members, which can be declared all on one line separated by commas, or each member declared on its own line prefixed with the case keyword. Let's consider an example of grades Kindergarten through Fifth grade as an enum, shown in Listing 12.1.

LISTING 12.1   Basic Enum in Swift

```
01:   enum GradesKTo5 {
02:       case Kindergarten, First, Second, Third
03:       case Fourth, Fifth
04:   }
05:   let thirdGrade = GradesKTo5.Third   // displays "(Enum Value)"
```

In line 1 of Listing 12.1, we declare the enum called GradesKTo5. Then, in lines 2 and 3, we declare our members to consist of grades Kindergarten to Fifth grade. Notice there is no comma at the end of line 2, even though we continue with another case statement on line 3. After closing the curly brace to end the enum definition, we declare a variable thirdGrade on line 5 to equal the value .Third.

As it is now, our example enum has no backing values; each member is a value in itself and can be compared against or assigned directly without needing a backing value. But there will be times when it is helpful to have backing values, such as for comparison reasons.

Raw Values

As mentioned already, Swift enums do not have backing values, or **raw values,** by default. However, there will be times when you need a raw value, and it is easy to designate an enum to have raw values for its members.

First, give the enum itself a type in the initial declaration statement. Then, you can assign values to each case. In the event of an Int-backed enum, Swift automatically does two things for you:

sets the first member's raw value to zero (0), and then auto-increments each following member's raw value. Raw values for other types must be explicitly assigned for each member.

Getting Raw Values from Enums

Let's continue with the Kindergarten to Fifth grade example. Listing 12.2 illustrates how to make the enum an `Int`-backed enum and how to retrieve the raw value by using the `.toRaw()` instance method.

LISTING 12.2   Assigning and Retrieving Raw Values

```
01:    enum GradesKTo5: Int {
02:        case Kindergarten, First, Second, Third
03:        case Fourth, Fifth
04:    }
05:    var thirdGrade = GradesKTo5.Third
06:    thirdGrade.toRaw()   // displays 3
```

Lines 1 through 5 were identical to Listing 12.1, although this time we declared `GradesKTo5` to be of type `Int`. Then, on line 6, we use the `toRaw()` function to retrieve the underlying raw value of the current member, which is 3. Remember enums are zero-based, so Kindergarten's raw value is `0`, One is `1`, and so on.

Setting Enum Values from Raw Values

Not only can you use the `toRaw()` instance method to obtain the raw value from an enum member, you can set an enum value from a raw value using `fromRaw(T)`. The placeholder `T` means we can use any type, and since `fromRaw(T)` is a type method, Xcode senses the type of enum with its auto-complete functionality and will supply the type hint for you while typing. Figure 12.2 shows Xcode's suggested hint for `fromRaw(T)` for our `GradesKTo5` enum scenario.

NOTE

Type Methods

So far we have discussed instance methods, which are functions that can be executed on an instance of a class or struct. Type methods are functions that can be executed at a type level and are not dependent upon an instance of any given type. We cover this topic more in Hour 15, "Adding Advanced Type Functionality."

It is important to notice here that `fromRaw(T)` returns an optional type. The reason for this is that you could easily enter `9` as the grade, and there is no raw backing value equal to `9` in this implementation. The result would be `nil`, and therefore `fromRaw(T)` must return an optional value to ensure that `nil` would not be returned to a nonoptional variable or constant.

```
enum GradesKTo5: Int {
    case Kindergarten, First, Second, Third
    case Fourth, Fifth
}
let firstGrade = GradesKTo5.fromRaw( Int )
               M  GradesKTo5? fromRaw(Int)
```

FIGURE 12.2
The `fromRaw(T)` type method in Xcode's auto-complete, suggesting the proper type based on the type of enum chosen.

Enum Shorthand Syntax

As with many things in Swift, enums can utilize shorthand syntax too. Enum shorthand syntax for accessing members is simple; just drop the type name and only enter the member name prefixed with a dot (.). This shorthand syntax can only be used *after* a variable or constant has been defined of an enum type. This example will best be understood by doing it yourself, so follow along in this next Try It Yourself section.

TRY IT YOURSELF ▼

Create an Enum with Raw String Values and Shorthand Syntax

Expand upon the `GradesKTo5` example by changing the enum to be backed by String raw values, and use shorthand syntax to reassign a variable.

1. Open Xcode 6 and create a new playground. Either a Mac or an iOS playground will work. Clear the contents of the playground.

2. Create the `enum` for `GradesKTo5` of type `String`.

   ```
   enum GradesKTo5: String {

   }
   ```

3. Create cases inside the enum for Kindergarten through Fifth, and assign each one a short `String` value.

   ```
   case Kindergarten = "K", First = "1st"
   case Second = "2nd", Third = "3rd"
   case Fourth = "4th", Fifth = "5th"
   ```

4. That's all for the enum. After the enum's closing curly brace, declare a variable named `myKid` and set it to the `Kindergarten` value initially. Call `toRaw()` to see its raw value.

   ```
   var myKid = GradesKTo5.Kindergarten
   myKid.toRaw()    // displays "K"
   ```

5. One year passes, and your kid grows up. He or she advances to first grade. Change `myKid` to the member value for First grade, using shorthand syntax. Call `toRaw()` to see its raw value.

```
myKid = .First
myKid.toRaw()      // displays "1st"
```

6. Examine the types when you assign a variable or constant to an enum member or to an enum member's raw value. Create two new constants, `secondGrade` equal to `GradesKTo5.Second` and `thirdGrade` equal to `GradesKTo5.Third.toRaw()`. Option-click each constant name and observe the data type of each.

```
let secondGrade = GradesKTo5.Second  // Option-clicking shows type as
➥GradesKTo5
let thirdGrade = GradesKTo5.Third.toRaw()  // Option-clicking shows type as
➥String
```

7. Use `fromRaw(T)` to create a new constant called `fourthGrade`. Then use optional binding to extract the value if it is not nil, and display its `toRaw()` value.

```
let fourthGrade = GradesKTo5.fromRaw("4th")
if let fourth = fourthGrade {
    println(fourth.toRaw())
}
```

If you finished the Try It Yourself section successfully, your playground should look like what is shown in Figure 12.3.

```
 ● ● ●              🔳 Ch12 Enum GradesKTo5 TIY.playground
 ┌──┐
 │  │  < > │ 🔳 Ch12 Enum GradesKTo5 TIY.playground > No Selection
 └──┘
 1   enum GradesKTo5: String {
 2       case Kindergarten = "K", First = "1st"
 3       case Second = "2nd", Third = "3rd"
 4       case Fourth = "4th", Fifth = "5th"
 5   }
 6
 7   var myKid = GradesKTo5.Kindergarten        (Enum Value)
 8   myKid.toRaw()                              "K"
 9   // 1 year passes...
 10  myKid = .First                             (Enum Value)
 11  myKid.toRaw()                              "1st"
 12
 13  let secondGrade = GradesKTo5.Second        (Enum Value)
 14  let thirdGrade = GradesKTo5.Third.toRaw()  "3rd"
 15
 16  let fourthGrade = GradesKTo5.fromRaw("4th") {(Enum Value)}
 17  if let fourth = fourthGrade {
 18      println(fourth.toRaw())                "4th"
 19  }
 20
```

FIGURE 12.3
The completed exercise from the Try It Yourself section for creating a `String`-backed enum, using shorthand syntax and using `toRaw()` and `fromRaw(T)`.

Associated Values

Swift enums have a feature that enables each member to store values called **associated values**. Associated values are a way to store additional information alongside the currently stored enum member value. Associated values can be thought of as if you were storing values, such as in the members of a struct, inside an individual member of an enum.

Associated values are defined with just their types inside parentheses, immediately after the name of a member inside an enum definition. There can be any number of associated values, and any number of types, defined with an enum member. Associated values are useful for when a member of an enum must be chosen, and corresponding information is helpful to be stored, but with a tighter relationship than just another instance property.

Listing 12.3 illustrates how to declare an enum with associated values for its members.

LISTING 12.3 Associated Values in Enums

```
01:  enum PhoneNumber {
02:      case TollFree(Int, Int, Int)
03:      case InternalExtension(Int)
04:  }
05:
06:  let customerService = PhoneNumber.TollFree(800, 555, 1212)
```

When an enum member has associated values, the arguments are given at the time of assignment. These associated values can later be accessed by either methods or other functionality inside the enum, which we explore later this hour, or in something like a `switch` statement. Let's discuss switching enum values next.

NOTE

Named Parameters in Associated Value Definition

Just like a struct's memberwise initialization, it is possible to declare an enum member's associated values with named parameters, requiring you to use them when you declare a variable with that respective enum member as its value. This can help with readability but doesn't provide you any usability benefit inside the enum. For instance, we could have had case `TollFree(areaCode: Int, exchange: Int, ext: Int)` in our enum definition, which would require us to use them in the declaration `let customerService = PhoneNumber.TollFree(areaCode: 888, exchange: 555, ext: 1212)`.

Switching Enum Values

In Hour 6, "Controlling Program Flow with Conditionals," the switch statement is a great way to clearly choose a path of execution based on meeting conditional criteria. Enums are particularly nice to switch on, because we can use their member values as the cases, and the Swift compiler is smart enough to sense when all cases have been considered, thus counting the switch statement as exhaustive.

Let's consider the GradesKTo5 example for switching enum member values. Listing 12.4 illustrates how we can do that to print a custom greeting to a student, depending on the student's current grade in school.

LISTING 12.4   Switching Enum Values

```
01:   enum GradesKTo5 {
02:       case Kindergarten, First, Second, Third, Fourth, Fifth
03:   }
04:
05:   let studentGrade = GradesKTo5.First
06:
07:   switch studentGrade {
08:   case .Kindergarten:
09:       println("Welcome to Kindergarten!")
10:   case .First:
11:       println("First grade will be awesome!")
12:   case .Second:
13:       println("You're in second grade? You must be smart!")
14:   case .Third:
15:       println("You'll master multiplication in third grade!")
16:   case .Fourth:
17:       println("Fourth grade spelling bee tryouts, first day!")
18:   case .Fifth:
19:       println("Fifth graders rule the school!")
20:   }

// displays "First grade will be awesome!"
```

In Listing 12.4, we assign GradesKTo5.First to the constant studentGrade, and then switch on that value in line 7. Line 10 passes the condition, so line 11 is executed. After execution, control is passed to line 20, which ends the switch block. Pretty easy.

We can also use bindings in our switch cases, for when we have associated values. This is when associated values can become valuable. Take a look at Listing 12.5, using the PhoneNumber example with associated values, and using bindings in the case statements to extract individual values from the member's associated values.

LISTING 12.5   Using Bindings with Associated Values

```
01:   enum PhoneNumber {
02:       case TollFree(Int, Int, Int)
03:       case InternalExtension(Int)
04:   }
05:
06:   let customerService = PhoneNumber.TollFree(800, 555, 1212)
07:
08:   switch customerService {
09:   case .TollFree(_, _, let ext):
10:       println("Toll-free number, extension: \(ext)")
11:   case .InternalExtension(let ext):
12:       println("Internal extension: \(ext)")
13:   }
```

Listing 12.5 is largely the same as before, but notice in line 9 how we extract just the ext value from the associated value inside the .TollFree option and bind that value to a local constant called ext so we can use it inside the case statement. This can be useful—as you write more apps you may have associated values containing RGBa values (Red/Green/Blue/alpha) for making a color, barcode information for 1D or 2D barcodes, phone numbers, or any of a multitude of possibilities for storing values in enums.

You might have figured out on your own that optional values in Swift are a type of enum with associated values. Some languages have a structure like this called **either**, where a value can be either the first value or the second value. A basic implementation of the optional type is represented in Listing 12.6.

LISTING 12.6   Crude Implementation of Optional Enum

```
enum STYOptional<T> {
    case None
    case Some(T)
}
```

As you know, constants and variables in Swift are either optional or non-optional. In previous examples, you've stored optional values inside variables, and it has looked like {Some 3}, because the associated value was not nil, and it was associated with the Some enum member. If a value was nil, the None member was returned. Swift provides shorthand syntax (the question mark) when indicating an optional, versus using .Some(value) or .None.

Adding Instance Methods to Enums

By this point, I'm sure you've become comfortable with functions, both by themselves and also as instance methods. It should not come as a surprise to you that enums can also have instance methods inside them. This is a big mental stretch for some who are accustomed to C-style enums where they store a logical progression of enumerated values, and that's it. Swift enums are much more flexible and powerful, and the ability to add instance methods is just one more ounce of proof of that.

Instance methods in Swift enums are basically identical to instance methods in a class or a struct. The structural syntax is the same. They are defined with the `func` keyword; you provide a name for the method, parameters, and a return type, and then the body goes inside curly braces. This enables you to perform actions based on the current instance of the enum, which can make it possible for you to do some pretty powerful things with very little code, since now you can encapsulate a lot of power directly inside an enum.

To access instance methods on an enum instance, you simply use the dot syntax just as with a class's or struct's instance methods. Let's walk through an example in this next Try It Yourself section, so you can get the feel for how enums can add powerful capabilities to your code.

▼ TRY IT YOURSELF

Adding Instance Methods to Enums

Extend the PhoneNumber enum type by adding an instance method to encapsulate a `switch` statement, utilizing associated values of the enums members. The function should provide the extension for the phone number provided.

1. Open Xcode 6 and create a new playground. Either a Mac or an iOS playground will work. Clear the contents of the playground.

2. Create the `PhoneNumber` enum in your playground to look like that in Listing 12.5.

   ```
   enum PhoneNumber {
       case TollFree(Int, Int, Int)
       case InternalExtension(Int)
   }
   ```

3. After the `case` statements, but before the enum's closing brace, declare a function called ext that takes no parameters and returns a `String`.

   ```
   func ext() -> String {

   }
   ```

4. Inside this method, switch the current value (`self`, since we're dealing with the current instance) and use binding to obtain the extension from either case. Use a `String` variable inside the method to keep track of the result to be returned. (Note: Even though we are retrieving the extension portion of a phone number, do not use the word `extension`, as it is a reserved keyword in Swift.)

```
var resultExtension = ""
switch self {
case .TollFree(_, _, let xtnsn):
    resultExtension = "Toll-free extension, \(xtnsn)"
case .InternalExtension(let xtnsn):
    resultExtension = "Internal extension, \(xtnsn)"
}
```

5. Return the `resultExtension` value from the method after the `switch` statement's closing curly brace.

```
return resultExtension
```

6. That's all for the instance method, and the enum as well. Now you can reuse the `switch` statement on any instance, not just once per variable or constant like Listing 12.5. Create a variable instance of `PhoneNumber`, assign it the `TollFree` member, and provide a phone number for the associated values. Then call the `ext()` instance method we just created.

```
var number = PhoneNumber.TollFree(800, 555, 1212)
number.ext()
```

7. Use shorthand syntax to reassign the number variable to `PhoneNumber.InternalExtension`, and provide a single `Int` as an associated value. Then, call the `ext()` instance method again and observe the value.

```
number = .InternalExtension(4357)
number.ext()
```

Upon completion of the Try It Yourself section, your code should look like the code in Figure 12.4.

Hopefully by now you're starting to see how all the concepts discussed thus far in the book are used and how they can be integrated with other concepts to create a powerful app with not much code. In this Try It Yourself section, we declare an `enum` with two members, each having associated values. We also have an instance method on that enum, with a `switch` block that uses binding to extract values and use them in the `case` statements. Then we declare a variable with an enum value, call the instance method, reassign the variable, and call the instance method again. This is all done in 20 lines of code.

```
      ● ● ●                    ⊡ Ch12 Enum Functions TIY.playground
     ▦  <   >   ⊡ Ch12 Enum Functions TIY.playground ⟩ No Selection
  1  enum PhoneNumber {
  2      case TollFree(Int, Int, Int)
  3      case InternalExtension(Int)
  4
  5      func ext() -> String {
  6          var resultExtension = ""                               (2 times)
  7          switch self {
  8          case .TollFree(_, _, let xtnsn):
  9              resultExtension = "Toll-Free extension: \(xtnsn)"  "Toll-Free extension: 1212"
 10          case .InternalExtension(let xtnsn):
 11              resultExtension = "Internal extension: \(xtnsn)"   "Internal extension: 4357"
 12          }
 13          return resultExtension                                 (2 times)
 14      }
 15  }
 16  var number = PhoneNumber.TollFree(800, 555, 1212)              (Enum Value)
 17  number.ext()                                                   "Toll-Free extension: 1212"
 18
 19  number = .InternalExtension(4357)                              (Enum Value)
 20  number.ext()                                                   "Internal extension: 4357"
 21
```

FIGURE 12.4
The completed Try It Yourself section, implementing enum functions.

Summary

This hour introduced a new type not yet used in this book called enums. Enumerations are great type choices when you need a data type to hold a particular value from a set of available options.

You learned that Swift enums can have a backing (or *raw*) value, or they can peacefully exist without one. A raw value can be of type Int, String, Character, Double, or Float, and Swift auto-increments Int-backed raw values, as well as starts them at zero if not explicitly defined. You also learned how to access raw values with the toRaw() method and select an enum member via the fromRaw(T) method, which returns an optional.

We also discussed shorthand syntax as a way to quickly and tersely assign an enum member to a variable or constant, while still maintaining meaning and readability. Then we discussed associated values, which are great for storing data alongside an enum member in an instance, rather than storing that data in a property somewhere else. Then we used switch statements to execute code based on the current enum value (self) and used binding inside switch cases to extract the associated values.

Finally, we discussed adding instance methods to enums, which greatly adds power to enums, a feature not in other languages. Adding instance methods to enums encapsulates enum-specific actions to the enum itself and keeps the responsibility of the code with the enum, rather than as separate entities in code.

In the next hour, we discuss initializers in Swift, and how they can be added and customized within classes, structs, and enums. Because of Swift's type safety, initializers play a big role in ensuring safe class construction and use.

Q&A

Q. What happens if I don't assign raw values to enumerations members of type `Character`?

A. You'll get a compiler error. If you create an enumeration with members of any non-`Int` type, you must assign raw values to each member.

Q. What's the difference between raw values and associated values?

A. You assign raw values to your enumeration's members when you create the enumeration. Once you set them, they cannot change. With associated values, you set the type when you create the enumeration, but no value is assigned until you create a variable based on one of your enumeration's members.

Q. Can an enum have both associated values and raw values?

A. No. Enums can have either associated values or raw values, but not both.

Q. Can I inherit from enumerations like I can from classes?

A. No. Enumerations do not allow inheritance in the way that classes do. You have to create a new enumeration from scratch.

Workshop

The workshop contains quiz questions and exercises to help you solidify your understanding of the material covered. Try to answer all questions before looking at the answers that follow.

Quiz

1. Are Swift enumerations value types or reference types?

2. Which instance method returns an enum's backing value?

3. What's wrong with the following code?

```
enum Day {
  case Sunday, Monday, Tuesday, Wednesday
  case Thursday, Friday, Saturday

  func isWeekday() -> Bool {
    switch self {
      case .Saturday, .Sunday:
        return false
      default:
        return true
    }
  }
}
```

```
}

let today: DayOfWeek = .Monday
today.isWeekday()
let tomorrow = .Tuesday
tomorrow.isWeekday()
```

4. Which types are legal to use as raw values? Which are legal as associated values?

Answers

1. Swift enumerations are value types. This means that they are copied when they are assigned to a variable or constant or when they are passed as an argument to a function.

2. The `.toRaw()` method.

3. We're trying to use enum shorthand notation when we assign a value to `tomorrow` before we establish what type `tomorrow` is. With no type assigned, the compiler doesn't know what `.Tuesday` means.

4. Raw values must be of type `String`, `Character`, `Int`, `Double`, or `Float`. Associated values can be of any type.

Exercise

Create a new OS X playground. We're going to model a standard deck of playing cards. Begin by creating an enum called Suit, with members Hearts, Diamonds, Clubs, and Spades. Write an instance method that determines the color of the card. Remember that hearts and diamonds are red, where clubs and spades are black.

Next, write an enum to hold the rank of the card. Valid ranks are One, Two, Three, Four, Five, Six, Seven, Eight, Nine, Ten, Jack, Queen, King, and Ace. Write an instance method that determines whether the card is a face card. Remember that face cards are Jacks, Queens, and Kings.

Last, create a PlayingCard class with properties of type Rank and Suit. Write a method called Description for the PlayingCard class that returns a string of the form: "The <RANK> of <SUIT> is a <COLOR> <FACE> card." Replace <RANK>, <SUIT>, and <COLOR> with the appropriate strings. Replace <FACE> with the word "face" if the card is a face card and with an empty string if the card is not a face card.

For example, if the card is the Ace of Spades, your description method should print "The Ace of Spades is a Black card." For the King of Diamonds, it should print "The King of Diamonds is a Red face card."

Think about how you might assign raw values to your enums to make this task easier.

Customizing Initializers of Classes, Structs, and Enums

What You'll Learn in This Hour:

▶ What the goal of initialization is
▶ How to create default and parameterized initializers
▶ How to use initializer delegation for value types
▶ How to use designated and convenience initializers
▶ What the rules of initialization are
▶ How to use and override inherited initializers

Throughout the book thus far, we have made do without mentioning much about initialization as a concept in itself, but we have used it, whether you knew it or not. All instances of any type must be initialized before use, not only for safety, but also to be a usable instance in general; it doesn't do you much good to have an uninitialized instance of anything because you wouldn't be able to reliably interact with the instance in either sending data to or getting data from it. In this hour we discuss many different methods and concepts of initialization. Initialization is a huge topic in itself, and probably more than what would fit in an hour's worth of reading. But in the interest of keeping the discussion of this topic to an hour while still conveying all pertinent and usable information to you, we cover enough of a foundation of initialization, which later hours extend, due to how they interact with initialization. Without further ado, let's dive into initialization in Swift.

Initialization

Each instance in Swift, whether an enum, class, or struct, must be initialized before use. **Initialization** is the method by which values inside the instance are set to either default values or values passed in as arguments. Initialization takes place in code through something called an **initializer**. An initializer is just an instance method, much like the instance methods we have written in the previous several hours, only it has specific syntax that differentiates it from normal instance methods. Let's take a look at the structure of initializers now.

The Goal of Initializers

The goal of initializers is simple: Set a value for every property inside the current instance. That is the *raison d'être* of initializers. They should perform no other actions than to ensure the instance is set up properly before use.

Listing 13.1 illustrates the syntax of a basic initializer. Unlike regular instance methods, the func keyword is not used here. Rather, only the init keyword and a pair of parentheses are used. Inside the curly braces is where you put initialization code.

LISTING 13.1 Basic Initializer Syntax

```
01:  class SampleClass {
02:      var sampleInt: Int
03:      init() {
04:          sampleInt = 0
05:      }
06:  }
```

In Listing 13.1, we create a sample class called SampleClass on line 1, with a single variable property called sampleInt, of type Int, on line 2. On line 3 we declare our initializer with the init() method. Inside the init() method, we simply set our instance property sampleInt to 0, which is a likely and common starting value for many numeric types.

Up until now, if you recall, we have always initialized our properties when we define them; otherwise, we get compiler errors (with the exception of structs, but we'll get to that shortly). An example of the compiler error we would receive if we had neither an initializer nor a default value for sampleInt is shown in Figure 13.1. Notice that Xcode offers a solution, in light gray text to the right of the Int keyword, which is to assign an initial value of zero (0) to sampleInt.

FIGURE 13.1
Xcode compiler error when using uninitialized properties in a class.

Double-clicking the blue Fix-it suggestion auto-completes adding the assignment to zero and silences the compiler error. Setting a value in a variable's or constant's definition statement is called setting its **default property value**. The reason for this is Swift's need for type safety. Returning an uninitialized instance could potentially cause your app to crash. As you see as we progress through this hour, initializers play a key role in properly setting up instances for use and ensuring your instances begin their lives with the proper initialized values.

We would expect that we would be able to change the value of a variable property, due to it being introduced with var rather than let. But what about constants, or even optionals? Constant properties can be set in their initializers *only*, if not set directly in their definition. A constant can be set and altered as needed inside an initializer, but once the initializer ends, the constant is immutable. The reason for this is that even though it is constant, it still needs an initial value, and inside the initializer or directly in its definition are the only safe places for that to happen. As for optionals, they don't have to be initialized inside an initializer or in their definition statement, because *they are optional*. By being declared optional, its value is nil until set otherwise.

There Is Always an Initializer

Swift enums, classes, and structs always have an initializer. Swift provides a **default initializer** for any struct, enum, or base class that provides default values for all its properties and doesn't implement an initializer itself. Because Swift provides a default initializer, we do not see it, but it is there behind the scenes. The best way to understand this is to examine how we create instances of these types. Recall that when we create a constant or variable of a type, we set the constant or variable equal to the name of the type, followed by a pair of parentheses. Using the parentheses after the type name is actually calling the initializer for that type. In the case of our SampleClass example in Listing 13.1, writing let a = SampleClass() would assign a new instance of type SampleClass to a, with a.sampleInt being equal to 0. But in this example, it is easy to see that there is an initializer, because we created it on line 3. Consider the following revised version of SampleClass:

```
class SampleClass {
    var sampleInt = 0
}
```

In this shortened version of SampleClass, since sampleInt is set to 0 upon definition, and there are no other properties to assign, there is no need to explicitly add an initializer. However, Swift implicitly adds an initializer to our class because Swift has to have at least one initializer per type to properly instantiate the instance.

Initializing Value Types

There are some differences between initializing value types, such as structs and enums, and reference types, such as classes. Let's cover value types first to grasp some key concepts and then move on to reference types, where we expand upon these concepts with more that only relate to classes.

Setting Default Values

Setting default values for structs is just as simple as either setting the property value directly in the definition statement, or by setting property values inside the initializer, as we have seen so far in this hour. Let's discuss how structs and enums can set default values.

Memberwise Initialization for Structs

If you recall from Hour 10, "Learning About Structs and Classes," when we created a struct called Point, we created an instance of it by using something called **memberwise initialization**. Listing 13.2 shows our Point struct and an example of creating an instance of Point.

LISTING 13.2   Using Memberwise Initialization on a Struct

```
01:   struct Point {
02:       var x: Double
03:       var y: Double
04:   }
05:   let point = Point(x: 2.0, y: 3.0)
```

Memberwise initialization is something Swift does by default when you do not provide any initializers. A memberwise initializer analyzes the current members in a struct and creates a default initializer requiring those members as parameters. Listing 13.3 illustrates what our Point struct would look like if we provided the exact same initializer as the memberwise initializer (although I changed the parameters to be xx and yy to show that we're using the new initializer and not the memberwise initializer).

LISTING 13.3   What a Memberwise Initializer Looks Like

```
01:   struct Point {
02:       var x: Double
03:       var y: Double
04:       init(xx: Double, yy: Double) {
05:           self.x = xx
06:           self.y = yy
07:       }
08:   }
09:   let point = Point(xx: 4.0, yy: 2.5)
```

The init(xx:, yy:) method on line 4 is just as it would appear if Swift provided its memberwise initializer explicitly, except xx would be x, and yy would be y. Inside the init(xx:, yy:) method, on lines 5 and 6, we set the struct instance's x and y properties to equal the parameters passed in as arguments, and the struct is initialized fully.

NOTE

Using `self`

In Listing 13.3, we refer to `self.x` and `self.y`, rather than just `x` and `y`. Using `self` refers to the instance itself, so you can interact with other parts of the instance directly. In Objective-C, it was required to use `self` before referring to a property or method inside the instance of a class, but in Swift using `self` is not required unless the statement could be ambiguous. The `init(xx:, yy:)` method in Listing 13.3 could have read `x = xx` and `y = yy` instead, since Swift knows `x` and `y` are its instance properties. If the `init(xx:, yy:)` method's arguments were `x` and `y`, we couldn't have `x = x` and `y = y`. That is unclear as to which `x` and `y` we are working with on the left-hand or right-hand side of the equation, so we would use `self.x = x` and `self.y = y` in that case instead.

Custom Initializers for Structs

As an alternative to having Swift provide a memberwise initializer for structs, you can provide one or more of your own initializers. By providing an initializer, Swift does not provide a memberwise initializer. Take Listing 13.4 for example. We create a simple `Rectangle` struct with just an `init()` method where we provide default values for the properties `width` and `height`.

LISTING 13.4 Initializing Structs with Default Values

```
01:  struct Rectangle {
02:      var width: Double
03:      var height: Double
04:      init() {
05:          width = 1.0
06:          height = 2.0
07:      }
08:  }
09:  var rectangle = Rectangle()    // rectangle is equal to {width: 1.0,
➥height: 2.0}
```

When we declare an `init()` method on line 4, we can no longer use the memberwise initializer. Line 9 shows how we now declare a variable of type `Rectangle`, with an initialized instance.

Custom Initializers for Enums

Enums are a little different than structs. Enums provide different cases that a property value could store, but so far no clear mechanism for setting which case should be set initially, if any. Since enums are value types just like structs, and Swift provides much more functionality to enums, we can also add our own initializers to enums. Listing 13.5 illustrates adding an `init()` method to an enum and setting a default value.

LISTING 13.5   Initializing Enums with Default Values

```
01:  enum GradesKTo5: String {
02:      case Kindergarten = "K", First = "1st", Second = "2nd"
03:      case Third = "3rd", Fourth = "4th", Fifth = "5th"
04:      init() {
05:          self = .Kindergarten
06:      }
07:  }
08:  let k = GradesKTo5()
09:  k.toRaw()                // displays "K"
```

Here, we reused the GradesKTo5 enum from the previous hour and added an initializer on line 4. The initializer takes no arguments, so its purpose is to simply set a default initial value, which we set to .Kindergarten. When we declare a constant value of the enum on line 8, rather than writing let k = GradesKTo5.Kindergarten, we simply call the enum's initializer with the parentheses after GradesKTo5. On line 9 we call the toRaw() method to show that our initializer did its job.

Let's walk through an example together to get more practice writing code with initializers in a Try It Yourself section.

▼ TRY IT YOURSELF

Using Initializers to Set Default and Custom Values

Create an enum holding different types of melons, and then create a Melon struct, with a property of the enum type, seed count, and weight. Use initializers to help properly set up the instances.

1. Open Xcode 6 and create a new playground. Clear the contents of the playground.

2. Create an enum, and call it MelonType, with a raw value type of String.

   ```
   enum MelonType: String {


   }
   ```

3. Inside the enum, create three case members: Watermelon, Cantaloupe, and Honeydew.

   ```
   case Watermelon = "Watermelon", Cantaloupe = "Cantaloupe", Honeydew =
   ➥"Honeydew"
   ```

4. Below the case statement, create an initializer without parameters that sets the default melon to Watermelon.

   ```
   init() {
       self = .Watermelon
   }
   ```

5. That's all for the enum. Next, create a struct called `Melon`.

```
struct Melon {

}
```

6. Define three variables: one for the melon type, one for the seed count, and one for the weight of the melon.

```
var melonType: MelonType
var seedCount: Int
var weightInPounds: Double
```

7. Create a default initializer that sets all values to zero, or their type's initial default state.

```
init() {
    melonType = MelonType()
    seedCount = 0
    weightInPounds = 0.0
}
```

8. Create a custom initializer that can be called when creating an instance of `Melon` that accepts all three parameters for the properties in our struct.

```
init(melonType: MelonType, seedCount: Int, weightInPounds: Double) {
    self.melonType = melonType
    self.seedCount = seedCount
    self.weightInPounds = weightInPounds
}
```

9. For our struct, create a description method that displays in a friendly format the data inside our `Melon` struct instances.

```
func description() -> String {
    return "My \(melonType.toRaw()) has \(seedCount) seeds and weighs
➡\(weightInPounds) lbs."
}
```

10. That's all for the struct and enum. Next, declare two instances of `Melon` using both initializers and then call their description methods to see their resulting data.

```
let defaultMelon = Melon()
let customMelon = Melon(melonType: .Honeydew, seedCount: 100,
➡ weightInPounds: 2.0)
defaultMelon.description()
customMelon.description()
```

After completing the Try It Yourself section, your code and results in the results pane should look like those in Figure 13.2.

FIGURE 13.2
The completed Try It Yourself exercise for creating default and custom initializers.

External Parameter Names in Initializers

By default, all parameters in initializers behave as both the external and internal parameter names. This means that you do not have to explicitly declare external parameter names in your initializers, and Swift requires the parameter names when declaring an instance of that type.

In some cases it may not make sense to have to explicitly state the initializer parameter name or names, or for succinctness and clarity the parameter name(s) could be removed. To do this, preface an initializer parameter name with the underscore (_) character and a space to indicate to Swift's compiler that the parameter name is not needed when declaring a new instance of a type. Listing 13.6 shows how this is done.

LISTING 13.6 Hiding Parameter Names in Initializers

```
01:   struct MilesPerHour {
02:       var rate: Double
03:       init(_ rate: Double) {
04:           self.rate = rate
05:       }
06:   }
07:   let mph = MilesPerHour(60)      // intent is clear, 60 MPH
```

Listing 13.6 looks like a pretty standard struct as we've seen already, but on line 3 we use the underscore (_) to denote that we don't need to enter the parameter name in the declaration on line 7. The intent is clear that we are creating an instance to hold a value representing 60 miles per hour.

Initializing Class Types

The initialization concepts and examples so far in this hour, minus memberwise initialization for structs, are available for classes as well. You get a default initializer when your class is a base class and all properties are assigned values in their definition statements. You can also create custom initializers, with or without parameters. Parameterized initializers require their parameters to be listed inside the parentheses when creating an instance. Finally, you can also hide parameter names with the underscore (_) and a space before the parameter name.

Later in this hour, we discuss some of the more powerful and advanced features of class initialization, such as how it works in multiple phases, delegation, and convenience and designated initializers. These concepts become clearer when we cover them if we cover their less-advanced partners for structs.

Advanced Initialization

Now that you have a pretty good foundational understanding of the basics of initializers, it's time to discuss some rules and patterns around initialization in Swift.

Initialization Delegation

Initializers of all types can use something called **delegation**, but the rules and methods of delegating initialization are slightly different for structure types and class types. To begin, we discuss delegation in terms of structs and enums.

NOTE

Initializing Enums

As we know, enums in Swift are value types just like structs. This means that, for the most part, the same concepts should apply to enums as to structs. Since Swift is such a new language, and since enums work so differently in Swift than any other language, best practices and accepted idioms have yet to be discovered. With that being said, examples in this book, when comparing value types and reference types, largely, but not always, use a struct-versus-class example, because enums and structs behave so similarly in Swift.

What Is Initialization Delegation?

Initialization delegation is the process of a particular initializer within a type partially completing initialization and then passing the remaining initialization responsibility to another initializer.

Delegating Initialization with Structures

In value types like structs and enums, you can only delegate across, meaning to another initializer in the same structure. This should make sense, since structs and enums can neither inherit nor be inherited from, so it should stand to reason that initializers can only delegate across within the same structure. Figure 13.3 shows a visualization of this, and then Listing 13.7 shows this written out in Swift code.

FIGURE 13.3
Diagram of initialization delegation for the Rectangle struct.

In Figure 13.3, the init() method points to the init(width:, height:) method. That may seem fuzzy to you for now, but examine Listing 13.7 to see how this is written in code.

LISTING 13.7   Initialization Delegation for Structs

```
01:  struct Rectangle {
02:      var width: Double
03:      var height: Double
04:      init(width: Double, height: Double) {
05:          self.width = width
06:          self.height = height
07:      }
08:      init() {
09:          self.init(width: 1.0, height: 2.0)
10:      }
11:  }
12:  let rect1 = Rectangle(width: 4.0, height: 6.0)   // rect1 is {width:
➡4.0, height: 6.0}
13:  let rect2 = Rectangle()                          // rect2 is {width:
➡1.0, height: 2.0}
```

Now the arrow pointing from `init()` to `init(width:, height:)` in Figure 13.3 should be clearer. Our `init()` method calls another initializer inside the same struct, `init(width:, height:)`. In other words, the `init()` method delegates the initialization responsibility to the `init(width:, height:)` method. You do not have to structure your initializers this way, but doing so helps keep your code clean and readable, as well as adhering to the Don't Repeat Yourself (DRY) principle for writing code.

CAUTION

Only Call `self.init()` from Inside Initializers

Keep in mind that you can only call `self.init()` (or any other initializer) from within an initializer, and not from anywhere else inside the structure or class. This is for safety and keeps you from re-initializing an instance, as it may be in use and have user data in it already.

Class Initialization Delegation

Classes can delegate the responsibilities of initialization slightly differently than structures can. In addition to delegating across, classes can also delegate up the inheritance chain. This is because classes can inherit from other classes, which means that a subclass inherits the properties and methods of a superclass, and thus all stored properties of the superclass *must* be initialized before use, as well as those in the subclass itself. Because of this, it is important to cover some preliminary vocabulary first.

Initializer Definitions

A **designated initializer** is the primary initializer of the class. The ultimate responsibility of initializing all property values and calling the appropriate superclass designated initializer belongs to the designated initializer. Every class must have at least one, even if it is inferred or inherited, and must be called at most once to properly instantiate the instance. A designated initializer has no special syntax to indicate it is a designated initializer.

A **convenience initializer** is a secondary initializer in a class and is not required like a designated initializer is. A convenience initializer can be used to set some sensible default values, or set properties from arguments passed in to it, by passing them along to the designated initializer or setting them once another initializer has returned execution to the convenience initializer. Convenience initializers are sometimes much nicer to use to create an instance when default values will suffice or if it can reduce code while still providing clear intent. Convenience initializers prefix the `init` method with the `convenience` keyword.

An **inherited initializer** is an initializer method that gets inherited from the superclass. This can be called directly from the subclass using the `self` keyword rather than `super`. However, it often is treated like a convenience initializer in a subclass due to the subclass having slightly different behavior or needs than its superclass, thus requiring a more custom designated initializer.

Initializer chaining is the process of creating relationships between initializers, whether inherited, convenience, or designated initializers.

The Rules of Initialization Chaining

Apple suggests several rules around initialization chaining, which can be summarized as follows:

▶ Designated initializers must always delegate up to their immediate superclass, if one exists.

▶ Convenience initializers must always delegate across, to either another convenience initializer or designated initializer, in the same class.

NOTE

Full List of Rules, Safety Checks, and Phases for Initialization

The Swift language has safety in mind always, as it is one of the primary cornerstones of the language. Apple maintains a full list of the three rules of initialization chaining, four safety checks initializers must pass, and two phases of initialization that occur before an instance can be used. This information can all be referenced in Apple's iBook *The Swift Programming Language*. For our purposes in this book, we cover key concepts to initialization and delegation that adhere to these guidelines, although we may not take the extensive amount of time to cover each of them in detail.

The Initialization Process

Let's examine what happens when we create an initializer chain with a class hierarchy. We start out with `Shape` as our base class with one initializer, which is also its designated initializer. Then we subclass that with a class called `Rectangle`, with a designated initializer and a convenience initializer. After that, we subclass `Rectangle` with a class called `Square`, also with a designated initializer and convenience initializer.

Let's look at the diagram of how this would look in Figure 13.4, and then we write the code to show how this looks in practice.

In Figure 13.4 we can see the class hierarchy of `Shape` => `Rectangle` => `Square`. Each blue block is a designated initializer for that class, and each red block is a convenience initializer for that class. If we were to declare an instance of `Square` using the convenience initializer, our code would call `Square`'s `init()` method, which delegates to `Square`'s designated initializer, `init(length:)`. Then `Square`'s designated initializer delegates up to `Rectangle`'s designated initializer, which performs steps relevant to the `Rectangle` class. Then `Rectangle`'s designated initializer delegates up to `Shape`'s designated initializer, which performs steps relevant to the `Shape` class. All these steps are in *phase one* of initialization.

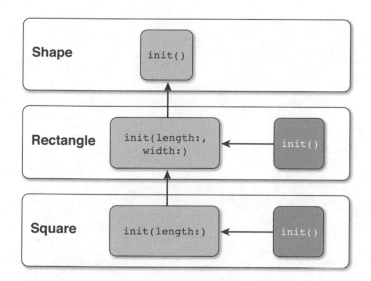

FIGURE 13.4
The diagram illustrating the inheritance chain, as well as initialization chain for initialization delegation.

Phase two of initialization begins on the way back down the initialization chain. After the Shape class's designated initializer finishes, execution returns to the point after which it was called, which is in Rectangle's designated initializer. Any code after the call to Shape's designated initializer is then executed, and control returns to the point after which Rectangle's designated initializer was called. This continues through to the last initializer, at which point the instance is then fully initialized and able to be used.

Now, let's take a look at implementing this in code, in the following Try It Yourself section.

TRY IT YOURSELF ▼

Implementing Initialization Chaining

Create the class hierarchy and initialization chain previously discussed.

1. Open Xcode 6 and create a new playground. Clear the contents of the playground.

2. Create a Shape base class, provide a property called numberOfSides of type Int, and inside the class's designated initializer set numberOfSides to 0. Create a description() method, too, which each subclass overrides.

```
class Shape {
    var numberOfSides: Int
    init() {
        numberOfSides = 0
    }
    func description() -> String { return "I am a shape with no sides." }
}
```

3. Create a `Rectangle` class that inherits from `Shape`. Create a property of type `Int` for the length and another for the width.

```
class Rectangle: Shape {
    var length: Int
    var width: Int
}
```

4. Inside the `Rectangle` class, after the `width` definition, create a designated initializer for `Rectangle` that takes length and width parameters of type `Int`. Set the class's `length` and `width` properties to the length and width parameter values first and then call `super.init()`, since a designated initializer must always call its immediate superclass's designated initializer. After the call to `super.init()`, set `numberOfSides` equal to 4.

```
init(length: Int, width: Int) {
    self.length = length
    self.width = width
    super.init()
    numberOfSides = 4
}
```

5. Create a convenience initializer called `init()`, which calls `self.init(length:, width:)`. This must be overridden because the superclass's designated initializer is `init()`. Then set `numberOfSides` to 0, because technically a rectangle with no length or width has no sides.

```
override convenience init() {
    self.init(length: 0, width: 0)
    numberOfSides = 0
}
```

6. The `Rectangle` initializers are created now, so override the `description()` method to show the values of the current instance where we can verify our initializers worked properly.

```
override func description() -> String {
    return "I am a rectangle with \(numberOfSides) sides,
➥\(length)x\(width), area: \(length * width)"
}
```

7. That's all for the `Rectangle` class. Next, create a `Square` class that inherits from `Rectangle`.

```
class Square: Rectangle {
}
```

8. Inside the `Square` class, create a designated initializer that takes a length parameter of type `Int`. The initializer only needs to call `super.init(length:, width:)`. Calling `super.init(length:, width:)` sets the `length` and also `numberOfSides` properties, so we don't need to repeat setting those properties inside `Square`.

```
init(length: Int) {
    super.init(length: length, width: length)
}
```

9. Create a convenience initializer that calls our designated initializer. Note that this `init()` method does not need to be prefixed with the `override` keyword because the superclass's `init()` method is not a designated initializer. Then set `numberOfSides` to 0, again because a square with zero length and width has no sides.

```
convenience init() {
    self.init(length: 0)
    numberOfSides = 0
}
```

10. That's all for the `Square` initializers, so override the `description()` method to show the values of the current instance to verify our initializers worked properly.

```
override func description() -> String {
    return "I'm a square with \(numberOfSides) sides,
➥\(length)x\(length), area: \(length * length)"
}
```

11. Our classes are done. Create two instances of `Square`, one using the designated initializer and one using the convenience initializer. Call the `description()` method on both instances to view their properties after initialization.

```
let square = Square()
square.description()    // "I'm a square with 0 sides, 0x0, area: 0"
let square2 = Square(length: 5)
square2.description()    // "I'm a square with 4 sides, 5x5, area: 25"
```

12. Create two instances of the `Rectangle` class, one using the designated initializer and one using the convenience initializer. Call the `description()` method on both instances to view their properties after initialization.

```
let rectangle = Rectangle()
rectangle.description()    // "I'm a rectangle with 0 sides, 0x0, area: 0"
let rectangle2 = Rectangle(length: 3, width: 4)
rectangle2.description()    // "I'm a rectangle with 4 sides, 3x4, area: 12"
```

Once you've finished the Try It Yourself section, your code and results should look like those in Figure 13.5.

FIGURE 13.5
The completed Try It Yourself section implementing class initialization delegation.

There are a few key points of note in this example. First, notice how the initialization delegation takes place. Creating an instance of `Square` with the convenience initializer sets all the values in the class instance to zero for us; all we need to do is instantiate it by calling `Square()`. This calls the same class's designated initializer, which then sets property values and calls its superclass's designated initializer. This repeats until initialization hits the top of the class hierarchy, where it then traverses back down to resume execution.

Notice that when the second phase of initialization (the coming back down the hierarchy) is executing, `numberOfSides` gets assigned the value 4. Then down in `Square`, `numberOfSides` gets assigned back to zero because we used the convenience initializer. That may not be the most efficient method for real-world apps, but I did it this way to make a point; execution resumes after the call to `super.init()` finishes in the `Rectangle` designated initializer, which means `numberOfSides = 4` gets executed before resuming execution in `Square`'s designated initializer. You see, when your initializers call another initializer, execution of the current initializer halts until the call to the other initializer returns; then execution resumes. Throughout this example this happens several times, which ultimately produces our properly instantiated instances. Keep this hierarchy and structure in mind when you are developing apps and planning how your instances should get initialized.

The second thing to note is that `Rectangle`'s `init()` is defined with the `override convenience` modifiers, but `Square`'s `init()` is defined with just the `convenience` modifier keyword. This is because if you are creating an initializer in a subclass with the same name as the superclass's designated initializer, you must override it, even if the subclass is using it as a convenience initializer. If the initializer exists in the superclass but is not a designated initializer in the superclass, the subclass can implement its own version but technically is not overriding it, because convenience initializers cannot call initializers in their superclass.

Summary

The topic of initializers is deceivingly large. What seems like a topic to flippantly say "Yeah, okay, hurry up and initialize my data, because I need to use it!" about turns out to be incredibly deep, as you learned if you made it through this hour. Initializers are important, especially with Swift's requirement for safety. Initialization ensures that instances are appropriately assigned values, whether provided or defaults, before being used. This ensures you'll never get returned an instance that has garbage in it or even nil for a non-optional type.

You learned about initialization for structs, enums, and classes, and the similarities and differences therein. Structs and enums can call or delegate to initializers within the same structure, whereas classes can not only delegate across but must also delegate up to their superclass's designated initializer, if one exists. Structs also receive memberwise initializers by default, based on the properties defined within it. Also we learned that external parameter names are provided by default, the same as with internal parameter names, or you can hide them by adding an underscore and a space before the parameter name.

You also learned about designated initializers, convenience initializers, and inherited initializers, and the rules each one must follow. When using these initializers, you learned what happens to control flow of our apps and how to gauge when to initialize properties of the current class or set properties of a superclass.

The best part of this all is that Xcode can really help you with meaningful messages if you are ever stuck or unsure which initializer is the designated initializer, which should be overridden or not, which should be a convenience initializer, and so on. By doing the examples in this hour, you should have a much clearer understanding of how initializers can help make setting up your instances easier and more efficient.

Q&A

Q. Can I have default values assigned where I declare my properties and still use an initializer to set those properties?

A. You certainly can. As long as each stored property has been assigned a value when class initialization is finished, you won't get an error.

Q. Can a class have more than one designated initializer?

A. Yes, as long as the method signatures are different, a class can have as many designated initializers as you want. Because subclasses can only call designated initializers in super-classes, this can be useful when you want subclasses to have more than one way to initialize your class.

Q. If I'm creating a subclass, when should I call `super.init()` in my initializer?

A. You can only call an initializer in a superclass after you have fully initialized your own stored properties. This is to prevent your superclass from accidentally trying to access a property that has not been initialized and thereby causing an error. Consider the case in which you have overridden a method so that it changes the value of a stored property introduced in your subclass. If `super.init()` calls this overridden method, it invokes the subclass's version instead of its own and tries to set a property that hasn't been initialized yet, which would cause an error.

Q. Are initializers inherited from a parent class?

A. If you provide default values for every stored property in your class and provide no initializers, your class will inherit its superclass's initializers. Otherwise, you will not inherit any initializers and you will have to provide your own.

Workshop

The workshop contains quiz questions and exercises to help you solidify your understanding of the material covered. Try to answer all questions before looking at the answers that follow.

Quiz

1. If you write a custom initializer for a struct, is the default memberwise initializer still available to you?

2. Do you have to use external names for all initializer parameters?

3. What's wrong with the following code?

```
class QuizClass {
  var x: Int
```

```
    init(x: Int) {
      self.x = x
    }

    init() {
      self.init(x: 4)
    }
}
```

4. Can a convenience initializer call another convenience initializer in the same class?

Answers

1. No, the struct's default memberwise initializer is no longer available, but you can write an initializer that behaves like the default if you want.

2. No. By default, Swift requires that external names be used when calling initializers, but you can override this behavior by explicitly setting the external name to underscore (_).

3. A designated initializer cannot call another designated initializer. The initializer that takes no parameters should be marked with the `convenience` keyword.

4. Yes, convenience initializers can call other convenience initializers in the same class as long as a designated initializer is the last initializer called for the class.

Exercise

Create a new OS X playground. See if you can create a class to store some information about triangles. Create a Triangle class with properties to store the length of each side. Triangles are called scalene when all three sides are of different lengths, isosceles when two sides have the same length, or equilateral when all three sides have the same length.

Create an initializer for your class that takes three arguments and properly sets the class properties. Next create a second initializer to use when your triangle is equilateral. Remember that all three sides will be the same length, so this method should only take one argument, but should still set all three properties. Try writing this initializer as a designated initializer first and then convert it to a convenience initializer.

Finally, we want an initializer for isosceles triangles that takes two arguments. Think about how you should set up the external names for your parameters to make it clear which value will be used for two sides.

Consider other ways you might solve this problem. Could you use subclasses of Triangle to represent isosceles and equilateral triangles instead of using a single class with multiple initializers? Was setting up the isosceles initializer a good idea, or does it just confuse the class? Would the answers to these questions change if you were working on a larger, more complex program? If so, how?

Digging Deeper with Properties

What You'll Learn in This Hour:

▶ How to use stored properties and computed properties

▶ What lazy properties are and how to use them

▶ How to customize getters and setters

▶ How to observe changes in properties

▶ How to override getters, setters, and observers

Throughout this book you have been using properties inside classes and structs without yet learning how they are implemented. That is the job of this hour; we cover the basics of properties for storing data in or providing data from instances, observing changes and taking actions based on change, and more. We also cover properties from an instance perspective, as well as a type perspective. Properties provide a great benefit to classes, structs, and enums, so let's get started and learn how to take advantage of properties in Swift.

Properties are a way to associate values with a particular instance of a class, struct, or enum. Each instance has its own properties, relative to the instance in which they are stored. A quick analogy for this is that we are all humans, and we (for the most part) have similar attributes but just different values for those attributes. We all have a height. I am 6'5", but you may be a different height. I have brown hair, but yours may be black, blonde, red, some other color, or none. Humans share a lot of attributes, but the values of those attributes may be different. That is how properties in Swift are handled, too. You can designate properties in a class, struct, or enum that you are creating, and each instance will have its own values for its properties.

There are two categories of properties in Swift: **stored properties** and **computed properties**. Let's take a look at the differences between them now.

Stored Properties

Stored properties in Swift do just as the name suggests: store values as constants or variables in a specified instance. These properties remain as part of the instance until the instance is deallocated from memory. Stored properties can belong to structs and classes but not enums.

As you are familiar with safety in Swift, you know that properties must be initialized to some value before use. You can set values for stored properties during definition or inside an initializer. If your property is a constant (defined with the `let` introducer) your property cannot change after it has been initialized. But if your properties need to change, use the `var` introducer. Stored properties of the same type and same mutability can be declared on the same line, separated by commas, even with default values.

Stored properties can also be optional, defined with the question mark after the type name. This enables data to be represented in an instance that is not yet known upon instantiation or initialization. If not initialized, optionals contain `nil`.

The code in Listing 14.1 shows an example of declaring several types of stored properties in a sample struct.

LISTING 14.1 Declaring Stored Properties

```
struct Square {
    var length = 0.0, width = 0.0
    var name: String?
}
```

Instance Variables

If you are coming from Objective-C, it has **instance variables** that are the backing value to stored properties. The idea is that you have an instance variable that is of a certain type, and it is what stores values in your instances. On top of that, Objective-C has properties (like we know them in Swift) that provide a layer of abstraction on top of instance variables. Objective-C properties provide safety for instance variables, plus they give clues to the compiler (that you must declare) as to how it should handle memory for that particular instance variable. They also enable you to create custom accessors to assist with getting or setting a property's instance variable. The widely accepted practice was to label the instance variable with a prefixed underscore to the property name, so that you could identify the instance variable in code apart from the property.

While Objective-C properties are great, they don't prevent you, the developer, from directly accessing the backing instance variable, which could prove to be unsafe in some cases during execution.

Swift does not allow access to a property's backingstore, for safety reasons. To enable you to customize a property's behavior or observe changes to it, Swift provides several methods for that, which we discuss later in this hour.

Lazy Stored Properties

Another type of stored property in Swift is called a **lazy stored property**. A lazy stored property, or just a lazy property for short, is a property of a struct or class that is known to have a value when it is needed but won't actually initialize itself until it is first called or accessed. This is useful for situations where you may have a property that has an expensive operation such as loading data from a file on disk, creating or retrieving a lot of data after a particular button is tapped or clicked in an app, or making a lengthy network request, and you don't want this processing happening at the time of initialization.

To define a property as lazy, simply add the `lazy` keyword in front of the `var` introducer. The lazy property must be a `var` since it may be called after initialization, and all constants must not change after initialization. A lazy property can be assigned an instance of another class, struct, or enum. Listing 14.2 illustrates an example of a lazy stored property.

LISTING 14.2 Lazy Stored Properties

```
01:   class SomeClassWithExpensiveOperation {
02:       func doSomeHeavyLifting() -> [String : String] {
03:           var aDictionary: [String : String] = [:]
04:           // lift heavy things and assign to aDictionary
05:           aDictionary["Test key"] = "Test Value"
06:           return aDictionary
07:   }
08:
09:   class SomeClassWithLazyVar {
10:       lazy var dataFromNetwork = SomeClassWithExpensiveOperation()
11:   }
12:
13:   let someClass = SomeClassWithLazyVar()              // displays {nil}
14:   someClass.dataFromNetwork.doSomeHeavyLifting()  // displays
➡ ["Test Key" : "Test Value"]
```

The example in Listing 14.2 uses a lazy property in the `SomeClassWithLazyVar` class, and it is defined on line 10. Line 13 declares and initializes an instance of our class, but the `dataFromNetwork` property is not initialized until we access it on line 14, because it is lazy. Since the method we call, `doSomeHeavyLifting()`, returns an instance of type `[String : String]`, we see the resulting dictionary in the results pane of a playground.

Lazy properties can also be assigned a closure instead of an instance of a class or struct. The closure can have whatever code may take a substantial amount of time or processing power. Then after the closing curly brace, you must add open- and closed-parentheses, which executes the closure. Remember, closures are just unnamed functions, and executing a function requires the parentheses to call it.

Listing 14.2 could be rewritten to move the heavy lifting tasks from the SomeClassWithExpensiveOperation class to inside the dataFromNetwork lazy property as a closure. Let's see how that's done in Listing 14.3.

LISTING 14.3   **Using Closures with Lazy Stored Properties**

```
01:  class SomeClassWithLazyVar {
02:      lazy var dataFromNetwork: [String : String] = {
03:          var aDictionary: [String : String] = [:]
04:          // lift heavy things and assign to aDictionary
05:          aDictionary["Test key"] = "Test Value"
06:          return aDictionary
07:      } ()
08:  }
09:
10:  let someClass = SomeClassWithLazyVar()   // displays {nil}
11:  someClass.dataFromNetwork                // displays ["Test Key" :
➥"Test Value"]
```

In the preceding example, on line 2, we define the dataFromNetwork to be lazy as was done in Listing 14.2, but then we assign a closure rather than another class instance. The code that once was executed as part of another class is now inside the closure on lines 3 through 6. Line 7 ends the closure and appends the parentheses to execute the closure once the lazy property is accessed.

Now that we have done this, it is interesting to note the results in lines 10 and 11. On line 10, we declare someClass and assign it to an instance of SomeClassWithLazyVar and initialize it. But the results pane reads {nil}. Why is that? We only have one property in our class, and it is lazy, so there is nothing to our class yet, hence the {nil} result. Once we access the lazy property dataFromNetwork on line 11, the closure executes, and we now have data.

Using a lazy property with a closure reduces the number of lines of code we need, and also removes a class, thus removing potential places where we could introduce bugs. Doing more with fewer lines of code is always a great feeling!

Computed Properties

The concept of stored properties is easily understood: They simply store values related to the instance to which they belong. Another type of property in Swift is called a **computed property**. Computed properties do not actually store any value. Rather, they return a calculated value each time they are called. Also, unlike stored properties, computed properties can belong to not only structs and classes but also enums. Computed properties cannot be declared with the `lazy` modifier—that would result in a compiler error.

There is no difference in the way you access a stored property or a computed property. Both use dot syntax, and Swift's compiler analyzes when you are retrieving data or assigning data and calls the respective getter or setter. Let's look at property accessors now.

Property Accessors

Computed properties enable you to provide a **getter** method to retrieve data, and optionally you can provide a **setter** method to set values of other properties indirectly. These are called **property accessors**. The property accessors of stored properties are inherently created for you, and you cannot alter them; they are provided by Swift so that you have the capability to get and set data inside the property. Computed properties, however, enable you to customize the behavior of a property.

Getters

A getter is a method that returns a value for a computed property. Getters are denoted with the `get` keyword and a pair of curly braces surrounding the code calculating the return value. If you only provide a getter for your computed property, your computed property is treated as read-only, and no assignment can occur. This is useful for when you have a property that you want to provide to external instances, but you do not want them changing the value. Listing 14.4 shows a struct named `Square`, and we use a computed property to calculate and retrieve the area of the `Square` instance.

LISTING 14.4   Using Getters in Computed Properties

```
01:   struct Square {
02:       var length: Double
03:       var area: Double {
04:           get {
05:               return length * length
06:           }
07:       }
```

```
08:    }
09:
10:    let square = Square(length: 4)
11:    square.area                          // displays 16.0
```

The struct in Listing 14.4 is straightforward, and you already learned everything included, outside of lines 3 through 7. Line 3 introduces the computed read-only property, `area`, of type `Double`. A computed property then has curly braces surrounding the code that will be computed and returned. On line 5, we return the product of `length * length`, which gets returned when the `area` property is called on line 11.

NOTE

Omit `get` Keyword in Read-Only Computed Properties

If you are only providing a getter for your computed property, you can safely omit the `get` keyword and curly braces. The resulting effect would turn lines 3 through 7 into one line, `var area: Double { return length * length }`.

Setters

A setter is a method with which you can set the values of other stored properties, based on the value given to the setter. The syntax for creating a setter is the same as a getter, although the `set` keyword is used, and curly braces surround the setting code. You can designate a name for the new value sent to the computed property by including it inside parentheses after the `set` keyword; otherwise, Swift provides the `newValue` constant for you, which includes the value assigned to the computed property. Either `newValue` or the name of the value you designate can only be used within the setter; otherwise, you get a compiler error.

If you provide a setter, you must provide a getter, and you cannot omit the `get` keyword.

Let's expand our Square example by adding a setter in the following Try It Yourself example.

▼ TRY IT YOURSELF

Provide Custom Setter for `Square` Struct

Take the preceding `Square` struct example and expand it to add a custom setter to alter the `length` property in the `Square` struct.

1. Open Xcode 6 and create a new playground, either iOS or Mac will work. Clear the contents of the playground.

▼

2. Import the Foundation framework, as we need the square root function later in this example.

```
import Foundation
```

3. Create the `Square` struct and provide a `length` variable property of type `Double`.

```
struct Square {
    var length: Double
}
```

4. Create a computed property named `area`, of type `Double`, and provide the same getter as in Listing 14.3 for returning the area of the square.

```
var area: Double {
    get {
        return length * length
    }
}
```

5. After the getter's closing curly brace, add a setter with the `set` keyword, and inside the setter's curly braces, set the `length` property to equal the square root of the new value.

```
set(newArea) {
    length = sqrt(newArea)
}
```

6. That's all for the struct. Create an instance of `Square` and give it an initial length of 4.

```
var square = Square(length: 4)    // Swift converts the Int 4 to a Double 4.0
```

7. Accessing the `area` property should now return the proper area of the square.

```
square.area     // displays 16.0
```

8. Now set the area of the square to 25.

```
square.area = 25
```

9. Call the `length` property of the square to ensure that the `length` property changed accordingly.

```
square.length      // displays 5.0
```

The completed Try It Yourself code and results should look like those in Figure 14.1.

```
                    ▣ Ch14 Custom Setter TIY.playground
⊞  〈  〉 │ ▣ Ch14 Custom Setter TIY.playground 〉 No Selection
 1   import Foundation
 2
 3   struct Square {
 4       var length: Double
 5       var area: Double {
 6           get {
 7               return length * length            16.0
 8           }
 9           set(newArea) {
10               length = sqrt(newArea)            {length 5.0}
11           }
12       }
13   }
14
15   var square = Square(length: 4)               {length 4.0}
16   square.area                                  16.0
17   square.area = 25
18   square.length                                5.0
19
```

FIGURE 14.1
The completed Try It Yourself example with computed property accessors.

Notice in step 5 of the preceding Try It Yourself example that we explicitly declared the name
for the newly assigned value for our setter, with set(newArea) {...}. If we had not specified
newArea, and just written set {...}, we could use newValue instead. Adding an explicitly
named parameter in the setter is more for self-documentation, so your code is clearer about what
its intent is, and it is not mandatory to provide a custom name for the value to be set.

Computed properties are great for things that should be properties, yet perform some actions
or calculations to derive their data, such as the area property in our example. Other examples
would be a description property or a center coordinate of a square on a Cartesian coordinate
graph. A function might not make sense for these values, since functions are more geared
toward performing a particular action, not returning or setting a simple value.

Property Observers

To observe changes in property values, Swift provides **property observers** that you can customize. There are two ways to observe changes in a property: before the change happens and after
the change happens. To respond before the change takes place, use the willSet keyword, followed by a closure encapsulating the code to execute before the property value changes. To
respond after the change takes place, use the didSet keyword with a closure, such as willSet.

NOTE

Initialization Does Not Trigger Property Observers

Properties that get their values at definition or via an initializer do not trigger property observers. Observers are only triggered when a property is set after initialization.

The syntax for a property observer is similar to the syntax of a computed property, except you are not assigning the closure to the property with an assignment operator (=). The closure containing willSet and/or didSet immediately follows the defined type of the property, and there are no ending parentheses after the closing curly brace.

Swift provides the new value in the willSet observer as newValue, and the old value of the property in the didSet observer as oldValue. This enables you to validate a property change, monitor the difference between the old and new values, or use it however you need for your app. The oldValue and newValue values cannot be changed.

A reason you may want to observe changes in a property could be to calculate the difference between the old and new property values upon a given interval, such as with a speed limit. Let's say we are driving on a highway, and the speed limit is 65 miles per hour (MPH). To be good law-abiding citizens, we are also driving 65 MPH. But suddenly the speed limit decreases to 55 MPH as we enter city limits. We need our app to respond to the change and decrease our speed limit to 55 MPH. Let's look at how this is done in Listing 14.5. If you're following along in a playground, either an iOS or Mac playground will work, as this example does not require any external frameworks.

LISTING 14.5   Observing the Speed Limit

```
01:  class Vehicle {
02:      var speed: Int
03:      var speedLimit: Int {
04:          willSet {
05:              println("Preparing to change speed to \(newValue) MPH")
06:          }
07:          didSet {
08:              var changeSpeed: () -> () = (speed > speedLimit) ? slowdown
�: speedup
09:              while speed != speedLimit {
10:                  changeSpeed()
11:              }
12:              println("Now I'm driving \(speed) MPH because the speed limit
➡changed to \(speedLimit) MPH from \(oldValue) MPH\n")
```

```
13:                }
14:           }
15:        init(speedLimit: Int, speed: Int) {
16:             self.speedLimit = speedLimit
17:             self.speed = speed
18:             println("Speed limit is \(speedLimit) MPH, I'm driving:
➡\(speed) MPH")
19:           }
20:        func speedup() {
21:             println("Speeding up to \(++speed) MPH...")
22:           }
23:        func slowdown() {
24:             println("Slowing down to \(--speed) MPH...")
25:           }
26:      }
27:
28:   let car = Vehicle(speedLimit: 65, speed: 65)
29:   car.speedLimit = 55
30:   car.speedLimit = 70
```

There is a lot happening in the preceding example, so let's break it down. We create a Vehicle class, with two properties: speed and speedLimit. speed and speedLimit are both stored properties, and speedLimit has custom observers in place, as seen by willSet and didSet on lines 4 and 7, respectively. This is because we want to have some action (either speed up or slow down) occur when the speed limit changes.

The willSet observer simply tells the driver to prepare to change speed to the new speed limit and uses newValue, which is provided by Swift and holds the new value assigned to speedLimit. The didSet observer creates a variable on line 8 of type () -> (), meaning a function that has no parameters and returns void, and then uses a ternary conditional operator to gauge whether the speed should decrease or increase and assign the corresponding function slowDown or speedUp to changeSpeed. Finally, we use a simple while loop to execute while speed is not equal to speedLimit and call the changeSpeed() function inside on line 10, which changes the speed of the car until the driver is driving the speed limit.

Opening the console output viewer in the Assistant Editor shows that our speed limit started at 65 as well as our speed, since those are the values we provided in our initializer. Changing the speedLimit property on lines 29 and 30 displays the results of our property observer performing the actions needed to change our speed to match the speed limit. Press Command+Option+Return to open the Assistant Editor, and the console output should look like Figure 14.2.

```
╳                          Console Output
  Speed limit is 65 MPH, I'm driving 65 MPH
  Prepare to change speed to 55 MPH
  Slowing down to 64 MPH...
  Slowing down to 63 MPH...
  Slowing down to 62 MPH...
  Slowing down to 61 MPH...
  Slowing down to 60 MPH...
  Slowing down to 59 MPH...
  Slowing down to 58 MPH...
  Slowing down to 57 MPH...
  Slowing down to 56 MPH...
  Slowing down to 55 MPH...
  Now I'm driving 55 MPH because the speed limit changed to 55 MPH from 65 MPH

  Prepare to change speed to 70 MPH
  Speeding up to 56 MPH...
  Speeding up to 57 MPH...
  Speeding up to 58 MPH...
  Speeding up to 59 MPH...
  Speeding up to 60 MPH...
  Speeding up to 61 MPH...
  Speeding up to 62 MPH...
  Speeding up to 63 MPH...
  Speeding up to 64 MPH...
  Speeding up to 65 MPH...
  Speeding up to 66 MPH...
  Speeding up to 67 MPH...
  Speeding up to 68 MPH...
  Speeding up to 69 MPH...
  Speeding up to 70 MPH...
  Now I'm driving 70 MPH because the speed limit changed to 70 MPH from 55 MPH
```

FIGURE 14.2
The Assistant Editor console output for the speed limit example in Listing 14.5.

Inheriting and Overriding Accessors

Not only can you create custom accessors in your class, but you can override them in any subclass. If you create a subclass, any source properties can be overridden in the subclass, whether stored or computed. As we saw in Hour 11, "Implementing Class Inheritance," to access anything in the superclass, you use the `super` keyword, followed by the name of the property or method.

Because Swift only needs to know the name of the property and its type, it doesn't care whether the property you are overriding is stored or computed; you can create your own computed version in your subclass. If a property is read-only in the superclass, you can make the property read-write in the subclass, but you cannot make a read-write property in the superclass a read-only property in your subclass.

NOTE

Preventing Override

Remember from Hour 11 that to prevent a property from being overridden in a subclass, you must prefix the definition in the superclass with the `final` keyword.

Overriding accessors only applies to classes and not structs or enums. This is because it requires you to inherit from another class, and structs and enums cannot inherit from other structs and enums.

Let's work through overriding a property in the following Try It Yourself example.

▼ TRY IT YOURSELF

Override a Property and Create Custom Accessors

Inherit a class called `Square` from a base class called `Shape`, and override the `area` property on the superclass with a custom getter and setter relative to the area of a square.

1. Open Xcode 6 and create a new playground, either a Mac or an iOS playground will work. Clear the content of the playground.

2. Because we need the square root function, import the Foundation framework at the top of the playground.

   ```
   import Foundation
   ```

3. Create the base class, called `Shape`, with a property named `area`, assigned to 0.0.

   ```
   class Shape {
       var area = 0.0
   }
   ```

4. Create the subclass, called `Square`, and provide a `length` property of type `Double`. Add an initializer that takes a length parameter of type `Double` and assigns it to our `length` property.

   ```
   class Square: Shape {
       var length: Double
       init(length: Double) {
           self.length = length
       }
   }
   ```

5. Override the `area` property and provide both a getter and setter. Use the default `newValue` keyword in the setter to access the value assigned to the `area` property. Place the overridden property after the `length` property, before the `init` method, to keep the properties all together.

```
override var area: Double {
    get {
        return length * length
    }
    set {
        length = sqrt(newValue)
    }
}
```

6. That's all for the `Square` subclass. After the closing curly brace, create a constant of type `Shape` and check its `area` property's value.

```
let shape = Shape()
shape.area              // displays 0.0
```

7. Create a constant of type `Square` with an initial length of 10. Check the `area` property to get its value; then set the value to 49 and check the length.

```
let square = Square(length: 10)
square.area                     // displays 100.0
square.area = 49
square.length                   // displays 7.0
```

After completing the preceding Try It Yourself example, your code and results should look like those in Figure 14.3.

Inheriting and Overriding Observers

You can also override property observers in Swift, and the process is similar to the process of overriding a property. Supply `willSet` and/or `didSet` closures to your inherited property definition, and the structure is exactly the same as the `speedLimit` property in Listing 14.5; just add the `override` keyword in front of the property definition.

If you are overriding the custom getter and setter already, there is no need to provide `willSet` and `didSet` implementations; you can perform the desired actions inside your setter. You also cannot provide custom observers to inherited constant stored properties or to inherited read-only computed properties.

```
● ● ●                  ⬛ Ch14 Override Accessor TIY.playground
⊞  <  >  ⬛ Ch14 Override Accessor TIY.playground ⟩ No Selection
 1   import Foundation
 2
 3   class Shape {
 4       var area = 0.0
 5   }
 6
 7   class Square: Shape {
 8       var length: Double
 9       override var area: Double {
10           get {
11               return length * length              100.0
12           }
13           set {
14               length = sqrt(newValue)             {{area 0.0} length 7.0}
15           }
16       }
17       init(length: Double) {
18           self.length = length
19       }
20   }
21
22   let shape = Shape()                             {area 0.0}
23   shape.area                                      0.0
24
25   let square = Square(length: 10)                {{area 0.0} length 10.0}
26   square.area                                     100.0
27   square.area = 49                               {{area 0.0} length 7.0}
28   square.length                                   7.0
29
```

FIGURE 14.3
The completed Try It Yourself example code and results for overriding a property with custom accessors.

Listing 14.6 illustrates overriding a property that has property observers in it and adding additional property observers in the subclass. When a subclass and its superclass both provide property observers for a property, both observers are called in a chaining fashion much like how initialization occurs; the subclass's `willSet` observer is called and then the superclass's `willSet` observer is called. The property value gets changed, since technically it exists in the superclass. Then the superclass's `didSet` observer is called and then back down the chain the subclass's `didSet` observer is called. It is important to understand this concept so you understand what is happening to properties and you know where to look if you are noticing unexpected behavior when customizing a subclass's property observers.

Extra `println(...)` have been added to the `Vehicle` class to give you visual feedback in the console when different observers are called. If you are following along in your own playground, you can use either a Mac or an iOS playground.

LISTING 14.6 Overriding Property Observers

```
01:  class Vehicle {
02:      var speed: Int
03:      var speedLimit: Int {
04:          willSet {
```

```
05:                  println("willSet for Vehicle. Preparing to change speed
➡ to \(newValue) MPH")
06:              }
07:          didSet {
08:              println("didSet for Vehicle.")
09:              var changeSpeed: () -> () = (speed > speedLimit) ? slowdown
➡ : speedup
10:              while speed != speedLimit {
11:                  println("Increasing by 1")
12:                  changeSpeed()
13:              }
14:              println("Now I'm driving \(speed) MPH because the speed limit
➡ changed to \(speedLimit) MPH from \(oldValue) MPH\n")
15:          }
16:      }
17:      init(speedLimit: Int, speed: Int) {...}  // init unchanged from
➡ Listing 14.5
18:      func speedup() {...}                     // speedup unchanged from
➡ Listing 14.5
19:      func slowdown() {...}                    // slowdown unchanged from
➡ Listing 14.5
20: }
21:
22: class Porsche : Vehicle {
23:      override var speedLimit: Int {
24:          willSet {
25:              println("willSet for Porsche.")
26:          }
27:          didSet {
28:              println("didSet for Porsche.")
29:              var changeSpeed: () -> () = (speed > speedLimit) ? slowdown
➡ : speedup
30:              let porscheSpeedLimit = speedLimit + 10
31:              while speed != porscheSpeedLimit {
32:                  println("Increasing by 2 because Porsches are fast.")
33:                  changeSpeed()
34:                  changeSpeed()
35:              }
36:              println("Porsches should always go faster than the speed limit")
37:          }
38:      }
39: }
40:
41: let porsche = Porsche(speedLimit: 65, speed: 65)
42: porsche.speedLimit = 70
43: porsche.speed              // displays 80
```

As you can see in the preceding example, our `Porsche` instance increases its speed by 2 on lines 33 and 34. It doesn't happen only by 2, because the superclass's `didSet` observer increments by 1. You need to be aware of this behavior. The `Porsche` instance also adds 10 to the suggested speed limit, because who wants to drive the speed limit in a Porsche? On line 30 we create the temporary constant of a new speed limit, because if we simply set our own `speedLimit` property to `speedLimit += 10`, it would recursively call its property observer infinitely, because setting the value each time would call its own property observers. Finally, we can see the results in the console output in the Assistant Editor by pressing Command+Option+Return. Figure 14.4 shows the console output for the preceding example.

```
×                        Console Output
Speed limit is 65 MPH, I'm driving 65 MPH
willSet for Porsche.
willSet for Vehicle. Prepare to change speed to 70 MPH
didSet for Vehicle.
Increasing by 1
Speeding up to 66 MPH...
Increasing by 1
Speeding up to 67 MPH...
Increasing by 1
Speeding up to 68 MPH...
Increasing by 1
Speeding up to 69 MPH...
Increasing by 1
Speeding up to 70 MPH...
Now I'm driving 70 MPH because the speed limit changed to 70 MPH from
65 MPH

didSet for Porsche.
Increasing by 2 because Porsches are fast
Speeding up to 71 MPH...
Speeding up to 72 MPH...
Increasing by 2 because Porsches are fast
Speeding up to 73 MPH...
Speeding up to 74 MPH...
Increasing by 2 because Porsches are fast
Speeding up to 75 MPH...
Speeding up to 76 MPH...
Increasing by 2 because Porsches are fast
Speeding up to 77 MPH...
Speeding up to 78 MPH...
Increasing by 2 because Porsches are fast
Speeding up to 79 MPH...
Speeding up to 80 MPH...
Porsches should always go faster than the speed limit.
```

FIGURE 14.4
The Assistant Editor console output for the Porsche example in Listing 14.6.

Summary

Properties are powerful and flexible constructs in Swift. In this hour you learned how to define properties with or without initial values, declare lazy properties, and create computed properties. You also learned how to customize behavior when a property is set by creating custom accessors, called getters and setters, as well as observing value changes by providing custom actions before and after a property changes.

Finally, you learned how to override properties, both stored and computed, as well as override observers and the effective chain of observation when a subclass instance's value changes.

In the next hour, we discuss adding type properties and type methods that can function without an instance of a type. We also cover subscripts and more.

Q&A

Q. When would I want to use a lazy property?

A. Lazy properties are useful when you want to delay the calculation or retrieval of a property. Suppose our class provides access to movie reviews from five different sources, but we aren't sure ahead of time whether the user will request all five reviews. Loading them all ahead of time might result in extra network traffic that we didn't actually need. It would be better in this case to only load the information when the user actually requests it and avoid the extra traffic.

Q. If I write my own accessors, when do I have to provide both set and get?

A. If you only provide a get accessor, your computed property is read-only. The only time you have to provide a set is if you are overriding a mutable property. When the property you override is read-write, your overridden property must also be read-write.

Q. Why would I want to explicitly name parameters in my accessors instead of using the default names provided by Swift?

A. Naming your parameters makes your code more readable. It may save you a few keystrokes to use the default names, but if it makes it easier for you to understand the flow of your program, it's worth the extra typing. You'll find that you spend much more time getting the logic of your program correct than you do actually typing code, and the extra keystrokes are a small price to pay for more clarity.

Q. How are `willSet` and `didSet` different?

A. Property observer `willSet` is called before your property changes and has a default parameter named `newValue`, where `didSet` is called after your property has been changed and has a default parameter named `oldValue`.

Workshop

The workshop contains quiz questions and exercises to help you solidify your understanding of the material covered. Try to answer all questions before looking at the answers that follow.

Quiz

1. Can constant stored properties be lazy?

2. Of classes, enums, and structs, which can have computed properties?

3. What's wrong with the following code?

```
class QuizClass {
  var xVal: Int = 1
  var x: Int {
    set { xVal = newValue }
  }
}
```

4. If you don't explicitly assign a name to the argument in a setter, what variable name is used by default?

Answers

1. No. All constant properties must have a value assigned at the end of initialization.

2. Classes, enums, and structs can all have computed properties, but only classes and structs can have stored properties.

3. `QuizClass.x` has a setter, but no getter. If a computed property provides a setter, it must also provide a getter.

4. By default, the parameter is named `newValue`.

Exercise

Create a new OS X playground. Create a `Triangle` class with properties to store the length of each side. If you did last hour's exercise, you can use the class you constructed there. Next, add a read-only computed property named `isEquilateral` that checks to see whether all three sides are the same length and returns true if they are and false if they are not.

Next, add observers so that if the length of a side changes and the triangle becomes equilateral, a message is printed to the console.

Add similar read-only properties to check for scalene (all three sides are different lengths) and isosceles (at least two sides have the same length), and then update your observers to watch for these new triangle types.

Adding Advanced Type Functionality

What You'll Learn in This Hour:

▶ How to use type properties and type methods

▶ How to create type aliases

▶ How to create custom subscripts

▶ What is the significance of `Any` and `AnyObject`

▶ How to cast and downcast types

We have discussed types at length over the past several hours, and there are a few smaller but important concepts to combine in this hour. We cover type properties and methods, type aliases, subscripts, and casting types up or down. After this hour is complete, you should feel comfortable in your understanding of types and how important all the different components of types are.

Type Properties and Methods

Let's start this hour with discussing **type properties** and **type methods**. Type properties and methods belong to the type itself, rather than an instance of that type and can be applicable to all instances of that type.

Type Properties

Properties can belong to a type, and not necessarily an instance of a type. The syntax for type properties differs slightly between reference types and value types. Classes prefix a type property with the `class` keyword, while structs and enums prefix a type property with the `static` keyword.

CAUTION

Class Properties Are Not Yet Supported

At the time of this writing, class properties are not yet supported. Trying to create one will result in a compiler error. We suspect they should be supported in a future release of the language.

Type properties are useful when you want to declare a property that has a value applicable to all instances of a type. For instance, a `Square` struct may have a static property named `numberOfSides`, which is equal to 4, since there will never be greater than or less than four sides to a square. Type properties are also useful if you have a maximum or minimum bound that all instances should not cross, such as music volume levels, bowling scores, and so on.

Type properties can come as stored properties or computed properties, and type computed properties can be read-only or read-write. Type properties can be overridden by subclasses, much like you saw in Hour 14, "Digging Deeper with Properties."

Listing 15.1 illustrates how to use a type property in a struct. The syntax would be identical if we defined a type property inside an enum.

LISTING 15.1 Type Properties in Structs

```
struct Square {
    static let numberOfSides = 4
}
let sides = Square.numberOfSides
sides      // displays 4
```

Listing 15.1 shows how to use a static constant in a struct to get access to the value, even without creating an instance of `Square`. You can integrate type properties and instance properties to be used in an instance of the type, but you cannot access instance properties from a type or any type properties or methods. Take a look at Listing 15.2 for an example that builds on Listing 15.1, where an instance property accesses a static property.

LISTING 15.2 Accessing Type Properties from Instance Properties

```
01:  struct Square {
02:      static let numberOfSides = 4
03:      var length: Int
04:      var area: Int {
05:          return Square.numberOfSides * length
06:      }
07:  }
08:
09:  let square = Square(length: 4)
10:  square.area                        // displays 16
```

As you can see on line 5 of the preceding example, to access the type property from within an instance property or method, use the `TypeName.typeProperty` style syntax.

Type Methods

The structure, syntax, and concept of type methods are not too dissimilar from those of type properties. Type methods, of course, are methods and not properties, but the syntax is the same; prefix the definition of a type method with the `class` keyword for a class method or the `static` keyword for a struct or enum. As of the time of this writing, class methods are supported, whereas class properties are not yet.

A conventional use for type methods is to return an initialized default instance of a particular type, often referred to as a **factory method**. This is common in Apple's Cocoa and Cocoa Touch frameworks. Using type methods for this is useful in that it not only reduces a few lines of code to one single line, but another benefit is that you get returned a properly structured instance of that type.

In type methods, you can use the `self` keyword to reference the type itself. This is in contrast to using the `self` keyword inside an instance method, computed property, or initializer, where the `self` keyword refers to the instance itself. Another feature of class methods is that you do not need to qualify calling another class method from within a class method with the `TypeName.classMethodName()` syntax. Rather, you can simply call `classMethodName()` directly.

Take a look at Listing 15.3. In it, we declare a class named `AClass`, with two class methods and an instance method. If you're following along, either a Mac or an iOS playground will do. Once you finish, press Command+Option+Return to view the console output in the Assistant Editor to verify your results.

LISTING 15.3   A Class with Class and Instance Methods

```
01:  class AClass {
02:      class func aClassMethod() {
03:          println("I am a class method")
04:      }
05:      class func bClassMethod() {
06:          aClassMethod()
07:      }
08:      func anInstanceMethod() {
09:          println("anInstanceMethod. Calling bClassMethod().")
10:          AClass.bClassMethod()
11:      }
12:  }
13:
14:  AClass.aClassMethod()          // displays "I am a class method"
15:
```

```
16:   let aClass = AClass()
17:   aClass.anInstanceMethod()      // displays "anInstanceMethod. Calling
➥bClassMethod()."
                                     //          "I am a class method"
```

Listing 15.3 shows several points to discuss. There are two class methods, defined on lines 2 and 5, and one instance method defined on line 8. Class methods can be called from outside the class by using the `TypeName.classMethodName()` format, such as on line 14, or from within a class, too. If called from within a class definition, instance methods must call a class method by prefixing the type name and using dot syntax. A class method, though, may call another class method directly any of three different ways:

▶ Without qualifying the type name, as seen on line 6

▶ By using `AClass.aClassMethod()`

▶ By using the `self` keyword with `self.aClassMethod()`

Type methods can alter type properties. Even though type properties do not belong to an instance directly, they can hold state information of a class, struct, or enum. Listing 15.4 illustrates having a static property on a struct and having a static method modifying the static property.

LISTING 15.4   Modifying Type Properties with Type Methods

```
struct Counter {
    static var count = 0
    static func increaseCountByOne() {
        ++count
    }
}

Counter.count                  // displays 0
Counter.increaseCountByOne()
Counter.count                  // displays 1
```

Let's solidify your knowledge of type properties and type methods in this next Try It Yourself section.

▼ TRY IT YOURSELF

Use Type Properties and Type Methods

Create a struct that controls audio volume. Use static properties to set upper and lower volume limits that every instance must adhere to.

1. Open Xcode 6 and create a new playground. Either Mac or iOS will work. Clear the contents of the playground.

2. Create a struct named `Volume` and initially give it two static constant properties: one named `minVolume` set to 0 and one named `maxVolume` set to 20.

```
struct Volume {
    static let minVolume = 0
    static let maxVolume = 20
}
```

3. Create a stored variable property named `volume`, an `Int` set to 0, with an observer after the value has been set to ensure it is not above the max or below the min volume levels. Place this after the two static constant definitions, inside the struct.

```
var volume: Int = 0 {
    didSet {
        if volume > Volume.maxVolume || volume < Volume.minVolume {
            volume = oldValue
        }
    }
}
```

4. Now that we have property validation happening inside the `didSet` property observer, and our `volume` property will never go above `maxVolume` or below `minVolume`, we can set simple methods for increasing or decreasing the `volume` property. Create one for each.

```
mutating func turnItUp() {
    ++volume
}
mutating func turnItDown() {
    --volume
}
```

5. That's all for the struct. Create a new variable instance of the `Volume` struct. Set the `volume` property to 1. Then turn it down to ensure we can adjust our volume properly.

```
var volume = Volume()
volume.volume = 1
volume.turnItDown()
volume.volume          // displays 0
```

6. Call the `turnItDown()` method again on the `volume` instance and ensure the `volume` property remains at 0 and does not equal -1.

```
volume.turnItDown()
volume.volume          // volume.volume should equal 0
```

7. Do the same to test turning up the volume. Set `volume` to 19 and then turn it up. Check to ensure the volume did go up. Then turn it up once more. Did the value change?

```
volume.volume = 19
volume.turnItUp()
volume.volume              // volume.volume should equal 20
volume.turnItUp()
volume.volume              // volume.volume should still equal 20
```

8. Because our struct enables our `volume` property to be set directly, any other part of an app this struct belongs to could set the `volume` value without using `turnItUp()` or `turnItDown()`. But we safeguarded our value with the `didSet` observer. Set `volume` directly to 30 to ensure that the actual stored value does not go above the maximum allowed.

```
volume.volume = 30
volume.volume              // volume.volume should equal 20
```

The completed Try It Yourself example code and results should look like those in Figure 15.1.

```
●  ●  ●            Ch15 Type Audio Volume TIY.playground

⊞  <  >  | Ch15 Type Audio Volume TIY.playground ⟩ C Volume

 1   struct Volume {
 2       static let minVolume = 0
 3       static let maxVolume = 20
 4
 5       var volume: Int = 0 {
 6           didSet {
 7               if volume > Volume.maxVolume || volume < Volume.
                     minVolume {
 8                   volume = oldValue                              (3 times)
 9               }
10           }
11       }
12
13       mutating func turnItUp() {
14           ++volume                                              (2 times)
15       }
16       mutating func turnItDown() {
17           --volume                                              (2 times)
18       }
19   }
20
21   var volume = Volume()                                         {volume 0}
22   volume.volume = 1
23   volume.turnItDown()
24   volume.volume                                                 0
25   volume.turnItDown()
26   volume.volume                                                 0
27   volume.volume = 19
28   volume.turnItUp()
29   volume.volume                                                 20
30   volume.turnItUp()
31   volume.volume                                                 20
32   volume.volume = 30
33   volume.volume                                                 20
34
```

FIGURE 15.1
The completed Try It Yourself example of using type methods and properties.

Type Aliasing

Swift has a concept called **type aliasing**, which means that you can create an alias to an existing type with whatever name you choose. This enables you to use your custom type in a more meaningful manner in your code to provide a clearer intent than with a more generic type name or to provide a shorter name for perhaps something such as a really long type name.

In its simplest form, you use the `typealias` keyword, followed by the alias you choose, and use the assignment operator (=), and then the type for which you want to create an alias. In the `Volume` example from the preceding Try It Yourself section, it might have provided a clearer intent if we had set a type alias called `VolumeLevel` equal to `Int`. Even though the term `VolumeLevel` is longer than using `Int`, it is clearer to anyone reading your code what type the `volume` property is. Listing 15.5 shows how we could do that.

LISTING 15.5   Using Type Aliasing

```
typealias VolumeLevel = Int
var volume: VolumeLevel = 0
```

Type aliasing can also be used to better document the type of a function. Sometimes when you are reading through code, function syntax can get a little difficult to decipher. This is where type aliasing can shine. Let's alias a function type and use it in a function parameter in Listing 15.6. Suppose we have a function that receives a function for a completion handler to be executed once our function has finished performing a long process. Our function has one parameter, which is our completion handler, and it is of the type we alias.

LISTING 15.6   Using Type Alias with Functions

```
typealias ArrayCompletion = ([Int]?) -> ()

func downloadLotsOfData(completion: ArrayCompletion) {
    var someData: [Int]?
    // download lots of data
    completion(someData)  // execute the completion handler
}
```

As you can see, type aliasing can be beneficial for maintaining readable and understandable code. Once you know the type that the alias really is, you can read your code more easily like a sentence.

Type Access Control

Access control provides some security around the visibility of certain properties, methods, initializers, or subscripts in classes, structs, and enums. There are three levels of access you can apply to properties, methods, and subscripts in your code: **public**, **private**, and **internal**.

Public access enables your properties, methods, or subscripts to be accessed and used from anywhere within the module that defines them, or from any external module that imports the module in which the public entity is defined. Public access is often used for elements you want to be visible in the public-facing interface of a framework, as it is the least restrictive. Public access is defined by prefixing the property, method, or subscript with the `public` keyword. The following code snippet illustrates how to declare a property as public.

```
class MyClass {
    public myVar: String = "Hello"
}
```

Private access, denoted with the `private` keyword, restricts visibility to your properties, methods, initializers, or subscripts to only your class, struct, or enum *file*. This means that you can hide implementation from being accessible by other source files in the module or target. This is often used when you declare a helper method that may help a current method with some sort of calculation but shouldn't be visible to instances of that type to use. The following code snippet illustrates how to declare a method as private. Note that if you try this in a playground, you can use `helperMethod()` from an instance, because it is within the same source file.

```
class MyClass {
    private func helperMethod() -> Int {
    // do some calculation and return an Int
    }
    func needSomeHelp() -> String {
        // Doing something, but I need some help
        var myInt = helperMethod()
        return "\(myInt)"
    }
}
```

Internal access, denoted with the optional `internal` keyword, restricts access to any property, method, initializer, or subscript inside a source file to only other source files within the current module. The internal keyword is optional because this level of access is the default if no access modifier is declared. For many projects, you may only have one module, so internal access means that any source file elements can access the element declared as internal. All properties, methods, initializers, and subscripts we have used until now have been internal, because we have not declared them to be either public or private, and Swift inferred them to be internal.

Not only can properties, methods, initializers, and subscripts be made public, private, or internal, but so can classes, structs, and enums themselves. The same rules and syntax apply to types as they do to elements inside a type and use the same three access keywords.

Subscripts

Most programming languages provide a way to access elements in an array or dictionary, including Swift, by using something called **subscripts**. A subscript is shorthand for directly accessing or modifying an element at a particular index in an array, dictionary, or collection.

Throughout this book, we have used subscripts, and the concept should be familiar to you by now. Writing `anArray[3]` would return the fourth element in an array, and writing `aDictionary["username"]` would return the value for the "username" key. Likewise, you can use subscripts to modify elements at an index of an array or add or modify elements at a particular key in a dictionary.

Swift enables you to create your own subscripts for any class, struct, or enum you create. This can be useful when you want to create a custom grid, such as for a board game, a quick way to perform a calculation through a particular mathematic equation, or whatever functionality your app needs. The syntax for creating a subscript in Swift is almost identical to defining an instance method or computed property. The only difference is that you use the `subscript` keyword rather than the `func` keyword, and subscripts do not have names. Subscripts take parameters with names and types, and even return a value or values with provided type or types. As with instance methods, subscripts can also receive variadic parameters.

Listing 15.7 illustrates how we can create a subscript to calculate the power of a given number. If we know that we want to cube any number that comes to us, we can create a subscript that returns any number we provide to the power of three. Creating a subscript for this purpose gives the impression of behaving like a pre-populated array of cubes, just without needing to store the actual values.

LISTING 15.7 Creating a Subscript to Cube a Number

```
01:   struct CubeANum {
02:       subscript(num: Int) -> Int {
03:           return num * num * num
04:       }
05:   }
06:
07:   let cubeANum = CubeANum()
08:   cubeANum[2]          // displays 8
09:   cubeANum[5]          // displays 125
```

In Listing 15.7, we declare the subscript on line 2, taking only one parameter of type Int and returning an Int. Like a computed property, there is an implicit getter, since we are only writing a read-only subscript.

Let's do an example together in the following Try It Yourself section. Suppose the user of your app is a second grade teacher, and he has assigned his class of six students to write a paragraph about their favorite topic. Because the teacher is busy, he can only grade three papers at a time from the stack of papers. Let's create an example of using subscripting to retrieve a particular number of papers from the stack at a time, rather than one at a time. If you are unfamiliar with stacks in computer programming terms, stacks are **LIFO** (last-in-first-out), meaning you can only remove the top item. You **push** items onto a stack to add, and **pop** them off to remove, one at a time.

▼ TRY IT YOURSELF

Use Subscripts to Help a Teacher Grade Papers Faster

Create a stack of papers and use subscripts to allow the teacher to get three or any number of papers at a time.

1. Open Xcode 6 and create a new playground. Either Mac or iOS playground will work. Clear the contents of the playground, as we will not need it.

2. Create a struct named Paper to store each student's paper. To keep the example brief, only create student and topic properties, constants of type String.

```
struct Paper {
    let student: String
    let topic: String
}
```

3. Create a class named StackOfPapers. Create a variable array of type [Paper] and initialize it to an empty array.

```
class StackOfPapers {
    var papers = [Paper]()
}
```

4. Inside the StackOfPapers class, after the papers definition, create a method named push that takes an item of type Paper and adds it to the papers array.

```
func push(paper: Paper) {
    papers.append(paper)
}
```

5. After the `push` method, create a method named `pop` that takes no parameters but returns an item of type `Paper` that it removed from the end of the `papers` array.

```
func pop() -> Paper {
    return papers.removeLast()
}
```

6. Create the `subscript` method inside the `StackOfPapers` class after the `pop()` method that takes a parameter of type `Int` and returns an array of type `[Paper]`.

```
subscript(number: Int) -> [Paper] {
    var tempPapers = [Paper]()
    for _ in 0..<number {
        tempPapers.append(self.pop())
    }
    return tempPapers
}
```

7. Create a computed property below the subscript named `count` so we can easily see how many papers are left to grade.

```
var count: Int {
    return papers.count
}
```

8. That's all for the stack. Declare an instance of `StackOfPapers` and add six students and their topics to the stack.

```
let stack = StackOfPapers()
stack.push(Paper(student: "Susie", topic: "Sea Creatures"))
stack.push(Paper(student: "Bobby", topic: "Music"))
stack.push(Paper(student: "Madeline", topic: "Jungle Cats"))
stack.push(Paper(student: "Blake", topic: "Soccer"))
stack.push(Paper(student: "Cole", topic: "Bicycling"))
stack.push(Paper(student: "Marion", topic: "Boating"))
```

9. Call our `count` computed property to ensure there are six papers in the stack. Then grab the top three papers to be graded.

```
stack.count       // should equal 6
stack[3]          // should display three students and topics,
➥in reverse order
```

10. Call our `count` property again, to ensure there are three papers left. Grab the next stack of papers to be graded.

```
stack.count       // should equal 3
stack[3]          // should display three more students and topics
```

11. Call our `count` property once more, to ensure it is now 0.

Upon completion, the code and results from the preceding Try It Yourself example should look like those in Figure 15.2.

FIGURE 15.2
The completed Try It Yourself section creating a stack with subscripts for grading papers.

Subscript Overloading

Suppose we not only want to return the cubed value of integers but also of floating-point numbers. We can overload subscripts, just like we did with functions in Hour 8, "Using Functions to Perform Actions," with different parameters. Taking the cube example from Listing 15.7, let's re-implement the structure with another subscript that takes a parameter of type `Double` (see Listing 15.8).

LISTING 15.8 Overloading Subscripts

```
01:  struct CubeANum {
02:      subscript(num: Int) -> Int {
03:          return num * num * num
04:      }
05:      subscript(num: Double) -> Double {
06:          return num * num * num
07:      }
08:  }
09:
10:  let cubeANum = CubeANum()
11:  cubeANum[2.5]              // displays 15.625
12:  cubeANum[2]               // displays 8
```

Listing 15.8 has two subscripts now: one that takes an Int and returns an Int, and another that takes a Double and returns a Double. On line 11 we call the subscript that takes a Double and returns a Double on line 5, because we provided a value of type Double inside the subscript, and the results pane displays 15.625. On line 12, we call the subscript that takes an Int and returns an Int, because we provided a value of type Int inside the subscript. The results pane displays 8, not 8.0, so we can easily see that the proper overloaded subscript was called.

NOTE

Don't Repeat Yourself

The Listing 15.8 is functional, but repeating code like that is a sign of poor implementation. These two subscripts do exactly the same thing; they return the parameter provided to the third power. There is a much more succinct and reusable way to express this—by using generics. You learn about generics in Hour 20, "Introducing Generics."

Overriding Subscripts

Subscripts can be overridden as well in a subclass that inherits from a superclass that contains a subscript. The same rules of overriding apply as discussed in previous hours in this book. All you must do is provide the override keyword in front of your subscript definition in the subclass. Remember, this can only be done from classes, because structs and enums do not inherit from any other type.

Type Casting and Non-Specific Types

The term **type casting** refers to treating an instance of a particular type as if it were of a different type in its own hierarchy temporarily. Type casting does not actually change the type of the value, since once a value's type is set, Swift does not allow it to be changed for safety reasons.

Determining an Instance's Type

Swift provides an operator called the **type check operator**, denoted with the is keyword. Using this operator enables you to determine whether an instance *is* of a particular type or subclass type. If you are an Objective-C programmer, you may be familiar with this concept from using the isMemberOfClass: and isKindOfClass: methods.

Suppose you have a room full of marching band instruments, and you want to organize and track them. It would be great to know the name of the instrument, the type (brass, woodwind, and so on), and how many keys or valves it has. We could store these items in an array. But arrays in Swift must have an explicit type, and clarinets have traits that trumpets don't, and vice-versa. How can we do this?

Each item has a common trait; it has a name. Take a look at Listing 15.9 for how to build this by creating a common superclass that both Woodwind and Brass inherit from and adding them to an array. If you are a percussionist or like any other type of instrument better, feel free to substitute to suit your style.

LISTING 15.9   **Determining Type of Marching Instruments**

```
class Instrument {
    var name: String
    init(name: String) {
        self.name = name
    }
}

class Brass: Instrument {
    let valves: Int
    init(name: String, valves: Int) {
        self.valves = valves
        super.init(name: name)
    }
}

class Woodwind: Instrument {
    let keys: Int
    init(name: String, keys: Int) {
        self.keys = keys
        super.init(name: name)
    }
}

let marchingInstruments = [
    Brass(name: "Trumpet", valves: 3),
    Brass(name: "Trombone", valves: 0),
    Woodwind(name: "Clarinet", keys: 18),
    Woodwind(name: "Alto Sax", keys: 22),
    Brass(name: "Piccolo Trumpet", valves: 4)
]

var brassCount = 0, woodwindCount = 0

for instrument in marchingInstruments {
    if instrument is Brass {
        ++brassCount
    } else if instrument is Woodwind {
        ++woodwindCount
```

```
        }
    }

brassCount        // displays 3
woodwindCount     // displays 2
```

Inside the for-in loop in Listing 15.9 is where we use the type checking operator (`is`). This is sometimes referred to as **introspection**. By checking the type of each instrument, we can come up with how many of each type of instrument is in our room.

Downcasting

Instances in Swift may be of one type, but under the hood they may actually be of a subclass of that type. For instance, if we have a function that takes a parameter of type `Instrument`, and we pass an argument of type `Brass`, the parameter inside the function knows the variable is of type `Instrument`, but under the hood it is really a `Brass` instance. We can find this out by using the **type cast operator**, denoted with the `as` keyword.

The `as` keyword can be used in one of two ways: first, by just using the `as` keyword, or second, by using the optional type cast syntax, `as?`. When using the `as` keyword, you are literally forcing the cast, which may fail if the type you are checking is not in the class hierarchy of the instance's type. In situations where you aren't sure whether downcasting will succeed, use the operational type cast operator, which returns nil wrapped in an optional value. This means that you can check for successful downcasting and unwrapping with `if let` syntax.

Continuing with the preceding marching instrument example, Listing 15.10 illustrates how we could use type casting in a function to extract type-specific information from the parameter passed in. This is a continuation of Listing 15.9, if you are following along. Place the following code at the end of your playground.

LISTING 15.10 Type Casting

```
func displayInstrumentInfo(instrument: Instrument) {
    if let brass = instrument as? Brass {
        println("Brass: \(brass.name). Valves: \(brass.valves)")
    } else if let woodwind = instrument as? Woodwind {
        println("Woodwind: \(woodwind.name). Keys: \(woodwind.keys)")
    }
}

displayInstrumentInfo(marchingInstruments[0])   // displays "Brass:
➥Trumpet. Valves: 3"
displayInstrumentInfo(marchingInstruments[2])   // displays "Woodwind: Clarinet.
➥Keys: 18"
```

In Listing 15.10, we use the `as?` operator, because we cannot always be sure that we will know whether we received a `Brass` or `Woodwind` instance, or even `Percussion` if we had implemented that.

Using the `as` keyword without the `?` character forcibly downcasts the type in question. As mentioned earlier, this may fail, so only use this operator when you are sure your downcasting will succeed. Many times, the documentation for an API states that a particular type is used, or your code may be structured well enough for the needs of your app, so you can confidently downcast with the `as` keyword.

Non-Specific Types

Type casting can be useful when working with Cocoa APIs, because much of the framework is built to use a generic type called **id**. id is a pointer to any type of object. This works well in Objective-C, because Objective-C is not a **strongly-typed** language, meaning it does not have to explicitly state what type an object should be at compile time.

To work with the Cocoa and Cocoa Touch frameworks when dealing with type id, Swift provides the **Any** and **AnyObject** keywords for non-specific types. The Any keyword refers to an instance of any type, not including function types. The AnyObject keyword refers to an instance of any class type.

When working with JSON (JavaScript Object Notation), you may not always know what each value's type for each key is, so typically JSON either is stored as AnyObject or needs to be casted to AnyObject first before being downcasted to an array, dictionary, or any other type.

CAUTION

`Any` and `AnyObject` Are Not Superclasses

AnyObject is not a superclass. AnyObject represents an instance of any class type. Likewise, Any is not a superclass either. Any represents an instance of any type, whether class, struct, or enum, but not function types. You can use Any and AnyObject without any interaction with the Cocoa frameworks, but you often use them when working with Cocoa due to the widespread use of id in Cocoa.

For instance, you could declare an array of type `[Any]` and append values such as 3.14, 7, "car", and so on. You could also declare an array of type `[AnyObject]` and append values such as instances of `Instrument`, `Brass`, `Woodwind`, or even `Square` and `Circle` from examples in previous hours. Be careful when doing this, because this removes Swift's capability to ensure type safety. It is highly suggested that you always downcast when possible to use a safe type.

Summary

This hour contained a lot of information pertaining to types with respect to the additional capabilities enabled in Swift. You learned about type properties and methods, which enable you to access functionality and stored data appropriate for all instances of a type. You also learned about type aliasing, enabling you to create more succinct and readable code, while simplifying the actual writing of code.

Next you learned about access control and how to determine which source files should have what level of access to your classes, enums, and structs, and even the properties, methods, initializers, and subscripts of those types, too.

Then you learned about subscripts and how you can leverage their shorthand syntax to access property values inside your types easily. Subscripts can be overloaded and even overridden.

Finally you learned about type casting, type checking, downcasting, and how Swift handles non-specific types with the `Any` and `AnyObject` keywords.

In the next hour, we discuss memory management in Swift. You learn how Swift manages memory and how to manage different reference types.

Q&A

Q. How are type properties and instance properties different?

A. Each instance of a type has its own set of instance properties, but all instances of a type share the same set of type properties. For example, if you create an `Employee` class, each `Employee` has his or her own name. Changing one person's name should not change the name of any other person in the system, so name should be an instance variable. But suppose we want our `Employee` class to know how many employees there currently are. Then we might create a static property named `employeeCount` and increase it by one each time someone joins our company and decrease it by one whenever someone leaves our company. Because there is only one `employeeCount` shared by all employees, we only have to update our count in one place.

Q. Do I set a value for stored type properties in `init()` like I do with stored instance properties?

A. Remember that `init()` is called when a new instance of a type is created, but type properties exist before we create the first instance of a given type. This means that unlike stored instance properties, you must always assign a default value to stored type properties. You can still update or change the value of a type property at initialization, but you don't have to.

Q. Can type methods access instance properties?

A. No, they can't. Type methods are not called using an instance of the type, so it would be unclear which instance variables should be used. Additionally, because a type method can be called before any instance is instantiated, there is no guarantee that any instance property will have a value.

Q. If no access level is specified, which level is used by default?

A. Generally, the internal access level is specified. There are a few specific exceptions to this rule, but they are beyond the scope of this book. Refer to Apple's documentation for more information.

Workshop

The workshop contains quiz questions and exercises to help you solidify your understanding of the material covered. Try to answer all questions before looking at the answers that follow.

Quiz

1. Can a type property be computed, or does it have to be stored?

2. Can you define a type with multidimensional subscripts in Swift?

3. What's wrong with the following code?

```
let myArray:[Any] = [1,2,3,4,5]
let myOtherArray = [1,2,3,4,5]
let x = myOtherArray[1] + myArray[2]
```

4. What keywords do you use to define a type parameter for a struct, an enum, and for a class?

Answers

1. Type properties can be either computed or stored.

2. Yes. Subscripts can take any number of parameters.

3. Even though we assigned an array of integers to `myArray`, it is still of type `Any`. When we try to add an element of `myArray` to an `Int` in line 3, we get a compiler error. We can fix the code by changing `myArray[2]` to `(myArray[2] as Int)` at the end of line 3.

4. For structs and enums, use the `static` keyword. For classes, use the `class` keyword.

Exercise

Create a new OS X playground. Many times a class will contain an array or dictionary that stores the most relevant data in the class, with the rest of class there to support operations on or with the internal array. When this happens, we might want to use subscripts on the class instance to access the array directly. Let's look at an example by modeling a company's employee database for an HR system.

Create an `Employee` class with properties for name (a String), job title (a String), and employee ID (an Int). Next, create a `Company` class that contains an array of Employee objects and methods to add and remove employees to the array. Define a computed property for the `Company` class that takes a job title and returns an array of employees who have the matching job title.

Finally, define a subscript on the `Company` class that takes an integer and returns the employee who has the matching employee ID.

Is there anything you might change about this design? For example, could we have made the job title an enum, and how would that change our class?

Understanding Memory Allocation and References

What You'll Learn in This Hour:

▶ How to deinitialize class instances

▶ The basics of Automatic Reference Counting (ARC)

▶ The difference between strong, weak, and unowned references

▶ How to identify and avoid reference cycles

▶ How to create capture lists inside closures

Reference types in Swift, such as classes and closures, have different rules for memory allocation, retention, and disposal than value types. In fact, value types in Swift do not require any extra attention to these concepts at all. Reference types, on the other hand, require us to be mindful of how we are using them in our code. We haven't yet had a need to specifically manage memory settings in Swift, as our examples thus far have been relatively small and self-contained. But when apps get larger, and dependencies on other instances come into play, you must be more mindful of how memory is managed and sometimes tell Swift explicitly how to manage references to instances. In this hour we cover these concepts, starting with how any instance gets deinitialized and deallocated.

Deinitialization

In Hour 13, "Customizing Initializers of Classes, Structs, and Enums," we discussed initializers, which are called immediately after memory for an instance has been allocated and provide setup instructions for instances of a particular type. **Deinitialization** is the process of cleaning up anything necessary before an instance gets completely deallocated from memory.

Deallocation is not the same as deinitialization. When an instance gets deinitialized, you still have access to the properties inside the instance and can manipulate them as needed before the instance totally goes away. When an instance gets deallocated, however, it is set to `nil` and removed from memory completely. An instance of a reference type gets deallocated from memory when no other instances hold a **strong reference** to it. More about strong references shortly.

To customize a class's deinitializer, use the `deinit` keyword followed by open and closed curly braces, similarly to an `init` method. However, `deinit` takes no parameters. Superclass deinitializers are inherited from an instance's superclass and are executed immediately following the subclass instance's deinitializer method. Swift's **Automatic Reference Counting** (ARC) mechanism calls `deinit` on instances of reference types automatically, when the last strong reference to the instance is removed.

CAUTION

Never Call a Deinitializer Directly

Swift's ARC mechanism calls `deinit` automatically, so you should never call `deinit` directly.

The following code snippet shows the syntax of a `deinit` method.

```
deinit {
    // code goes here, if any, to free up resources or modify properties
➥before deallocation
}
```

When a variable or constant reference to a class instance is set to `nil`, and there are no other variables or constants referencing the instance, its **reference count** (sometimes referred to as a **retain count**) is zero and the instance is deallocated from memory. Swift handles this for us, but it is important to understand what is going on.

At the time of this writing, Xcode playgrounds do not use ARC in the same way that an actual compiled app or the REPL does, so let's use the Swift REPL to watch what happens when we initialize and deinitialize a class instance in memory.

▼ TRY IT YOURSELF

Initializers and Deinitializers in Action

Use the Swift REPL to examine when initializers and deinitializers are called and observe the results. I have included line numbers as you would see them in the REPL.

1. Open Terminal.app and open the Swift REPL by typing `xcrun swift` at the prompt.

   ```
   $ xcrun swift
   ```

2. Create a class named `TestClass` and provide a variable property named `title` of type `String`.

   ```
   1> class TestClass {
   2.     var title: String
   ```

3. Provide a basic initializer that sets the `title` property to the title parameter. Print a line to the console here that tells us when we are in the `init` method.

```
3.     init(title: String) {
4.         self.title = title
5.         println("\(title) is initialized.")
6.     }
```

4. Provide a deinitializer that just prints a line to the console that tells us when our instance is about to be deallocated. Then end the class with a final curly brace.

```
7.     deinit {
8.         println("\(title) is being deinitialized.")
9.     }
10. }
```

5. Create three variables of type `TestClass?` (*optional* `TestCase`). The REPL output from each line is shown immediately following without a line number.

```
11> var test1: TestClass?
test1: TestClass? = nil
12> var test2: TestClass?
test2: TestClass? = nil
13> var test3: TestClass?
test3: TestClass? = nil
```

6. Initialize `test1`, then assign `test2` and `test3` to `test1`. This effectively creates three references to the same instance of `TestClass`.

```
14> test1 = TestClass(title: "testing")
testing is initialized.
15> test2 = test1
16> test3 = test1
```

7. Assign each reference to nil, one at a time. Observe what happens after each assignment and when the actual deinitialization occurs.

```
17> test1 = nil
18> test2 = nil
19> test3 = nil
testing is being deinitialized.
```

You may be wondering after performing step 7, "Wait, we assigned a new `TestClass` instance to `test1`, why did nothing happen when we assigned `nil` to `test1`?" Remember that when an instance gets created, it exists in memory somewhere. And because classes are reference types, our variables don't actually hold an instance themselves; they hold a *reference* to the instance in memory. Figure 16.1 shows what essentially happened in step 6.

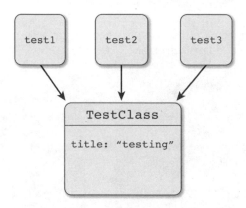

FIGURE 16.1
Three variables referencing the same class instance from the Try It Yourself example.

Even though we declared that `TestClass(title: "testing")` is assigned to the `test1` variable, we assigned that same instance's reference to `test2` and `test3`, creating three references to the same instance. Then, once we began assigning `nil` to each variable, each respective reference went away. Assigning each variable to `nil` is like removing each variable's arrow pointing to the `TestClass` instance in Figure 16.1. After the last reference (`test3`) was set to `nil` in step 7, our instance's reference count was zero, and right before ARC removed the instance from memory, it called our `deinit` method, which printed to the console `"testing is being deinitialized."` The completed REPL code and results should look like the following code and results in Figure 16.2.

```
● ● ●                    1. xcrun swift (lldb)
→ ~  xcrun swift
Welcome to Swift!  Type :help for assistance.
  1> class TestClass {
  2.     var title: String
  3.     init(title: String) {
  4.         self.title = title
  5.         println("\(title) is initialized.")
  6.     }
  7.     deinit {
  8.         println("\(title) is being deinitialized.")
  9.     }
 10. }
 11> var test1: TestClass?
test1: TestClass? = nil
 12> var test2: TestClass?
test2: TestClass? = nil
 13> var test3: TestClass?
test3: TestClass? = nil
 14> test1 = TestClass(title: "testing")
testing is initialized.
 15> test2 = test1
 16> test3 = test1
 17> test1 = nil
 18> test2 = nil
 19> test3 = nil
testing is being deinitialized.
 20> █
```

FIGURE 16.2
The completed Try It Yourself example of initialization and deinitialization in the REPL.

A classic example of the usefulness of deinitialization is when writing content to a file on disk. You don't want the instance doing the writing to get deallocated without closing the file for writing or no one else or no other process can edit the file. Placing code in your class's deinitializer to close or release the file handler would be beneficial, so that any file your instance writes to does not retain a permanent write-lock on the file. Another example could be when a player leaves a game. Their `Player` instance gets deinitialized, and the `deinit` method could return any coins or points the player has to a central bank or repository before the player instance gets deallocated.

Automatic Reference Counting

Several years ago, Apple introduced the aforementioned Automatic Reference Counting (ARC), to manage the allocation and deallocation of objects in memory. Objective-C programmers remember times before ARC, when you had to manually tell the compiler when to retain a reference to an Objective-C object and when to release it with the `retain` and `release` keywords, respectively. This was a point of confusion for a lot of developers, and misunderstanding proper memory management rules led to retain cycles and memory leaks, and even crashing apps. ARC was created to resolve these issues.

How ARC Works

What ARC does is analyze the code for creation of instances, places where they are referenced, and expected lifetimes of the instances via the number of references to them, and automatically keeps track of retaining and releasing references to instances. Then, as mentioned already, once an instance's reference count gets to zero, the instance is deallocated. In other words, when no property, variable, or constant strongly references an instance, ARC deallocates the instance. But what is a strong reference?

Reference Relationships and Behaviors

Rather than explicitly retaining instances ourselves, we tell the compiler the *behavior* a reference should have or what kind of *relationship* to have with another instance. We can do that by telling Swift what type of relationship a property, variable, or constant should have with another class or closure instance. The three types of relationships are **strong**, **weak**, and **unowned**. We will get to weak and unowned shortly, first let's discuss strong references.

Strong references maintain a strong hold on an instance. As long as at least one strong reference to an instance exists, ARC will not deallocate that instance. When you assign a property, variable, or constant to a class instance, a strong reference is created by default.

Optional type variables, constants, and properties behave the same way, but only once a reference to an instance is assigned. Declaring a property, constant, or variable of an optional type sets its initial value to `nil` until it is assigned a reference to an instance.

Reference Cycles

Our examples thus far haven't been too advanced, so we haven't had to worry about the implications of strong references. There may be times, though, when you have a class property that strongly references an instance of another class, and that property's class instance needs a reference back to the first instance. Such an occasion could be when a person buys an iPhone; a person would want to strongly hold onto a reference to that iPhone, and likewise the iPhone should only have one owner. Neither instance can get deallocated because each holds a strong reference to the other, creating a **strong reference cycle**.

The code in Listing 16.1 creates two classes, a `Person` class and a `Phone` class. After they are created, an instance of each is created.

NOTE

Do Not Use Playgrounds for Testing Memory Management

Remember that Xcode playgrounds do not use ARC in the same way the Swift REPL or an actual compiled app does. When testing ARC's capabilities to ensure instances get deallocated properly without creating strong reference cycles, you may find the easiest solution is to use the REPL. If you're a more advanced Xcode user, you may find using some advanced debugging methods easier, but those are not covered in this book.

If you're following along, we use the Swift REPL. You can either add the code directly in the interactive REPL, or you can add the code to a file with the .swift extension and then run the following command at a command prompt to test your code in the REPL:

```
$ xcrun swift test.swift
```

I prefer to write my code in a .swift file and then execute it in a separate tab of the Terminal app to avoid constantly closing the .swift file, executing the .swift file, and then reopening the file for editing. Feel free to do whatever is easiest for you.

NOTE

Known Issue in Xcode Command Line Tools

At the time of this writing, Xcode 6.0.1 is the latest public release. However, there is a known issue that the REPL cannot run using the Xcode 6.0.1 command line tools, and you must use those of Xcode 6.1. Xcode 6.1 is in beta and not yet released to the public, so if you have an Apple Developer account, you can download it and install the command line tools. If not, you may have to wait for Xcode 6.1 to be released. The version of command line tools can be changed in Xcode by opening the Xcode menu, then click Preferences. From there, click to open the Locations tab, then choose an option from the drop-down selection for Command Line Tools.

LISTING 16.1   Creating Classes with Dependent Properties

```
enum iPhoneModel: String {
    case iPhone4 = "iPhone4", iPhone4S = "iPhone4S", iPhone5 = "iPhone5"
    case iPhone5C = "iPhone5C", iPhone5S = "iPhone5S", iPhone6 = "iPhone6"
}

class Phone {
    let model: iPhoneModel
    var owner: Person?
    init(model: iPhoneModel) {
        self.model = model
        println("\(model.toRaw()) is being initialized.")
    }
    deinit {
```

```
            println("\(model.toRaw()) is deinitializing.")
        }
    }

class Person {
    let name: String
    var phone: Phone?
    init(name: String) {
        self.name = name
        println("\(name) is being initialized.")
    }
    deinit {
        println("\(name) is deinitializing.")
    }
}

var aPerson: Person?
var aPhone: Phone?

aPerson = Person(name: "Steve")     // displays "Steve is being initialized."
aPhone = Phone(model: .iPhone6)     // displays "iPhone6 is being initialized."

aPerson = nil                       // displays "Steve is deinitializing."
aPhone = nil                        // displays "iPhone6 is deinitializing."
```

Listing 16.1 shows a standard example of defining two classes, an enum to help with the model of iPhone and declaring an instance of each class. This example uses optionals so that we can assign to nil for the purposes of illustrating deinitialization and deallocation.

All works as planned in the preceding example, and both instances get deinitialized and deallocated once assigned to nil. But watch what happens if we assign aPerson to aPhone's owner property, and aPhone to aPerson's phone property in Listing 16.2. Place the following code immediately before the lines assigning nil to each variable.

LISTING 16.2   Creating a Strong Reference Cycle

```
// ... the iPhoneModel enum, Phone class, and Person class from Listing 16.1

aPerson!.phone = aPhone
aPhone!.owner = aPerson

aPerson = nil                       // nothing is displayed
aPhone = nil                        // nothing is displayed
```

In Listing 16.2, the only change we made was to assign `aPhone` to `aPerson!.phone` and `aPerson` to `aPhone!.owner`. Remember, since these are optional values, we had to forcibly unwrap the variables to assign anything to their properties. Look at the results when we assign each variable to `nil`. Wait, there aren't any results! This is because while we removed the references from our variables (`aPerson` and `aPhone`) to their respective instances in memory, each instance also had strong references to each other from their properties.

Figure 16.3 illustrates an abstract of how our instances would look in memory as separate instances and no dependence upon each other, just like Listing 16.1. Figure 16.4 and Figure 16.5 show the same instances with references to each other, creating a strong reference cycle, just like Listing 16.2, and what happens after the variables are assigned `nil`.

FIGURE 16.3
The `Person` and `Phone` instances with only strong references from a respective single variable.

FIGURE 16.4
A strong reference cycle between `Person` and `Phone` instances.

FIGURE 16.5
The strong reference cycle remains even after the variables are assigned to `nil`.

The preceding figures illustrate what happened in our code with respect to the strong references from each variable or property to an instance of a class. Your app's code may need to reference several other instances throughout its lifecycle, so how do we avoid strong reference cycles? There are two other types of memory relationships: weak and unowned.

Resolving Strong Reference Cycles

Strong reference cycles can be resolved by changing the type of relationship that variables, constants, and properties have with their instances. Since the preceding example had properties that wouldn't let go of the other instance, neither instance could be deallocated from memory, causing a **memory leak**. A memory leak is when an app never lets go of an instance or instances in memory, so that memory never gets returned to the operating system.

Weak References

To fix this, we can specify one of those references to be a **weak reference**, meaning that property holds a reference to a respective instance as long as some other property holds a strong reference to that instance. If the last strong reference to an instance goes away and only a weak reference remains, the weak reference is set to `nil` and the instance is deallocated.

Using the `Phone` and `Person` example from earlier, modify the `Phone` class so that the owner variable property is weak by prefacing the definition with the `weak` keyword. Then execute the .swift file with the REPL. Listing 16.3 illustrates what this change looks like.

LISTING 16.3   Resolving Strong Reference Cycles with Weak References

```
// reusing code from Listing 16.1 and 16.2
class Phone {
    let model: iPhoneModel
    weak var owner: Person?
```

```
    // remainder of Phone class...
}
// remainder of code from example

// Now, at the command line, execute your .swift file, e.g.
➥ch16_weak_reference.swift
$ xcrun swift ch16_weak_reference.swift
// results:
//    Steve is being initialized.
//    iPhone6 is being initialized.
//    Steve is deinitializing.
//    iPhone6 is deinitializing.
```

Now that we made the owner property a weak reference, the strong reference cycle is broken, and both instances can be deallocated after each variable is set to nil. Figure 16.6 shows the new diagram of our instances with a weak reference, enabling both instances to deallocate safely.

FIGURE 16.6
Using weak references to resolve strong reference cycles.

Weak references must be optional because they may be set to nil at runtime, and because they must be optional, they must be variables, so you cannot have a constant weak reference. Also, because they may be set to nil at runtime, you should check whether a reference is nil before attempting to access the instance to which it refers.

Consider using weak references when instances do not expect to have the same lifetimes. For example, our Person instance could live for years (as we would hope), but iPhones certainly don't live as long as humans. Their life expectancies are different, so it is appropriate to use a weak reference in this case.

Unowned References

The final type of memory relationship is called an **unowned reference**. Unowned references are a new concept if you are an Objective-C programmer, as you are most likely only familiar with strong and weak references. An unowned reference is a reference that is not strong but yet intends to have the same life expectancy as the instance it references, as the instances depend on each other. An unowned reference behaves as if to say "I depend on you, but I will not strongly hold on to you." To use an unowned reference, insert the unowned keyword in front of a property, variable, or constant definition, exactly the same way you use weak.

Since unowned references expect to live as long as the instances they refer to, they cannot be nil. Unowned references must always have a value and be defined as a non-optional type.

For example, let's say at your job you hire a new employee. That employee will always have an email address as long as they're employed, and that email address will only belong to that employee. They should have the same life expectancy (in terms of employment, not to cast ill will upon your new employee). Listing 16.4 illustrates such a scenario, that when your new employee is created in the HR system, an email instance is also created and attached to the employee. Again, since we cannot test ARC inside a playground, if you intend to follow along, I suggest you write the code in a .swift file and execute the file with the Swift REPL.

LISTING 16.4 Creating Reference Cycle with Employee and Email

```
01:  class Employee {
02:      var name: String
03:      let email: Email!
04:      init(name: String, emailAddress: String) {
05:          self.name = name
06:          self.email = Email(address: emailAddress, employee: self)
07:          println("\(name) is being initialized.")
08:      }
09:      deinit {
10:          println("\(name) is being deinitialized.")
11:      }
12:  }
13:
14:  class Email {
15:      var address: String
16:      var server = "imap.company.com"
17:      let employee: Employee
18:      init(address: String, employee: Employee) {
19:          self.address = address
20:          self.employee = employee
21:          println("\(address) is being initialized.")
22:      }
23:  }
```

```
24:
25:   var employee: Employee? = Employee(name: "BJ", emailAddress:
➥"BJ@company.com")
26:   employee = nil

// Displays:
//   BJ@company.com is being initialized.
//   BJ is being initialized.
```

Notice in the initializer for `Employee` that on line 6 we reference `self` by passing it as an argument to the `Email` initializer. We are allowed to do this because the `name` property is given a value on line 5, and the `email` property is an implicitly unwrapped optional (line 3), so its initial value is `nil`, and the `Employee` instance is considered fully initialized after line 5. We cannot use the `self` keyword until the instance is completely initialized, unless it is to differentiate similarly named parameters, such as `self.name = name`.

There is a problem, though. When you execute the .swift file, you see that the results show only initialization and no deinitialization when we set our `employee` variable to `nil`.

The proper way to resolve this reference cycle is to use the `unowned` keyword. Because these instances should stay alive as long as the other is alive but not hold each other strongly, we should set one to be an `unowned` reference. Modify the code in Listing 16.4 to add the `unowned` keyword at the beginning of line 17.

```
17:      unowned let employee: Employee
```

Now execute your .swift file again in the Swift REPL. You should see the deinitialization happen as soon as the employee variable is set to `nil` on line 26.

NOTE

Analyze What Behavior and Relationship Is Needed

It is always best to analyze what type of relationship is needed for properties, constants, and variables to instances of reference types. In the preceding example, we could have set the employee as a weak optional `Employee` instance, but that would imply that we could change the employee to another non-nil employee at a later time, and we don't want that behavior. This is why you must think about intended behavior of what each property, variable, or constant must have, and also what type of memory management relationship it will have with its respective instance.

Closures and Strong Reference Cycles

Closures in Swift are also reference types. That means that closures are also susceptible to strong reference cycles just like class instances. Since a closure *captures* the properties, variables, and constants from its surrounding context, it has the potential to capture a strong reference to self or another instance that has a strong reference to it, creating a strong reference cycle. We can overcome a strong reference cycle with closures by providing a **closure capture list**.

Closure Capture Lists

Closure capture lists are comma-separated lists that go inside a closure at the head, immediately after the opening curly brace and before the parameter list and return type. If there is no parameter list or return type, the closure capture list is placed before the in keyword, before the body of the closure. Closure capture lists provide what references should have what type of relationship, all inside a pair of square braces. Since strong is the default, you do not need to specify strong references inside the closure capture list, or anywhere for that matter. Rather, you can specify weak or unowned followed by the reference's name and list as many as needed, separated by commas.

Since closures are reference types just like a class, we can easily think of closures having the capability to create instances of other types inside their braces, as well as reference self, since the closure may need access to properties inside the class in which the closure belongs.

Let's create an example in the following Try It Yourself section that creates a class with a built-in math function, as well as some parameters to accept values upon initialization. In the example, we also create a deinitializer, so we can tell when our instance gets deinitialized before deallocation.

▼ TRY IT YOURSELF

Use Closure Capture Lists to Resolve Reference Cycles in Closures

Using the Swift REPL, create a class named MathFunction and provide a mathematical function inside a closure that can be called on an instance of MathFunction. Examine how ARC will or won't deallocate memory when we provide a closure capture list.

1. Open a text editor and create a file named Ch16_UnownedClosure.swift.

2. Create a class named MathFunction and create two variable properties of type Int.

```
class MathFunction {
    var firstNum: Int
    var secondNum: Int
}
```

3. Create a lazy variable property of type `()  -> Int` and return the product of the two instance properties. This lazy property should be placed after the `secondNum` definition statement.

```
lazy var multiply: () -> Int = {
    return self.firstNum * self.secondNum
}
```

4. Create an initializer that accepts two integers and assign them to the instance properties.

```
init(firstNum: Int, secondNum: Int) {
    self.firstNum = firstNum
    self.secondNum = secondNum
    println("initializing.")
}
```

5. Create a deinitializer that just prints to the console when the instance is being deinitialized.

```
deinit {
    println("deinitializing.")
}
```

6. That is all for the class. Create a variable of type *optional* `MathFunction` and assign a newly created instance.

```
var math: MathFunction? = MathFunction(firstNum: 3, secondNum: 5)
```

7. Since the `multiply` property is a lazy property, it has not been initialized yet, even though the instance itself has been initialized. This means the closure is not in memory and there is no reference to it yet. Assign `nil` to the `math` variable and observe ARC initializing and deinitializing our `MathFunction` instance.

```
math = nil
```

8. Now try to print the result of the `multiply` property, right before assigning `nil` to `math` on the last line. The `MathFunction` class instantiates the closure in memory, and since the closure references `self`, a strong reference is created from the closure to the class instance.

```
println(math!.multiply())
math = nil
```

9. At this point, the output from executing your .swift file should be two lines: "initializing" and "15". But we don't see "deinitializing." Try capturing a `weak` reference to `self` in a closure capture list. Execute your .swift file and observe the output. Do you get an error?

```
// Add closure capture list to end of 'lazy var multiply' line
lazy var multiply: () -> Int = { [weak self] in
// remainder of file...


// at the command line:
$ xcrun swift Ch16_UnownedClosure.swift
```

10. Executing the file with the weak reference in the closure capture list displays an error, "'MathFunction?' does not have a member named 'firstNum'". This is because assigning the reference as `weak` means that we would need to unwrap `self` before using it (as it is of an optional type). While we could do this, `unowned` is a more appropriate choice, because once the lazy variable has been initialized, it should never be `nil` and should exist as long as the class instance exists. Change the `weak` keyword to the `unowned` keyword inside the closure capture list. Then re-execute your .swift file. You should now see "initializing", "15", and then "deinitializing".

```
lazy var multiply: () -> Int = { [unowned self] in
// remainder of file...


// at the command line:
$ xcrun swift Ch16_UnownedClosure.swift
```

Once you've completed the Try It Yourself section, your code and results should look like those in Figure 16.7.

```
1. vim Ch16_UnownedClosure.swift (vim)

vim

class MathFunction {
    var firstNum: Int
    var secondNum: Int

    lazy var multiply: () -> Int = { [unowned self] in
        return self.firstNum * self.secondNum
    }

    init(firstNum: Int, secondNum: Int) {
        self.firstNum = firstNum
        self.secondNum = secondNum
        println("initializing.")
    }

    deinit {
        println("deinitializing.")
    }
}

var math: MathFunction? = MathFunction(firstNum: 3, secondNum: 5)
println(math!.multiply())
math = nil

..H/Playgrounds

→ Playgrounds  xcrun swift Ch16_UnownedClosure.swift
initializing.
15
deinitializing.
→ Playgrounds []
```

FIGURE 16.7
The completed Try It Yourself example code and REPL results for using unowned references inside a closure capture list.

Summary

In this hour you learned about deinitialization and how to clean up instances before they are deallocated. You also learned about Automatic Reference Counting (ARC), and how it is an automated mechanism for managing the number of references to instances in memory, allocating memory for them, and deallocating them from memory when done.

From ARC, you learned about strong, weak, and unowned references, the behaviors they maintain, and when it makes sense to use each one. You then learned how to identify and resolve strong reference cycles in memory.

Finally, you learned about closure capture lists as a way to mitigate risks of strong reference cycles in closures. Since closures are reference types just like class instances, they are susceptible to strong reference cycles as well. Providing closure capture lists suggests to Swift how you would like to manage the relationships between instances and closures.

While memory management isn't the most glamorous of topics, it is important as you write software for any platform, let alone for mobile platforms, which are more resource-constrained than desktop platforms and for which the implications of poorly managed memory can be noticed more frequently.

Although a lot of memory management is handled for you in Swift's ARC mechanism, you certainly still have a lot of power at your fingertips with this knowledge. Make sure you understand these concepts and their implications, because you want happy users of your apps, and apps crashing from poor memory management make for unhappy users.

In the next hour, we discuss protocols. Protocols enable you to add functionality to types to define what a particular implementation should provide, so that the instance asking for information can guarantee that appropriate information is provided.

Q&A

Q. Do structs have `deinit` methods?

A. Structs do not have deinitializers in the same way that classes do. If you try to declare one, Swift gives you a compiler error.

Q. When does my class need a deinitializer?

A. Unfortunately, it's not possible to provide a comprehensive list of when a `deinit` method is required; most of the time your class won't need a deinitializer. Generally, you need a deinitializer when you perform some manual cleanup and release extra resources when your class is about to be deallocated. For example, if your class has open network connections you'll want to close them before your class becomes unavailable.

Deinitializers can also be useful in debugging your application. It is sometimes helpful to have a class display or log information about itself just before it is deallocated so you can check that its state is as it should be.

Q. What causes a memory leak and how can I find them?

A. A memory leak occurs when an application allocates memory for an object but never releases it. Strong reference cycles are the most common cause of memory leaks in reference-counted languages such as Swift. Xcode provides excellent debugging and analysis tools, but they are beyond the scope of this book. If you're interested, look into the Instruments application, which comes bundled with Xcode.

Q. When should I use an unowned reference instead of a weak reference?

A. You should only use an unowned reference when you're sure that the reference will never be nil. If an unowned reference is set to nil and you try to use the reference, your app will crash.

Workshop

The workshop contains quiz questions and exercises to help you solidify your understanding of the material covered. Try to answer all questions before looking at the answers that follow.

Quiz

1. What are the three reference types available in Swift?

2. If no reference type is specified, which type is used by default?

3. Can weak references have an optional type?

4. Does a deinitializer have access to the class's properties?

Answers

1. Strong, weak, and unowned.

2. By default, references in Swift are strong.

3. Not only can weak references have an optional type, they must have an optional type.

4. Yes. Deinitialization occurs before deallocation, so all properties in the class are still available to `deinit`.

Exercise

For this exercise, you can either work in a playground or use the REPL like you did for the Try It Yourself sections of this hour.

Let's take a look at how deinitializers are called in a class and its subclasses. Create a class called `Parent` with a `title` property and write an `init` and `deinit` method for your class. These methods should print messages containing the `title` to the console and indicate that the object was initialized or deinitialized.

Next, write a subclass of `Parent` called `Child`. `Child` should have a property called `subtitle` and should have its own set of `init` and `deinit` methods. These should print messages containing the `subtitle` to the console and indicate that the object was initialized or deinitialized. Don't forget to call `super.init()` and pass on the `title` parameter.

Create an optional `var` of type `Child` and assign a child object to it. It shouldn't surprise you that the superclass's `init` message appears before the subclass's. This is the same thing we saw when we covered initializers in Hour 13. Now, set your `var` to `nil` and watch the `deinit` messages.

Think about the code you just wrote. Did you have to use the `override` keyword in any of your `init` methods? How about in the `deinit` methods? Why do you think that is? Were you surprised by the order of the `deinit` messages? Why or why not?

Using Protocols to Define Behavior

In this hour we discuss protocols as a way to define additional behavior a type should exhibit. Protocols are not a new concept if you are familiar with Objective-C. Even other languages have similar constructs called contracts or interfaces. Protocols are used frequently throughout the Cocoa and Cocoa Touch frameworks, so the knowledge you learn here will help you gain a better understanding of how to interact with different areas of Mac and iOS development.

Defining Protocols

Let's begin the topic with a definition of protocols. A **protocol** is an outline, or contract, of behavior that a type can implement. A protocol itself does not have any implementation; it is only a blueprint of methods and properties. Any type can **adopt** a protocol to help give it extra functionality to accomplish a particular task or set of tasks.

Adopting a protocol is similar to a class inheriting from a superclass, although there is nothing to inherit with protocols. Rather, you adopt a protocol as a way of agreeing to abide by the contract it defines. Also, adopting protocols is not limited to classes like it is in Objective-C; Swift structs and enums can also adopt protocols. A type that adopts a protocol and implements its defined behavior is said to **conform** to the protocol. Before we go any further with adopting and conforming to protocols, let's take a look at how a protocol is structured.

The syntax of a protocol is similar to type definitions we have seen already, just with the `protocol` keyword, the name to give the protocol, and a pair of curly braces. Inside the curly braces are the properties, methods, and any other information that should be implemented by whatever type adopts the protocol. The following snippet shows the basic syntax of defining a protocol.

```
protocol MyProtocol {
    // ...property definitions, method definitions, and so on go here
}
```

Creating and Adopting Protocols

To declare that a type adopts a protocol, you use the same syntax as if you were inheriting a class from a superclass. Separate the name of your type with a colon and then the name of the protocol. If you are inheriting a class from a superclass but also need to conform to a protocol, list the superclass first, then any protocols second, and so on, separated by commas. Then, inside your type's implementation, fulfill the defined behavior of the protocol. But what does it mean to fulfill the defined behavior of the protocol? Let's start with a basic protocol with only a few properties defined. Then we create a struct to adopt the protocol and make our struct conform to the protocol by fulfilling the protocol's definition. We do this in Listing 17.1. If you are following along, you may use either a playground (Mac or iOS is fine) or the Swift REPL.

LISTING 17.1   Creating and Adopting a Protocol

```
protocol Rentable {
    var title: String { get }
    var barcode: String { get set }
}

struct Book : Rentable {
    let title: String
    var barcode: String
    var chapterCount: Int
}

let book = Book(title: "Sams Teach Yourself Swift in 24 Hours",
➥barcode: "12345678", chapterCount: 24)
```

The syntax for defining a property in a protocol looks a bit strange, but that's because there is no implementation. It is structured exactly as a computed property is, just without any implementation. Let's discuss properties in protocols in greater detail now.

Fully Conform to Adopted Protocols

If your class, struct, or enum declares that it adopts a particular protocol, you must implement all required defined functionality in the protocol. Failing to do so results in a compiler error. Figure 17.1 shows an example of what you might see if your type does not conform to a protocol.

```
15
16    protocol MyProperty {
17        var myTypeVar: String { get }
18    }
19
20    struct MyStruct : MyProperty {          ⓘ Type 'MyStruct' does not conform to protocol 'MyProperty'
21
22    }
23
```

FIGURE 17.1
A type not fully conforming to a protocol results in a compiler error.

Properties

To require a gettable property, you simply provide the `get` keyword inside the curly braces, like the `title` property. To require a gettable and settable property, provide both the `get` and `set` keywords inside the curly braces, separated by a space, such as `{ get set }`, like the `barcode` property. Property requirements are always introduced with the `var` keyword inside a protocol, even if they may be declared as constants in the conforming type.

Properties in a protocol designed to be read-write must be implemented with the `var` introducer and also must provide a getter and setter in the conforming type's implementation. Read-write properties cannot be implemented as constants or with just a getter. Conversely, a protocol property defined as read-only, with just a getter, can be implemented in the conforming type as read-write, with a getter and a setter, if it makes sense to do so.

Notice in Listing 17.1 that the `title` property is defined with just a getter, and the `barcode` property is defined with a getter and a setter, but neither property has a custom accessor in the implementation. The `title` property's implementation is as a constant, and a value is assigned during initialization, so it is read-only and satisfies that requirement. The `barcode` property's implementation is as a variable, and even though it is set during initialization, it can be reassigned at any time during runtime, so that requirement is satisfied as well. You can, however, provide custom accessors, if it makes sense to do so.

Notice also in Listing 17.1 that the `Book` struct has an extra property, `chapterCount`. Types that adopt and conform to protocols often have more implementation than just what is defined in the protocol or protocols they adopt.

Protocols can define instance properties and type properties. Type properties are defined with the `class` keyword, even if the conforming type is a struct or enum. In the actual implementation inside your struct or enum, you would use the `static` keyword when providing the implementation for the type property from the protocol, whereas classes still use the `class` keyword for implementing type properties. Type properties in protocols could be useful if you are creating a game and you want the maximum number of damage sustainable to be provided to not only your player but also any enemies. That way each type can define its max, and because each type conforms to the protocol, you know each instance is guaranteed to be able to access that value.

Defining Methods in Protocols

Method definitions inside protocols look exactly like they do in a class, struct, or enum; they just don't have any implementation, just like properties. You still use the `func` keyword, give the method a name, and then a list of parameters and a return type—no curly braces, no implementation.

When you provide your implementation, you do not need to write the `override` keyword, because you are not inheriting the method from a superclass; you are merely implementing a method you promised you would implement when you adopted the protocol. Listing 17.2 adds to our example in Listing 17.1 by adding a method signature to the protocol, which requires any conforming type to implement that method.

LISTING 17.2 Adding Methods to Protocols

```
protocol Rentable {
    var title: String { get }
    var barcode: String { get set }
    func rent()
}

struct Book : Rentable {
    let title: String
    var barcode: String
    let chapterCount: Int
    func rent() {
        println("Please return \(title) in 3 weeks.")
    }
}

let book = Book(title: "To Kill A Mockingbird", barcode: "87654321",
➥chapterCount: 31)
book.rent()      // displays "Please return To Kill A Mockingbird in 3 weeks."
```

We could also add parameters to the function and specify a return type in the protocol. The syntax to do this is exactly what you would expect, minus the implementation. Listing 17.3 continues with our `Rentable` scenario to add parameters and a return type to the protocol, and conforming type, `Book`.

LISTING 17.3   **Adding Parameters and a Return Type to Protocol Methods**

```
protocol Rentable {
    var title: String { get }
    var barcode: String { get set }
    func rent(forWeeks weeks: Int) -> Bool
}

struct Book : Rentable {
    let title: String
    var barcode: String
    let chapterCount: Int

    func rent(forWeeks weeks: Int) -> Bool {
        println("Please return \(title) in \(weeks) weeks.")
        return true
    }
}

let book = Book(title: "Goodnight Moon", barcode: "12344321", chapterCount: 1)
book.rent(forWeeks: 2)     // displays "Please return Goodnight Moon in 2 weeks."
```

To define mutating functions, such as those required in structs to alter the state of a property inside an instance, you provide the `mutating` keyword in front of the definition inside the protocol. This is true for any method that needs to mutate properties, even if the conforming type is a class, where the `mutating` keyword is not necessary. You must add the `mutating` keyword in the protocol, but in the case of a conforming class, you can safely omit the `mutating` keyword in front of method declarations.

As with type properties, you must declare a type method with the `class` keyword in the protocol. If the conforming type is a struct or enum, use the `static` keyword in the actual implementation.

You can also define initializers in protocols. When implementing an initializer from a protocol, the initializer must be prefixed with the `required` keyword. Everything else about the initializer is the same as you have learned about initializers.

Using Protocol Names as Types

Although protocols are not a fully implemented type, they can be used as a type in parameter lists, return types, constants, and variables, as an indication that no matter what class, struct, or enum an instance is, it is expected to have a certain set of behaviors based on conformance to a protocol. This can be useful when you have arrays or dictionaries with instances of inconsistent types but yet which conform to a common protocol, for example.

Let's say we need to encapsulate any rentable types into an array. Listing 17.4 creates two new structs, DVD and AudioCD, both adopting the Rentable protocol, and we create an array of instances with all the different types.

LISTING 17.4 Using Protocol Names as Types

```
protocol Rentable {
    var title: String { get }
    var barcode: String { get set }
    func rent(forWeeks weeks: Int) -> Bool
}

struct Book : Rentable {
    let title: String
    var barcode: String
    let chapterCount: Int

    func rent(forWeeks weeks: Int) -> Bool {
        println("Please return \(title) in \(weeks) weeks.")
        return true
    }
}

struct DVD: Rentable {
    let title: String
    var barcode: String
    let lengthInMinutes: Int

    func rent(forWeeks weeks: Int) -> Bool {
        println("Please return \(title) in \(weeks) weeks.")
        return true
    }
}

struct AudioCD : Rentable {
    let title: String
```

```
    var barcode: String
    let audioTracks: Int

    func rent(forWeeks weeks: Int) -> Bool {
        println("Please return \(title) in \(weeks) weeks.")
        return true
    }
}

let brownBear = Book(title: "Brown Bear, Brown Bear, What Do You See?",
➥barcode: "13243546", chapterCount: 1)
let clue = DVD(title: "Clue: The Movie", barcode: "64534231", lengthInMinutes: 94)
let incubus = AudioCD(title: "If Not Now, When?", barcode: "09876543",
➥audioTracks: 11)

let items: [Rentable] = [brownBear, clue, incubus]

for item in items {
    println("Item: \(item.title) is rentable. Barcode is \(item.barcode)")
}
```

The example in Listing 17.4 shows how we can have multiple types conforming to a single protocol, and then have an array of type Rentable. The array is represented by instances of three different structs. Yet they all commonly adopt and conform to the Rentable protocol, so the array is of type [Rentable]. Since we can guarantee that each item can provide a title and a barcode, as they are specified in the protocol's definition, we iterate through the array and ask each item for its title and barcode without any problem. This is part of what makes protocols so powerful; they can make disparate types behave in a common fashion.

There should be something wrong staring you in the face in the preceding example: We repeated the same code in all three structs. A lot of this implementation should be extracted out into a common superclass, which adopts the Rentable protocol. This calls for not only class inheritance but protocol inheritance.

Adopting and Inheriting Multiple Protocols

To fix the preceding example, we still need the individual properties particular to each type, such as audioTracks on AudioCD, but the protocol methods and properties can be offloaded to the superclass to reduce redundancy. Also, we need to change the types from structs to classes to take advantage of inheritance. And to show that we can create types that not only inherit from a superclass but also adopt multiple protocols, we add a protocol named Optical to identify what type of disc we have. Let's build this example in the following Try It Yourself section.

▼ TRY IT YOURSELF

Class Inheritance and Multiple Protocol Inheritance

Recreate the Library example from preceding examples to create classes rather than structs to implement a class hierarchy, as well as to adopt multiple protocols.

1. Open Xcode 6 and create a new playground. Either an iOS or a Mac playground will work. Clear the contents of the playground.

2. Begin by creating the `Rentable` protocol, same as in earlier examples.

```
protocol Rentable {
    var title: String { get }
    var barcode: String { get set }
    func rent(forWeeks weeks: Int) -> Bool
}
```

3. Create the `Optical` protocol. This is used to define what type of optical media a rentable item is.

```
protocol Optical {
    var discType: OpticalDiscType { get }
}
```

4. Create an enum that holds the types of optical media and satisfies the type of the property in the `Optical` protocol.

```
enum OpticalDiscType {
    case CD, DVD, BluRay
}
```

5. Create the superclass, named `Media`. Adopt the `Rentable` protocol and fulfill the protocol's defined requirements.

```
class Media : Rentable {
    let title: String
    var barcode: String
    init(title: String, barcode: String) {
        self.title = title
        self.barcode = barcode
    }
    func rent(forWeeks weeks: Int) -> Bool {
        println("Please return \(title) in \(weeks) weeks.")
        return true
    }
}
```

6. Create the `Book` class as a subclass to `Media`. Add a `chapterCount` property of type `Int`, along with an initializer. Because `Book` inherits from `Media`, which conforms to the `Rentable` protocol, the `Book` class, by definition of inheritance, also conforms to the `Rentable` protocol.

```
class Book : Media {
    let chapterCount: Int
    init(title: String, barcode: String, chapterCount: Int) {
        self.chapterCount = chapterCount
        super.init(title: title, barcode: barcode)
    }
}
```

7. The `Book` class looks much cleaner. Create the `DVD` class, subclassing from `Media` and also adopting the `Optical` protocol. Then add an `OpticalDiscType` property to conform to the `Optical` protocol. Remember, a class can inherit from only one direct superclass, but it can conform to multiple protocols. You must list the class first if you inherit from both a class and protocol(s).

```
class DVD : Media, Optical {
    let lengthInMinutes: Int
    let discType: OpticalDiscType = .DVD
    init(title: String, barcode: String, lengthInMinutes: Int) {
        self.lengthInMinutes = lengthInMinutes
        super.init(title: title, barcode: barcode)
    }
}
```

8. The `DVD` class now inherits from `Media` and conforms to both the `Rentable` and `Optical` protocols. Do the same by creating an `AudioCD` class, with a property named `audioTracks` of type `Int`, set the `discType` property, and create the initializer.

```
class AudioCD : Media, Optical {
    let audioTracks: Int
    let discType: OpticalDiscType = .CD
    init(title: String, barcode: String, audioTracks: Int) {
        self.audioTracks = audioTracks
        super.init(title: title, barcode: barcode)
    }
}
```

9. Now that our classes are created, let's create instances of them and populate an array with the newly created instances. Also, try to rent *The Notebook* for 3 weeks. You should be able to do so because of inheritance.

```
    let theNotebook = Book(title: "The Notebook", barcode: "44445555",
    ➥chapterCount: 12)
    theNotebook.rent(forWeeks: 3)
    let majorLeague = DVD(title: "Major League", barcode: "66667777",
    ➥lengthInMinutes: 107)
    let incubus = AudioCD(title: "Monuments and Melodies", barcode:
    ➥"88889999", audioTracks: 12)

    let items: [Rentable] = [theNotebook, majorLeague, incubus]
```

10. Iterate through the array of rentable items and print a basic description to prove that you are able to access protocol properties on any type that conforms to that protocol. Create an `if` statement to check whether a title is equal to a favorite of yours and output your favorite song, scene, or chapter.

```
for item in items {
    println("Item: \(item.title) is rentable. Barcode is \(item.barcode).")
    if item.title == "Monuments and Melodies" {
        println("My favorite song on \(item.title) is Black Heart Inertia.")
    }
}
```

A key take-away from the preceding Try It Yourself example is that you can always inherit from multiple protocols whether your type is a class, struct, or enum. If your type is a class, you can only inherit from one class, but you can still conform to multiple protocols. You just need to list the superclass first before listing protocols your type will adopt.

Another key take-away is that no matter what type an instance is, if it conforms to a protocol, you can ask it for properties and methods defined in that protocol. An example of this is with Apple's MapKit framework. You are probably familiar with seeing a map on an iPhone or iPad and interacting with red pins to show locations of places. Those pins are represented by any instance that conforms to the `MKAnnotation` protocol. The protocol defines a title, subtitle, and a coordinate location, which is all it needs to place a pin on the map. It is convenient to create an extension on your model types to conform to this protocol, reducing the need to create special instances just of the type `MKAnnotation`. We discuss extensions in Hour 18, "Using Extensions to Add Type Functionality."

The completed code results from the preceding Try It Yourself example should look like those in Figure 17.2.

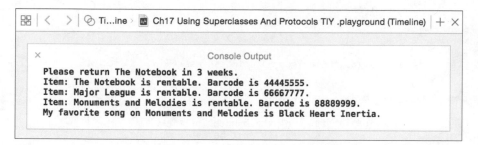

FIGURE 17.2
The results from the completed Try It Yourself example using class inheritance and multiple protocol inheritance.

If we needed to reference an instance that conformed to multiple protocols, such as for a parameter of a function, and the function body accessed properties or methods from multiple protocols, we could use **protocol composition** to ensure our parameter type was defined properly. This is done using the `protocol` keyword, followed by the protocols needed inside open and closed angle brackets, separated by commas. Protocol composition can be used to define any instance property, constant, or variable, and is not limited to just parameters. The following code snippet is an example of protocol composition.

```
func SomeMethod(composedProperty : protocol<ProtocolOne, ProtocolTwo>) { }
```

Optional Protocol Properties and Methods

Much like protocols in Objective-C, Swift provides the `optional` keyword to be inserted before a property or method definition inside a protocol. An optional property or method is not the same as an optional type (by adding the question mark character after a type name); an optional property or method inside a protocol means that the conforming type does not *have* to implement that property or method, but it *could*.

A protocol with any optional members must itself be marked with the `@objc` modifier in front of the `protocol` keyword. Even though you may not be interacting with Objective-C, the keyword is still required. If you mark your protocol with the `@objc` attribute, it can only be used by class types, and not structs or enums. This is discussed at greater length in Hour 21, "Adding Interoperability with Objective-C."

An example of this is the `MKAnnotation` protocol. If you open a playground and `import` `MapKit`, type `MKAnnotation` on an empty line. Then Command+click the word `MKAnnotation`. You should see the code listed in Figure 17.3.

```
2    //
3    //  MKAnnotation.h
4    //  MapKit
5    //
6    //  Copyright (c) 2009-2014, Apple Inc. All rights reserved.
7    //
8
9    protocol MKAnnotation : NSObjectProtocol {
10
11       // Center latitude and longitude of the annotation view.
12       // The implementation of this property must be KVO compliant.
13       var coordinate: CLLocationCoordinate2D { get }
14
15       // Title and subtitle for use by selection UI.
16       optional var title: String! { get }
17       optional var subtitle: String! { get }
18
19       // Called as a result of dragging an annotation view.
20       @availability(iOS, introduced=4.0)
21       optional func setCoordinate(newCoordinate: CLLocationCoordinate2D)
22    }
23
```

FIGURE 17.3
The MKAnnotation protocol definition, with optional properties and an optional method.

The only required property is the `coordinate` property of type `CLLocationCoordinate2D`.
It is not *required* to implement the `title` and `subtitle` properties, or the
`setCoordinate(newCoordinate:)` method, although you can. If you do provide those prop-
erties and methods in your conforming type, they can be used in the greater implementation.
If they aren't provided by you, the properties are ignored and the method is never called by
MapKit.

But wait, where is the `@objc` modifier? Notice on line 3 of Figure 17.3 that `MKAnnotation.h`
is written, the ".h" meaning that it is from an Objective-C file. `MKAnnotation` is already an
Objective-C protocol, but Xcode makes it look like Swift code for us by automatically generating
the Swift representation of an Objective-C protocol. A purely Swift protocol with optional members would look like the example in Listing 17.5, which is my version of the `MKAnnotation` protocol, called `BJMAnnotation`.

LISTING 17.5   Adding Optional Members to Protocols

```
import MapKit

@objc protocol BJMAnnotation : NSObjectProtocol {
    var coordinate: CLLocationCoordinate2D { get }
    optional var title: String! { get }
    optional var subtitle: String! { get }
    optional func setCoordinate(newCoordinate: CLLocationCoordinate2D)
}
```

How to Check for Protocol Conformance

Swift provides a mechanism for checking a type's conformance to a protocol, and it is the exact same syntax for type checking and type casting from Hour 15, "Adding Advanced Type Functionality," using the `is` and `as` operators. The `is` keyword returns true if the given instance conforms to the protocol in question and false if not. The `as` keyword temporarily downcasts the protocol type forcibly. Remember this can cause a runtime error if the downcasting fails.

You can also use the `as?` operator, which attempts to downcast the instance in question to the protocol's type and returns an optional value of the protocol's type if successful. It returns `nil` if the downcasting is unsuccessful.

The only alteration you must make to the type you are checking for conformance is to preface the protocol's definition with the `@objc` attribute.

Since the syntax and the concept are the exact same as type checking and type casting in Hour 15, see the "Type Casting and Non-Specific Types" section of Hour 15 for a full understanding. Simply substitute the protocol type where there is a regular type when using `is`, `as`, or `as?`, and you experience the same behavior.

Using Protocols for Delegation

Delegation is a common design pattern, and it is used frequently in the Cocoa and Cocoa Touch frameworks. Apple defines a delegate as "an object that acts on behalf of, or in coordination with, another object when that object encounters an event in a program." This means that an application may have certain events that occur, such as the start or end of a game, that can notify a delegate object to customize the response returned to the application.

Take table views on iOS for example. A table view is a list of items viewed onscreen, such as your music list, or a list of emails. The table view is an instance of `UITableView`, and it has two types of delegates: One is an action-based delegate (simply called its **delegate**) and the other is its **data source** delegate. The table view's delegate can respond to calls such as when a row in a table view is selected or deselected, editing or deleting a row, and tapping on the accessory button on the right-hand side of a table cell to show more information. The table view's data source can respond to calls such as returning a configured cell for an index path in the table view, a title for the header of each section, and number of rows in each section of the table view. The aforementioned delegate and data source responsibilities are typical for their definitions; delegates often are responsible for taking action on behalf of another instance, and a data source is responsible for providing for a particular criteria and not necessarily performing actions.

So what do delegates have to do with protocols? Because the instance that offloads tasks to its delegate doesn't care what type of instance it is, delegate instances typically conform to a given protocol, versus relying on a class, struct, or enum structure. As long as whatever type of instance the delegate or data source is conforms to the protocol, both instances happily communicate with each other.

NOTE

Dependency Inversion Principle

The Dependency Inversion Principle is one of the SOLID principles of object-oriented programming. A key point of this principle is to depend on abstractions and not on concretions. While every app is different and some implementations call for different design patterns, the Dependency Inversion Principle is a good guideline to follow to ensure loose coupling of objects in your code, making code more flexible and easier to maintain. Using protocols in Objective-C and Swift is one way to implement this principle. For more information on this topic, see the article on Wikipedia at http://en.wikipedia.org/wiki/Dependency_inversion_principle.

Let's look at a quick example of this in Listing 17.6. We create a class that delegates some actions to a delegate instance that conforms to a protocol we specify.

LISTING 17.6   Delegating Responsibilities

```
protocol ButtonDelegateProtocol {
    func didTapButton(button: Button)
}

class ButtonDelegate : ButtonDelegateProtocol {
    func didTapButton(button: Button) {
        println("You tapped the button labeled \(button.title).")
    }
}

class Button {
    let title: String
    let delegate: ButtonDelegateProtocol

    init(title: String, delegate: ButtonDelegateProtocol) {
        self.title = title
        self.delegate = delegate
    }

    func buttonTapped() {
        self.delegate.didTapButton(self)
    }
}

let button = Button(title: "Tap Me!", delegate: ButtonDelegate())
button.buttonTapped()    // displays "You tapped the button labeled Tap Me!"
```

As you can see in the results pane if you were following along, when you call `button.button-Tapped()`, the output is displayed saying what the label is of the button that was tapped. This is because when we tapped the button, the `Button` class didn't care what happened when the button was tapped; it offloaded that responsibility to the `ButtonDelegate` class, which conforms to the `ButtonDelegateProtocol` protocol.

NOTE

Protocols Guarantee Behavior

The `ButtonDelegate` class in the preceding example could very well have implemented the `buttonTapped()` method if `delegate` was an instance of type `ButtonDelegate`, and the example would still have worked if no protocols were involved. However, because we introduced the protocol, it is our way of guaranteeing that the delegate *must* implement that method, plus we loosen the coupling between our classes, and we program to an abstraction versus a concretion. Without the protocol, we cannot guarantee that the method would be implemented, and the app may not compile, or even worse, if it sneaks past your compiler, the app could crash at runtime.

Now that you have a better understanding of how protocols and delegates work, let's do a larger example together. This is a mini reimplementation of *The Legend of Zelda* (one of my all-time favorites). If you're not familiar with the game, here's the basic premise: You are Link, and you are saving Princess Zelda from the evil enemy Ganon. You battle different enemies along your journey as you search for Zelda and must gauge your health along the way (determined by how many hearts you have). The game is over if you have zero hearts.

We create a protocol for objects that can heal Link and for the game beginning and ending. We also create an enemy struct and a class that manages Link and his journey. Let's get started.

 TRY IT YOURSELF ▼

Using Protocols and Delegates

Create a small rendition of *The Legend of Zelda* using protocols and delegates.

1. Open Xcode 6 and create a new playground. Either a Mac or an iOS playground will work. Clear the contents of the playground.

2. Create the `Healable` protocol, with a `healableName` variable of type `String` and a `heartsRestores` variable of type `Double`.

```
protocol Healable {
    var healableName: String { get }
    var heartsRestores: Double { get }
}
```

3. Create a `BluePotion` struct and a `Heart` struct, each identifying itself in the `healableName` property, and restoring 4 hearts in `BluePotion` and 1 heart in `Heart`.

```
struct BluePotion : Healable {
    var healableName: String { return "blue potion" }
    var heartsRestores: Double { return 4.0 }
}

struct Heart : Healable {
    var healableName: String { return "heart piece" }
    var heartsRestores: Double { return 1.0 }
}
```

4. Create a simple struct for an enemy, with properties for a `name` and `damage` points.

```
struct Enemy {
    let name: String
    let damage: Double
}
```

5. Create the protocol to manage game events. Name it `GameManagerDelegate` and provide the blueprint for two functions: one for game start and one for game end. Each function should take a parameter of the type that we specify for the game, which we haven't created yet, so just enter the type here. The compiler may give you an error until you declare the type later.

```
protocol GameManagerDelegate {
    func gameDidStart(game: TheLegendOfZelda)
    func gameDidEnd(game: TheLegendOfZelda)
}
```

6. Create the `TheLegendOfZelda` class. This will be a long one, so in the interest of being brief, we create the whole class implementation here. Start with declaring the maximum and minimum heart containers Link can have and then set properties for the delegate, player name, sword, heart containers, and hearts. Validate the `hearts` property in `didSet` to make sure it stays within the number of hearts available. Create an initializer, a function to take damage, and finally a function to heal with a `Healable` item.

```
class TheLegendOfZelda {
    let maxHeartContainers = 20
    let minHearts = 0.0
    let delegate: GameManagerDelegate
    let name = "Link"
    var sword: String?
    var heartContainers = 3.0
    var hearts: Double = 0.0 {
        didSet {
            if hearts > heartContainers {
```

```
                    hearts = heartContainers
                }
                if hearts <= minHearts {
                    hearts = minHearts
                }
            }
        }
        init(delegate: GameManagerDelegate) {
            self.delegate = delegate
            self.delegate.gameDidStart(self)
        }
        func takeDamage(fromEnemy enemy: Enemy) {
            hearts -= enemy.damage
            println("\(name) lost \(enemy.damage) hearts from \(enemy.name),
    ➥\(hearts) hearts left.")
            if hearts == 0 {
                self.delegate.gameDidEnd(self)
            }
        }
        func heal(#item: Healable) {
            hearts += item.heartsRestores
            println("\(name) gained \(item.heartsRestores) hearts from a
    ➥\(item.healableName), and has \(hearts) hearts left.")
        }
    }
```

7. The last class we need to implement is the GameManager, which adopts the
   GameManagerDelegate protocol. Provide the methods necessary to conform to the
   protocol.

```
class GameManager : GameManagerDelegate {
    func gameDidStart(game: TheLegendOfZelda) {
        println("It's dangerous to go alone. Take this.")
        game.sword = "Wooden"
        game.hearts = 3.0
    }
    func gameDidEnd(game: TheLegendOfZelda) {
        println("GAME OVER. RETURN OF GANON.")
    }
}
```

8. Now it's time to create an instance of TheLegendOfZelda and play the game. Watch
   your console output as you type each line here, to observe which delegate methods get
   called, which properties get adjusted, and when the game starts and ends.

```
let link = TheLegendOfZelda(delegate: GameManager())
let keese = Enemy(name: "Keese", damage: 0.5)
let dekuBaba = Enemy(name: "Deku Baba", damage: 1.0)
let ganon = Enemy(name: "Ganon", damage: 2.0)
link.takeDamage(fromEnemy: keese)
link.heal(item: BluePotion())
link.takeDamage(fromEnemy: keese)
link.takeDamage(fromEnemy: dekuBaba)
link.heal(item: Heart())
link.takeDamage(fromEnemy: ganon)
link.takeDamage(fromEnemy: ganon)
```

As you can see, the preceding example is crude, and there is much room for improvement. But it gets the point across about how to use delegates that conform to protocols to make your code less complex and more loosely coupled, rather than depending so tightly on a particular type. Pressing Command+Option+Return displays the Assistant Editor with the console output results for you to see your work in action. The results of your code should look like those in Figure 17.4.

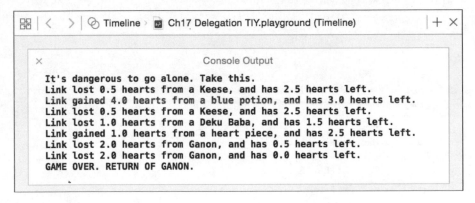

FIGURE 17.4
The console output results from the preceding Try It Yourself section using delegates that conform to protocols.

Summary

In this hour you learned about protocols, which are used as a contract to guarantee that a particular conforming type will respond to being asked for property information or execute methods. You learned the basics of the syntax and structure of protocols, and how to make a class, enum, or struct adopt one or more protocols.

Next, you learned how to use protocols as types when specifying that a constant, variable, or property that conforms to a protocol should be used. Using protocols as types can also be used in collection types. You also learned how to adopt multiple protocols mixed with class inheritance. Following that, you learned how to check conformance to a protocol with the is, as, and as? operators in the exact same way, and how to use the @objc attribute on a protocol if you are checking for conformance during runtime or if your protocol contains any optional members.

Finally, you learned about delegation and the role protocols play in delegation. Delegates and data sources are found throughout the Cocoa and Cocoa Touch frameworks and are typically reliant upon any type that conforms to the respective protocol versus a concrete implementation.

In the next hour, we discuss extensions as a way to add, or extend, functionality in types, along with some neat examples of the power this gives you to create concise, meaningful, and powerful code.

Q&A

Q. Why would I want to use protocols? It seems easier to use subclasses or just make new classes instead.

A. When an object adopts a protocol, it is making a promise that it will provide certain functionality. This allows objects that are otherwise unrelated fill a similar role. For example, both a car and a classroom might provide information about maximum capacity, but they probably don't belong in the same class structure.

Swift is a single inheritance language, which means that a class can only have a single superclass. But a class, enum, or struct can adopt multiple protocols, which enables more flexibility in your code.

Q. Can a protocol specify a default implementation of a method?

A. No. A protocol only specifies which methods must be present, not how they should work.

Q. If I use the @objc keyword, do I have to write Objective-C instead of Swift?

A. No, @objc is just a hint to the compiler that the protocol is doing something that it needs to be aware of. You still write your code in Swift.

Q. Can protocols inherit other protocols?

A. Yes, they can! Protocols can inherit one or more other protocols if you need them to. Any class that adopts the child protocol must also satisfy the requirements of the parent protocol.

Workshop

The workshop contains quiz questions and exercises to help you solidify your understanding of the material covered. Try to answer all questions before looking at the answers that follow.

Quiz

1. Do you need to use the `override` keyword when implementing a method required by a protocol your class adopts?

2. True or false? Properties defined in a protocol must always be defined with the `var` keyword, even when they're constants.

3. What's wrong with the following code?

```
protocol CoolProperty {
  var coolFactor: Bool { get set }
}

class Student {
  var name = "Default Name"
}

class Senior : CoolProperty, Student {
  var coolFactor = true
}
```

4. If a protocol defines a read-write property, can my class implement it as read-only?

Answers

1. No, you can just implement the method in your class.

2. True. Always use `var` in property definitions.

3. In the `Senior` class, the superclass must be listed before any adopted protocols. Here, we list the protocol `CoolProperty` before the superclass `Student`.

4. No, if the property is read-write in the protocol definition, it must be read-write in the adopting class.

Exercise

Create a new OS X playground. Define a protocol named `Nameable` that specifies a `describe` method and a property called `name`. The `describe` method should take no arguments and return a string. Next, define a protocol named `Debugable`, which specifies a method named `showDebug`. This method should take no arguments and return a string. When you adopt these protocols, have `name()` and `showDebug()` display useful information about the object.

Create three classes, one that adopts `Nameable`, one that adopts `Debugable`, and one that adopts both protocols. Now create arrays of types `Namable`, `Debugable`, and the composition of those two protocols.

Practice adding objects of each type to these three arrays and then calling `describe` and `showDebug` on the contents. What happens if you try to add a class that doesn't adopt `Describable` to an array of type `Describable`? What would be different if you were using enums or structs instead of classes? Can you add a class that adopts both protocols to the `Describable` array? Try it out and see.

HOUR 18
Using Extensions to Add Type Functionality

What You'll Learn in This Hour:

▶ How to define extensions

▶ How to add initializers with extensions

▶ How to add methods, computed properties, and subscripts with extensions

▶ How to adopt a protocol to an existing type

In this hour we discuss a feature of Swift called **extensions**. Types provided by Apple in the Swift programming language are closed, unable to be modified by us, and extensions help overcome that roadblock. You learn how to add functionality of multiple different facets to existing types and the implications of doing so. Let's take a look at what extensions are and how to use them.

Defining Extensions

A Swift extension is a way to add functionality, but not override existing functionality, to an existing type. You can add extensions to types that you create, as well as to types provided by Swift, such as `Int`, `Double`, `String`, `Array`, and so on.

Why would you want to add functionality with an extension? There are several reasons why you might want to add extensions to your types. You might not have access to the actual source implementation of types, which is exactly the case with Swift's built-in types of `Int`, `String`, and so on. Your company might have a policy in place as well that disallows you from accessing standard structures of types for modification. Such examples are said to be *closed for modification*, but with extensions, these types are now able to be extended because they are *open for extension*.

NOTE

Open/Closed Principle

The Open/Closed Principle, coined by Bertrand Meyer, states that "software entities should be open for extension, but closed for modification." In keeping with good software development methodologies, extensions provide a tremendous way to extend existing type functionality without altering the actual implementation of a type.

There are also instances in developing apps for Mac and iOS platforms where you may use a framework called Core Data. Core Data is a way to use model objects and an object graph to persist data, rather than dealing with a SQLite database (or whatever backing store) directly. When you create your model objects with Xcode's visual editor, you then create NSManagedObject subclasses that represent your model objects. These NSManagedObject subclasses can get recreated any time your data model is updated. Since these subclasses get overwritten frequently, it doesn't make much sense to put any extra logic inside them, so extensions are a perfect solution for an example such as this.

Basic Structure of Extensions

Extensions in Swift do not get a special name; they only need to reference the type they are extending. The syntax for defining an extension is simply the extension keyword followed by the type name that you want to extend, and, finally, curly braces to include the code you're extending onto the type. Figure 18.1 shows the general structure of an extension.

```
extension TypeNameToExtend {
    // ... functionality to add
}
```

FIGURE 18.1
The general structure of an extension in Swift.

You can also have more than one extension for a particular type. In fact, in the interest of good software design, it may behoove you to create multiple extensions separated by each having a single responsibility. For example, if you Command+click the Int keyword in Xcode, Xcode navigates you to the definition of the Int struct and all its extensions. There are many extensions, each responsible for providing a single solution, such as for providing the hashValue property and also the description property, as shown in Figure 18.2.

```
2456
2457   extension Int : Hashable {
2458       var hashValue: Int { get }
2459   }
2460
2461   extension Int : Printable {
2462       var description: String { get }
2463   }
2464
```

FIGURE 18.2
Two extensions on the Int struct showing how functionality can be extracted out to separate components with extensions and protocols.

Adding Functionality with Extensions

There are several pieces of functionality we can add to types with extensions, which include adding new computed instance and type properties, instance and type methods, subscripts, initializers, nested types, and protocol conformance. Adding these pieces of functionality is treated as if you were adding them directly to the type itself, so there really is no difference in syntax; the only difference is that you're adding them to an extension inside an extension definition. Since we are adding functionality to existing types and dealing with instance properties or instance methods, we can refer to the instance itself with the self keyword. Let's discuss each one and cover examples to illustrate how each piece of functionality can be added.

Computed Instance and Type Properties

You may add computed instance and type properties to a type with extensions. You cannot, however, add stored properties. An example of adding computed properties could be if you wanted to add instance properties on the Double type to convert gallons to quarts, pints, and cups, or on the String type to return the string instance broken into an array of Character instances.

NOTE

Extensions Add Functionality to All Instances of a Type

Remember that adding an extension to a type adds that functionality to all instances of that type, even if they were created before the instance was created, such as an instance from permanent storage.

Let's take a look at how we can add a computed instance property to the `String` type. Remember, adding functionality with an extension is just as if we were adding the functionality directly into the type like normal, so the syntax should all look the same to you for concepts learned thus far.

Listing 18.1 illustrates how to add an extension to the `String` type to return an instance's representation as an array of characters.

LISTING 18.1   **Extending the String Type with Computed Properties**

```
extension String {
    var asArray: [Character] {
        var result = [Character]()
        for character in self {
            result.append(character)
        }
        return result
    }
}

let chars = "Hello".asArray    // chars is equal to ["H", "e", "l", "l", "o"]
let dog = "Fido"
let dogChars = dog.asArray     // dogChars is equal to ["F", "i", "d", "o"]
```

In the preceding example, we simply add a computed instance property to the `String` type, which we can then use with dot syntax to get the result. Simple, right? Notice that we can also use our extended computed property directly on a string literal in addition to a variable. This is because string literals are still of type `String`, so any property or method can be accessed just as if it were on a variable or constant.

Let's create another example on a numeric type, to see how extensions can be used to add some powerful functionality in just a few lines of code. Say that we have used the `typealias` keyword to create a type alias to `Double`, for working with miles per hour of a car. We can even extend an aliased type. Listing 18.2 illustrates how to do this.

LISTING 18.2   **Extending Aliased Types**

```
typealias MPH = Double
extension MPH {
    var kmPerHour: Double { return self * 1.60934 }
    var milesPerMinute: Double { return self / 60.0 }
}

let speed: MPH = 60
let kmH = speed.kmPerHour      // kmH is equal to 96.5604
let mpM = speed.milesPerMinute // mpM is equal to 1.0
```

Creating custom computed properties for types inside extensions can greatly increase functionality of a type and its instances, while keeping code separated by responsibility and modularized. Think about how computed properties could be added to other types and experiment on your own!

Instance and Type Methods

Methods are another piece of functionality that we can add to types via extensions. Again, methods (both instance and type) are added with their normal syntax, without any special modifications. If you are creating a method that would mutate a struct or enum, you must add the `mutating` keyword, as you normally would.

A classic example of adding a method to a type is by adding a method to the `Int` type with a trailing closure that gets executed as many times as the integer value equals. The method takes a single parameter, of type `()  ->  ()`, and looks like the example in Listing 18.3.

LISTING 18.3   Adding Methods with Extensions

```
extension Int {
    func repeat(closure: () -> ()) {
        for _ in 1...self {
            closure()
        }
    }
}


3.repeat { println("I'm being printed!") }
```

That is a common example for extensions on the `Int` type, but how could you use this in a practical application? Listing 18.4 shows how to use this extension for quickly adjusting a player's score in a game. Because the `repeat(closure:)` method takes a function with no parameters and returns void, we can send any method or function that fits that description.

LISTING 18.4   Adding Methods with Extensions for a Game

```
// use extension from Listing 18.3
struct Player {
    var score = 0
    mutating func increaseScore() {
        ++score
    }
    mutating func decreaseScore() {
        --score
    }
}
```

```
var player = Player()
// while playing game, player wins 5 points
5.repeat { player.increaseScore() }
player.score                 // displays 5
```

Adding Subscripts in Extensions

Another functionality that can be added to extensions is the capability to add subscripts. You can give subscripts their own meaning inside your apps by creating custom subscripts to be applied to any type, but with extensions, you can add them to existing types. Let's try an example in the following Try It Yourself section to add subscripting capability to the String type so we can obtain the character at a particular index in the string.

▼ TRY IT YOURSELF

Extend the String Type to Add Subscripts

Add a subscript function to the String type to obtain the character at a particular index.

1. Open Xcode 6 and create a new playground; either an iOS or a Mac playground will work. Clear the contents of the playground.

2. Recreate the asArray computed property from Listing 18.1, as that provides a convenience for our subscript extension.

```
extension String {
    var asArray: [Character] {
        var result = [Character]()
        for character in self {
            result.append(character)
        }
        return result
    }
}
```

3. Now that we have self as an array instance, we can easily return the character at a particular index by using a subscript function inside a new extension. Create a subscript with only a getter to return the character at a given index.

```
extension String {
    subscript(index: Int) -> Character {
        return self.asArray[index]
    }
}
```

4. There's a problem with this subscript, though. Can you see it? What happens if the string is empty or if the index provided is out of bounds? Fix the subscript to check the string and index first, and return `nil` if these criteria are not met. Because we could return `nil`, change the return type from `Character` to `Character?`.

```
extension String {
    subscript(index: Int) -> Character? {
        if !self.isEmpty && index < countElements(self) && index >= 0 {
            return self.asArray[index]
        }
        return nil
    }
}
```

5. Create an instance of `String`, and access a subscript on that string. Then create an empty string and try to access a subscript on the empty string.

```
let words = "Cuyahoga River"
let fifthChar = words[4]!
let emptyString = ""
let badIndex = emptyString[0]
```

By using extensions and reusing code, we easily created a powerful construct to use any time we need to quickly access the *nth* element of a string, and we don't need to have a lot of repeated code in our app since our extensions apply to all `String` instances in our module. The completed Try It Yourself section code and results should look like those in Figure 18.3.

```
     ● ● ●                    Ch18 Subscripts TIY.playground
     ⊞  <  >   Ch18 Subscripts TIY.playground ⟩  C  String
 1   extension String {
 2       var asArray: [Character] {
 3           var result = [Character]()                    0 elements
 4           for character in self {
 5               result.append(character)
 6           }
 7           return result                                 ["C", "u", "y", "a", "h",…
 8       }
 9   }
10
11   extension String {
12       subscript(index: Int) -> Character? {
13           if !self.isEmpty && index < countElements(self) && index >= 0 {
14               return self.asArray[index]                {Some "h"}
15           }
16           return nil                                    nil
17       }
18   }
19
20   let words = "Cuyahoga River"                          "Cuyahoga River"
21   let fifthChar = words[4]!                             "h"
22   let emptyString = ""                                  ""
23   let badIndex = emptyString[0]                         nil
24
```

FIGURE 18.3
The completed Try It Yourself example illustrating using extensions on the `String` type to return the character at a particular subscript.

Adding Custom Initializers with Extensions

By now you should be familiar with the extension concept and syntax, in that you can add mostly any functionality you need by adding an extension on a particular type. Another piece of functionality that you would expect to be written exactly as it is normally and behave the same way is initializers. And you're right, initializers can be added to types via extensions, but there are two caveats: You cannot add a designated initializer with an extension, and you cannot provide a deinitializer.

If you have a struct that provides default values for its properties without a custom initializer, your extended initializer can call either the default initializer or the memberwise initializer. Let's take a look at how that is done in Listing 18.5.

LISTING 18.5 Creating Initializers in Extensions

```
import Foundation

struct Circle {
    var radius = 0.0
    var circumference: Double {
        return 2 * radius * M_PI
    }
}
```

```
extension Circle {
    init(circumference: Double) {
        let radius = circumference / (2 * M_PI)
        self.init(radius: radius)
    }
}


let circle = Circle(circumference: 31.42)
circle.radius                           // displays 5.0006483....
```

Since a class type must have a designated initializer inside its main implementation, you cannot add one in an extension. Creating initializers inside extensions of class types must use the `convenience` keyword since they should, by default, be convenience initializers, as the designated initializer must reside inside the class implementation directly. That also means that your convenience initializer *must* call the designated initializer or another convenience initializer in the same type to complete full initialization of the instance before use. Failure to do so generates a compiler error. Listing 18.6 shows adding a convenience initializer in a class extension.

LISTING 18.6 **Creating a Convenience Initializer in a Class Type Extension**

```
class Person {
    var fullName: String
    init(fullName: String) {
        self.fullName = fullName
    }
}


extension Person {
    convenience init(firstName: String, lastName: String) {
        let fullName = firstName + " " + lastName
        self.init(fullName: fullName)
    }
}


let person = Person(firstName: "George", lastName: "Washington")
person.fullName              // displays "George Washington"
```

Creating an initializer in an extension for a class type is equally as easy and syntactically the same as if it were inside a class implementation directly. Remember that since you cannot add a designated initializer in an extension to a class type, any initializers you add must be convenience initializers.

Adding Nested Types to Extensions

Although we haven't discussed **nested types** yet, the concepts discussed here pertain just as if they were added directly to a type without an extension. Nested types are types that help support a larger type and are only accessible to instances of that larger type. Nested types are not accessible to types outside the type inside which they are encapsulated.

An example of when you would use a nested type could be with a deck of cards, for a quick and simple way to obtain data whether a card is a face card or a numeric card. Listing 18.7 shows how we could use a nested type inside a Rank enum.

LISTING 18.7   **Adding Nested Types in Extensions**

```
01:   enum Transformers : String {
02:       case OptimusPrime = "Optimus Prime"
03:       case Bumblebee = "Bumblebee"
04:       case Ratchet = "Ratchet"
05:       case Megatron = "Megatron"
06:       case Starscream = "Starscream"
07:   }
08:
09:   extension Transformers {
10:       enum TransformerType {
11:           case Autobot, Decepticon
12:       }
13:
14:       var type: TransformerType {
15:           switch self {
16:               case .OptimusPrime, .Bumblebee, .Ratchet:
17:                   return .Autobot
18:               default:
19:                   return .Decepticon
20:           }
21:       }
22:   }
23:
24:   let transformer = Transformers.Bumblebee
25:   switch transformer.type {
26:       case .Autobot:
27:           println("\(transformer.toRaw()) is an Autobot.")
28:       case .Decepticon:
29:           println("\(transformer.toRaw()) is a Decepticon.")
30:   }
```

Since nested types are new to us in this book, as well as a new concept for us to cover with regard to extensions, let's discuss some key lines in Listing 18.7. We created a standard enum on line 1 with a backing value of type `String`. But suppose after the `Transformers` type is created we want to add a description of whether the `Transformers` instance is an Autobot or Decepticon. On line 9 we extend the `Transformers` enum, and on line 10 we create a nested type. The nested type is another enum, and the enum is only available to instances of the `Transformers` type. A nested type can be added to a main type implementation and used just as you see here if not used in an extension—the syntax and usage are exactly the same.

Then on line 14 we create a computed property to return a value of our nested type. If you were following along in the REPL or in a playground, try changing the enum value from `.Bumblebee` to another `Transformers` case on line 24, to watch the `switch` statement find the appropriate description for the Transformer in question.

Protocol Adoption and Conformance in Extensions

The final concept in this hour with regard to what can be added with extensions is about protocols. As you learned in Hour 17, "Using Protocols to Define Behavior," protocols are a blueprint to functionality and behavior that a type must conform to if it adopts the protocol. It is a contract stating that any type that conforms to this protocol can and will provide the necessary information outlined in the protocol.

Adding adoption and conformance to a protocol in an extension is just as simple as everything else we have done in extensions this hour, combined with the simplicity of declaring and conforming to a protocol. Whether you're creating a new protocol to make a type conform to or conforming to an existing protocol, you simply add the protocol name after the type name and a colon in the extension declaration, as shown in the following snippet.

```
extension ExistingType : ProtocolName {
    // ...add protocol properties or methods here...
}
```

If a type already has the properties and/or methods that belong to a protocol's definition but does not yet adopt the protocol, you can simply create an extension of the type that adopts the protocol and then provide an empty pair of curly braces, as shown in the following snippet.

```
extension ExistingType : ProtocolName { }
```

The preceding snippet may be beneficial in cases where you have a model object in your app that contains information about the instance that happens to be the same information required by a protocol. Imagine your model object also has a title, subtitle, and coordinate. Despite having the information needed to drop a pin on a map view, the model object's type may not have adopted the protocol, so the map view cannot use it as a pin annotation on the map. By providing an empty extension for your model's type that adopts the `MKAnnotation` protocol, it can then be shown on the map as a pin annotation, because the map view can only place instances that adopt and conform to the MKAnnotation protocol to the map.

Let's try a small example of adopting and conforming the Int type to a protocol in the following Try It Yourself example.

▼ TRY IT YOURSELF

Extend Int to Adopt and Conform to a Protocol

Create a protocol that has a function to square an integer. Then extend the Int type to adopt the protocol. Finally, add the method to conform to the protocol.

1. Open Xcode 6 and create a new playground; either an iOS or a Mac playground is fine. Clear the contents of the playground.

2. Start by creating the protocol. Call it Squarable and provide a function definition that takes no parameters and returns an Int.

```
protocol Squarable {
    func squared() -> Int
}
```

3. Create an extension for the Int type and adopt the Squarable protocol. Then conform to the protocol by implementing the squared() function and return the squared value of the given integer.

```
extension Int : Squarable {
    func squared() -> Int {
        return self * self
    }
}
```

4. Finally, try out your new instance method from your extension on a number.

```
5.squared()      // displays 25
```

In just a few lines, you added a lot of power to the Int type. Now any instance of an Int can call the squared() instance method and immediately get the squared value of itself. The completed code and results from the preceding Try It Yourself section should look like those in Figure 18.4.

```
● ● ●               🄰 Ch18 Protocol Extension TIY.playground
⊞  |  <   >  |  🄰 Ch18 Protocol Extension TIY.playground ⟩ No Selection
 1    protocol Squarable {
 2        func squared() -> Int
 3    }
 4
 5    extension Int : Squarable {
 6        func squared() -> Int {
 7            return self * self                          25
 8        }
 9    }
10
11    5.squared()                                         25
12
```

FIGURE 18.4
The completed Try It Yourself example code and results from adding protocol conformance via extensions.

Summary

This hour introduced extensions, a Swift feature enabling you to add functionality to built-in or custom types. You learned about many different capabilities that can be added to types with extensions including computed properties, methods, subscripts, initializers, nested types, and protocols.

As you saw in the many examples in this hour, the code to add these behaviors to types is exactly the same as if they were added directly to the type itself.

In the next hour, we discuss optional chaining, which is a powerful way to traverse paths of optional properties and fail gracefully if nil is encountered.

Q&A

Q. When would I want to use extensions instead of just making a subclass and adding the new functionality there?

A. Extensions enable you to modify an existing class without creating a new one. This means that the changes you make are available to every object of the type being extended. If you make a subclass, the new functionality is only available to that new subclass. For example, in this hour, we added new properties to integers, and those changes affected all integers in our program.

Q. Can an extension override a method that already exists in the class, structure, or enumeration type?

A. No. If you try to override an extension or property that already exists, you get an invalid redeclaration error.

Q. Can I use access control (public, private, internal) in an extension?

A. Yes. You can specify any level of access control you need to when creating an extension. The same access control rules that we saw in Hour 15, "Adding Advanced Type Functionality," apply to extensions.

Q. If I define an extension on a class, is that extension available to its subclasses too?

A. Yes. Your extension adds new functionality to the base class, and that functionality is passed on to subclasses.

Workshop

The workshop contains quiz questions and exercises to help you solidify your understanding of the material covered. Try to answer all questions before looking at the answers that follow.

Quiz

1. Can there be more than one extension for a single type?

2. True or false? You can add designated initializers using extensions, but not convenience initializers.

3. Can extensions be used to adopt protocols?

4. True or false? Mutating methods are not allowed in extensions for structs or enums.

Answers

1. Yes, as long as the extensions are adding different things.

2. False. You can add a convenience initializer, but just like any other convenience initializer, it must ultimately call a designated initializer.

3. Yes, but if a protocol is adopted, all the normal conformance rules apply. The class, struct, or enum must be extended to implement all required methods and properties.

4. False. Methods defined in extensions can mutate a struct or enum's properties as long as the mutating keyword is used in the method definition.

Exercise

Create a new OS X playground. Create an extension to `String` that produces the string in reverse order. For example, `"My String".reverse` should give us "gnirtS yM" back. If you get stuck, look at the `toArray` method we created earlier.

For more of a challenge, create an extension to `String` that converts a string of digits to an integer. For example, `"1397".toInt` should return the integer 1397. What do you think your extension should do if the string contains something other than integers? This might be a good time for an optional.

HINT: Remember that 1397 = 7 + 90 + 300 + 1000

Working with Optional Chaining

What You'll Learn in This Hour:

▸ What optional chaining is

▸ When to use optional chaining

▸ How to chain properties, methods, and subscripts

▸ How to verify optional chaining success or failure

In this hour we cover optional chaining. This concept is new to most programmers, as it only makes sense in the context of working with optional values, which is a new concept itself to some programmers, and sort of new to most Objective C programmers. You learn the basics of optional chaining, when and how to use it, and how to verify success or handle failure. This hour builds on the concepts of optional values discussed in Hour 5, "Understanding Optional Values," so if you need to brush up on optionals first, I suggest you do so before continuing with this hour. If not, let's discuss optional chaining in Swift.

Defining Optional Chaining

As you recall, Swift provides functionality for dealing with nil, or the absence of a value, called optional values. Think of an optional value as a box. The box may have something inside, or it may be empty. The same goes for optional values in Swift. To continue the box metaphor, if you have an optional string, denoted by String?, the box is of type String?, and it may have an actual value (a present), or it may be empty (nil).

Optional chaining is the process of checking optional values by calling or querying properties, methods, and subscripts of an optional type to perform a specific task or return nil. If an optional value that you call or query is not nil, the call or query succeeds. If the optional value is nil, the call or query fails gracefully and returns nil. Since there is a possibility for the call or query to return nil, the result of an optional chaining is always of an optional type. An optional chain can be used instead of several nested optional binding statements.

Optional chaining can be thought of like Matryoshka dolls (also known as Russian nesting dolls). You can see the outer doll, but you don't know whether there is another doll or dolls inside. You open the doll, and if there is another doll, you can attempt to use or open that doll too. If there is no other doll inside you stop, as if you encountered nil.

The reason for stating in the beginning of the hour that this is sort of new to Objective-C programmers is that in Objective-C you can message or query nil and it will fail gracefully, so Objective-C programmers use it to their benefit. There are differences, though, in how Swift handles optional chaining and Objective-C handles messaging nil. Mainly, Swift can chain optionals of any type, and return nil for any type, not just class instances like Objective-C. You can also have an instance of a class be equal to nil in Objective-C without being wrapped, but that is not considered safe in Swift. So all nil values must be wrapped, or else the app will crash at runtime.

Optional chaining returns an optional value of the type specified by the instance being called or queried. This means that if you query a property of type `String?`, you receive a `String?` instance back, even if there is a value inside the optional. This is actually helpful, because if you receive nil from the call or query, you know that the call or query failed. And if the optional contains a value, your call or query succeeded. The same goes for a property, method, or subscript that returns a non-optional type; the result will still be an optional because the call or query could have failed along the chain and returned nil.

Chaining Optional Properties

Often you have properties in a class, struct, or enum of an optional type. The types that those properties reference or contain could also be optional, and you may find yourself needing to access values two, three, or more levels down the property relationship chain. Optional chaining gives you a safe way to determine whether a value is nil at any point along the way to calling or querying your final property, and if so, fail safely by returning nil. Not only can you use optional chaining for calling or querying properties, but you can also set properties using optional chaining.

Let's take a look at a simple example of how optional chaining works. Say we have a `Person` class representing a possible owner of a `Dog` instance. The person may or may not have a dog, so we would make this property an optional type. For simplicity's sake, all you dog lovers, we keep the person to one dog for now. Using optional chaining, we try to retrieve the name of the person instance's dog. Listing 19.1 illustrates this example.

LISTING 19.1   Basic Optional Chaining of Properties

```
01:   class Person {
02:       var dog: Dog?
03:   }
04:
```

```
05:   class Dog {
06:       var name: String
07:       init(name: String) { self.name = name }
08:   }
09:
10:   let susie = Person()
11:   let dogsName = susie.dog?.name    // returns nil
```

In Listing 19.1, we declare two classes, Person and Dog, just like normal. On line 10 we declare an instance of Person and set it to the constant susie. Then on line 11, we try to get the dog's name from susie's dog instance's name property. Since susie's dog property is of an optional type, we need to place the question mark after the dog property before we try to access the dog's name property. susie has no dog yet, so dogsName is of type String? and contains nil.

If we were to assign an instance of Dog to susie's dog property, we would see the optional chaining call on line 11 with a different result. Let's do that in Listing 19.2 by inserting a creation of a Dog instance between lines 10 and 11 from the preceding example.

LISTING 19.2 **Assigning a Dog**

```
// reuse classes declared in Listing 19.1
let bobby = Person()
bobby.dog - Dog(name: "Cletus")
let dogsName = bobby.dog?.name        // returns {Some "Cletus"}
```

As you can see, now that bobby's dog property is not nil, there is now a name to be accessed via optional chaining. Do you see how the resulting value assigned to dogsName is {Some "Cletus"}? That is because even though there is a value for the name property of the Dog instance, bobby's dog property is of type Dog?, and thus the returned value must be optional, as a String?, too.

The preceding examples illustrate how the syntax works for optional chaining, but let's deviate to a larger example, one that may represent an enterprise problem that needs solved with your Swift programming expertise. To start, let's discuss accessing and modifying subscripts with optional chaining.

Subscripts

Recall that subscripts are a way to set and get values of types such as arrays and dictionaries, and the syntax for subscript access is implemented by including an integer index or hashable key inside a pair of open- and closed-square brackets.

In my experience, I have worked a lot in the administration realm of Microsoft SharePoint Server. You may have used SharePoint at some point in your career for document management, team collaboration, or any other feature it provides. This book isn't going in the direction of educating you on the inner workings of Microsoft SharePoint Server, but concepts in it can be applied to our topic of optional chaining. Rather than continuing to refer to Microsoft SharePoint Server, I will henceforth refer to it and any similar collaboration tool as simply a *collaboration tool.*

NOTE

The SharePoint Object Model

We discuss objects similar to the hierarchy of SharePoint but not anything specific from the SharePoint Object Model. The concepts here can apply to many other collaborative systems, but I reference SharePoint because of its generally ubiquitous understanding in the tech world.

When accessing subscripts through optional chaining, it is important to take a second to think about what portion or portions of the optional chain should have the optional chaining operator (?), and where in relation to the property, method, or subscript syntax it should be placed. You should always place the optional chaining operator after the portion or portions that can be optional, not necessarily after the entire expression. For example, accessing an element at a particular index of an optional array means that you should put the optional chaining operator immediately after the name of the optional array, but before the index, because the array itself is optional, not necessarily the element at the index. In code, it would look like the following code snippet.

```
let someValue = someInstance.someArray?[0] // correct
let anotherValue = anotherInstance.anotherArray[0]?  // incorrect
```

NOTE

Delegates Are Often Optional

Remember using the delegate pattern in Hour 18, "Using Extensions to Add Type Functionality," and how we set the delegate directly in the initializer? That was so that the delegate could not be nil. There may be times, however, where the delegate may never be set, because all properties and methods on a particular protocol are optional, and the instance calling the delegate can operate without having a delegate respond to any messages. Using a delegate is a prime example of using optional chaining, by checking whether the delegate is nil first before calling or querying any properties or methods on the delegate.

Let's say we are writing an app that integrates with a collaboration tool and we need a few classes to store data and perform actions for us, such as a site, document library, and document. Each site can have zero or more document libraries, and each document library can have zero or more documents. There are many other things that these objects could do in real-world collaboration tools, but these few examples are sufficient for this hour. Figure 19.1 illustrates what a collaboration scenario might look like structurally.

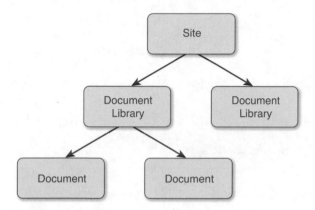

FIGURE 19.1
An example collaboration hierarchy diagram of a site, document libraries, and documents.

Let's create this example in code in the following Try It Yourself section. You walk through creating the classes with optional array properties and then how to access data using optional chaining.

Using Optional Chaining with Subscripts

Create an object model that reflects the collaboration tool hierarchy previously discussed. Then use optional chaining to set and get elements down the chain.

1. Open Xcode 6 and create a new playground, either iOS or Mac will work. Clear the contents of the playground.

2. Start by creating the `Site` class. Provide a variable property named `title` of type `String`. Then create a variable property that is an optional array of `Library` instances. Don't initialize the array. Provide an initializer to set the `title` property.

```
class Site {
    var title: String
    var libraries: [Library]?
    init(title: String) { self.title = title }
}
```

3. Create the `Library` class. This class has a variable `title` property of type `String` and an optional array of type `Document`. Create an initializer for the `title` property.

```
class Library {
    var title: String
    var documents: [Document]?
    init(title: String) { self.title = title }
}
```

4. Create the `Document` class. This class also has a variable `title` property of type `String` and an initializer for the `title` property.

```
class Document {
    var title: String
    init(title: String) { self.title = title }
}
```

5. That's all for the model classes. Create an instance of type `Site` and call it "Accounting".

```
let acctSite = Site(title: "Accounting")
```

6. Create an instance of a document library for documents related to auditing and use optional chaining to append it as the first instance in the `acctSite`'s `Library` array. But before we do that, we have to initialize the `acctSite`'s `Library` array before we can use it.

```
let auditLibrary = Library(title: "Audit Library")
acctSite.libraries = []
acctSite.libraries?.append(auditLibrary)
```

7. That is how we can use optional chaining for assignment. If the `libraries` array was nil, `auditLibrary` would not have been appended, and the expression would have returned nil signifying to us that the optional chaining failed. Repeat step 6 but with creating a document and adding it to the `documents` array in the `auditLibrary` instance, and initialize the `documents` array first.

```
let document = Document(title: "Audit Report November 2014.txt")
auditLibrary.documents = []
auditLibrary.documents?.append(document)
```

8. Now that we have a non-nil hierarchy of site > library > document, use optional chaining with subscripts to grab the document name for use in a constant. Use multiple levels of optional chaining to retrieve the document name. Try using `[0]` and also `first` to get the first element.

```
let docName = acctSite.libraries?[0].documents?[0].title  // or...
let docName = acctSite.libraries?.first?.documents?.first?.title
```

9. Notice how you had to add `?` after `first` also? That is because there may not be an item in the first element, so that computed property returns an optional. Also, even though the `title` property on `Document` is not optional, `docName` *is* optional, because it was retrieved using optional chaining, and any point along the way could have failed and returned `nil`. Use optional binding to extract the value and print an appropriate message.

```
if let name = docName {
    println("Document name is \(name).")
} else {
    println("Could not retrieve document name.")
}
```

10. For fun, comment out the line in step 6, `acctSite.libraries = []`. Now what results do you get? You should get nil, because optional chaining encountered a nil value in its chain before it got to the document's `title` property.

The completed Try It Yourself example code and results should look like those in Figure 19.2.

```
class Site {
    var title: String
    var libraries: [Library]?
    init(title: String) { self.title = title }
}

class Library {
    var title: String
    var documents: [Document]?
    init(title: String) { self.title = title }
}

class Document {
    var title: String
    init(title: String) { self.title = title }
}

let acctSite = Site(title: "Accounting")                          {title "Accounting" nil}

let auditLibrary = Library(title: "Audit Library")                {title "Audit Library" nil}
acctSite.libraries = []                                           {title "Accounting" {0 eleme...
acctSite.libraries?.append(auditLibrary)                          {(0 elements)}

let document = Document(title: "Audit Report November 2014.txt")  {title "Audit Report Novemb...
auditLibrary.documents = []                                       {title "Audit Library" {0 elem...
auditLibrary.documents?.append(document)                          {(0 elements)}

//let docName = acctSite.libraries?[0].documents?[0].title   // or...
let docName = acctSite.libraries?.first?.documents?.first?.title  {Some "Audit Report Nove...

if let name = docName {
    println("Document name is \(name)")                           "Document name is Audit R...
} else {
    println("Could not retrieve document name")
}
```

FIGURE 19.2
The completed Try It Yourself example with optional chaining using subscripts and multiple levels of optional chaining.

Another utilization of subscripts with optional chaining is with dictionaries. This is another place where you need to pay close attention to the placement of the optional chaining operator, whether it is before or after the subscript, but luckily Xcode is good about suggesting how to fix your code if you don't put the ? in the right place.

Let's say you are creating an app to track bowling scores, so you have a dictionary with the bowlers' names as the keys and their scores in an array for their key's value. Listing 19.3 utilizes optional chaining using dictionaries to adjust a value of one of the values in a player's array of scores.

LISTING 19.3   **Using Optional Chaining with Dictionary Subscripts**

```
var bowlingScores = [ "Jane" : [190, 180, 172], "John" : [165, 156, 214] ]

bowlingScores    // displays ["John": [165, 156, 214], "Jane": [190, 180, 172]]

// pin counter mis-counted Jane's last game by 1
bowlingScores["Jane"]?[2]++

bowlingScores    // displays ["John": [165, 156, 214], "Jane": [190, 180, 173]]
```

By using optional chaining, we are able to directly set an array's value inside a dictionary's value for a specific key. Remember that a dictionary can return nil when we ask it for a value at a particular key, because that key may not exist yet, so there obviously is no value. We must use optional chaining to access the element at index two of the array stored for key "Jane" to increment it.

Methods

Accessing methods in Swift using optional chaining works in much the same way as accessing properties; you just need to add the parentheses after the method name when you call it. If the method returns a non-optional value, the result will still be an optional value if it was accessed using optional chaining, just as with properties. If the method returns an optional value, the resulting value is not doubly wrapped; a method that returns String? when called using optional chaining does not return String??. A returned value is either optional or non-optional.

Something special happens, however, when you call a function that doesn't have a return type. Swift infers this type of function to return an empty tuple, or (), as we discussed in Hour 8, "Using Functions to Perform Actions." The actual type for this is Void, and since when we use optional chaining we always get a return type as an optional, we are returned Void?. Usually if a function returns nothing, we don't have any need for an empty tuple or anything of type

`Void`, but with optional chaining, we can use this as a way to verify whether our function was actually executed by checking it against `nil`.

Going back to the collaboration tool example, we can add instance methods to these classes, such as for adding a new document and checking out or checking in a document. By adding a method on `Library` to add a new document, we can also lazily instantiate the `documents` array and alleviate the caller of that responsibility, like we had to do in the preceding Try It Yourself example. If you're following along, feel free to open up your playground file from the Try It Yourself example and adjust your code with me as shown in Listing 19.4. Notice in line 40 of Listing 19.4 that a warning is produced; this is expected and is explained in the paragraph following the listing.

LISTING 19.4 Using Optional Chaining to Call Instance Methods

```
01:  class Site {
02:      var title: String
03:      var libraries: [Library]?
04:      init(title: String) { self.title = title }
05:      func addNewLibrary(#title: String) -> Library {
06:          var library = Library(title: title)
07:          if libraries == nil {
08:              libraries = []
09:          }
10:          libraries?.append(library)
11:          return library
12:      }
13:  }
14:
15:  class Library {
16:      var title: String
17:      var documents: [Document]?
18:      init(title: String) { self.title = title }
19:      func addNewDocument(#title: String) -> Document {
20:          var document = Document(title: title)
21:          if documents == nil {
22:              documents = []
23:          }
24:          documents?.append(document)
25:          return document
26:      }
27:  }
28:
29:  class Document {
30:      var title: String
31:      var checkedOut = false
32:      init(title: String) { self.title = title }
33:      func checkOut() { checkedOut = true }
```

```
34:        func checkIn() { checkedOut = false }
35:    }
36:
37:    let acctSite = Site(title: "Accounting")
38:    acctSite.addNewLibrary(title: "Audit Library")
39:    let addDoc = acctSite.libraries?.first?.addNewDocument(title: "Audit Report")
40:    let checkout = acctSite.libraries?.first?.documents?.first?.checkOut()
```

In the preceding example, we add two new instance methods, one on `Site` and one on
`Library`, on lines 5 and 19, respectively. These create a new instance of the type contained in
their array properties and lazily instantiate the arrays if they are nil, on lines 7 through 9 and
21 through 23, respectively. On line 37 we create the site, and then on 38 we add a new library
to its `libraries` array. On line 39 we ask the first library in `acctSite.libraries?` to add
a document using optional chaining, which returns `Document?` to `addDoc`. We could check
`addDoc` for `nil` to see whether it succeeded. On line 40, we use optional chaining for calling a
method again and attempt to check out the first document in the first library in the site. Xcode 6
provides a warning, stating that the inferred type of our optional chaining call to `checkOut()` is
`()?`, and Xcode suggests explicitly adding the type annotation to silence the compiler warning,
as seen in Figure 19.3. Xcode's Fix-it suggestion is a good safety feature to ensure we intended to
be returned the inferred type.

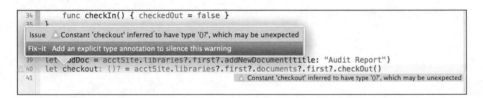

FIGURE 19.3
Xcode compiler warning suggesting explicit type annotation for `()?`.

Summary

In this hour you learned what optional chaining is and how to understand it by thinking of the
Matryoshka dolls, in that the outer doll wraps around a possible inner doll, and so on.

You also learned how to use optional chaining to perform many different tasks. First we discussed accessing and setting properties using optional chaining, both at a single level of chaining and also multiple levels of chaining. A great use case of optional chaining with properties
is with delegates and data sources, by offloading responsibilities to other instances and using
optional chaining to determine whether a delegate or data source has been assigned before calling it.

Then you learned how to use optional chaining with subscripts in the collaboration tool example. Remember to think about placement of the optional chaining operator (?) with respect to which expression is optional.

Finally, you learned how to use optional chaining with methods and how to use the `Void?` return type to your advantage, in addition to any return type other than nil, to verify that calling a particular method succeeded.

In the next hour we discuss using generics to create functions that can operate the same set of tasks on many different types. This can be used to significantly reduce the amount of repeated code in your app. When you feel comfortable with the content in this hour, let's move on to generics!

Q&A

Q. Why do I need optional chaining? Aren't `susie.dog?.name` and `susie.dog!.name` doing the same thing?

A. No. Suppose that Susie doesn't have a dog and so `susie.dog = nil`. In that case, `susie.dog!.name` is forcing the unwrapping of an optional and trying to access the name property on a `nil` value. This results in a runtime error. When you use `susie.dog?.name`, optional chaining is used and instead of a runtime error your code returns an optional value containing `nil`.

Q. When I call `susie.dog?.name` the `name` property is a `String`, not an optional `String`. Does that mean that I'll get a non-optional `String` back?

A. No. The result of optional chaining is always an optional, even when the final property or return type is not an optional.

Q. When should I use optional chaining?

A. Any time you need to access properties or methods contained in an optional type, you should use optional chaining.

Workshop

The workshop contains quiz questions and exercises to help you solidify your understanding of the material covered. Try to answer all questions before looking at the answers that follow.

Quiz

1. True or false? If the result of optional chaining is not nil, the value is automatically unwrapped for you, so you only get an optional when the result is nil.

2. Which of the following is the correct way to perform optional chaining on an element of an optional array:

   ```
   01: var myInt = myObject.intArray[0]?
   02: var myOtherInt = myObject.intArray?[0]
   ```

3. True or false? Optional chaining can only be used to retrieve values, not to set values.

4. If a function has no defined return value, what does it return?

Answers

1. False. The result of optional chaining is always an optional.

2. Line 02 is correct.

3. False. Optional chaining can be used to both set and retrieve values.

4. A function without a defined return value returns an empty tuple, which is written as `()`.

Exercise

Create a new OS X playground. We're going to create a model for a message board. Our model consists of a single class that contains an array of replies.

Create a class called `Post` with string properties for the post's `author`, `title`, and `body`, and an integer property for the post's `score`. Add a property called `replies`, which should be an array of post objects.

Test your new class using the following code:

```
let rootPost = Post(author: "Christine", title: "My First Post", body: "This is the
➡body of my post!")


var replyAuthor = rootPost.replies.first?.author // Should be nil


let firstReply = Post(author: "Sarah", title: "Great Post!", body: "That's one heck
➡of a post!")


rootPost.addReply(firstPost)


replyAuthor = rootPost.replies.first?.author // Should be {Some "Sarah"}
```

If you've done everything correctly, you get the indicated output.

HOUR 20
Introducing Generics

What You'll Learn in This Hour:

▶ How to create generic functions
▶ How to create generic types
▶ How to set type constraints
▶ How to extend generic types
▶ How to add associated types for generic protocols

This hour focuses on a concept in Swift called **generics**, which Apple calls one of Swift's most powerful features. Generics exist in other languages such as C# and Java, and also in C++ where they are called templates. You have come a long way in learning the Swift language and its concepts, and by now you are hopefully familiar with many core principles and rules utilized in Swift. And with that knowledge, throughout this book you have hopefully thought to yourself "that example seems to repeat a lot of code," or "couldn't that example be done in a much more concise way?" This is the hour you've been waiting for. There are many places where generics can solve these problems, so let's get going and learn how to understand and use generic code to solve these problems and write better code.

An Introduction to Generics

Generics are a way to create flexible and reusable code to avoid a lot of repetitive code that exists merely to satisfy type requirements. Generics enable you to create code that works with any type or any kind of types you specify. As you see shortly, generics can also increase type safety by setting expected types during declaration and using those expected types throughout the function, class, struct, or enum.

Recall that in Hour 9, "Understanding Higher Order Functions and Closures," we created a function called mapEachElement(inArray:, withFunc:), which iterated over an array of Ints and returned a new Int array. This function worked well for arrays of type [Int], but what if we need to perform the same function on each element of an array of type [Double]? Or even [String]?

This is the big problem that generics solve. You may have several types of data that could benefit from using the same functions, classes, structs, or enums, and it is inefficient and error-prone to create a separate function and so on for every single case you can think of. Let's take a look at the structure of a generic function.

Type Parameters and Placeholder Types

A key to generics in Swift is their flexibility. Remember that Swift is a strongly typed language, meaning that outside of using Any or AnyObject, every instance has a specific type. To create generic functions, we must specify a **placeholder type** inside a **type parameter list** at the beginning of the function, class, struct, or enum definition. A placeholder type can be any unused term you choose (typically a single capital letter, such as T, U, and so on), and the type parameter list is a list of placeholder types inside angle brackets, with multiple placeholder types separated by commas, such as <T, U>. The type parameter list is inserted immediately after the name of the function, class, struct, or enum, and before the function's parameters, if any.

Think of type parameters as you would think of parameters to a function—you are just providing types instead of values. A generic function, class, struct, or enum needs to know what types will be represented by its placeholder types. Placeholder types can be used in functions as parameter types, return types, or types used within the body of the function.

Before we get into reconstructing the mapEachElement(inArray:, withFunc:) function mentioned earlier, let's take a look at a small example to illustrate the syntax for defining generic functions. Listing 20.1 shows a generic function that prints the value of any given argument of any type.

LISTING 20.1   Generic Function Structure

```
func printWeather<T>(value: T) {
    println("Today should be \(value)")
}

let val1: String = "beautiful"
let val2: Int = 72

printWeather(val1)          // displays "Today should be beautiful"
printWeather(val2)          // displays "Today should be 72"
```

As mentioned, the placeholder type T is inside the type parameter list immediately following the name of the function and before the function's parameter list. Then, inside the parameter list, we define a parameter named value of type T. This means that whatever type we designate as T, value will be of that type. If our function called for it, we could declare variables or constants of type T inside the function, and the T placeholder type would represent the given type from the type parameter list.

You may look at that example and think, "What's the big deal? The println() function already does that for us!" And you're right; it does—because it is a generic function. Suppose we had a more detailed function. We would have had to implement printWeather(value: Int), printWeather(value: String), and so on. Implementing a generic function potentially saved us a great amount of code.

A different function would be to compare equality of two instances. Let's examine how that would look as a generic function in Listing 20.2. First create two functions that have identical functionality but take parameters of different types, and then create the generic function that will replace them. If you're following along in your own Swift REPL or playground, watch to see what error you get and on what line you receive the error.

LISTING 20.2   Comparing Equality with a Generic Function

```
01:    func areIntsEqual(first: Int, second: Int) -> Bool {
02:        return first == second
03:    }
04:
05:    func areStringsEqual(first: String, second: String) -> Bool {
06:        return first == second
07:    }
08:
09:    func areTheseEqual<T>(first: T, second: T) -> Bool {
10:        return first == second
11:    }
```

Did you get an error on line 10? The error is a little cryptic, stating "Cannot invoke '==' with an argument list of type '(T, T)'." This means that Swift cannot infer what *is equal to* means (with the == operator) with certain types, and since T can literally mean *any* type, Swift does not have enough information to know when some types are equal or not. To get this to work we need to add **type constraints**.

Specifying Type Constraints

Type constraints are used to specify what behavior a type should exhibit or what class a type should inherit from. The syntax for type constraints is similar to how you specify a variable or constant of a certain type—you use a colon after the placeholder type name, and then either the protocol or protocol composition that the type should adopt and conform to, or the class the

placeholder type should be a subclass of. Writing this inside the type parameter list looks similar
to the following snippet.

```
func someFunction<T: ProtocolA, U: ClassB> { ... }
```

To fix Listing 20.2 to be able to create the generic equality function we wanted, we need
to ensure that whatever type T represents adopts the Swift standard library protocol called
Equatable. The Equatable protocol enables Swift to determine whether two values of the same
type are considered to be equal by ensuring each instance of the given type implements the ==
operator. If a type adopts the Equatable protocol it must implement a function for the == operator to properly conform to the protocol.

Let's fix the error in Listing 20.2 by adding the type constraint to the generic function of making
sure our placeholder adopts the Equatable protocol, and then add some examples in Listing
20.3. The areIntsEqual() and areStringsEqual() functions have been omitted for brevity
but are used for reference.

LISTING 20.3   Adding a Type Constraint

```
func areTheseEqual<T: Equatable>(first: T, second: T) -> Bool {
    return first == second
}


let a = 6, b = 7, c = 6
areIntsEqual(a, b)                          // returns false

let hi = "hi", hello = "hi", bonjour = "bonjour"
areStringsEqual(hi, hello)                  // returns true

areTheseEqual(a, c)                         // returns true
areTheseEqual(hello, bonjour)              // returns false
```

By refining the broad range of types that T could be, we limit it to only those types that conform
to the Equatable protocol. If you try to create two dictionaries, whether containing equal key-
value pairs or not, and try to compare them in the areTheseEqual() function, you get an error
that the dictionaries' types do not conform to the Equatable protocol. So you can see that this
equality function works for many types but not all since Dictionary does not conform to the
Equatable protocol.

Try out what you learned so far in the next Try It Yourself example. This example combines
declaring a generic placeholder type inside the type parameter list, constraining it to conform to
a protocol, and using the placeholder type inside the function parameter list, return type, and
body. In this example you return an array of unique elements from an array passed in with
potentially duplicate elements. To do this, you need to create a hash table (dictionary) with the

elements of the array as the keys in the hash table. Because they will be keys, they need to be hashable, so we have to have our generic type placeholder constrained to only allow types that conform to the `Hashable` protocol.

Create a Generic Function to Return a Unique Array

Using the concepts discussed so far, create a generic function that produces an array with unique elements.

1. Open Xcode 6 and create a new playground. Either a Mac or an iOS playground will work. Clear the contents of the playground.

2. Create a function called `unique` and accept a placeholder type `T` that conforms to the `Hashable` protocol inside its type parameter list. The function should take one parameter of type `[T]` and a return type of `[T]`. Leave the function empty for now.

```
func unique<T: Hashable>(array: [T]) -> [T] {

}
```

3. Declare a temporary variable dictionary for us to use inside the function as our hash table. Since the elements in the array parameter will be the keys of the hash table, they should be of type `T`. The value can be anything non-nil, since we only care to know whether a value exists or not, so `Int` will do for the value type.

```
var results = [T : Int]()
```

4. Use the `map()` array instance method for mapping a function to each element in an array and provide a closure that sets the value at the current key in the results table to 1. Use shorthand closure syntax `$0` to access the current item being mapped.

```
array.map { results[$0] = 1 }
```

5. Now that the hash table has keys for every unique element in the array, return the keys of the hash table as an array of type `[T]`. Remember that the `keys` property in a dictionary is of type `LazyBidirectionalCollection` and not an array itself, so we need to ask it for its `array` property.

```
return results.keys.array
```

6. That's all for the function. Create three arrays of differing types with some duplicate elements in each.

```
let numbers = [-8, 0, 1, 3, -8, 5, 3]
let greetings = ["Aloha", "Hello", "Aloha", "Bonjour", "Ciao", "Ciao"]
let bools = [true, false, true]
```

7. Call the generic `unique` function with each array and examine the results. You should see unique arrays for each type, since each array contains hashable types.

```
let uniqueNumbers = unique(numbers)
let uniqueGreetings = unique(greetings)
let uniqueBools = unique(bools)
```

As you can see, generics are a powerful concept and implemented with not too much extra code. The syntax can get a little difficult to understand sometimes, but it always helps to read it aloud since most things in Swift are structured to read easily: "a function named `unique` that handles data of some type `T` which conforms to the `Hashable` protocol, accepts an array of type `[T]`, and returns an array of type `[T]`."

The completed Try It Yourself example code and results should look like those in Figure 20.1.

```
                          Ch20 Unique Array TIY.playground
    ⊞  <  >     Ch20 Unique Array TIY.playground › No Selection

 1  func unique<T: Hashable>(array: [T]) -> [T] {
 2      var results = [T : Int]()                     (3 times)
 3      array.map { results[$0] = 1 }                 (19 times)
 4      return results.keys.array                     (3 times)
 5  }
 6
 7  let numbers = [-8, 0, 1, 3, -8, 5, 3]             [-8, 0, 1, 3, -8, 5, 3]
 8  let greetings = ["Aloha", "Hello", "Aloha", "Bonjour",   ["Aloha", "Hello", "Aloha", "Bonjour", "Ciao", "Ciao"]
        "Ciao", "Ciao"]
 9  let bools = [true, false, true]                   [true, false, true]
10
11  let uniqueItems = unique(numbers)                 [-8, 0, 1, 3, 5]
12  let uniqueGreetings = unique(greetings)           ["Hello", "Ciao", "Aloha", "Bonjour"]
13  let uniqueBools = unique(bools)                   [false, true]
14
```

FIGURE 20.1
The completed Try It Yourself example using a generic function to return a unique copy of a provided array.

You may have realized that `Array` and `Dictionary` are generic types, too. They can contain any type of instance for their values. Take a look at the `Dictionary` type definition, by typing `Dictionary` onto an empty line of Xcode, and then press Command and click the word `Dictionary`. You see that the type parameter list for the `Dictionary` type is `<Key: Hashable, Value>`. You are not constrained to just a single letter (such as `T`) when defining placeholder types inside your type parameter list; you can have meaningful names too, as long as they are defined inside the type parameter list, make sense, and are used consistently throughout your generic implementation.

NOTE

Conforming Custom Types to the `Hashable` Protocol

You are not limited to Swift's built-in types when you need a hashable value to serve as a key in a dictionary or anywhere else a hashable value is required. You can adopt the `Hashable` protocol in any type you create and implement the `hashValue` computed property defined in the `Hashable` protocol to ensure your type conforms to the protocol. Your `hashValue` computed property should always return a unique value.

Creating Generic Types

So far this hour we have created generic functions, and while they are useful, they may be better served inside a struct, class, or enum to provide a greater benefit. So if we can put generic functions inside types, can we make the types themselves generic? Yes we can!

Generic types are just that; they are types that can use a placeholder type throughout their implementation for properties, methods, and subscripts they provide. You have used generic types already by using `Array` and `Dictionary`.

Recall in Hour 15, "Adding Advanced Type Functionality," in the second Try It Yourself example, you created a collection called a **stack** that contained instances of type `Paper` so the teacher could grade a stack of papers. A stack is a great example of a type that can be generic so that you can reuse that structure for any type that needs the capability to have a last-in-first-out storage characteristic to it.

Listing 20.4 illustrates a basic stack implementation to show what a generic type implementation might look like. If you are following along in a playground or the REPL, note that the last line is just an example to show that any custom type we have can be used.

LISTING 20.4   Generic Stack Type Implementation

```
struct Stack<T> {
    var items = [T]()
    mutating func push(item: T) {
        items.append(item)
    }
    mutating func pop() -> T? {
        if items.isEmpty { return nil }
        return items.removeLast()
    }
}
var myIntStack = Stack<Int>()
var myStringStack = Stack<String>()
var myCustomStack = Stack<SomeCustomType>()   // just an example
```

Declaring an instance of a `Stack` is easy, as seen in the last three lines of the preceding example. This stack implementation is fairly common; there is an instance property to contain all the values and functions to push and pop values. Adding the type parameter list after the type name enables us to reuse this collection for any type of data we want to store in it.

Creating generic types is just as simple as creating generic functions. However, the scope of the placeholder types reaches throughout all methods, properties, and subscripts inside the type, rather than just a single function.

A different example of a generic type to create is called a **set**. Cocoa provides a class called `NSSet`, which is an unordered and unique set of values. Sets are useful constructs and are used in Core Data model relationships, representing touches on an iOS device screen and in many more places. But, there is no `Set` struct in Swift. In the next Try It Yourself example create a simple `Set` struct. (The actual implementation is most likely different, but our version will work for the purpose of this example.) The `Set` struct needs an empty initializer, a variable array of type `[T]` to store its values, a computed property to return the current count of items, and mutating functions to add items to and remove items from the storage array. The function to add items is responsible for ensuring the array contains only unique items. The placeholder type in `Set` must have the capability to be compared for equality with other instances to ensure uniqueness with the `Equatable` protocol. This example will be built upon throughout the remainder of this hour, but we will not reproduce the entire `NSSet` class.

▼ TRY IT YOURSELF

Create a Set Type to Store Unique Unordered Values

Create a type called `Set` that stores a unique and unordered collection of values. It should have the capability to add and remove values, as well as provide a computed variable to return the current count.

1. Open Xcode 6 and create a new playground. Either a Mac or an iOS playground will work. Clear the contents of the playground.

2. Define the `Set` struct with an equatable placeholder type `T` in the type parameter list.

   ```
   struct Set<T: Equatable> {

   }
   ```

3. Define the private array variable property, an empty initializer, and the `count` computed property. Mark the array as `private`; even though it doesn't make a difference in a playground, it would in a real application, and it's good to practice good habits.

   ```
   private var items = [T]()
   init() { }
   var count: Int { return items.count }
   ```

4. Create the `add` function. This takes a value of type `T` as its only parameter and has no return value. Ensure that the item does not exist before adding it. (Hint: Use the global function `contains(seq:, x:)`.)

```
mutating func add(value: T) {
    if !contains(items, value) { items.append(value) }
}
```

5. Create the `remove(value:)` function. The `remove(value:)` function first checks for the nonexistence of the requested item, and if not found then returns `nil`. Otherwise, find the index of the item, remove it from the array, and return the item in case the calling instance needs that value for comparison or validation.

```
mutating func remove(value: T) -> T? {
    if !contains(items, value) { return nil }

    var foundIndex = 0
    for (index, item) in enumerate(items) {
        if item == value {
            foundIndex = index
            break
        }
    }

    items.removeAtIndex(foundIndex)
    return value
}
```

6. That's all for the `Set` type. Create an instance of `Set`. Add items, remove items, and check the count to ensure the proper number is being added. Try adding duplicate items to ensure uniqueness.

```
var set = Set<Int>()
set.remove(9)        // nil, since 9 did not exist in the set
set.add(5)
set.count            // displays 1
set.add(5)
set.count            // displays 1, since we ensured uniqueness
set.add(4)
set.add(3)
set.count            // displays 3
set.remove(5)        // displays {Some 5}, because remove returns an optional
set.count            // displays 2
set.remove(7)        // displays nil, since 7 did not exist in the set
set.count            // displays 2
```

I hope you can see how the Set struct could be beneficial to you in your career as a programmer. But we're not done with it yet. As you continue learning a few more concepts about generics in this hour, we add more functionality to it to make it even more useful.

The completed Try It Yourself example code and results look like what you see in Figure 20.2.

```
1   struct Set<T: Equatable> {
2       private var items = [T]()
3       init() { }
4       var count: Int { return items.count }        (5 times)
5
6       mutating func add(value: T) {
7           if !contains(items, value) { items.append(value) }
8       }
9
10      mutating func remove(value: T) -> T? {
11          if !contains(items, value) { return nil }    (2 times)
12
13          var foundIndex = 0                           0
14          for (index, item) in enumerate(items) {
15              if item == value {
16                  foundIndex = index                   0
17                  break
18              }
19          }
20
21          items.removeAtIndex(foundIndex)              5
22          return value                                 {Some 5}
23      }
24  }
25
26  var set = Set<Int>()                                 {0 elements}
27  set.remove(9)                                        nil
28  set.add(5)
29  set.count                                            1
30  set.add(5)
31  set.count                                            1
32  set.add(4)
33  set.add(3)
34  set.count                                            3
35  set.remove(5)                                        {Some 5}
36  set.count                                            2
37  set.remove(7)                                        nil
38  set.count                                            2
39
```

FIGURE 20.2
The completed Try It Yourself example creating the basis of a Set struct.

Extending Generic Types

Extending a generic type is done in the exact same manner as if you were extending a regular type. There is no special syntax in the extension definition, and all the same placeholder types are available to you in addition to what is normally available to you in extensions such as the type's properties, methods, and subscripts.

NSSet has a class method on it called setWithArray(array:), which takes an array of some type as a parameter and returns a new instance of an NSSet object. Listing 20.5 shows how we can do that in Swift using native Swift syntax and utilizing our placeholder type T.

LISTING 20.5   Extending the Set Struct

```
// reuse the Set struct from the Try It Yourself example
extension Set {
    static func setWithArray(array: [T]) -> Set<T> {
        var set = Set<T>()
        array.map { set.add($0) }
        return set
    }
}
let items = [1, 2, 3, 3, 3, 4, 5]
let set = Set.setWithArray(items)      // displays {[1, 2, 3, 4, 5]}
```

In the preceding example, we simply create a static function on Set to return a new instance of Set with unique elements.

You may be thinking at this point, "This is great, but what if I want to get access to the items in the set without removing them?" That's a good question, and it's one we can solve by extending the Set struct and doing so by conforming to a protocol. But first, you need to learn what to expect from getting at the data inside a set.

Due to the unique and unordered nature of sets, there is no index or subscript defined, nor is there a first or last computed property. However, you can ask a set for *any object* or *all objects*, and then return any object or all objects from the set. Let's create two computed properties called any and allObjects by extending our Set struct with a protocol.

NOTE

Why Are We Extending Set Versus Modifying It?

The any and allObjects properties do not have to be added via a protocol, and you could modify the Set struct to add them directly. However, you may not have access to the Set source code where you work, or it may not be open for modification, thus a protocol is a perfect solution.

Using Associated Types in Protocols

Before we go straight into the code to add the properties, we need to discuss **associated types** in protocols. Associated types are a way to have generic placeholder types in protocols. This is similar in effect to, but slightly different syntax than, the type parameter list you learned about so far.

To use an associated type in a protocol, you declare the type with the `typealias` keyword inside the protocol definition. Anywhere in the protocol you need to reference the generic type, you provide the associated type you defined in the `typealias` expression. Then, in the implementation that conforms to the protocol, you set the associated type equal to whatever type you need, if it is not inferred by Swift. From that point on, anything defined in the protocol uses your type as its associated type, and the protocol is happy, and Swift remains type-safe.

Now that you know how protocols behave with respect to generic types by using associated types, let's create a protocol and extend the `Set` struct to return any value and all values from computed properties. Also, so that we can see the results at any given time, add a computed property called `description` that returns a representation of the current state of the `items` array but not in the protocol; the description is merely for the convenience of this example, to enable you to see your results as you make changes to the set.

LISTING 20.6   Using Associated Types in Protocols

```
// reuse the combined Set struct and the extension from Listing 20.5
import Foundation

protocol Returnable {
    typealias ItemType
    var any: ItemType? { get }
    var allObjects: [ItemType] { get }
}

extension Set : Returnable {
    typealias ItemType = T    // Swift infers this line from the any: T?
➥implementation
    var any: T? {
        if items.isEmpty { return nil }

        let randomNumber = Int(arc4random_uniform(UInt32(items.count)))
        return items[randomNumber]
    }
    var allObjects: [T] {
        return items
    }
}

extension Set : Printable {
    var description: String { return "\(items)" }
}
```

```
let fish = ["One", "Fish", "Two", "Fish", "Red", "Fish", "Blue", "Fish"]
var set = Set.setWithArray(fish)
set.any            // see what value you get returned
set.add("Dr. Seuss")
set.description    // displays "[One, Fish, Two, Red, Blue, Dr. Seuss]"

let allObjects = set.allObjects
allObjects         // displays ["One", "Fish", "Two", "Red", "Blue", "Dr. Seuss"]
```

Adding the `description` computed property gives us a nice way to view all the contents of the set in case we needed to verify or validate during debugging, because sometimes having just the count is not enough to verify the proper contents are being added to or removed from a set. Also, we could have created the description computed property without adopting the `Printable` protocol, but if our set is ever used by another object that expected to use any instances that conformed to the `Printable` protocol, our set would behave nicely and print a quick description of its contents, or whatever message we wanted to return. Again, adding this protocol is in the name of good practice.

Using the `allObjects` computed property is useful when you are iterating over the set and need to quickly get access to all instances or pass the set as an array to some other instance for processing. Using `any` is useful when you just need one instance from the set, but you don't care which one, such as detecting a touch event. The user interface may be paused, say in a game, and any type of touch with any number of fingers could trigger the game to resume. So getting any touch from a set of received touches would unpause the game.

Summary

In this hour you learned about the basics of generic programming in Swift. You learned how to define and use generic functions by using type parameter lists and placeholder types to represent the type that will be used at runtime. You then learned how to use those placeholder types inside functions in the parameter list, as return types, and inside the body if necessary.

Then you learned how to use type constraints to refine what kind of type could be used in a generic function. You can constrain placeholder types by declaring that they must be a subclass of a particular class or conform to a protocol or protocol composition.

You also learned that not only can generics be used in functions, but with class, struct, and enum types as well. The placeholder types defined in the type parameter list can be used within the scope of the type, not just a single function. Once you learned that, you learned how to extend generic types with extensions, as well as extensions that adopted protocols.

Finally, you learned about associated types and how they can be used as generics inside protocols to be defined fully by the conforming type. This allows for many different types to adopt protocols and still implement the required functionality, but also enables generic types to adopt and conform to the protocols as well.

In the next hour, we take a look at interoperability between Swift and Objective-C. Even though this book is about learning Swift, if you pursue a career as a Swift developer you will doubtless run across Objective-C code, so it is good to have some familiarity with it and how to integrate the two languages.

Q&A

Q. What if I need to use more than one generic type in a single function?

A. You can use as many generic types as you need. Just use multiple type parameters. For example, `func foo<T,U>(first: T, second: U) { ... }` would take two generic types, `T` and `U`.

Q. If I use more than one generic type, does the order that I list the placeholder types in the type parameter list declaration matter?

A. No. As all of the generic types are listed, the order doesn't matter. For example, if we rewrite `foo` from the previous question this way: `func foo<T,U>(first: U, second: T) { ... }` it functions exactly the same way.

Q. If my method takes two parameters, and the first is a generic type, does the second one have to be generic too?

A. No. You can mix generic types in with non-generic parameters if you want. For example, `func foo<T>(first: T, second: Int) { ... }` defines a function that takes a generic type `T` and an `Int` as parameters.

Q. Are generics in Swift the same as generics in C# and Java?

A. Swift's generics are similar to generics in C# and Java, and to templates in C++. There are some minor differences, which are beyond the scope of this book, but they serve roughly the same purpose in each language.

Workshop

The workshop contains quiz questions and exercises to help you solidify your understanding of the material covered. Try to answer all questions before looking at the answers that follow.

Quiz

1. Do generic placeholder types have to be declared with a single letter?

2. Can we write extensions that use generic types?

3. True or false? Only functions and methods can use generic types.

4. True or false? We can use classes, protocols, or protocol compositions as type constraints.

Answers

1. No, it is customary to use a single capital letter as a placeholder type, but you can use longer names if you want.

2. Absolutely. Extensions for generic types work in the same way as other extensions.

3. False. You can use generic types with classes, structs, and enums as well.

4. True. Classes, protocols, and protocol compositions are all valid type constraints.

Exercise

Create a new OS X playground. In this hour we created a `Set` struct that maintained a list of unique elements. `Set` defined `add`, `remove`, and `setWithArray` methods as well as `any` and `allObjects` properties.

For this exercise, create an extension on `Set` that defines `union` and `intersection` methods. The `union` method should take a set as an argument and return a new set that contains all the elements from both sets.

The `intersection` method should take a set as an argument and return a set containing only those elements that appear in both sets.

Test your extension with the following code:

```
let oddNumbers = Set.setWithArray([3,5,7,9,11,13,15])
let primeNumbers = Set.setWithArray([2,3,5,7,11,13])
let setUnion = oddNumbers.union(primeNumbers) // {[2, 3, 5, 7, 9, 11, 13, 15]}
let setIntersection = primeNumbers.intersection(oddNumbers) // {[3, 5, 7, 11, 13]}
```

Adding Interoperability with Objective-C

What You'll Learn in This Hour:

▶ How to create a basic Objective-C class

▶ How to translate types between Swift and Objective-C

▶ How to use bridging headers

▶ How to use id and AnyObject between languages

▶ How to call Objective-C methods and properties from Swift

In this hour we discuss several concepts with regard to interoperability between Swift and Objective-C. The encompassing topic is huge in and of itself, and we will not be able to cover everything in just one hour. Throughout this book, I have made the assumption that you do not necessarily have an Objective-C background, so some of the concepts in this hour may be too basic for you if you do; feel free to skip anything you may already know. The position taken this hour is to familiarize you with Objective-C by comparing certain aspects of it to what you have learned in Swift thus far. Also, I want you to have a basic understanding of Objective-C when you see it, so that you know how to access an existing Objective-C code base from Swift. If you plan to be a Swift developer, you will doubtless encounter Objective-C code, and you must know how to integrate Swift and Objective-C. Let's start with some basics.

Objective-C Basics

Before we begin integrating Swift and Objective-C, let's take a few minutes to cover some quick basics about Objective-C. Objective-C notoriously uses a lot of @ signs and square brackets ([]), so I hope that doesn't bother you.

Also, since Xcode playgrounds are not compatible with Objective-C, we do not use any playgrounds in this hour. There is a project on GitHub set up for you to clone to your computer that we will walk through, adding Swift functionality to an existing app written in Objective-C. You can find the project at https://github.com/STYSwiftIn24H/Examples/ in the Ch21 folder.

File Structure

The first thing to note about Objective-C is that, unlike Swift class files, there are two files: a **header file** (filename.h) and an **implementation file** (filename.m). The header file, sometimes called the **public interface file**, is where you define publicly accessible properties and methods of your class. The implementation file is where your implementation code is written. You can also have an optional **private interface** at the top of the implementation file, which is a place to define private properties and methods to be used inside the implementation but not publicly accessible. Elements inside the implementation file are not accessible publicly unless publicly defined in the header file. Listing 21.1 illustrates a simple model object interface. We cover the implementation shortly. Both Song.h and Song.m appear in the Models group in the Xcode project, if you are looking at them in the project. There are minor differences between what is in the project and Listing 21.1 in order to keep the book examples small.

LISTING 21.1   Sample Objective-C Model Interface

```
01:  // Song.h
02:  #import <Foundation/Foundation.h>
03:
04:  @interface Song : NSObject
05:  @property (nonatomic, strong) NSString *title;
06:  @property (nonatomic, strong) NSString *artist;
07:  - (instancetype)initWithTitle:(NSString *)title artist:(NSString *)artist;
08:  @end
```

A lot happened in Listing 21.1, so let's break it down so you understand all the pieces. Lines 1 through 8 define the public interface for the Song class, inside the Song.h file. Lines 10 through 27 belong inside Song.m and are the implementation of the class. Breaking each down further, let's start with the header interface.

Objective-C Header Files

Line 2 imports the Foundation framework, similarly to what we have done with the import Foundation statements in Swift. That is necessary to create a class in Objective-C since all classes in Objective-C must have a root class, which is most often NSObject (or a subclass thereof), and NSObject is part of the Foundation framework. Did you see that there is no class or @class keyword to define a class, rather just an @interface statement? That is how Objective-C creates classes and ends the interface with the @end statement.

Inside the @interface section is where we declare any properties and/or methods that we want to publicly expose. On lines 5 and 6 we define two properties, of type NSString * (the * is important—see the next note) and have nonatomic and strong property attributes. nonatomic means that we simply want to return or set the property values directly without any locking mechanism, which would prevent multiple process threads from accessing or changing the value while we may be reading or writing the property's contents. The `strong` keyword is exactly the same as the `strong` keyword we discussed in Hour 16, "Understanding Memory Allocation and References," in that we tell Objective-C that we want to retain a strong reference to that property. We must specify this in Objective-C, whereas in Swift, `strong` is the default. Sometimes you may see the `copy` attribute as opposed to a `strong` attribute, which still is a `strong` reference but a copy of the object is returned. This helps keep the actual model object safe from accidental mutation. For our example, using `strong` is perfectly fine.

NOTE

Why Is the Asterisk Important?

Remember that Objective-C is a strict superset of the C language and to reference memory in the heap (which is where all Objective-C instances are stored) you must reference that memory location by using the `*` character. The type is often said to be "an `NSString`," but strictly speaking the type is `NSString *`, meaning a pointer to an `NSString` object.

NOTE

Custom Getters and Setters

Objective-C provides default getters and setters in a process called **synthesizing**. Prior to auto-synthesizing properties, Objective-C programmers had to write getters and setters for every property, or just use the backing instance variable directly, which is often not safe. If you want to provide custom getters and setters, you can, but you need to add `@synthesize propertyName;` in the implementation file so Objective-C could create a backing instance variable to be used by your properties and handle its memory management. Xcode is fairly good about warning you when you need to specifically synthesize properties.

On line 7 we define a custom initializer that we provide code for inside the implementation. All methods in Objective-C are prefaced with either a plus sign (+) for a class method or a minus sign (-) for an instance method. After the class/instance sign, the return type is listed inside parentheses. This is different from Swift where the return type is at the end of the function or method definition. Inside the parentheses is the keyword `instancetype`, which is a special return type for `init` methods and is a reference to the type of the receiver object. Since a class could be subclassed but use the superclass's initializer, `instancetype` returns the proper type of object.

Notice the syntax of the initializer on line 7. The parameter names and types are intermixed with the arguments just like in Swift, just without commas. Listing 21.2 shows the same initializer definition in Swift and Objective-C.

LISTING 21.2   Initializers in Swift and Objective-C

```
// Objective-C
- (instancetype)initWithTitle:(NSString *)title artist:(NSString *)artist;


// Swift
init(title: String, artist: String)
```

The functionality of these two `init` methods is identical. Swift's method syntax is a little more succinct than Objective-C's, but the Objective-C `init` method should be easily readable now that you've learned Swift's method syntax with relation to the inline parameter names, types, and arguments. Objective-C's convention for method naming with parameters is to provide a meaningful explanation of what the method does, while intermixing the parameters inline, as seen by `initWithTitle:(NSString *)title artist:(NSString *)artist`. Notice also that Objective-C does not separate parameters with commas like Swift. Rather, a single space separates the parameters.

Objective-C Implementation Files

The implementation of the `Song` class in Objective-C from Listing 21.1 is shown here in Listing 21.3.

LISTING 21.3   Sample Objective-C Model Implementation

```
01:   // Song.m
02:   #import "Song.h"
03:
04:   @interface Song ()
05:   // this is where the private interface code goes, if any
06:   @end
07:
08:   @implementation Song
09:
10:   - (instancetype)initWithTitle:(NSString *)title artist:(NSString *)artist {
11:       if (self = [super init]) {
12:           self.title = title;
13:           self.artist = artist;
14:       }
15:       return self;
16:   }
17:
18:   @end
```

The file begins by importing the Song.h header file on line 2, so that the implementation file can use the information from the public header in case any properties or methods are declared publicly and used in the private implementation.

Lines 4 through 6 define a private interface, where private properties and methods can be declared before being used. This section is particularly useful when you need to maintain private data that you don't want to expose to other classes but need to use inside this class. In our example nothing is listed there, but declaring private properties and methods is identical to declaring them in the public interface. However, the Objective-C compiler knows not to expose them. This is akin to using the `private` attribute in Swift.

Line 8 begins the implementation with the `@implementation` keyword, and then on line 10 we define our initializer's implementation. First, we ask our superclass to perform its initialization process and assign `self` to the result with `self = [super init]`. We check the result of that inside an `if` statement, because in Objective-C, the initialization process could fail and return `nil`. If our superclass initializes properly and is assigned to `self` properly, we finish our own class's initialization by setting our instance property values. After the `if` statement, we return `self`, just like we do in Swift, but we return `self` after the `if` statement because if our call to `[super init]` failed, `return self` would return `nil`, which is 100% okay in Objective-C.

NOTE

Failable Initializers in Swift

Failable initializers are not a part of Swift as of Xcode 6 and Swift 1.0, but they have been added in Xcode 6.1 and Swift 1.1, released on October 20, 2014. This topic is outside the scope of this book, but you can read more about it on Apple's Swift blog at https://developer.apple.com/swift/blog/?id=17.

NOTE

Order of Initialization

Did you see that in Objective-C we call `[super init]` first before initializing any of our own class's properties? This is because the object needs to get allocated in memory first, which our superclass chain takes care of, before we can set any properties of our own. This is different from Swift, where our instance needs to be initialized before calling `super.init()`. Swift classes do not need a superclass, so Swift handles the memory allocation automatically, and you are responsible for initializing your instance first before calling `super.init()`.

Allocation and Initialization

While Swift takes care of the memory allocation for you, as discussed in Hour 16, Objective-C does not do that for you. Listing 21.4 shows the differences in instantiating objects in Swift and Objective-C.

LISTING 21.4   Instantiating Objects

```
// Objective-C

Song *song = [[Song alloc] initWithTitle:@"Happy" artist:@"Pharrell"];

// Swift
let song = Song(title: "Happy", artist: "Pharrell")
```

In Objective-C, we have to pass the `alloc` message to the `Song` class, which allocates a space in memory for a new object of type `Song`. Then we pass `initWithTitle:artist:` to the newly allocated object, which initializes the object and sets the values we passed in as arguments.

Notice that to declare a constant or variable of an Objective-C type in Swift, you do not need to enter `init` or even `With`. The `init` keyword is assumed when you use parentheses after a type name. The compiler automatically strips out `With` as well, because it doesn't make sense grammatically to have a floating `With` since `init` was stripped out.

NOTE

Nested Method Calls in Objective-C

The square brackets can get a bit confusing to keep straight sometimes in Objective-C. Each method call is really a *message* sent to the object or class name inside the brackets. Objective-C's compiler executes the nested message first, and the result of that is then used within the outer message. So for instance, `[Song alloc]` is executed, and the result of that is an uninitialized object of type `Song`, which is then sent the `initWithTitle:artist:` message. While it looks a little weird at first, it becomes second nature after a while. This type of message sending syntax is structured after SmallTalk.

One more quick note about initializers in Objective-C that are used in Swift is that Objective-C class methods that return an instance of that type (sometimes referred to as **factory methods**) are mapped to be convenience initializers in Swift. Such an example is shown in Listing 21.5. Before ARC, factory methods in Objective-C were helpful with memory management in that they would automatically release an object when it went out of scope, which was one less object for you to manage with `retain` or `release` keywords.

LISTING 21.5   Objective-C Factory Methods Are Convenience Initializers in Swift

```
// Objective-C
NSURL *url = [NSURL urlWithString:@"https://github.com"];

// Swift
let url = NSURL(string: "https://github.com")
```

The Objective-C factory method takes care of the alloc/init process for you and returns a reference to a newly instantiated NSURL object. As mentioned, this translates to a convenience initializer in Swift. Since you don't have to specifically execute an alloc statement this can all happen in an initializer.

Bridging

In a moment we get to implementing Swift code in an existing Objective-C app, but first we need to cover a concept called **bridging**. With regard to the interoperability of Swift and Objective-C, bridging takes on a few different meanings under different contexts, the first bridging context being the module or API level and the second being the type level. Let's cover module/API bridging first.

Module Bridging

Any Objective-C framework (or C framework) accessible as a module can be imported into Swift, using the import SomeModuleName statement. This makes available to Swift all publicly declared APIs in an Objective-C or C module. You can also make Objective-C classes available to Swift via a **bridging header**, which Xcode automatically creates for you when it senses that you are about to mix languages in the same project. Xcode offers to create a bridging header when you are about to add an Objective-C file to a Swift app or a Swift file to an Objective-C app. We create a bridging header shortly when we get into our example.

When you need to import Swift code into Objective-C, Xcode auto-generates a header file named using a generated filename consisting of the name of the product module plus "-Swift.h". To use this in Objective-C, you would then have a statement at the top of either your .h or .m file, #import "YourProductModule-Swift.h".

Type Bridging

Many of the types used in Objective-C are actually from the Cocoa framework. The Cocoa framework consists of the Foundation Kit, Application Kit (often referred to as AppKit), and Core Data frameworks. The Cocoa Touch framework is similar but contains UIKit instead of AppKit. The types included in these frameworks are mostly recognized by their naming convention of starting with the two letters NS. This naming convention stemmed either from NeXT-Sun's creation of OpenStep or NeXTSTEP's term for the OpenStep framework (Wikipedia, http://en.wikipedia.org/wiki/Cocoa_(API)#History). Unless I need to differentiate between the two, I will henceforth refer to Cocoa and Cocoa Touch as simply "Cocoa."

Most Cocoa types are inherently bridgeable to Swift without any extra work. For instance, NSString is bridgeable to String and vice-versa. Being a bridged data type means that it can be used interchangeably or is convertible to its equivalent counterpart. This is useful if you have an existing Swift type, such as a `String` or an `Array` and you are working with an Objective-C API that requests an `NSString` or `NSArray`, respectively.

Also, remember in Hour 15, "Adding Advanced Type Functionality," we discussed non-specific type specifiers such as `Any` and `AnyObject`. `Any` and `AnyObject` aren't really types; they are protocols. `AnyObject` is a protocol that describes any instance of a reference type. Since all objects in Objective-C are reference types, all Objective-C objects are `AnyObject` compatible by default when using them in Swift. The Objective-C equivalent to `AnyObject` is `id`, which is a pointer to any Objective-C object.

Following are several Swift types and their Objective-C compatible equivalents. There is a lot of information on these topics that could be covered, but here we only cover some main highlights.

`String` and `NSString`

Swift's `String` type and Objective-C's `NSString` class are bridgeable as well as interchangeable. Wherever you see `NSString` in Objective-C, you can insert a Swift `String` and vice-versa. To enable the bridging in a Swift file, simply import the Foundation framework. You can also cast `String` instances to `NSString` and vice-versa, and you do not need to use the optional `as?` operator since the cast is guaranteed to succeed between the two types. This may seem a little odd at first because technically `String` is a value type (struct) and not a reference type, yet it is still interchangeable with `NSString`, which is a reference type. The work to bridge these types has been done for you to provide a seamless coexistence between the two, so just imagine the Jedi-wave with Apple telling you "You don't need to see Swift's internal implementation."

Numeric Types and `NSNumber`

Several numeric types in Swift are directly interchangeable with `NSNumber` objects in Objective-C. These Swift types include `Int`, `UInt`, `Bool`, `Double`, and `Float`. Whenever a method or object defines the need for an `NSNumber` object, you can freely pass in one of the aforementioned Swift numeric types. The difference, however, is that you cannot pass an `NSNumber` object to a method or object that defines the need for an `Int`, `UInt`, `Bool`, `Double`, or `Float`, because the compiler cannot guarantee that whatever number inside the `NSNumber` object is compatible with the Swift type. For example, if a function parameter takes an `Int`, you cannot send an `NSNumber` object because the compiler cannot guarantee that the `NSNumber` is not really a `Bool`, or some other non-`Int` type.

`Array` and `NSArray`

When converting an `NSArray` instance to an `Array` instance, an array of type `[AnyObject]` is returned. This is because `NSArray` objects contain objects of type `id`, and all Objective-C objects are `AnyObject` compatible, so Objective-C returns `[AnyObject]` to Swift to remain type-safe. When converting from `Array` to `NSArray`, each element in the array must be `AnyObject` compatible, meaning it must be of a class type (or reference type).

Once you have an [AnyObject] array, you can downcast it to a more defined type if you need to, such as from [AnyObject] to [Int]. This is done with the as? operator, because the downcast could fail if the types of objects inside are not compatible with the intended casted type. If you are sure of the type cast, you can use the as operator, but just know that if it fails your app will crash reliably.

Dictionary **and** NSDictionary

Converting an NSDictionary object to a Swift Dictionary results in a dictionary of type [NSObject : AnyObject]. Just as with arrays, you can downcast a dictionary to a more specific type for the keys and values, but the conversion is not always guaranteed to succeed, so use the as? operator for safety. When converting from a Swift Dictionary to an NSDictionary, all keys and values must be instances of classes or bridgeable to instances of classes. In other words, if the keys or values are structs (like String), they should be bridgeable to an Objective-C class type (like NSString).

Integrating Swift into an Objective-C App

In lieu of separate Try It Yourself sections, let's take the remainder of this hour to build an app together that uses both Objective-C and Swift. This way, I can explain things a lot better along the way, and with screenshots, and basically make one long Try It Yourself section. So follow along, and let's get rolling.

Download the Starter Project

To start, clone the repository for this book's example code from GitHub. Open Terminal.app, or whatever app you use to access a Unix shell, and enter the following command:

```
$ git clone git@github.com:STYSwiftIn24H/Examples.git
```

Once the cloning has completed, change the directory to the Examples/Ch21/ObjCInterop folder and then open the Xcode project by entering the following commands:

```
$ cd Examples/Ch21/ObjCInterop
$ open ObjCInterop.xcodeproj
```

Xcode should now be open to the ObjCInterop project. Don't feel too overwhelmed by everything in Xcode if you're not familiar with it; I will walk you through what you need to do for this app.

TIP

Completed Project Is Available For Reference

If you get stuck or need to see the project in its entirety, the completed project is available in the Examples/Ch21/ObjCInterop-Final folder. Only use it if you need to!

The ObjCInterop project lists a few songs, with the artist and rating information below it (the ratings are made up). So far, it is written solely in Objective-C. Hold down the Command key and press R to run the app. The app opens in the iOS Simulator, and an app appears that looks like the one in Figure 21.1.

FIGURE 21.1
The ObjCInterop app upon first run, as solely an Objective-C app.

Clicking on any of the list items pushes, or **segues**, a new view controller onto the screen, showing detailed information about whatever song you tapped. Right now, what is displayed should look similar to <Song: 0x7fd0b1e5bb40>, because the app hasn't implemented a pretty way to display the song tapped. We implement that in Swift shortly. Hold the Command key and press Q to quit the iOS Simulator.

In the Xcode Navigation Pane on the left-hand side, expand the ObjCInterop grouping and then expand the Models grouping. Inside the Models grouping, you see two files: Song.h and Song.m. Click Song.h, and in the content area you see the public header interface for the Song class. In it, song title, artist, and rating properties are defined, as well as a custom initializer. Notice that the Song class inherits from NSObject, since all Objective-C classes must have a superclass, most commonly NSObject or a subclass thereof. Next, click on Song.m and notice that we have nothing in the private interface, and we provide a simple implementation for our initializer. Song is our model class and is used to populate the elements in each cell in the table view.

Our MasterViewController class provides the list of songs to the table view interface, and the DetailViewController class currently displays detailed information about whatever element belongs to the cell tapped in the master view controller. Right now, the DetailViewController class is not implemented, so select both DetailViewController.h and DetailViewController.m and delete them. If Xcode prompts you to remove references or move to trash, select Move To Trash. We recreate this class in Swift.

Create a Swift Class and Bridging Header

In Xcode, click to select the ObjCInterop grouping (with the folder, not the project icon, at the very top of the Navigation Pane). Click File > New > File (or hold down the Command key and press N). In the template picker under iOS, select Source, choose Swift File, and then click Next, as shown in Figure 21.2.

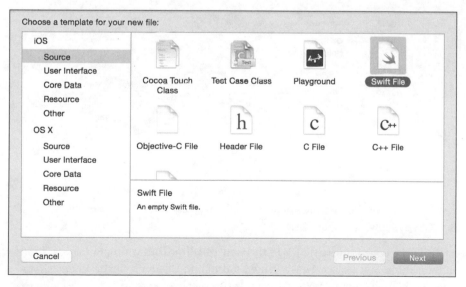

FIGURE 21.2
Choosing to create a Swift file from Xcode's template picker.

On the next dialog, in the Save As text field, name the file DetailVC and then click Create, as shown in Figure 21.3. DetailVC is short for DetailViewController, but I wanted to name it differently to illustrate using the Swift file versus anything left over from the `DetailViewController` Objective-C class we deleted.

FIGURE 21.3
Save the new Swift file with the name DetailVC.

Xcode prompts you with a question about whether you want to configure an Objective-C bridging header. Click Yes, as shown in Figure 21.4.

The newly created DetailVC.swift file is shown in the content editor with a simple `import` `Foundation` statement inside it. Select the ObjCInterop-Bridging-Header.h file and notice there is nothing in it yet but some comments. We add to this file later.

Would you like to configure an Objective-C bridging header?

Adding this file to ObjCInterop will create a mixed Swift and Objective-C target. Would you like Xcode to automatically configure a bridging header to enable classes to be accessed by both languages?

| Cancel | No | Yes |

FIGURE 21.4
Click Yes to create an Objective-C bridging header.

Now we can create the `DetailVC` class inside the DetailVC.swift file. Click to select the DetailVC.swift file in the Navigation Pane. In the content area, create the class by entering the code exactly as listed in Listing 21.6.

LISTING 21.6   Creating the `DetailVC` Class in Swift

```
01:    import UIKit
02:
03:    class DetailVC : UIViewController {
04:        @IBOutlet weak var detailDescriptionLabel: UILabel!
05:
06:        var detailItem: AnyObject? {
07:            didSet {
08:                self.configureView()
09:            }
10:        }
11:
12:        func configureView() {
13:            detailDescriptionLabel?.text = detailItem?.description
14:        }
15:
16:        override func viewDidLoad() {
17:            super.viewDidLoad()
18:            self.configureView()
19:        }
20:    }
```

On line 1, we replace the Foundation framework with the UIKit framework so we can have our `DetailVC` class be a subclass of `UIViewController` (necessary for controlling the scene in the storyboard and displaying a view onscreen) and also have access to types such as `UILabel`.

Then on line 3 we define the `DetailVC` class as a subclass of `UIViewController`. You should be familiar with everything on line 4 except that weird `@IBOutlet` attribute. `@IBOutlet` declares to Xcode that this property will be used as an **outlet** to an interface element and will be responsible for changing that UI element. The outlet property is set to be `weak`, because when the `UILabel` gets placed onscreen, a strong reference will be held on to it already, so we don't need another strong reference ourselves. It is also an implicitly unwrapped optional, which is by default set to nil in case the outlet never gets set. But once it is set, it lives until the view controller is deinitialized, so the outlet will never get set back to nil.

On lines 6 through 10 we define a stored property called `detailItem` of type `AnyObject?`. Ultimately `detailItem` will be an instance of `Song`. The reason for this is that if you open MasterViewController.m and look at the `-prepareForSegue:sender:` method, it sends the `setDetailItem:` message to the `destinationViewController` object, passing a `Song` instance, and the interface *segues* to the destination view controller, as seen on line 50 in Figure 21.5. The `detailItem` property was from the `DetailViewController` class that we deleted, so we just redefined it here in Swift. We also use a property observer to notify our interface to update when the property gets set.

```
43
44   #pragma mark — Segues
45
46   - (void)prepareForSegue:(UIStoryboardSegue *)segue sender:(id)sender {
47       if ([[segue identifier] isEqualToString:@"showDetail"]) {
48           NSIndexPath *indexPath = [self.tableView indexPathForSelectedRow];
49           NSDate *object = self.songs[indexPath.row];
50           [[segue destinationViewController] setDetailItem:object];
51       }
52   }
53
```

FIGURE 21.5
The `prepareForSegue:sender:` method that gets executed before segueing a new view controller on screen.

Continuing the explanation of Listing 21.6, lines 12 through 14 define the `configureView()` method, which simply updates the `detailDescriptionLabel`'s `text` property (which is what gets updated in the UI) using optional chaining assignment and sets it equal to the optionally chained value on `detailItem` called `description`. We haven't implemented any description computed properties yet, but we will do that shortly.

Finally, on lines 16 through 19 we override a method from `UIViewController` called `viewDidLoad()`. This important method gets called immediately before the view comes onscreen, after every outlet has been connected to an interface element, if necessary. Inside the method we simply call its superclass implementation to make sure any other view hierarchy setup gets executed, and then we call `configureView()` to update the UI.

Running the app right now would not prove fruitful, because we have to tend to a few errors and also update the UI to use our new Swift class. Let's do a few more things to finish our implementation, starting with some housecleaning.

Housecleaning

Now that we have created the Swift `DetailVC` class and file, we need to remove references to the `DetailViewController` files we removed and update `#import` statements with our new Swift file. Select the MasterViewController.m file from the Navigation Pane to edit it. Xcode should be greeting you with an error already, which is good. Remove the `#import` `"DetailViewController.h"` line and replace it with the following:

```
#import "ObjCInterop-Swift.h"
```

ObjCInterop-Swift.h is the **generated header file** that Swift creates for interoperating with Objective-C. You do not need to create this header file; it is automatically regenerated any time there is a change to anything publicly or internally declared in any Swift file.

CAUTION

Xcode Auto Complete Suggests Incorrect Header

Be careful not to choose the ObjCInterop-Bridging-Header.h file that is auto-suggested by Xcode. This is the wrong header file, and the rest of the project will not work correctly if you import the bridging header instead of the generated header file. Make sure your import statement reads `#import` `"ObjCInterop-Swift.h"`.

Next, select AppDelegate.m from the Navigation Pane, and you see a similar error in Xcode. This `#import` statement, however, does not need to be replaced for our needs, so just remove it.

Exposing Objective-C Classes to Swift

To add the `description` computed property to the Song class as an extension, we need to make the `Song` class available to Swift. In the Navigation Pane, select the ObjCInterop-Bridging-Header.h file to edit the file. Add the following line to the bridging header.

```
#import "Song.h"
```

This statement imports the `Song` class's public interface properties and methods to Swift and enables them to be used by Swift.

Extending an Objective-C Class with Swift

Extending an Objective-C class with Swift is just as easy as adding an extension normally in Swift. To do this, let's create the extension in its own dedicated file.

Hold down the Command key and press N to create a new file. From the template chooser, choose another iOS Swift file and click Next. Name the file SongDescription and click Create. Listing 21.7 shows the code that you need to enter into the extension. Note that you can remove the import Foundation statement, as it is not necessary for this extension.

LISTING 21.7   Extending the Song Class

```
01:   extension Song : Printable {
02:       public override var description: String {
03:            return "\(artist) sings the song \(title), \(rating) stars."
04:       }
05:   }
```

As mentioned in Hour 20, "Introducing Generics," we do not *need* to adopt the Printable protocol, but it is good practice since we're conforming to it anyway on line 2, and some other object may want to communicate with our Song instance via that protocol. The computed property must be declared public because it is overriding a public property on Song. Since all instances inheriting from NSObject (which Song does) have a description property already, we must declare it with the override keyword too, because we are overriding the existing description implementation. Then on line 3 we simply return the String value we want to show in our detail view controller. Notice that we are returning a String and not an NSString, even though our Song class is declared in Objective-C.

You're almost there, just one more small thing to do and then we can see the fruits of our labor.

Update the Class in the Storyboard

Since we deleted the provided DetailViewController class and created our own, we need to change the class type of the scene in the storyboard. Select the Main.storyboard file in the Navigation Pane to edit it. You may have four panes in this view: the Navigation Pane on the far left, the Scene Pane to its right, the actual storyboard layout in the third pane, and the Inspector Pane on the far right. In the Scene Pane, expand Detail Scene. Click to select Detail (with the yellow icon). Click View > Utilities > Show Identity Inspector, which then shows the Identity Inspector in the right-hand Inspector Pane. In the Class drop-down field, change the value from DetailViewController to DetailVC, as shown in Figure 21.6.

Run the App

If you have done everything so far as outlined, you should be able to run the app in the Simulator. Hold the Command key and press R to run the app. You may have to choose a device first, which you can do from the device picker in the top bar of Xcode, as shown in Figure 21.7. To the right of the Run and Stop buttons, you see the name of the app (which is the Scheme Picker) and then the device type. Click the device type button, which may say "iOS Device" or any of the devices listed in Figure 21.7. I chose iPhone 6; feel free to choose whichever device you want.

FIGURE 21.6
Change the class in the Identity Inspector to DetailVC.

FIGURE 21.7
Choose a Simulator to execute your app on.

Once your app begins running, you should see three songs listed; they are the three songs we hard-coded into MasterViewController.m. Tapping any one of them should perform the segue from the master view controller to the detail view controller, which is our new Swift class, DetailVC. Since we created the extension to Song and provided a description property, we get a nice, easy-to-read output in the detail view controller. The detail view controller should look like Figure 21.8.

FIGURE 21.8
The detail view controller showing the description of the song you tapped.

Summary

The topic of interoperability with Objective-C and Swift is too much to cover within the bounds of this hour. The goal for this hour was to acquaint you with Objective-C, using similarities to what you have learned already with Swift, and to help you learn how to recognize some things about Objective-C to know how to write Swift to integrate with it.

In this hour you learned some basics of Objective-C including class file structure, the differences between public and private interfaces, and what a class implementation looks like. With this, you learned about Objective-C property definitions and how to create an initializer method. Then you learned the structure of an Objective-C class and how to instantiate an instance of a class using the alloc/init pattern.

Next you learned about bridging, both in terms of modules and APIs, as well as types. You learned how Swift and Objective-C bridge similar types, such as `String` and `NSString`, and how to make APIs available from Objective-C to Swift with bridging headers. There is also an auto-generated header file that the compiler creates to allow Objective-C to access Swift APIs, which is the name of the application or module, plus `"-Swift.h"`. That must get imported using the `#import` statement wherever you need Swift APIs in an Objective-C class file.

Finally, we walked through adding Swift code to an existing Objective-C app. You learned how to create an extension on an Objective-C class, which you used to display customized output to the detail view controller's user interface (UI). There are many more resources on learning Objective-C if you are interested, such as *Sams Teach Yourself Objective-C in 24 Hours,* 2nd edition, by Jesse Feiler, as well as the highly acclaimed *Objective-C Programming: The Big Nerd Ranch Guide,* 2nd edition, by Aaron Hillegass and Mikey Ward.

In the next hour, you learn more about interacting with user interfaces and Swift. You learn how to create a UI and hook up Swift code to control the UI. Great job making it through this hour! When you're ready to move on to the next hour, let's go!

Q&A

Q. I see that a Swift `Bool` bridges to Objective-C's `NSNumber`. Why does that happen?

A. The Bool type in Objective-C is actually a typedef of a signed char, and a signed char is a numeric type. This means that in Objective-C YES actually has a value of 1 and NO has a value 0.

Q. I see a folder called ObjCInteropTests in the sample project. What is that?

A. When you create a new project Xcode creates a Tests folder for you automatically. This is where you place your project's unit tests. Unit tests are small bits of code that you can use to make sure that your program is behaving the way you expect it. Unit testing is a deep and interesting topic but is beyond the scope of this book.

Q. I have an `NSArray` and I know it contains only `NSString` objects, but when I try to use it, Xcode tells me that `AnyObject` is not convertible to `String`. I thought `NSString` bridges to `String` automatically.

A. `NSString` does bridge to `String` automatically, but `NSArray` bridges to `[AnyObject]`. This means that you have to cast the elements of the array to the correct type before you can use them. You can cast the entire array at once using `myArray as? [String]` or cast the individual elements as you access them.

Workshop

The workshop contains quiz questions and exercises to help you solidify your understanding of the material covered. Try to answer all questions before looking at the answers that follow.

Quiz

1. What are header files (filename.h) used for an Objective-C project?

2. When converting an `NSDictionary` to a Swift object, what is the type of the resulting dictionary?

3. Which Swift types can you pass to an Objective-C method that expects an `NSNumber`?

4. True or false? If an object is written in Objective-C, you can only create subclasses in Objective-C, never in Swift.

Answers

1. Header files define the publicly accessible methods and properties for a class.

2. `NSDictionary` converts to a dictionary of type `[NSObject: AnyObject]`.

3. `Int`, `UInt`, `Bool`, `Double`, or `Float`.

4. False. You are free to create subclasses of Objective-C obƩjects in Swift.

Exercise

For this exercise, we continue using the project from the hour examples. The `Song` class is written in Objective-C, but we create a subclass in Swift and use it in our project. Add a new Swift file to the project called `PopSong.swift` and in that file define a class called `PopSong`, which is a subclass of `Song`. Don't forget to `import Foundation`.

Add a stored property called `chartPosition` of type `Int` to your class. Next, add an initializer that takes title, artist, rating, and chart position as arguments. This initializer is going to be called from Objective-C, so think carefully about what types your `init` method should take; will you need `Int` or `NSNumber`? In the initializer, set the `chartPosition` variable in the `PopSong` class and pass the rest of the arguments along to `super.init()`.

Next, override the description method so that it returns a string containing the artist, song title, rating, and chart position. Use the description method in `SongDescription.swift` as a guide.

Now go to `MasterViewController.m` and change the song "Happy" to be type `PopSong` instead of a `Song` and give it a `chartPosition` of 1. Don't forget to change the class in the `alloc` statement too.

After you make the changes, compile and run your application. When you click on Happy, you should see the new description string that you wrote instead of the original one.

Interacting with User Interfaces

What You'll Learn in This Hour:

▶ How to create a user interface in a storyboard

▶ The basics of constraints, size classes, and adaptive layout

▶ How to use actions and outlets

▶ How to populate elements with data onscreen

In the previous hour, you downloaded a precreated project from GitHub that had an interface already built, and you added Swift code to an existing Objective-C app. In this hour, you learn how to create an app from scratch (this time using Swift only!), create a user interface (UI) in a storyboard, and learn some basics about how to set up the interface. Then you learn about actions and outlets that enable your code to interact with visual elements in the UI. You also learn how to populate data from a data source and show that data in the UI. Basically, you create your first app from start to finish!

Like the previous hour, this hour does not have any Try It Yourself sections. You build an app throughout the course of this hour, so the entire hour is essentially a big Try It Yourself section.

Interface Introduction

A **user interface** (UI) is the term for any sort of interface that presents data to a user, whether visual with a graphical user interface (GUI), audio, a game controller, or what have you. Even though this hour focuses on building a graphical user interface using Xcode, I simply call it a UI. One hour is not long enough to cover everything about interfaces, so we touch on some basics and then cover how Swift interacts with your UI.

Xcode provides a place for you to create a UI called a **storyboard**. Storyboards were introduced in Xcode 4.2 for iOS 5. With the release of Mac OS X 10.10 Yosemite and Xcode 6, storyboards can now be used to create Mac apps as well. This is great news for Mac developers, and the information in this hour can be used across both Mac and iOS platforms. Even though you create storyboards in Xcode, the visual storyboard editor is sometimes referred to as **Interface**

Builder, or IB, because Interface Builder used to be a separate app alongside Xcode for building interfaces.

Storyboards are a way to visually design not only the way the screens look in your apps but also how each view and/or controller connects with others in the same app. With storyboards, you can visualize the entire flow of your app from screen to screen, which is a great tool for identifying what classes need to communicate with each other and how the app flows when using it.

Interface Definitions

Let's start with some definitions to acquaint you with the terminology we use throughout this hour.

- **Scene**—Each screen in a storyboard is called a scene. Each scene is comprised of elements from a single view controller.

- **Element**—A scene can have many different UI elements inside it, such as buttons, toolbars, sliders, date pickers, labels, text fields, and much more.

- **Segue**—The transition between each scene is called a segue. When an event occurs that displays a new view controller onscreen, such as tapping an email to view or a song to play, the current view controller segues to a new view controller with more detailed information.

- **View controller**—A class responsible for managing the interaction between model objects, views onscreen, and other controllers. Typically, this class is the "C" in the MVC (Model-View-Controller) paradigm.

- **Action**—The response to a tap, gesture, or event that calls a target method. A function that responds to an event by a UI element is defined with the `@IBAction` parameter so that Xcode knows the method is callable from the UI. An example would be a Save button that triggers a `save()` method in code.

- **Outlet**—A link between a class property and an element in the UI such that the UI element can be altered when the outlet changes state. An example would be a progress bar that updates its completed portion onscreen when a progress property value gets updated. These properties are defined with the `@IBOutlet` parameter.

- **Constraint**—Constraints are rules that define the layout behavior of an element. Elements in scenes use constraints to define their size and placement in a scene with respect to other elements, or even themselves. Constraints are useful for supporting devices with different screen sizes, rather than hard-coding origin points and size attributes explicitly.

These definitions make a lot more sense when you see them in action. Let's build a project using the Master-Detail template so you can see what some of these items look like.

Building an Interface

To explain building a UI, it is much easier to open Xcode and see for yourself. Let's examine what a storyboard with a template interface looks like.

Open Xcode, and at the Welcome screen choose Create a New Xcode Project. In the template chooser, select iOS, Application; then select Master-Detail Application and click Next. On the next screen, enter a name for your project, such as Ch22UI, in the Product Name field, make sure the language is set to Swift and Universal is selected in the Devices list, and then click Next. Finally, choose a location on your hard drive to save the project to and click Create. Once your project loads, click Main.storyboard from the left-hand Navigation Pane to open the storyboard for editing in the main content area. Your storyboard should look similar to Figure 22.1.

FIGURE 22.1
The standard Master-Detail template storyboard.

If you are using a MacBook Air or MacBook Pro with a multitouch trackpad or have an external trackpad, you can use the pinch gesture to zoom in and out of the storyboard. You can also open the Editor menu, expand Canvas, expand Zoom, and then choose an option there. To edit a scene, simply double-click it, and Xcode zooms in to that particular scene and provides editing tools. To view the tools available, open the Object Library by clicking the View menu, expanding Utilities, and then clicking Show Object Library (or press Control+Option+Command+3).

The tools appear in the bottom-right corner of Xcode. Scroll through the list to see what types of objects are available for you to drag-and-drop right into your interface.

To the left of your storyboard interface is an area called the **Document Outline**. If the Document Outline is hidden, click the Editor menu and then click Show Document Outline. You will find the Document Outline helpful while designing interfaces in storyboards because storyboards tend to get large, and it's difficult to fit everything on your computer's screen. Using the Document Outline is a great way to quickly access the elements in the scenes to link elements, create constraints, or set properties of elements in a hierarchical list, rather than in the storyboard where elements could be placed quite a distance apart. The Document Outline for your app should look like the one in Figure 22.2.

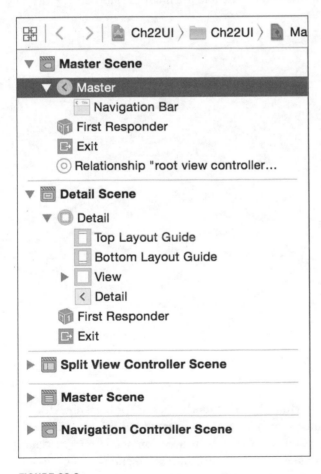

FIGURE 22.2
The Document Outline for the Master-Detail template storyboard.

Creating Your Own Project

Close the existing project by selecting File > Close Project (or by pressing Command+Option+W). Create a new Xcode project by selecting File > New > Project (or by pressing Command+Shift+N). Under iOS and Application, select Single View Application and then click Next. Enter a name, such as "Songs" in the Product Name field, make sure Swift is the language and Universal is set for the Devices drop-down, and then click Next. On the next dialog, save the project to a location on your hard drive and then click Create.

Adding UI Elements

With your new Songs project open, locate the Main.storyboard file in the left-hand Navigation Pane and select it to edit the storyboard in the main content area. In the storyboard, double-click the View Controller scene, which should be the only scene in the storyboard. It should look like a square, with a row of icons along the top; the yellow icon on the left represents the controller itself, the middle icon represents the First Responder (which we won't discuss in this book), and the right-hand icon is the Exit icon. Exit is used for **exit segues**, which are a way to handle dismissing a view controller from the screen. This View Controller scene is managed by the ViewController.swift class in our project, which is a subclass of UIViewController.

Every view controller scene has a view in it by default and a corresponding view outlet property referencing the view from the view controller's class. This view controller is a standard view controller, capable of arranging elements in it anywhere you want, almost like a blank slate. While we use this type of view controller later, we don't need it now, so select the View Controller from the View Controller Scene in the Document Outline and press the Delete key on your keyboard. Open the Object Library by pressing Command+Option+Control+3 and drag a new Table View Controller to the storyboard. The Table View Controller looks similar to the View Controller we just removed but with a few new things of note: There is a header labeled Prototype Cells and a prototype table view **cell** below it. List items in a table view are called cells, just like in the Mail or Music apps, and they can be configured however you or your clients want.

NOTE

Many UI Elements Have Similar APIs

Apple designed many elements with similar or familiar APIs so that learning about a few different UI elements helps you understand how most other elements interact with code. In other words, many different UI elements adopt similar patterns, such as using common delegate and data source patterns or a target-action pattern.

This prototype cell is used by Xcode within our table view to populate content in the UI, since all the cells we use have the same layout. If we need different cell prototypes, we can simply create more and design them to look how we want. We will eventually populate song information in each cell, similar to what we did in Hour 21, "Adding Interoperability with Objective-C."

Since we deleted the View Controller scene from the storyboard, we can delete the corresponding view controller class file from the project, so in the Navigation Pane select the ViewController.swift file and press the Delete key on your keyboard. If prompted, send the file to the Trash. Next, we need to create a new Swift view controller, this time a subclass of `UITableViewController`, so we can relate it to the Table View Controller scene we just added to the storyboard. Press Command+N to create a new file. Under iOS and Source, select Cocoa Touch Class and then click Next. Name the class `SongsTableViewController`, subclass of `UITableViewController`, make sure Swift is the language, and then click Next. On the next screen save the file by clicking Create. Yes, `SongsTableViewController` is a long name, but it is descriptive of what it is and what it displays.

The new class has several methods already provided for you, as well as comments hinting as to how to use each method. Not all of them are necessary for our example, or even for your app, but they are provided to give you a good starting point.

Populating Data

Let's put some test data into the table view so we can see how the table view controller actually displays data onscreen. First, we need to connect our newly created class to the Table View Controller scene we added in the storyboard, so Xcode knows which of our classes we want to control the scene.

Open the storyboard and select the Table View Controller from the Document Outline. Open the Identity Inspector on the right side of the screen by opening the View > Utilities > Show Identity Inspector (or by pressing Command+Option+3). Currently, the class selected for the Table View Controller scene is a base `UITableViewController` class. But since we created our own subclass of `UITableViewController`, let's change it to our new class. In the Class drop-down, select the `SongsTableViewController` class, as shown in Figure 22.3. Notice how the name of our scene changes in the Document Outline from Table View Controller to Songs Table View Controller. Xcode parses our class name for us.

We need to make one more small change, and that is to make the Songs Table View Controller scene the **initial view controller** in our storyboard. Since the View Controller scene was originally the initial view controller but we deleted it, we need to tell Xcode which view controller is our initial view controller when the app launches. With the Songs Table View Controller scene still selected, press Command Option+4 to open the Attributes Inspector, and in the View Controller section, make sure the Is Initial View Controller check box is selected.

FIGURE 22.3
The Identity Inspector for the Table View Controller where you can change the class.

Now that the class is set, select Cell below Table View in the Document Outline and press Command+Option+4 to review the cell's options in the Attributes Inspector. Change the Style to Subtitle, and enter "Cell" in the Identifier text field. This identifier is called the **reuse identifier**, which our `SongsTableViewController` class uses to identify which cells can be reused from its queue.

NOTE

Reuse Identifiers and Queues

The `UITableViewController` class has an efficient means of reusing cells to avoid constantly deallocating and reallocating new instances as you scroll through a table view. Say you have 1,000 songs in your Music app and you flick through the list of songs. The table view controller only creates as many instances of `UITableViewCell` as are visible onscreen, plus one or two more. The table view controller gets cells from a queue of reusable cells and updates the content of the next song in line in the newly dequeued cell. Any cell that goes offscreen gets queued for reuse. This improves performance and reduces lag, as only a finite number of cells ever gets instantiated, and it is less processor and power intensive to simply update the properties of an existing cell than to be constantly removing and recreating new cells.

Save the storyboard and switch back to the SongsTableViewController.swift file. At the time of this writing, Xcode and Swift are still undergoing changes with respect to removing the implicitly unwrapped optional operator from Cocoa types inside function definitions. This is a known issue documented in the Xcode 6 release notes for the Swift language. Xcode warns you when it senses an implicitly unwrapped optional where a non-optional type should be, so you can use Xcode's suggested solution to fix it by clicking on the yellow warning icon and double-clicking Fix It – Remove the '!' to Make the Parameter Required, as shown in Figure 22.4. Fix both warnings in the `SongsTableViewController` class.

```
29
30    override func numberOfSectionsInTableView(tableView:     ⚠ Overriding instance method parameter of type 'UITa...
         UITableView) -> Int {
31
32    Issue   ⊙ Overriding instance method parameter of type 'UITableView' with implicitly unwrapped optional type 'UITableView!'
33    Fix-it  Remove '!' to make the parameter required
34
35    Fix-it  Add parentheses to silence this warning
36    override func tableView(tableView: UITableView!, numberOfRowsInSection section: Int) -> Int {
37        // #warning Incomplete method implementation.   ⚠ Overriding instance method parameter of type 'UITableView' with implicitly...
38        // Return the number of rows in the section.
39        return 0
40    }
41
```

FIGURE 22.4
Remove the ! character to make the parameters required.

The two methods you fixed are defined in the `UITableViewDataSource` protocol. While our class does not specifically state adoption to the protocol, `UITableViewController` adopts the protocol, so our subclass can safely conform to it by providing the necessary methods. `numberOfSectionsInTableView(_:)` and `tableView(_:numberOfRowsInSection:)` tell our table view scene how many sections and rows in those sections to display. A section is a grouping, such as in the Music app in the Artists tab with the artists sorted alphabetically, and you see the first letter of each artist's name at the top of the table view.

NOTE
_____

Method Naming With Underscores and Commas

The underscore (_) character in the aforementioned method names indicate there is an argument sent, but the parameter name is not used, similar to what we discussed in Hour 8, "Using Functions to Perform Actions," in the "External Parameter Names" section. I have seen Apple use commas in their method parameter lists when referring to a method by name in some places, but without a comma in other places. The goal is for you to understand what method we are referring to.

_____

We need one more method to make a fully functioning table view, and it is provided already, just inside a comment block. Remove the `/*` and `*/` surrounding the function `tableView(_:cellForRowAtIndexPath:)`. This method also needs to have the `!` character removed to change the types from implicitly unwrapped optional types to non-optional types. What `tableView(_:cellForRowAtIndexPath:)` does is dequeue a cell from the queue of reusable cells and enable you to configure the cell before it is displayed onscreen. To put some quick test data into the app to ensure that we made all the connections properly and the table view's data source protocol methods are responding properly, make sure that the three methods in Listing 22.1 are the same in your app.

LISTING 22.1   Providing Table View Data Source Methods

```
01:  override func numberOfSectionsInTableView(tableView: UITableView) -> Int {
02:      return 3
03:  }
```

```
04:
05:   override func tableView(tableView: UITableView, numberOfRowsInSection
➡section: Int) -> Int {
06:       return 5
07:   }
08:
09:   override func tableView(tableView: UITableView, titleForHeaderInSection
➡section: Int) -> String? {
10:       switch section {
11:       case 0:
12:           return "Section A"
13:       case 1:
14:           return "Section B"
15:       case 2:
16:           return "Section C"
17:       default:
18:           return nil
19:       }
20:   }
21:
22:   override func tableView(tableView: UITableView, cellForRowAtIndexPath
➡indexPath: NSIndexPath) -> UITableViewCell {
23:       let cell = tableView.dequeueReusableCellWithIdentifier("Cell",
➡forIndexPath: indexPath) as UITableViewCell
24:       cell.textLabel?.text = "Row \(indexPath.row)"
25:       let detail = self.tableView(tableView, titleForHeaderInSection:
➡indexPath.section) ?? ""
26:       cell.detailTextLabel?.text = "In \(detail)"
27:
28:       return cell
29:   }
```

Now build and run the application to see the results of your hard work thus far. Make sure a Simulator (or your device if you have one plugged in) is selected from the device list in Xcode and then press Command+R to build and run. The example app should look like the app in Figure 22.5.

This looks great, except for the top. Why is the Section A heading overlapping the status bar? In iOS 7, a more full-screen table view controller was introduced, enabling content to be seen on more of the screen rather than skeuomorphic design taking up valuable real estate. With that change, though, it leaves an awkward overlap at the top, so the best thing to do in this case is to **embed** our Songs Table View Controller inside a **navigation controller**. A navigation controller is simply a **container view controller** that manages the navigation stack and provides mechanisms for managing the back button at the top-left of the screen when you tap on a cell for more detail. Whatever view controller is currently onscreen is the navigation controller's **top view controller**.

FIGURE 22.5
A table view in an example app showing three sections and five rows in each section.

Let's embed our Songs Table View Controller scene inside a navigation controller and watch our UI change for the better. Open the storyboard file, select the Songs Table View Controller scene in the Document Outline, and open the Editor menu. Expand Embed In and then select Navigation Controller. The storyboard added a scene for the navigation controller and now has an arrow pointing to our Songs Table View Controller scene. Build and run the app again by pressing Command+R to see the new UI. Figure 22.6 shows the top portion of the iPhone screen showing the change from embedding the Songs Table View Controller scene inside a navigation controller.

FIGURE 22.6
The Songs Table View Controller embedded inside a navigation controller.

That's much better. The UI looks clean and easily readable. But if you notice, tapping on any of the cells does nothing but highlight it. That's because we haven't implemented any methods to tell our app what to do when a user taps on a cell. We have two options: First, we could implement a table view delegate method called `tableView(_:didSelectRowAtIndexPath:)`, or second, we could implement a navigation method called `prepareForSegue(_:sender:)`. Because we want to segue to another view controller to show more details, `prepareForSegue (_:sender:)` is a more appropriate choice (although, if our app required it, we could implement both).

In SongTableViewController.swift, remove the comment lines surrounding `prepareForSegue(_:sender:)`, and notice the comment inside the method:

```
// Get the new view controller using [segue destinationViewController].
// Pass the selected object to the new view controller.
```

These comments help you to understand the purpose of the method and what you should expect to provide to the method. The code in the comment, `[segue destinationViewController]`, is still the Objective-C style of accessing the `destinationViewController` property getter on the `segue` instance. But now that you know how to recognize Objective-C code from Hour 21, you should know that you can simply use dot-syntax in Swift and access the property by using `segue.destinationViewController`.

In the `prepareForSegue(_:sender:)` method, we need to prepare our destination view controller with a `Song` instance, so we need a `Song` instance to pass, which means we need to create a `Song` type. Let's create a `Song` struct.

Press Command+N to create a new Swift file and name it Song. The `Song` struct should look like what is shown in Listing 22.2.

LISTING 22.2   The `Song` Struct

```
struct Song {
    var title: String
    var artist: String
    var rating: Double
}
```

Now that you have a `Song` struct to use, we should now create the destination view controller to display the song data. Press Command+N to create a new file. On the template chooser screen, select Cocoa Touch Class and then click Next. In the next dialog, make the class a subclass of `UIViewController`, name it `SongDetailViewController`, make sure the language is Swift, and then click Next. Save the file by clicking Create. When the new class file is created, remove everything inside the `SongDetailViewController` class except the `viewDidLoad()` method. The `SongDetailViewController` class should look like Listing 22.3.

LISTING 22.3   `SongDetailViewController` Class

```
import UIKit

class SongDetailViewController : UIViewController {

    override func viewDidLoad() {
        super.viewDidLoad()
    }

}
```

With the `SongDetailViewController` class created, let's update the storyboard to use the new class. Open the storyboard, drag a new View Controller object from the Object Library to the storyboard, and place it to the right of the Songs Table View Controller scene. Press Command+Option+3 to open the Identity Inspector, and change the scene's class to `SongDetailViewController`.

Now create a segue between the Songs Table View Controller scene and the Song Detail View Controller scene. In the Document Outline, expand Songs Table View Controller and then expand Table View. Hold down the Control key on your keyboard and then drag the cursor from Cell down to the Song Detail View Controller in the Document Outline, as shown in Figure 22.7. Choose the Show option in the Selection Segue section of the menu that pops up. This creates a **show segue** (also known as a **push segue**) between the Songs Table View Controller scene and the Song Detail View Controller scene that is activated whenever any of our cells in the table view is tapped.

FIGURE 22.7
Creating a show segue in the storyboard.

Notice that an arrow appears in the storyboard between the Songs Table View Controller scene and the Song Detail View Controller scene. Select the arrow and then press Command+Option+4 to display the segue's Attributes Inspector on the right. In the Identifier field, enter showSongDetails.

NOTEV

Checking Segue Identity

Segues do not need to have a name, but naming them is highly suggested. Your app may grow in size, and with that growth may come new segues to new view controllers. Inside prepareForSegue(_:sender:) you can check a segue's identity with the segue.identifier property and send different parameters to destination view controllers or prepare different destination view controllers depending on the identity of the segue activated.

Add Labels to the UI to Display Song Data

Now we need to add a few labels to the Song Detail View Controller scene so we can see the data being sent from the `SongsTableViewController` class. Select the Song Detail View Controller from the Document Outline. Press Control+Option+Command+3 to open the Object Library and scroll to find a Label object. Drag three labels into the Song Detail View Controller scene, one on top of another, centered vertically. Each time you should see blue lines helping you snap the labels into place, as shown in Figure 22.8.

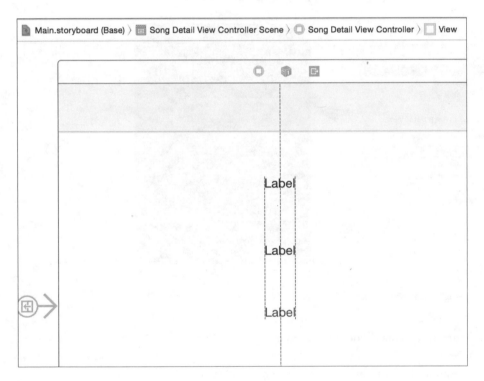

FIGURE 22.8
Adding three labels to the scene, centered vertically using Xcode's alignment guides.

With three labels in the Song Detail View Controller scene, we need to link them to outlets in our `SongDetailViewController` class, so that we can control the UI from our class with outlet properties. Make sure the Song Detail View Controller scene is selected and then press Command+Option+Return to open the Assistant Editor. The Assistant Editor opens directly to our class implementation. Hold down the Control key on your keyboard and drag your mouse or touchpad from each label to an empty space inside the class and above the `viewDidLoad()` method. Blue helper lines show where the code will be inserted. Let go of the Control key and the mouse or touchpad, and a menu displays. In the menu, choose Outlet for the Connection type, provide a name (we need three, so one will be `titleLabel`, one `artistLabel`, and one `ratingLabel`), make sure the Type is UILabel and the storage is weak, and then click the Connect button. The `@IBOutlet` property is automatically added for you. The sequence of steps is shown in Figure 22.9.

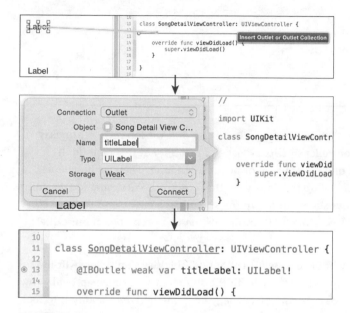

FIGURE 22.9
The sequence of connecting a UILabel element to a class as an `@IBOutlet` property.

Just a few more things to do and then we can see our app in action. We need to finish our `prepareForSegue(_:sender:)` method in the `SongsTableViewController` class and then update the UI from our `SongDetailViewController` class. Since we're already in the `SongDetailViewController` class, make your class look like the code shown in Listing 22.4.

LISTING 22.4 `SongDetailViewController` Class and Updating UI

```
import UIKit

class SongDetailViewController: UIViewController {

    var song: Song?

    @IBOutlet weak var titleLabel: UILabel!
    @IBOutlet weak var artistLabel: UILabel!
    @IBOutlet weak var ratingLabel: UILabel!
```

```
override func viewDidLoad() {
    super.viewDidLoad()
    self.updateView()
}

func updateView() {
    titleLabel.text = song?.title
    artistLabel.text = song?.artist
    ratingLabel.text = "\(song?.rating) / 5 stars"
}

}
```

In Listing 22.4, we declare an instance property of type `Song?` so that we can have a property
to be fulfilled by the sending view controller's `prepareForSegue(_:sender:)` method. It is
optional because it may contain nil and never be set or be set to nil later. Then we have our
three `@IBOutlet` properties that were set up previously. In the `viewDidLoad()` method we call
`super.viewDidLoad()` as you always should to set up the superclass's views, and then we call
`self.updateView()`. The `updateView()` method simply sets the text properties of our outlets
to values from our `song` property.

Save the SongDetailViewController.swift file and select the SongsTableViewController.swift file to
edit it. If you have not done so already, you can delete all the commented functions provided by
the file template. Navigate to the `prepareForSegue(_:sender:)` method and modify it to look
exactly like Listing 22.5.

LISTING 22.5   Prepare for Segue

```
override func prepareForSegue(segue: UIStoryboardSegue, sender: AnyObject!) {
    let detailViewController = segue.destinationViewController as
➥SongDetailViewController
    detailViewController.song = Song(title: "Trippin' on a hole in a paper
➥heart", artist: "Stone Temple Pilots", rating: 4.0)
}
```

Please pardon the extremely long arguments, but I did that to ensure that our labels can
handle really long text. Notice that we downcast `segue.destinationViewController`
to `SongDetailViewController`. This is so that we can set the `song` property, because the
`AnyObject` type (which `destinationViewController` is) does not have a `song` property.

Press Command+R to build and run the app in the Simulator and then click on any cell in
the table view. Your segue works! But why do the labels look so screwed up? We didn't set any

constraints in the storyboard scene to tell Xcode how we want our layout to show up. I had you pass in long argument names to show that the labels won't auto-resize and aren't centered in the display, even though when you dragged them onto the scene, you snapped them to the visual guides to center horizontally. Let's add some constraints and finish this part of the app for this hour.

Adding UI Constraints

As mentioned, constraints are rules that define where one element should be located relative to another, its size, if and/or how it should shrink or expand to fill space, and so on. Constraints can be a different way of thinking if you are coming from springs and struts (an older way of defining UI behavior) or setting a UI element's origin point and size values explicitly. Constraints are part of building an adaptive layout; as screen sizes continue to change, hard-coding your UI can prove to be difficult to manage and lead to poor looking layouts. Using constraints forces you to think about how a UI element should behave with respect to other elements, rather than giving it explicit traits.

Thankfully, the implementation of adding constraints is easy. To add constraints, you can either Control-drag from one element to another and choose a behavior or property from the ensuing pop-up window or use the auto layout constraint bar at the bottom of the storyboard, as shown in Figure 22.10. I don't believe that it has an official name from Apple, so we will call it the auto layout bar. There are four menu buttons on the right side of the auto layout bar, from left to right: Align, Pin, Resolve Auto Layout Issues, and Resizing Behavior.

☐	wAny hAny	⊟ ⊡ ⊣⊢ ⊒

FIGURE 22.10
The auto layout bar at the bottom of the storyboard.

NOTE

Size Classes

In the center of the auto layout bar, you will see **wAny hAny**. This is where you can choose what size class interface to modify. We do not cover size classes in this book except to say that there are two classes: **Compact** and **Regular**. Compact is for smaller dimensions, and Regular is for larger dimensions. You can also specify **Any**, which can be either Compact or Regular, thus providing nine options for customizing layout dimensions. This way you can customize how a UI is laid out based on the size and orientation of the user's device at any given time. For more information on size classes, check out the WWDC 2014 session 411 video, "What's New in Interface Builder."

Open the storyboard file and select all three labels in the Song Detail View Controller scene. Click the Align button in the auto layout bar. Select the Horizontal Center in Container check box, and then click the Add 3 Constraints button. You should now see an orange line going through the center of each label, and each label is surrounded in an orange frame. This means that Xcode's Auto Layout does not have enough information to properly place these labels at runtime without any sort of ambiguity. We centered the labels horizontally but did not give any clue to vertical spacing, so let's do that now.

Select the topmost label and click the Pin button in the auto layout bar. There are four drop-down boxes surrounding a plain white square, and dotted-lined I-beams between the drop-down boxes and the center square. The center square represents the current UI element we have selected, and we can pin the element in any certain direction. Click the orange I-beam on the top of the square, and then click Add 1 Constraint. Now the constraints to our topmost label are blue, indicating that Auto Layout is happy with our constraints. Repeat this I-beam pinning process for the remaining two labels.

Now that our labels have enough layout information provided to Auto Layout to be centered horizontally and spaced far enough away from the top and each other, we can run the app again. Press Command+R to build and run the app on the Simulator. Tap any cell in the list to see our song info display in the Song Detail View Controller. The results of our Auto Layout work can be seen in Figure 22.11.

Everything looks great, except the rating says "Optional(4.0)/5 stars". I'll leave that as an exercise for you to figure out where you should fix that so the proper non-optional amount of stars, if any, displays in the label.

The code and completed project for this hour can be found in the book's GitHub repository, https://github.com/STYSwiftIn24H/Examples, in the Ch22 folder.

FIGURE 22.11
The Song Detail View Controller with correct Auto Layout constraints.

Summary

In this hour you learned many things about creating a UI in Xcode's storyboard. You learned some primary definitions used in creating a UI and some examples to assist in understanding. Next, you learned how to create a new Xcode project from a template and observed how storyboard files can really help to visually diagram interfaces and program flow, as well as how the Document Outline can be used to see a hierarchical list of UI elements for quick access.

You then learned where to locate objects in the Object Library and how to use them to create a basic UI. You used a new Table View Controller element to visually represent a table view controller class and adjust the prototype cell to fit the needs of our app. Then you populated data into the table view controller by using data source methods to provide the data needed to display in the UI.

You also learned about segues and how to use the `prepareForSegue(_:sender:)` method to prepare any data to be sent to the destination view controller. After segues you learned about how constraints can be used to lay out the elements in the UI how you want them, relative to other elements, through a mechanism called Auto Layout.

In the next hour, we reuse this app and expand upon it by introducing actual song data retrieved from iTunes and learn about asynchronous programming to make for a more efficient app and better user experience.

Q&A

Q. Do I have to use storyboards when I design a user interface?

A. No, it is possible to create an entire user interface in code, but storyboards handle most of what you need to do. Unless you're already an experienced Mac or iOS developer, you should stick with storyboards for now.

Q. What is a first responder?

A. A responder object is an object that can recognize and handle events in your application. As the name suggests, the first responder is designated to receive events before other responder objects. If the first responder does not handle the event, it travels along the responder chain until it finds a responder that can. An example of a first responder is a text field, and it can be the first responder to keyboard input. For more information check Apple's documentation on responder objects and responder chains.

Q. When I run the app in the Simulator, there are a bunch of rows but only one cell in my storyboard. What's going on?

A. We created a prototype cell in our storyboard that defines the behavior of a generic cell in our table. When we populate the table in `SongsTableViewController.swift` we're using that prototype cell as a template to build all the cells in our table.

Workshop

The workshop contains quiz questions and exercises to help you solidify your understanding of the material covered. Try to answer all questions before looking at the answers that follow.

Quiz

1. What is a segue?

2. What is the purpose of the `@IBOutlet`?

3. Why do we need UI constraints?

4. What is the keyboard shortcut you use in Xcode to build and run your application? (It's an important one!)

Answers

1. A segue defines a transition from one scene to another.

2. @IBOutlet tells Xcode that a property in our class will be used to populate a designated UI element.

3. UI constraints enable us to define where UI elements appear in our application. Using constraints makes it possible for our application to automatically adjust its layout to fit the size of the device it's running on.

4. Command+R builds and runs your application. This is one of the most frequently used shortcuts in Xcode, and it's worth memorizing.

Exercise

For this exercise, we continue using the project from this hour's examples. Let's try adding a new property to our Song structure and then hooking it up to a label using our storyboard. Start by adding an Integer property called chartPosition to the Song struct in Song.swift. Try to build and run your application and you see that there are now errors in your project. Click on the red Error icon to find and correct the error, and then build and run your application again. At this point, your new property is in place, but it isn't showing up in the application.

Now add a new label to the Song Detail View Controller in your storyboard and set the constraints just like you did for the other labels. Once you have the constraints in place, hook up an outlet to the SongDetailViewController class and check that the new label shows up as expected.

If you get stuck at any point, just look back at the steps we took when we added the other labels for a hint.

You can also try playing around with the placement of labels in the view controller. Can you place two of the labels next to each other? You have to adjust your UI constraints to get this to work, but you'll learn a lot about storyboards by just playing with the positioning of the UI elements.

Asynchronous Programming in Swift

What You'll Learn in This Hour:

▶ What concurrency is and how OS X and iOS manage concurrency

▶ The difference between synchronous and asynchronous programming

▶ How to use Grand Central Dispatch

▶ How to use NSOperation and NSOperationQueue

▶ How to make synchronous and asynchronous network calls

In Hour 22, "Interacting with User Interfaces," you built an app from scratch using Swift. It wasn't necessarily an app that you would want to brag to your friends about, though, since it only contained test data. In this hour you learn about concurrency and how to use asynchronous programming to efficiently make network calls and load images. You also learn how to apply these concepts to the Songs app. You learn several different methods of managing tasks asynchronously. Using the knowledge about asynchronous programming you learn this hour, you adapt your Songs app to contact the iTunes API and load information gathered from an iTunes search in an effective and efficient manner.

The Problem That Concurrency Solves

Concurrency is the concept of improving responsiveness of code by ensuring that the main thread is free to respond to user events or leverage more cores to do more work in the same amount of time. But before we get too far into what that actually means, I need to provide you with a brief history of processors and computing.

Our current technological landscape is highly advanced compared to what we used to have in terms of processing power. Depending on how old you are, you may or may not remember the days when computers had only single-core processors (CPUs). Believe it or not, telephones used to be connected to walls also. And I know, some of you had to walk uphill both ways in the snow just to get to school and back. But let's get back to the single-core CPUs.

Apps are comprised of one or more **threads** of execution. A thread is simply a lightweight path of execution. Single-core CPUs could not efficiently multitask without complex thread management code that often was up to the developer to manage per app. As CPUs got faster, and thread management systems became more available to developers, developing concurrent apps became slightly easier, but there was still a lot to manage.

CPUs, because of thermal constraints and power consumption, could only get so fast, so chip manufacturers began creating multicore CPUs. By having multiple cores per CPU, threads could execute on separate cores simultaneously, versus serially or sequentially. But the problem of thread management in software remained.

Apple introduced a system to manage concurrency using **asynchronous design** called **Grand Central Dispatch** (GCD). An asynchronous function or task does some work to begin its operation and then offloads the task to another thread and may return execution to the next statement before the operation finishes in the background. You get to work an example of this shortly. GCD contains the thread management code that once was the responsibility of you and me and pushes that responsibility down to the system level. Mac OS X and iOS now contain this thread management system, freeing you from that responsibility so you can focus on writing more meaningful code.

I mentioned the **main thread** in the definition of concurrency earlier. The main thread of execution is the thread that the operating system creates to run your app's code from your app's starting point. In Cocoa and Cocoa Touch apps (which I just refer to as Cocoa for the remainder of this hour), the UI is executed on the main thread, as well all other tasks you create in code, unless explicitly specified to execute on another thread. Have you ever used an app that seemed to be sluggish and jittery as you scrolled through a list or interacted with the UI? It could be that the app did not offload some of its work to another thread to be executed asynchronously, and the UI suffered from being blocked while those processes ran on the main thread. The good news, though, is that you don't have to manage threads at all in Cocoa apps; you use **queues**.

Different Types of Queues

Concurrency in Cocoa apps comes in two different flavors: **dispatch queues** and **operation queues**. You learn about these concepts as we explore these APIs in more detail shortly.

Dispatch Queues

Dispatch queues are used by Grand Central Dispatch. They are a C-based mechanism for executing tasks. In Swift, you place the work to be done asynchronously inside a closure and hand the closure to a GCD dispatch queue. The dispatch queue handles scheduling of the task execution for you; you just need to specify what queue on which you want the task executed (that is, a background queue or the main queue). Dispatch queues schedule tasks to get executed serially or concurrently on a first-in-first-out (FIFO) basis.

Dispatch queues are nice in that you can quickly create a queue and fire off a closure onto that queue without creating any special handling objects. You can also create tasks inside closures to get executed on a different queue from within your initial closure. Such an example of that would be creating networking code that gets executed serially and placing that code inside a closure. Then hand the closure off to a background dispatch queue. Inside the closure, you know that when the code completes the network request you want to update the UI with what was downloaded, so you create a new closure inside the existing closure and dispatch the new closure to the main queue so the UI can get updated. If that seems confusing, be patient; we walk through this exact scenario in code later, which should help you understand.

NOTE

Threads Versus Queues

As you research concurrency using asynchronous design, you will most likely come across resources that intermix the terms **thread** and **queue**. While work on a background queue gets scheduled to execute on a background thread, and likewise work on the main queue gets scheduled to execute on the main thread, you typically never have to manage threads—only work with queues. Think of a thread as a conveyor belt and the queue is where work gets scheduled to be put onto the conveyor belt.

Operation Queues

Operation queues are a Cocoa abstraction of the lower-level GCD APIs, which use the NSOperationQueue class to manage operations. While they too operate on a FIFO basis, they can also take into account operation priority as well as dependency on other operations.

Operations in an operation queue are typically subclasses of NSOperation. NSOperation is an abstract class, which means that you don't create an instance directly of type NSOperation, but rather you subclass it to provide your own logic and set of tasks to execute. Cocoa provides two concrete subclasses you can use without going through the trouble of subclassing NSOperation yourself; NSBlockOperation and NSInvocationOperation. Adding an operation to an operation queue is easy; create an operation with some work to execute and then use the addOperation() method on an instance of NSOperationQueue. Alternatively, you can bypass using the NSOperationQueue instance and call start() on the operation itself. However, since much of the functionality gained by using operations is due to operation queues, it is most often preferred to use operation queues rather than calling an operation's start() method directly.

Which Queues Should You Use?

Dispatch queues and operation queues are each tools for the job of asynchronous programming. There are considerations, however, when choosing which one to use.

Creating NSOperations and using NSOperationQueues provide non-trivial overhead to asynchronous programming; while GCD is closer to the metal, so to speak, operations and operation queues are an abstraction on top of that and have extra memory and performance implications due to being Cocoa objects that have to get allocated and be managed. There are benefits to using operation queues; you can set properties such as maximum number of concurrent operations, easily access the main queue with familiar dot-syntax, set priorities, cancel requests, set completion blocks, and use familiar Swift syntax.

Dispatch queues in GCD can get ugly quickly, due to their C-style syntax. Having closures inside closures inside closures can get difficult to manage and troubleshoot. The benefits, though, to working with GCD are that you can quickly fire off closures to queues and with minimal overhead. Often using a lightweight GCD dispatch is more convenient and quicker than building an NSOperation and instantiating an NSOperationQueue.

If your app calls for it, you can also use a mix of the two. You are not limited to using *only* GCD or *only* operations queues.

Asynchronous Programming in Action

To see how concurrency works using asynchronous programming, let's quickly create a sample app to show this in action. Since GCD doesn't work well in playgrounds, let's create a simple app to examine using GCD to illustrate how it works.

Open Xcode and create a new project. Under iOS and Application, choose Single View Application and then click Next. Enter AsyncTest for the product name, choose Swift as the language, and click Next. Save the project on your hard drive by clicking Create.

In your new project, select ViewController.swift to edit it. Make some room to type inside the viewDidLoad() method and enter the code in viewDidLoad() as shown in Listing 23.1. When complete, press Command+R to build and run the app. The print() statements should show in the Debug Area at the bottom of Xcode's interface. If not, open View > Debug Area > Show Debug Area (or press Command+Shift+Y). Make sure the Show/Hide Console toggle button is selected with blue in the bottom-right corner of the Debug Area.

LISTING 23.1   Observing Serial Results

```
override func viewDidLoad() {
    super.viewDidLoad()

    for _ in 1...10 { print("A") }
    for _ in 1...10 { print("B") }
}
// displays "AAAAAAAAAABBBBBBBBBB"
```

The code in Listing 23.1 should be familiar to you by now. There is nothing special going on; we are simply printing "A" and "B" serially with for-in loops. Listing 23.2 shows what happens when we put each for-in loop inside its own background dispatch queue. Don't worry about the syntax for now—just know that each loop inside its closure is sent off to a background queue for execution. Update your viewDidLoad() method as shown in Listing 23.2.

LISTING 23.2   Observing Asynchronous Results

```
override func viewDidLoad() {
    super.viewDidLoad()

    dispatch_async(dispatch_get_global_queue(DISPATCH_QUEUE_PRIORITY_DEFAULT, 0)) {
        for _ in 1...10 { print("A") }
    }
    dispatch_async(dispatch_get_global_queue(DISPATCH_QUEUE_PRIORITY_DEFAULT, 0)) {
        for _ in 1...10 { print("B") }
    }
}
//  displays AAABBBBBBBBBBBAAAAAAA or some other variation
```

Run the app a few more times, and you see different results each time for the order in which the letters "A" and "B" are printed to the console. This is because when we send a task or set of tasks to a background queue, we cannot do much to manage their execution at that point. We can, however, set another set of tasks to execute once our initial set of background tasks executes by dispatching a new task inside our background dispatch. Rewrite the viewDidLoad() method as shown in Listing 23.3.

LISTING 23.3   Dispatching Tasks Inside Another Dispatch

```
override func viewDidLoad() {
    super.viewDidLoad()

    dispatch_async(dispatch_get_global_queue(DISPATCH_QUEUE_PRIORITY_DEFAULT, 0)) {
        for _ in 1...10 { print("A") }
        dispatch_async(dispatch_get_main_queue()) {
```

```
            for _ in 1...10 { print("B") }
        }
    }
}
// displays "AAAAAAAAAABBBBBBBBBB"
```

The code in Listing 23.3 is a common pattern when using GCD. This code dispatches a closure to execute on a background queue, just as in Listing 23.2. Even though the code inside the closure gets executed on an asynchronous queue, each line of code runs serially on that queue until it is finished. Since we only want to print 10 B's to the console *after* 10 A's have been printed from a background queue, we dispatch the closure printing the 10 B's to the main queue after 10 A's finish printing. An actual example of this would be putting a large network request in place of the for-in loop printing 10 A's, and when the large network request completes we dispatch a closure updating the UI in place of the for-in loop printing 10 B's. Nesting dispatch calls can get ugly but can be useful for sequencing tasks to execute after an asynchronous task completes.

NOTE

Why Nest Dispatched Closures?

Remember that asynchronously dispatched code sends the closure off to a background queue but returns control immediately to the next line of execution without waiting for the asynchronous task to complete. By nesting the dispatched code back to the main queue, you ensure that your work on the main thread executes upon completion of the asynchronous task.

So far these examples have been done using GCD. `dispatch_async` is the function to call when you want to execute a task asynchronously. Conversely, the `dispatch_sync` function dispatches a task synchronously, which means the lines of code following the closure must wait for the entire synchronous operation to finish and resume control. The first parameter of either function expects a queue of type `dispatch_queue_t`, so you can either create your own queue variable or use the `dispatch_get_global_queue()` function and pass two parameters. One is a quality of service identifier of type `long` (typically a constant provided by GCD—here we use `DISPATCH_QUEUE_PRIORITY_DEFAULT`), and the other is a value for the `flags` parameter of type `UInt` (flags aren't used yet; Apple's documentation states that they are reserved for future use, and to use zero (0) for this parameter). Then finally, we use trailing closure syntax to add the task or tasks we need to execute asynchronously inside the trailing closure.

Let's take a look at how Listing 23.2 and 23.3 would look using operation queues. Listing 23.4 recreates the same functionality of Listing 23.2 by using operations and operation queues.

LISTING 23.4 Asynchronous Programming with Operation Queues

```
override func viewDidLoad() {
    let queue = NSOperationQueue()
    class MyOp : NSOperation {
        var whatToPrint: String!
        override func main() {
            autoreleasepool {
                for _ in 1...10 { print(self.whatToPrint) }
            }
        }
    }
    let myOpA = MyOp()
    myOpA.whatToPrint = "A"
    let myOpB = MyOp()
    myOpB.whatToPrint = "B"
    queue.addOperation(myOpA)
    queue.addOperation(myOpB)
}
// displays "ABAABBABABABABABABAB"
```

As you can see from Listing 23.4, this method of creating asynchronous execution paths requires a lot more code. To subclass NSOperation and make your own class to perform tasks asynchronously, you must override the main() method. Since this block is running outside the memory pool created by the main thread, we must create our own auto-release pool inside main(). But there is power in what NSOperationQueue and NSOperations can provide. Listing 23.5 recreates Listing 23.3 using operation queues and implements a completion block in a much nicer and cleaner way than GCD.

LISTING 23.5 Using Completion Blocks with NSOperations

```
override func viewDidLoad() {
    let queue = NSOperationQueue()
    class MyOp : NSOperation {
        var whatToPrint: String!
        override func main() {
            autoreleasepool {
                for _ in 1...10 { print(self.whatToPrint) }
            }
        }
    }
    let myOpA = MyOp()
    myOpA.whatToPrint = "A"
    let myOpB = MyOp()
```

```
    myOpB.whatToPrint = "B"
    myOpA.completionBlock = { queue.addOperation(myOpB) }
    queue.addOperation(myOpA)
}
// displays "AAAAAAAAAABBBBBBBBBB"
```

Now that you understand the basics of asynchronous programming in Swift using either GCD or
NSOperations and NSOperationQueues, let's take a look at how we can add this to our Songs
app from Hour 22. We need to add functionality to it that makes a network request to the iTunes
API, parses the response in a format called JSON (JavaScript Object Notation), and displays the
results onscreen. Close the current AsyncTest project and open your Songs project.

Add iTunes Search to Songs App

In the Songs project, we need to clean up a few things first. It turns out that our client changed
his mind on what he wanted in the Songs app. The client does not want the song rating but does
want to add the album name and album artwork. Let's make those changes first.

In the Navigation Pane in Xcode, select Song.swift to edit it. Remove the `rating` property, as
well as any modifications regarding `chartPosition` from the exercises at the end of Hour 22,
and add constant properties for `albumName` and `artworkUrl`, both of type `String`. Save the file
and press Command+B to build the app, and see what errors we get from making this change.
You should see two errors in the status bar in Xcode, as shown in Figure 23.1. Click on the red
error indicator to show what the errors are in the Issue Navigator. Clicking any of the errors in
the Issue Navigator makes Xcode jump to the offending line(s) of code.

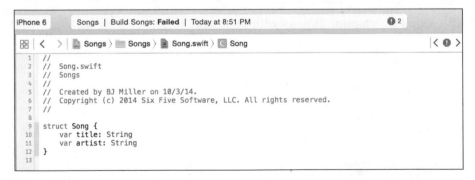

FIGURE 23.1
Xcode's status bar showing two errors.

Click on the error in the SongDetailViewController.swift file in the Issue Navigator first, and you
see that in `updateView()` we are using the previous `rating` property. Delete the entire line,

and delete the @IBOutlet line defining the ratingLabel outlet. Now we need to remove the rating label from the UI, so press Command+1 to open the Project Navigator, and select Main. storyboard. In the Document Outline, select Song Detail View Controller, select the label that displayed the rating (Hint: you can right-click each label to see what outlet it is currently referencing), and press the Delete key on your keyboard. Save your storyboard.

We still have one more error to fix, so click on the error indicator in the status bar to open the Issue Navigator. Click the remaining error to jump to the offending line of code. It is in SongsTableViewController.swift, inside the prepareForSegue(_:sender:) method; go ahead and delete that line.

While you're editing SongsTableViewController.swift, make the following modifications:

1. Add a mutable array of type [Song] and initialize it to an empty array.

2. Change the number of sections to 1.

3. Change the number of rows in the section to the current number of songs.

4. Remove all the code inside tableView(_:titleForHeaderInSection:) and simply return "Beatles Songs".

5. Delete the three lines of code in tableView(_:cellForRowAtIndexPath:) right before the return statement.

After you have made the listed modifications, your SongsTableViewController class should look like Listing 23.6.

LISTING 23.6 Preparing SongsTableViewController Class for iTunes Search

```
import UIKit

class SongsTableViewController: UITableViewController {
    var songs = [Song]()

    // MARK: - Table view data source
    override func numberOfSectionsInTableView(tableView: UITableView) -> Int {
        return 1
    }

    override func tableView(tableView: UITableView, numberOfRowsInSection
⮕section: Int) -> Int {
        return songs.count
    }

    override func tableView(tableView: UITableView, titleForHeaderInSection
⮕section: Int) -> String? {
```

```
        return "Beatles Songs"
    }

    override func tableView(tableView: UITableView, cellForRowAtIndexPath
➡indexPath: NSIndexPath) -> UITableViewCell {
        let cell = tableView.dequeueReusableCellWithIdentifier("Cell",
➡forIndexPath: indexPath) as UITableViewCell

        return cell
    }

    // MARK: - Navigation
    override func prepareForSegue(segue: UIStoryboardSegue, sender: AnyObject!) {
        let detailViewController = segue.destinationViewController as
➡SongDetailViewController
    }
}
```

Next, we need to talk to the iTunes search API and ask it for some results in the form of JSON.
To perform this task, we use a class called NSURLSession. NSURLSession was introduced
in iOS 7 and provides a means to download HTTP content asynchronously. NSURLSession
works by you creating an instance of it, providing a session configuration of type
NSURLSessionConfiguration, and then providing the session tasks to perform. Tasks by
default are in a suspended state, so you must call resume() on them to start them. Add the following code as shown in Listing 23.7 immediately after the songs property definition.

LISTING 23.7 Using NSURLSession to Download Data

```
01:  private func fetchData() {
02:      let url = NSURL(string: "http://itunes.apple.com/
➡search?term=beatles&country=us")
03:      let session = NSURLSession.sharedSession()
04:      let task = session.dataTaskWithURL(url, completionHandler: {
05:          data, response, error in
06:          if let taskError = error {
07:              // handle error
08:          } else {
09:              let httpResponse = response as NSHTTPURLResponse
10:              switch httpResponse.statusCode {
11:              case 200:
12:                  println("got 200")
13:                  println("data: \(data)")
14:              default:
15:                  println("request failed: \(httpResponse.statusCode)")
16:              }
17:          }
```

```
18:        })
19:        task.resume()
20:    }
21:
22:    override func viewDidLoad() {
23:        self.fetchData()
24:    }
```

Because we have not yet seen this class in action, let me walk through what happened. Inside the private `fetchData()` method, we create an `NSURL` instance on line 2 and provide its initializer with the URL we need for searching for Beatles songs in the U.S. iTunes store. Feel free to change to your country code as you see fit. Then on line 3 we get a reference to `NSURLSession`'s `sharedSession()` singleton session object, preconfigured with an `NSURLSessionConfiguration` instance already. Line 4 is where the work to be queued initiates, by calling session's `dataTaskWithURL(_:completionHandler:)` method. The task does not actually get scheduled to execute on a background queue until we call `task.resume()` on line 19. Let's take a close look at the completion handler.

The second parameter to the `dataTaskWithURL(_:completionHandler:)` function is the `completionHandler` argument. Here's a cool trick—when you're typing in the method name and you get the blue text bubble suggesting what parameters go in your `completionHandler` argument, double-click the blue text bubble and it automatically places the closure parameters and return type for you. When our data task finishes executing, it passes us back three objects: data (of type `NSData!`), response (of type `NSURLResponse!`), and error (of type `NSError!`). The closure we pass in is the completion handler to be executed as soon as program execution returns from the HTTP operation. On line 6 we check for an error, which you would want to handle in real-world apps, but we don't here. If there is no error, the `else` block on line 8 executes. First we cast response as `NSHTTPURLResponse` so we can switch on the `statusCode` to ensure the request is OK (the HTTP status code for an OK connection is 200). If the response is OK, we know we have good data. But when we print the data instance to the console, it looks like garbage. Why? `NSData` is an unformatted blob of data, and we haven't converted it to JSON yet. Let's do that now.

Parsing JSON

We need a helper method to parse the JSON for us, so right below the `fetchData()` method's ending curly brace, create a new function called `parseJson(data: NSData)`. Since parsing JSON is a new concept in this book and doesn't really have much to do with asynchronous programming, create the `parseJson(data:)` function as shown in Listing 23.8. Parsing JSON is something you most likely will need to do frequently as a developer, so doing your own research on this will benefit you greatly. Currently a lot of solutions are on the Internet for parsing JSON

in Swift, because Swift's type safety requirements make it a little more difficult than it was in Objective-C. Listing 23.8 illustrates just one way of doing it, but yet unforeseen best practices, or even functional approaches, may prove to be more efficient. Be sure to also update `tableView`
`(_:cellForRowAtIndexPath:)` as shown in Listing 23.8.

LISTING 23.8   Parsing JSON and Updating UI

```
01:  private func parseJson(data: NSData) {
02:      var error: NSError?
03:      let json: AnyObject? = NSJSONSerialization.JSONObjectWithData(data,
➥options: .AllowFragments, error: &error)
04:      if error == nil {
05:          if let unwrappedJson: AnyObject = json {
06:              parseSongs(json: unwrappedJson)
07:          }
08:      }
09:  }
10:
11:  private func parseSongs(#json: AnyObject) {
12:      songs = []
13:      if let array = json["results"] as? [[ String : AnyObject ]] {
14:          for songDictionary in array {
15:              if let title = songDictionary["trackName"] as? NSString {
16:                  if let artist = songDictionary["artistName"] as? NSString {
17:                      if let albumName = songDictionary["collectionName"]
➥as? NSString {
18:                          if let artworkUrl = songDictionary["artworkUrl100"]
➥as? NSString {
19:                              let song = Song(title: title, artist: artist,
➥albumName: albumName, artworkUrl: artworkUrl)
20:                              songs.append(song)
21:                          }
22:                      }
23:                  }
24:              }
25:          }
26:          dispatch_async(dispatch_get_main_queue()) {
27:              self.tableView.reloadData()
28:          }
29:      }
30:  }
31:
32:  override func tableView(tableView: UITableView, cellForRowAtIndexPath
➥indexPath: NSIndexPath) -> UITableViewCell {
33:      let cell = tableView.dequeueReusableCellWithIdentifier("Cell",
➥forIndexPath: indexPath) as UITableViewCell
34:
```

```
35:        let song = songs[indexPath.row]
36:        cell.textLabel?.text = song.title
37:        cell.detailTextLabel?.text = song.albumName
38:
39:        let data = NSData(contentsOfURL: NSURL(string: song.artworkUrl))
40:        let image = UIImage(data: data)
41:        cell.imageView?.image = image
42:
43:        return cell
44:    }
```

A lot happens here, so let's cover what takes place. Lines 1 through 9 are the parseJson() method, which accepts the raw data that was retrieved from the iTunes web service API and serializes the data into JSON using the JSONObjectWithData(_:options:error:) class method on the Cocoa NSJSONSerialization class on line 3. The class method returns an instance of type AnyObject?, so we first check for any error on line 4, and if there are no errors, use optional binding using if let syntax on line 5 to unwrap the JSON data if it is not nil. If the JSON data is not nil, we pass it to another private method on line 6, parseSongs(json:), to extract and work with each dictionary from the array of song dictionaries inside the JSON object.

The parseSongs(json:) method on line 11 does the actual work of creating Song instances by extracting out data from the JSON dictionaries. The JSON comes from Apple in the form of an array of dictionaries, each song (or whatever media type you choose) being represented by a dictionary of key-value pairs. Line 13 checks the JSON's results key to ensure that it is an array of dictionaries of type [[String : AnyObject]]. Then on line 14 we use a for-in loop to iterate over every song dictionary and use a series of nested if let expressions to ensure we have the proper data to populate into a Song instance. Once we are sure we do, line 19 creates a new Song instance, and line 20 adds it to our songs array, as that is our data source for the table view. We used the key "artworkUrl100" to download a larger image to illustrate lag when downloading for this example. This 100x100 image will have to get resized in every cell, wasting CPU cycles and battery power. In a real application, you would want to choose artwork sizes that are more suitable to your needs.

After the for-in loop finishes, and all the songs are correctly represented by Song instances inside the songs array, line 26 dispatches an asynchronous task to update the UI but this time to the main queue. The UI *must always* be updated on the main thread.

NOTE

Optional Downcasts to NSString

Notice that each if let expression optionally downcasts each value as an NSString object. This is because if we try to downcast to a Swift String, we get an error "'String' is not a subtype of '(String, AnyObject)'". Even though Swift strings are convertible to NSString objects, they do not conform to the `AnyObject` protocol because they are structs, so to get this to work we optionally downcast to `NSString`. Then, once we create the `Song` instance, we can use these `NSString` objects in places where the initializer expects Swift `String` instances, because at this point they are known to be convertible.

Finally, in lines 32 through 44, we tell our `tableView` how to display our cells with `Song` instances in the data source method `tableView(_:cellForRowAtIndexPath)`. An `NSIndexPath` object simply holds the section and row we need, and since we only have one section, we only care about the row. Once we know the row, we can get the corresponding song from the `songs` array by accessing the element at index `indexPath.row`. Once we have a constant of that song on line 35, lines 36 and 37 set the `textLabel.text` and `detailTextLabel.text` properties with the `song`'s `title` and `albumName` properties, respectively. Lines 39 through 41 do something we haven't yet seen; we want to display the album artwork in the left-hand side of our cell, a functionality that our cell provides for us. The image can be gotten from iTunes since we have the artwork URL, so line 39 uses `NSData`'s convenience initializer `NSData(contentsOfURL:)` and provides an `NSURL` with our `song.artworkUrl` property. Then line 40 converts that data to a `UIImage` instance with the convenience initializer `UIImage(data:)`. Line 41 simply sets the `cell`'s `imageView`'s `image` property with `cell.imageView.image` with our newly acquired image.

We have one more line of code to add, and that is inside the `case: 200` block of `fetchData()`. Remove the `println("data: \(data)")` line (line 13 in Listing 23.7) and replace it with the following:

```
self.parseJson(data)
```

Build and run the application by pressing Command+R. This looks awesome! But wait, why is it so jerky and choppy when you flick through the list? Something is blocking the main thread.

If you remember in `tableView(_:cellForRowAtIndexPath:)` we added code that gets the album artwork for each song. That's hitting the network every single time the table view is displaying a cell onscreen, and the network request is blocking the main thread every time. Asynchronous programming to the rescue!

Since this is a relatively small task without any dependencies or priorities, let's use GCD to encapsulate that network call. Change the `tableView(_:cellForRowAtIndexPath:)` method to look like the method in Listing 23.9. Also, add a private instance property equal to an instance of `NSCache`. `NSCache` is essentially a dictionary that we can use to store key-value pairs but has mechanisms for expiring caches and such automatically and is a good choice for our needs. You see why after the code listing.

LISTING 23.9   Dispatching a Network Call and Caching

```
01:   private let cache = NSCache()   // place at top of class below songs variable
➥definition
02:
03:   override func tableView(tableView: UITableView, cellForRowAtIndexPath
➥indexPath: NSIndexPath) -> UITableViewCell {
04:       let cell = tableView.dequeueReusableCellWithIdentifier("Cell",
➥forIndexPath: indexPath) as UITableViewCell
05:
06:       let song = songs[indexPath.row]
07:       cell.textLabel?.text = song.title
08:       cell.detailTextLabel?.text = song.albumName
09:
10:       if let image = cache.objectForKey(song.artworkUrl) as? UIImage {
11:           cell.imageView?.image = image
12:       } else {
13:           dispatch_async(dispatch_get_global_queue(
➥DISPATCH_QUEUE_PRIORITY_DEFAULT, 0)) {
14:               let data = NSData(contentsOfURL: NSURL(string: song.artworkUrl))
15:               let image = UIImage(data: data)
16:               self.cache.setObject(image, forKey: song.artworkUrl)
17:               dispatch_async(dispatch_get_main_queue()) {
18:                   self.tableView.reloadRowsAtIndexPaths([indexPath],
➥withRowAnimation: .Automatic)
19:               }
20:           }
21:       }
22:
23:       return cell
24:   }
```

Let's start with creating the cache on line 1. Here we simply create a private instance variable to handle the cache for the lifetime of our table view controller. Then inside `tableView` `(_:cellForRowAtIndexPath:)` we get a copy of the `Song` instance needed and set the `textLabel.text` and `detailTextLabel.text` properties as normal. On line 10 we check for the existence of an image for our `song.artworkUrl` value. If an image exists, we provide it to the `cell.imageView?.image` property. If it does not, we make an asynchronous call to the network, so that we don't block the main thread, and on line 16 we set the downloaded and converted image into the cache, for the `song.artworkUrl` key. Finally, line 18 is dispatched back to the main queue by the `dispatch_async()` function on line 17, which reloads just the row we are interested in, versus all rows.

NOTE

Operation Queue Alternative

The NSOperationQueue/NSOperation alternative to the dispatch_async section in Listing 23.9 is available in the project on GitHub, https://github.com/STYSwiftIn24H/Examples, in the Ch23 folder. The alternative code is commented out, so feel free to comment the dispatch_async section and uncomment the operation queue section.

There are several reasons we need a cache of images for this solution:

▶ **Local access**—Our former implementation of tableView(_:cellForRowAtIndexPath:) made a call to the network to download the artwork for every single row in our table. Our more efficient implementation checks for the existence of the image in the cache first on line 10 before making a network call on line 14 if the image is not in cache. This saves a lot of work, network bandwidth, and CPU cycles, which all help battery life and make for a happier user.

▶ **Cache expiry**—By expiring cached content automatically, our cache will not inflate to an enormous size if we have a lot of images or other pieces of data we are caching. When cached content expires, our method checks for its existence anyway, so it just re-downloads what it needs when it needs it, instead of keeping it around for a potentially long time.

▶ **Easy setup**—You do not need to get a handle to write the file to the file system or worry about placing the temporary files in any particular directory. Placing the images in the cache is ephemeral and takes care of the temporary storage and cleanup for you.

Build and run the app by pressing Command+R. Notice how smoothly the images load and how smoothly the table view scrolls. This is great! Your app should look like Figure 23.2.

The last thing we need to do is send the actual song tapped over to our detail view controller. Listing 23.10 shows the code needed in the prepareForSegue(_:sender:) method in the SongsTableViewController.swift file.

LISTING 23.10   Updating prepareForSegue with Tapped Song

```
01: override func prepareForSegue(segue: UIStoryboardSegue, sender: AnyObject!) {
02:     let detailViewController = segue.destinationViewController as
➥SongDetailViewController
03:     let cell = sender as UITableViewCell
04:     let indexPath = tableView.indexPathForCell(cell)!
05:     let song = songs[indexPath.row]
06:     detailViewController.song = song
07: }
```

FIGURE 23.2
The completed Songs app loading songs by the Beatles with album art.

Line 2 is the same as before, grabbing a reference to the segue.destinationViewController as our detailViewController constant. On line 3 we need to find out what cell was tapped; luckily we are provided with that in the method's parameter list. sender is of type AnyObject!. Many different objects can initiate a segue, but we know for our app that only a tap on a cell could initiate a segue, so we can downcast sender as UITableViewCell. Then on line 4 we use tableView's indexPathForCell() instance method to find the index path for the tapped cell. From there, since we know we can get the indexPath's row, we can get the respective song from the songs array and send that song to the detail view controller.

Now when you build and run the app by pressing Command+R you can tap on any cell and view details about the song. Congratulations, you built an entire app from scratch and using efficient asynchronous programming!

If you need the source code for the completed project, feel free to download it from GitHub at https://github.com/STYSwiftIn24H/Examples, in the Ch23 folder.

Summary

Asynchronous programming is not easy, but by Apple introducing Grand Central Dispatch (GCD) and operation queues, a lot of work that programmers had to do previously is no longer your responsibility. You can focus on writing code that matters versus difficult and potentially error-riddled thread management code.

In this hour you learned the differences between synchronous and asynchronous programming, and the two methods for implementing asynchronous programming: dispatch queues and operation queues. Dispatch queues are provided by GCD, and operation queues are provided by a Cocoa abstraction on top of GCD called NSOperationQueue, which executes subclasses of NSOperation onto its queue. Both methods are used by adding closures containing tasks to execute to their queues.

You then learned about nested closures and how to execute code on different queues from within a closure in GCD. A comparable action using operation queues is adding a completion block to an operation before adding it to the operation queue.

Finally, you learned how to use NSURLSession class to make asynchronous network calls and parse the JSON that is returned by using nested if let binding. The JSON turned into actual instances that you stored into an array and used as the data source for the table view.

You experienced a sluggish UI when we made network calls that blocked the main thread, and you learned how to identify the issue and encapsulate the blocking network call inside a GCD dispatch and update the UI using images from cache.

In the final hour, we discuss some of Swift's standard library functions and syntax. Many gems are in the standard library that can help you in your day-to-day work as a Swift developer and are a fun way to end this book.

Q&A

Q. **Why do I get different results each time I run the code in Listing 23.2?**

A. Once we start an asynchronous task, we lose control over when and how it executes. In Listing 23.2 we start two different asynchronous tasks and GCD takes control of the rest of the execution. This means that execution may appear to jump back and for the between the two threads at random, potentially resulting in different output each time we run the code.

Q. What is JSON and why do we need it?

A. JSON (JavaScript Object Notation) is an open standard that defines a way to convert data objects into plain text that can then be transmitted over a network and converted back to data after transmission. Even though JavaScript is in the name, the format is language independent, so we are able to parse and create JSON using a variety of languages.

Q. We used asynchronous tasks for retrieving network data in this hour. What are some other times we might need them?

A. You should use asynchronous tasks any time your application needs to perform a long operation, but you don't want to block the user from interacting with the application. Examples include long mathematical calculations, loading files from disk, or waiting on some external event to occur. Many frameworks already work asynchronously; for example, the `AVAudioPlayer` class enables you to play a sound while the user continues to interact with the application.

Workshop

The workshop contains quiz questions and exercises to help you solidify your understanding of the material covered. Try to answer all questions before looking at the answers that follow.

Quiz

1. What is Apple's concurrency management system called?

2. True or false? Operation queues operate at a higher level than dispatch queues.

3. By default, `NSURLSession` returns tasks in a suspended state. What method should you call to tell the task to continue?

4. True or false? A sluggish UI can always be solved by introducing asynchronous tasks into your application.

Answers

1. Apple's concurrency management system is called Grand Central Dispatch.

2. True. Operation queues are a Cocoa abstraction on top of the lower level dispatch queues.

3. The `resume()` method tells an `NSURLSessions`'s task to continue its execution.

4. This was a trick question! A sluggish UI can often be the result of long, CPU intensive, or network dependent tasks, which may be solved by introducing asynchronous tasks, but there can be other causes too. For example, low memory can cause poor performance in your application, but looking for parts of your program that might be helped by introducing asynchronous code is a good place to start.

Exercise

Let's explore asynchronous tasks a bit more. Start with the code in Listing 23.3 and print statements so that they provide a running count of the number of times the loop has run. For example, the first time through the first loop, you might print "1: A" instead of just "A", and the second time "2: A", and similarly the second print statement will print "1: B" then "2: B". You'll notice something strange happen when you run your code. The text is all jumbled up.

What do you think is going on? Can you fix the code so that the output is closer to what you expected?

HOUR 24
Learning Swift's Standard Library Functions

What You'll Learn in This Hour:

▶ Many of the functions available in the Swift standard library
▶ Which protocols are in the Swift standard library
▶ How to use functional programming functions
▶ How to use global functions

In this final hour, we explore some of the Swift standard library functions. The standard library reference documentation can be found on Apple's website, at https://developer. apple.com/library/ios/documentation/General/Reference/SwiftStandardLibraryReference/ SwiftStandardLibraryReference.pdf. We discuss some functions and features of the standard library that can be helpful to you in your career as a Swift developer, as well as some perhaps not so well known features. We explore some of the standard library that we haven't yet used in this book as well as rehash some that will prove to be useful. This hour should be light as we wrap up the book and full of many examples for you to follow along with if you so choose.

What Is a Standard Library?

A **standard library**, in terms of computer programming, is a library of commonly used functions, algorithms, and data structures available across implementations of a language. This means that without adding or importing any external framework, the standard library makes available certain features and functions that you can use to build an app. There isn't anything special, per se, about the standard library, but it contains many useful features and functions built right into the language for you to use from the start.

You have seen many standard library functions already and may not even have known it. Such functions include the `print()` and `println()` functions, operators such as `==` and `+=`, initializers, subscripts, and more. To see the entire standard library in code, open a new playground, type `import Swift`, and Command-click the word `Swift`.

Also, many standard library functions are available not only to instances of some types but also globally, to be sent any type of sequence or other argument and operate from a global perspective versus being an instance method or property. We see how some of those work shortly. Let's begin discussing what is in the standard library by covering numeric types.

Numeric Types

The standard library provides numeric types that you are familiar with by now: Boolean, integer, and floating point. We covered these thoroughly in this book, and there is nothing special that needs to be covered here, but let's just rehash the basics:

- ▶ **Boolean**—Boolean values evaluate to either `true` or `false`.

- ▶ **Integer**—The `Int` type is sensitive to the platform on which it is being used; an `Int` on a 32-bit platform is 32 bits in length, and an `Int` on a 64-bit platform is 64 bits in length. Smaller-bit and unsigned variants are available such as `UInt`, `UInt16`, `Int32`, and so on.

- ▶ **Floating point**—`Double` is the primary floating-point type in Swift, with 64-bit precision. `Float` is also available, with 32-bit precision.

String Type

Quite a bit of functionality is available to the `String` type in the standard library, such as with initialization, querying a string, converting strings, and string operators.

There are some convenient methods and properties on the `String` type for verifying or querying for data in a string, all of which return `Bool`s: `isEmpty`, `hasPrefix(prefix: String)`, and `hasSuffix(suffix: String)`. Listing 24.1 shows these in code.

LISTING 24.1 String Properties and Methods

```
let emptyString = ""
let name = "Steve Jobs"

emptyString.isEmpty        // returns true
name.isEmpty               // returns false

name.hasPrefix("Steve")    // returns true
name.hasSuffix("Martin")   // returns false
```

String Comparison

You have seen how to use the concatenating operator (+) with strings, but you may not have used the **lexicographical comparison operator**, <. Lexicographical comparison means the analysis and comparison of relationships within the lexicon or vocabulary. It's a really fancy way of verifying whether the characters of a string are less than, or have a Unicode value less than, others. Likewise, you can use > to verify whether the left-hand characters are greater than the right-hand characters. Listing 24.2 illustrates how to lexicographically compare strings.

LISTING 24.2 Lexicographically Comparing Strings

```
let zack = "Zack"
let kelly = "Kelly"
let screech = "Screech"

zack < kelly           // returns false, "K" appears before "Z" in the alphabet
kelly < screech        // returns true
screech > zack         // returns false
```

Protocols

Many protocols are available in the Swift standard library. Simply Command-clicking the word Swift in the import Swift statement mentioned earlier and then searching for the word *protocol*, you will see a plethora of protocol definitions. A few of the first ones you see are a type alias for Any and a protocol definition for AnyObject. The reason that Any is type aliased to equal protocol<> is so that Any can represent an instance of any type at all, excluding function types. The actual implementation is private, but at least you can see that AnyObject is indeed a protocol and Any is a type alias to protocol<>.

Another protocol you see in the library is ArrayLiteralConvertible. Literal convertible protocols, of which there are many to represent the many types in Swift, enable a literal of that type to be passed in as an initial value or appended to an existing value. For example, the following code snippet is made possible by the ArrayLiteralConvertible protocol:

```
let myArray = [1, 2, 3]
```

The following is a list of the literal convertible protocols used with their corresponding type.

▶ ArrayLiteralConvertible

▶ BooleanLiteralConvertible

▶ CharacterLiteralConvertible

▶ DictionaryLiteralConvertible

- ▶ ExtendedGraphemeClusterLiteralConvertible

- ▶ FloatLiteralConvertible

- ▶ IntegerLiteralConvertible

- ▶ NilLiteralConvertible

- ▶ StringLiteralConvertible

These protocols enable literals of the respective type to be assigned to an instance of that type. But why is there so much focus on protocols? Remember from Hour 17, "Using Protocols to Define Behavior," that protocols allow you to define the behavior of an instance of any type, rather than forcing an instance to be of a particular type? It turns out that defining behaviors with protocols lends itself to much more flexible and safer programming because you can guarantee an instance behaves in a particular way from the protocol definition. This also means that you could define a new type, like Set, make it conform to the ArrayLiteralConvertible protocol, and enable you to add instances to the set with array literal syntax.

NOTE

Naming Conventions with Protocols

Many protocols in the standard library end in –able or –ible in their naming, meaning the instance that conforms to that protocol is *able to* perform the requested method or respond to the requested property. This greatly helps with understanding what a protocol's purpose is and is self-documenting. Consider this naming convention when you create protocols. By saying an instance of a certain type is Printable, you know that it implements the description computed property and is able to print a description of itself to the console.

Another protocol listed in the standard library is Sliceable. Slice is actually a type, conforming to the Sliceable protocol, and represents a slice of (or an entire) array. The definition of both the Slice type and Array type is identical, other than the name, as shown in Listing 24.3.

LISTING 24.3   Slice and Array Type Definitions

```
struct Array<T> : MutableCollectionType, Sliceable {
    // implementation
}

struct Slice<T> : MutableCollectionType, Sliceable {
    // implementation
}
```

Both conform to the `MutableCollectionType` protocol and the `Sliceable` protocol. The `MutableCollectionType` protocol is a mutable interface variant of the `CollectionType` protocol, which only defines a getter. All collection types, such as `Array` and `Dictionary`, conform to the `CollectionType` protocol either directly or indirectly.

`Slice` can be used like a special kind of `Array`. In fact, range subscripts returned from instances of `Array` are returned as a `Slice<T>`. To see this in action, follow along in this next Try It Yourself section.

TRY IT YOURSELF ▼

Slicing an Array

Create an array with several elements and then extract a slice of that array using a range for the subscript index.

1. Open Xcode 6 and create a new playground. Either a Mac or an iOS playground will work. Clear the contents of the playground.

2. Create an array containing the Fibonacci series of numbers beginning with 1 and ending with 13.

   ```
   var fibonacci = [1, 1, 2, 3, 5, 8, 13]
   ```

3. Create a constant range of type `Range`, using the initializer that provides a start and end value. Start the range at 2 and end the range at 5. Notice in the playground's results pane that this range is a half-closed range, denoted by "2..<5".

   ```
   let range = Range(start: 2, end: 5)
   ```

4. Obtain a slice from the array of Fibonacci numbers, using the range you created in the previous step.

   ```
   let innerSlice = fibonacci[range]
   ```

5. While `Slice` and `Array` are not comparable like `String` and `NSString` are, you can create a new array by providing the `Slice` instance to its initializer.

   ```
   let innerArrayFromSlice = [Int](innerSlice)  // or Array(innerSlice)
   ```

The completed Try It Yourself code and results should look like those in Figure 24.1.

```
● ● ●                        ▣ Ch24 Slice TIY.playground
⊞  ⟨  ⟩ │ ▣ Ch24 Slice TIY.playground ⟩ No Selection
1   var fibonacci = [1, 1, 2, 3, 5, 8, 13]              [1, 1, 2, 3, 5, 8, 13]
2
3   let range = Range(start: 2, end: 5)                 "2..<5"
4   let innerSlice = fibonacci[range]                   [2, 3, 5]
5
6   let innerArrayFromSlice = [Int](innerSlice) // or Array(innerSlice)   [2, 3, 5]
7
```

FIGURE 24.1
The completed Try It Yourself exercise using `Slice` and `Array`.

Protocols and Overloading Operators

Swift enables you to override operators, something not available in Objective-C. By using protocols in Swift, this is made easy and available to you to do as you wish. Two protocols, `Equatable` and `Comparable`, enable you to do this with basic operators. The `Comparable` protocol requires you overload the less-than operator (<) and inherits from the `Equatable` protocol, which requires you overload the is-equal operator (==). So if your class, struct, or enum adopts the `Comparable` protocol, you must also implement both required operators, < and ==.

CAUTION

Overloading Operators Can Cause Confusion

A great deal of benefit can come from overloaded operators. However, a great deal of confusion also can come along with it. As a general rule, if you overload an operator, make sure that your team knows what it does and why, and that your overloading is documented. Accidental or unknowing use of an overloaded operator can cause unwanted behavior.

Let's say you have an app in which you need to sort answers to posts by whether the answer is the accepted answer and then by score, highest to lowest. Listing 24.4 illustrates a struct that conforms to the `Comparable` protocol and overloads both == and <. When you overload ==, you get != by default, and when you overload <, you get >, <=, and >= by default.

LISTING 24.4 `Comparable` Protocol Operator Overloading

```
struct Answer : Comparable {
    var text: String
    var score: Int
    var accepted: Bool
}


func == (lhs: Answer, rhs: Answer) -> Bool {
    return (lhs.accepted == rhs.accepted) && (lhs.score == rhs.score)
}
```

```
func < (lhs: Answer, rhs: Answer) -> Bool {
    if lhs.accepted {
        return false
    } else if rhs.accepted {
        return true
    } else {
        return lhs.score < rhs.score
    }
}


let answer1 = Answer(text: "I have the answer!", score: 100, accepted: true)
let answer2 = Answer(text: "Mediocre answer", score: 30, accepted: false)
let answer3 = Answer(text: "I have the answer!", score: 100, accepted: true)

answer1 == answer2    // false
answer2 != answer3    // true
answer1 == answer3    // true

answer1 < answer2    // false
answer2 < answer3    // true
answer1 >= answer3    // true
```

Even though our `Answer` struct adopts the `Comparable` protocol, the operator overloads are placed outside the struct's definition. You use the struct's (or class's or enum's) type inside the parameter list for the operator functions, denoted by `lhs` (for left-hand side) and `rhs` (for right-hand side). Since these comparison operators are infix operators, meaning they go in between two operands, it makes sense for us to label the parameters as `lhs` and `rhs`.

Many more protocols are defined in the Swift standard library. To learn more about the protocols defined, Command-click the word `Swift` in an `import Swift` line and search for the word *protocol*.

Functional Functions

Swift introduced some functional programming features in its standard library such as the `map()`, `reduce()`, and `filter()` functions to name a few, as seen in other functional programming languages. We have already discussed `map()` and `reduce()` briefly, but not `filter()`. You may end up using these functions extensively in your career as a Swift developer, so they are worth more explanation and examples.

Map

The map() function iterates over each element in a sequence and performs a transformation on that element that you provide in a closure as an argument. Batch arithmetic manipulation can be done using map(), as well as applying logic to instances of custom types, such as applying discounts to products as shown in Listing 24.5.

LISTING 24.5   Using map() to Apply a Discount

```
import Foundation  // needed only for String(format:)

struct Product : Printable {
    var name: String
    var cost: Double
    var description: String { return "\(name) is " + String(format: "$%.2f", cost) }
}

var product1 = Product(name: "Soap", cost: 5.0)
var product2 = Product(name: "Shampoo", cost: 8.0)
var product3 = Product(name: "Toothpaste", cost: 4.0)
var products = [product1, product2, product3]

products.map { println($0.description) }

println("\nApplying 20% discount\n")
var discountedProducts: [Product] = products.map { product in
    var discountedProduct = product
    discountedProduct.cost *= 0.8
    return discountedProduct
}
discountedProducts.map { println($0.description) }
```

As you can see in the example, we used map() to not only print the description of each product to the console but to apply a 20% discount to each product and store that information in a new array.

Reduce

The reduce() function takes a starting value and then iterates over the sequence, recursively building a return value. This is useful for building an aggregate sum of numeric values, but you can also build strings using reduce(). Listing 24.6 illustrates how to combine a rough sentence from words in an array.

LISTING 24.6   Using `reduce()` to Build a Sentence from Array Values

```
var goodMorning = ["Good", "morning,", "sweetie."]
let greeting = goodMorning.reduce("") { left, right in
    return left.isEmpty ? left + right : left + " " + right
}
greeting          // displays "Good morning, sweetie."
```

We start our reduction with an empty string. Inside the trailing closure, we obtain constants for the thus-far combined value (`left`) and the next value (`right`). Then, we assess whether the string is empty and return either just the concatenation of the two parameters or a concatenation separated by a space.

Filter

The `filter()` function returns a new sequence where each element is either filtered in or out of the new sequence based on the criteria provided in the closure argument. This is akin to using an `NSPredicate` object to filter a collection of items, if you've done that with Objective-C at some point. Listing 24.7 illustrates how to use `filter()` on dictionary keys and values to return arrays of desired values.

LISTING 24.7   Using `filter()` to Return a Filtered Array

```
var fooDictionary = ["fooOne" : 1, "two" : 2, "fooThree" : 3]
let foos = fooDictionary.keys.filter { startsWith($0, "foo") }
foos.array              // displays ["fooOne", "fooThree"]

let divisibleByTwo = fooDictionary.values.filter { $0 % 2 == 0 }
divisibleByTwo.array    // displays [2]
```

First we declare a dictionary of type `[String : Int]` and populate it with values. The constant `foos` gets assigned the result of calling `filter()` on the dictionary's `keys` property and returns a new array where any string starts with "foo". `startsWith()` is a global function in the Swift standard library. We discuss global functions in the next section.

Then we use `filter()` on the dictionary's `values` property, since that is a collection just like `keys` is, and this time we want an array where any value is evenly divisible by 2.

Global Functions

The Swift standard library comes with many global functions, too many to list and explain here. Many of these global functions operate on sequences or collections, such as arrays and dictionaries. In fact, several functions that are instance methods on sequences are also global functions in which you pass the sequence as the first parameter instead of calling the function as an instance method. `map`, `reduce`, and `filter` are examples, to name a few. To round out the hour, we cover a few functions that may prove useful for you.

Check Start of Sequence

To compare a value at the beginning of a sequence, use the global function `startsWith()`. To use this function, you provide the sequence and the value to check for existence, and the function returns a `Bool` whether the sequence starts with the value. Listing 24.8 illustrates several uses of the `startsWith()` function.

LISTING 24.8   Using the `startsWith()` Global Function

```
let constantArray = [1, 2, 3]
startsWith(constantArray, [1, 2])    // true
startsWith(constantArray, [1])       // true
startsWith(constantArray, [2])       // false

let macbook = "MacBook Pro"
let iPhone = "iPhone 6 Plus"
startsWith(macbook, "Mac")           // true
startsWith(iPhone, "Mac")            // false
```

Split

The `split()` function takes a sequence as its first argument and then a closure with an expression for how to match elements on which to split the array. Listing 24.9 uses the Fibonacci sequence from a previous example, with an extra set of numbers added in the middle for illustration.

LISTING 24.9   Splitting an Array

```
var fibonacci = [1, 1, 2, 3, 4, 4, 4, 5, 8, 13]
let splitFib = split(fibonacci, { $0 % 4 == 0 })
splitFib           // equals [[1, 1, 2, 3], [5], [13]]
```

Notice the returned sequence is a sequence of sequences. Also notice that I didn't say "array of arrays," because if you Option-click on `splitFib`, you see that its type is `[Slice<Int>]`. You can always convert a `Slice<T>` to an `Array<T>`.

Stride

A convenient way to iterate a range of numbers in a for-in loop is by using the stride() functions. There are a few options here: stride(from:to:by:) and stride(from:through:by:). These are similar to the half-closed range and closed range operators, but here you are given the option to increment by a value different than 1. Listing 24.10 illustrates using both of these functions.

LISTING 24.10   Stride To and Stride Through

```
for i in stride(from: 0, through: 10, by: 2) {
    println("i: \(i)")
}

for j in stride(from: 10, to: 0, by: -2) {
    println("j: \(j)")
}
// prints:
// i: 0
// i: 2
// i: 4
// i: 6
// i: 8
// i: 10
// j: 10
// j: 8
// j: 6
// j: 4
// j: 2
```

Using stride() functions can sometimes be more beneficial if you need to increment by something different than 1. Notice that you can also stride in a negative direction, whereas the closed range and half-closed range operators must only go in a forward or positive direction.

Sort and Sorted

Two sorting functions are in the standard library: sort() and sorted(). sort() does an in-place sort of the elements in a sequence, while sorted() returns a new sorted sequence instance. When using the sort() global function, since you are modifying the original sequence in place, you must pass the sequence as an in-out parameter using the & character. Xcode helps you if it senses you missed the & character. Listing 24.11 shows both sorting functions in action.

LISTING 24.11 The `sort()` and `sorted()` Functions

```
var array = [-8, 0, 5, 4, -1, 6]

let sortedArray = sorted(array) { $0 < $1 }
sortedArray                  // a new instance equaling [-8, -1, 0, 4, 5, 6]

sort(&array) { $0 < $1 }
array                        // modified original instance equaling [-8, -1,
➥0, 4, 5, 6]
```

Summary

The Swift standard library has many useful functions and features in it, and it is worth exploring further to find out what is provided out-of-the-box. By knowing what tools you have in your belt, you will be a better programmer. Many resources are available online for more explanations of the Swift standard library

In this hour you learned what the Swift standard library is and some of its useful built-in tools. You learned some of the basic type tools available in numeric types and strings. Then you learned how big a role protocols play not just in special cases but also in the fundamentals of Swift types. Protocols define behavior or instances and can be applied to any type that conforms to its requirements. With how engrained protocols are inside the Swift language, it is apparent how much Apple promotes their use.

You also learned about the `Equatable` and `Comparable` protocols and how to overload the `==` and `<` operators to perform custom comparison. Be careful, however, when overloading operators. Make sure that they have been clearly defined and documented to help prevent unwanted or accidental misuse of the operators.

Then you learned more about some of the functional functions in Swift, such as `map()`, `reduce()`, and `filter()`. These functions can prove to be incredibly helpful in day-to-day coding for simply, succinctly, and powerfully iterating through collections to perform operations upon them.

Finally, you learned about several global functions available in the standard library. There are many more global functions you can use, and I highly encourage you to research all the functions available to you and how to use them.

Congratulations are in order for having completed reading this book. I sincerely hope you learned a great deal of information about Swift and good programming practices and feel ready to take on learning more specifics about the Cocoa and Cocoa Touch frameworks to build useful apps for the Mac and/or iOS platforms. Best of luck to you in your endeavors building apps! And remember to check https://github.com/STYSwiftIn24H/Examples for up-to-date code examples from this book that will be updated for future revisions of Xcode and Swift. Thank you for reading this book.

Q&A

Q. Do my protocols have to end with –able or –ible as Apple's do?

A. You aren't required to follow Apple's naming conventions, but it's a good idea. It's clearer to talk about a class being `Comparable` than saying that it conforms to the Compare protocol. There are other naming conventions that you can use, such as starting method names with verbs like `String.hasPrefix()` and prefixing Boolean properties with is or has like `String.isEmpty`. These conventions are fundamental to good object-oriented design, and if you're interested in more information, consult a text on object-oriented programming techniques.

Q. What is the difference between `1..<5` and `Range(start:1, end:5)`?

A. There is no difference. These two statements produce identical range objects.

Q. The `Comparable` protocol enables me to use `>=` on my objects, but only requires me to implement `==` and `<`. How does it know what to do for `>=`?

A. Apple was clever in creating the protocols in the standard library. Checking for `>=` is the same as checking for `>` or `==`, and checking for `>` is the same as checking for not `<`. This means that all the comparison operators can be constructed using just the two required by the `Comparable` protocol.

Q. Is Swift a functional programming language?

A. Strictly speaking, Swift is not a functional programming language, but it does adopt a number of functional patterns. This enables you to structure Swift code to use functional techniques, imperative techniques, or some combination of the two depending on the requirements of your program.

Workshop

The workshop contains quiz questions and exercises to help you solidify your understanding of the material covered. Try to answer all questions before looking at the answers that follow.

Quiz

1. What is the difference between the `sort()` and `sorted()` functions?

2. Which function is best if you want to iterate over a sequence and apply the same transformation to each element? `map()`, `reduce()`, or `filter()`?

3. What's wrong with the following code:

```
var city = "San Diego"
if city.startsWith("San") { println("Nice and sunny today! ") }
else { println("How's the weather?") }
```

4. What value is stored in `result` at the end of this code?

```
var values = [1,2,3,4,5]
let result = values.reduce(0, { $0 + $1 })
```

Answers

1. The `sorted()` function returns a copy of the sequence in sorted order but leaves the original sequence unchanged. The `sort()` function modifies the original collection in place.

2. The `map()` function is best in this case.

3. `startsWith()` is a global function, not a method of the `String` class. Changing `city.startsWith("San")` to `startsWith(city, "San")` fixes the error.

4. The `reduce` statement here adds up all the numbers in the `values` array and stores the sum in `result`, so `result` is equal to 15.

Exercise

For this exercise, we use a playground to explore some of Swift's global functions. Start by replacing the contents of the playground with this:

```
let initialString = "1,2,3,4,5,6,7,8,9,10,11"
```

We apply a series of transformations to this string. First, use the `split()` function to chop up the string into an array of strings, each containing a number, and save the result in a variable called `numberStrings`. Your new array should look like this:

```
numberStrings // ["1", "2", "3", "4", "5", "6", "7", "8", "9", "10", "11"]
```

Use `map()` to convert all the strings to integers, and store the result in an array called `numbers`. Make sure you explicitly unwrap any optional values, and when you're finished you should have:

```
numbers // [1, 2, 3, 4, 5, 6, 7, 8, 9, 10, 11]
```

Use `filter()` to produce a new array that only contains numbers divisible by three, and store the result in an array called `multiplesOfThree` to get:

`multiplesOfThree // [3, 6, 9]`

Use `reduce()` to combine these numbers into a string and save the result in a variable called `finalString`. Now you should have:

`finalString // "359"`

Try rewriting this series of steps without using `map()`, `reduce()`, or `filter()` and see what your code looks like. Which way do you think is easier to read? Which way was easier to write?

Index

J-K

L

Sams **Teach Yourself**

When you only have time **for the answers**™

SAMS

REGISTER

THIS PRODUCT

informit.com/register

Register the Addison-Wesley, Exam Cram, Prentice Hall, Que, and Sams products you own to unlock great benefits.

To begin the registration process, simply go to **informit.com/register** to sign in or create an account. You will then be prompted to enter the 10- or 13-digit ISBN that appears on the back cover of your product.

Registering your products can unlock the following benefits:

- Access to supplemental content, including bonus chapters, source code, or project files.
- A coupon to be used on your next purchase.

Registration benefits vary by product. Benefits will be listed on your Account page under Registered Products.

THE TRUSTED TECHNOLOGY LEARNING SOURCE

Addison-Wesley | Cisco Press | Exam Cram
IBM Press | Que | Prentice Hall | Sams

SAFARI BOOKS ONLINE